Reflections of Invisible People:

A Struggle for Social Justice

A Memoir

Khaleeq Hodari

Printed in the United States of America
First printing 2021
Library of Congress Cataloging-in-Publication Data
Reflections of Invisible People: A Struggle for Social Justice. A memoir by Khaleeq I. I. Hodari
p. cm.
1. Hodari, Khaleeq I. I. 2. African American Biography

Author cover photo by Jamie Ortiz
Cover design by Hannah Linder
Interior formatting by Polgarus Studio

Published by Khaleeq I. I. Hodari

ISBN: 978-1-7364202-0-1 (Print)
ISBN: 978-1-7364202-1-8 (ebook)

This book is dedicated in memory of my beloved grandma, Viola Clarye Wright Jay for giving me vision necessary to soar beyond impossibilities.

Contents

Prologue: INVISIBLE PEOPLE 1

Chapter 1: BUSTER BROWNS 15

Chapter 2: A CRISIS AT HOME 26

Chapter 3: A SCENTILLA OF HOPE 34

Chapter 4: LICKIN STICK 53

Chapter 5: GET BACK 69

Chapter 6: BLUE-EYED DEVIL 75

Chapter 7: THE WHITE MAN'S BURDEN 84

Chapter 8: SEPARATE AND UNEQUAL 98

Chapter 9: REAL TRUTH 121

Chapter 10: IMPETUS FOR CHANGE 134

Chapter 11: CULTURE SHOCK 146

Chapter 12: ANGER AND BEYOND 167

Chapter 13: THE LEARNING CURVE 194

Chapter 14: SHUFFLE ALONG 215

Chapter 15: STORIES TO REMEMBER 226

Chapter 16: FORBIDDEN FRUIT 242

Chapter 17: SAME OLE CHANGES 258

Chapter 18: A FIRE THIS TIME 278

Chapter 19: MULE TRAIN 297

Chapter 20: MAGNIFICENT MOMENTS 311

Chapter 21: BUS STOP MOMENTS 324

Chapter 22: SAY IT LOUD 330

Chapter 23: RACE MATTERS 341

Chapter 24: LONESOME DOVE 366

Acknowledgements 383

Action without thought is empty.
Thought without action is blind.
-Kwame Nkrumah-

Prologue

INVISIBLE PEOPLE

One Saturday in June 1985 with scorching Florida sun at its peak, my shirt is drenched in sweat and my face is dripping faster than I can wipe it. Clutching my camera, I take shots of a newly designated historic African-American section of the city. But this morning in Orange Avenue's exclusive white business district, traffic and shoppers are scarce. Most major department stores are gone with boarded windows. Others struggle for shoppers. I expected it sooner.

"Clearance Sale." "Final Sale." "50% off Sale." "Going out of Business Sale." Numerous signs covering windows cry out desperately to a few potential customers. Looming in one direction on 8th Street and Orange Avenue, an old vacant Piggly Wiggly, once A&P grocery store, reminds me of when as a child, I was scorned for drinking from a "whites only" water fountain.

In another direction, Woolworth's 5 &10 department store with its art deco design is now a novelty shop. Within its doors lie historic moments of lunch counter sit-ins during the 60's Civil Rights Movement (none in Fort Pierce though). I can still hear stirring echoes of whites yelling for a burger and fries, yet I only get a sad refrain from Grandma, "Colored folk can buy here, but sho can't sit and eat here."

I walk briskly to avoid the heat from a hot sidewalk penetrating the soles of my shoes. I escape the sun's rays by walking under shady palm trees lining the sidewalk. In the distance, moving about aimlessly are homeless men carrying tote bags. Others form a line in front of a Salvation Army Shelter make-shift soup kitchen. Homeless men recently uncommon, now are permanent fixtures propped against storefronts laying in shady areas of empty parking lots. Others sit on sidewalks eating from Styrofoam trays. Some are old high schoolmates long forgotten.

A short distance away a peculiar looking man pushes a grocery cart with a large garbage bag filled with cans is approaching men on the sidewalk. Pushing his cart through men eating as they scramble hastily to avoid getting hit. "Yo brother!" "What's ya problem? Almost hit me wit that damn thing!" "Ya better check ya self, fast . . . I come close to kickin yo ass!" The brother launches a barrage of insults standing inches from the bagman's face.

The bagman unfazed, cool as a cucumber has the nerve to fake a smile, sticks out his tongue in a playful gesture. The brother's looking for a fight or out of his mind. Surprised by his behavior, the angry brother steps back. "Maaann you ain't worth it!" Slowly walks away.

The bagman stands at attention in a soldier's stance, smiles, salutes, pirouettes on his heels and marches pushing that cart and goes about his business. Homeless men explode in laughter at such an intense but comical scene.

I wander upon a familiar furniture store still doing business in the area. A sofa design African Kente cloth sits in a window with a large sign posted: "Yours only $250 half price off!" Fighting off the sun's glare, I curiously look inside. An elderly white man with a wide smile waves me in. I recognize him from earlier years. I'm not in the mood for an introduction. "You like that so. . . well it's on sale!" "It's yours!"Cool air from the air conditioner snaps me to my senses. "It's beautiful African print but doesn't match my mother's carpet," I blurt out. "Got some contemporary sofa's over there if you like." "No, I'm just browsing." "That's fine, take your time, and if you change your mind let me know." He walks toward another customer.

I head for the door as the last remaining customer gets ahead of me. I stop to tidy up my afro in a nearby dresser mirror, a flash of sunlight deflects off the chrome of a passing car dancing and casting a silhouette of a human figure off the wall nearby. Distracted for a

2

moment, I look back in the mirror and see the bagman, stooping over and staring through the window.

A sad face pinned against glass, both hands cupped around his face shielding sunlight make him difficult to recognize. I head for the door as he stares at me in heavy outdated clothing inappropriate for the summer's heat.

"I'll let you have it for a nice price!" "Going out of business!" "Everything's on sale!" The store manager says determined. "So, you said, perhaps another time." With patience wearing thin, my mind is on this curious brother staring at me.[1]

I get a fleeting thought and it comes. "Oh! By the way, I do have a question." "Go right ahead!" The manager says, pleasantly surprised. "Why are there so many sales going on around here today?" "Well." Carefully pondering over my question, I interrupt before he speaks, "Businesses are leaving, why is that?" "Well, this whole area is changing too fast for me. I just can't make a profit anymore." "You always have customers," I muse. A puzzled look appears on his face with a nervous grin quickly fading. "No business can make a decent profit in this area. I'm moving further south. Too many bums outside. There's one looking through the window!" he says angrily.

The owner exposes inescapable truths. Perhaps he has rehearsed this moment a hundred times over dinner in a gated area of Fort Pierce far removed from blacks. In attack mode, I counter his point. "Your business has done well for many years with poor African-American customers." "I think you're making excuses." "Who the hell are you coming in here speaking to me like this?" His

---

[1] Kente cloth is a fabric woven in silk and cotton first developed by the ancient Ashanti Empire of Ghana. The fabric was later worn during the rule of King Osei TuTu-1. Each design reflects Ghanaian culture and is historically and philosophically significant. Each color of the cloth is symbolic: gold=status, green=renewal, blue=pure spirit, harmony, yellow=fertility, red=passion, black=union with ancestors. Kwame Nkrumah, the first Prime Minister of Ghana popularized the cloth during a 1958 meeting with President Eisenhower at the White House, which caused a rebirth of the cloth's popularity in the US in the 1960s and again in the1980s and 1990s.

voice roars angrily. "Blacks supported your business through harder times during segregation." He ponders a moment. "You have a point but I'm losing money and other businesses are too. Your people are good to me. I don't know what to do." His face reddens in a heap of worry.

What I really want to say about race relations in Fort Pierce will be too involved, take too much time and will be intense. The way the old man looks, afraid he might slip into cardiac arrest. I back away and turn to leave the store. The bagman pulls off the speediest disappearing act I ever witnessed—out of site in all four directions. "Unbelievable!"

"Well . . . believe it." The store manager says, in hot pursuit on my heels. His voice shifts to a less convincing tone obstructing my departure. "Perhaps I'd like to stay. It'll be difficult don't you think?" "Yes," I say reluctantly. The owner listens unable to face the real issue: it is no longer black and white but one of coexistence with the influx of Haitians and some Mexicans moving into the area.

"Fear is the operative word," I say to him. "White businessmen and homeowners must overcome perceptions that people of color diminish property values and welcome crime, and that integrated neighborhoods area financial risk. Businesses leaving is indirectly responsible for the loitering because of abandoned buildings." When I finish, he looks gravely concerned.

"You raise interesting points." "Maybe I'm overreacting. These bums won't loiter around here if they were educated." "Knowledge brings economic power you know," he boasts. "Knowledge also erases fear," I retort. He forces a smile while offering a firm confident handshake. I watch him invite a few eager black customers inside. "Everything's on sale!" "Half price off!" Not a hint of frustration, though less enthusiastic than before.

I leave hoping our well-deserved debate is an eye-opener from an African-American perspective with redeeming value. Perhaps the white business owner will confront other white business owners about hidden agendas without feeling demonized on issues of racism. Deeply embedded stereotypes and false perceptions are all real precipitators of white flight. It is what contributes to his torment—the reality of losing a profitable economic base. Closing businesses on Orange and Delaware Avenues will cause a decline in economic growth, loss of jobs and more abandoned buildings. Inevitably this will bring a moral decline which will attract street people and crime.

Another telltale sign of de facto segregation is that ethnic groups are rapidly moving into enclaves of white exclusivity on the periphery of traditional business and school districts. The Mariel boatlift of 1980 brought Cubans, followed by Haitians and then Mexicans who were all joining African Americans and other islanders into once all-white traditional neighborhoods. The residential shift is reflected in the demographics of school districts where the majority are non-white students—little has changed.

As a deterrent, realtors may revert to the 60's blatant and illegal practice of block-busting. Unscrupulous agents selling homes at inflated prices for windfall profits may surely discourage integration as it did during the 60s in the city of Fort Pierce's urban renewal program. For Sale signs dot the yards from Delaware to Orange Avenues as far as Okeechobee Road which demonstrates that many white homeowners are anxious to leave. As people of color encroach on white neighborhoods, there's a perception that banks and other financial institutions will play along with what has been a historically successful discriminatory strategy—redlining. There won't be a gradual shift to gentrify anytime soon despite the trend in major cities with densely populated African-American communities.[2]

---

[2] Blockbusting is an illegal tactic used by real estate agents to encourage white homeowners to sell their homes below market value. To instill fear in the white homeowners, the agents claim that blacks and other minorities will move into their neighborhoods and the value of their homes will plummet. Once whites move out, the agents then sell the property at an inflated price to minorities. Redlining is an illegal, discriminatory and unconstitutional practice that banks, lending institutions, insurance agencies and other services used to color code non-white residential neighborhoods to refuse loans. In 1967 with the advent of school integration, the city of Fort Pierce must have realized the imminent passing of the Fair Housing Act. In 1968 when the act became law, a frantic slum clearance campaign began in the Lincoln Park community. I often questioned while riding the school bus through pristine white

Atlanta, where I live, illustrates this reality as weary white suburbanites who are stuck hours in gridlocked traffic are reclaiming (gentrifying or I should say less politically correct rapidly redistributing blacks or 'Negro removal') inner-city neighborhoods after decades of white flight to avoid living next to black folks. Gridlocked traffic is why they are rethinking where they want to live without realizing how they ended up living so far out of the city. Their narrow-mindedness and lack of historic knowledge doesn't come into play. Apparently hearts and minds haven't changed.

My mind sadly drifts from another time and place as the forces are still pushing back against school integration. Most whites and now some African-Americans and others are pushing back against busing; little has changed. How long will whites continue to flee when people of color arrive? With millions spent on a space station, could this be the next conspiracy theory? Will Mars be the newest frontier for whites to escape in the foreseeable future?

Ever wonder about the credibility of a department store chain's claim that they are closing its doors due to lost revenue? When the store is now full of black shoppers why do they claim to be losing revenue? Even when it's obviously making a profit? Ever think that it's because the neighborhood has become predominately black, even upwardly mobile black? Old strategies never die; their closing has all the underpinnings of racism. In this millennium, overt high-tech racism exists on many fronts.

Sixty-five years has passed since the Brown v. Board of Education decision. Despite the dreams of U.S. Supreme Court Justice Thurgood Marshall, court ordered school desegregation has never truly fostered school integration. As I scope out old familiar playgrounds, all the progress made, at least in theory, toward achieving racial equality still

---

neighborhoods with beautiful homes, paved streets, and well cared for parks, when our time would come. When would we achieve equality? Now as I write this book and I walk through these same neighborhoods I suspect the City of Fort Pierce was frantically clearing slums for new housing in hope of confining blacks to their own neighborhoods as a way to avoid white flight in theirs. As I walk through these neighborhoods African-Americans, Haitians, Mexicans and Islanders have moved in and whites again have fled.

hasn't resulted in school integration. In Fort Pierce and throughout the United States school segregation is alive and well. Eye-sores remain in the racial divide between the haves and the have nots. Endorsements by "the privilege race" still amasses exclusive advantages of economic power and influence over St. Lucie County's Board of Education. Years of accumulated wealth from generation to generation since the days of slavery make it impossible for the black masses to compete politically or economically.

As I walk with my camera in hand, I see how Fort Pierce and other small towns across America have reverted to defacto segregation and remain on a collision course with the progress that was made during the Civil Rights Movement. One step forward, two steps back is little progress indeed.

My lens captures a blurry and familiar figure, the bagman in the distance slowly pushing his grocery cart towards me on the sidewalk. Once again, we cross paths, but this time on the notorious one-mile strip of Avenue D. Once the center of a thriving African-American business district until the late sixties, when the push to integrate restricted public places moved blacks to abandon black-owned businesses and in doing so weakened our own. They were under the illusion that pastures were greener on the other side of the tracks.

Many years of economic abandonment has left the black community of Fort Pierce blighted, crime ridden and drug infested. But there's now a re-emergence of African-American and other ethnic businesses. The area is now being revitalized and designated a historic district as a resurgence of new businesses is gradually awakening, ironically not yet vibrant with life as it had been during Jim Crow segregation. We have, it seems in large measure, lost appreciation for, or have forgotten, how our segregated business empowered us. Blinded by brain-draining complacency and glittering opportunities integration brings, I suppose our people have forgotten a legacy of sustainable black business enterprises on Avenue D before integration. Fredrick Douglass' far-reaching words are still relevant. We must strive and learn from the past and make it useful for today and the future.

7

What defines any race of people is its own economic power base within the borders of its own community. Avenue D, "the strip" as it is known, is a major artery that extends over one mile to the east and to the west of the city to a quarter mile south to Thirteenth Street. A major black business hub during its heyday was a source of black pride and accomplishment.

We eagerly spend our dollars in other business communities owned by many who don't give a damn about us. We make lame excuses why we don't patronize African-American owned business: products sold in black owned stores are too costly, have a limited selection or of inferior quality. Those who complain don't and won't support our businesses in the first place. The issues of cost and quality—what other excuses will they offer now?

Seeking white acceptance and approval still lingers in the minds of many, but it will never be realized at the end of the rainbow. Before racial integration we seemed to be together with sustainable businesses and fewer social ills. The real challenge will occur through our autonomy and our resourcefulness to once again mobilize and rebuild our own institutions that instill racial pride.

My attention drifts once again to several vacant lots where Busy Bee Poolroom and George Jones Juke Joint once stood, evoking both good and bad memories. I stop to take a photo of the historic Lincoln Theater but the ubiquitous bagman obstructs my view. "Hey brother!" "Can you please move for just a minute?" I politely shout. The bagman approaches slowly pushing the cart with its wobbly tires and rattling cans. He gives me a peculiar stare. My intuition tells me that I know him. I take a few shots and leave.

Shooting scenes near a football teammate Chuck Scott's restaurant on Avenue D and Fifteenth, the bagman creeps up from behind and rests on the steps of an old church. Sitting motionless, he stares blankly into the distance. The tread on his shoes is badly worn with the mileage they've accumulated carrying goods of his trade. His heavy woolen sports coat is out of season. The hair on his head matted unlike conventional stylish dreadlocks but the real thing—natty, thick, long, ram like horns out of necessity. "You're Jessie Hawkins? How you doin brother? It's been a long time." He says nothing. "Do you remember Kenny Hurst?" I extend a hand. He keeps staring. "Are you alright Jesse?" He gives nothing but blank empty trance-like eyes. "Sorry to bother you brother," I impatiently say just inches from his face.

It's 95 degrees and I'm making no progress with the brother. I leave looking back into his weathered face. "Do you need help brother . . . hungry?" "Here's something to help you out." He doesn't twitch but takes a folded $10 between his fingers. Suddenly, with that mysterious stare he proceeds to slowly pull out a large 40-ounce can of malt liquor beer from inside his wool coat and takes a sip. "Oh! So that's it!" "You won't talk . . . want to chill and have a cold one . . . I interrupted your break time, right?" No response. The brother's unbelievably cool. I can't get a word out of him. Torn between compassion and impatience, I concede to the latter and walk away.

How can an unassuming man sit on the steps of God's house and drink a can of beer unless he's invisible? Powerless, stripped of hope, pride, and dignity. From a short distance, I turn and look one last time. The money remains between his fingers unchanged as he sips his beer.

I hear footsteps pounding the sidewalk in syncopation as a voice yells out, "Kenny . . . Kenny!" I turn and it's Curtis Jordan, a childhood friend. We embrace and share a few moments of laughter. "Who's that brother?" "Jesse Hawkins. You remember Jessie, don't you?" Curtis says softly out of earshot. "Jessie? I guessed right! Well, he won't speak, not sure he recognizes me." "I know," Curtis retorts. "What happened to him?" "I'll tell you about it." Speaking with reservation, we seek shelter under a shade tree protected from the hot Florida sun.

I try to dismiss Jesse's blank stare but can't erase what he has come to be. It has been twelve years since I last saw Jesse. Several weeks earlier he had been released from jail for loitering. Jesse has numerous loitering charges for sleeping in abandoned buildings; I surmise a few charges from the departed white storeowners who had abandoned their buildings. Jesse's one of many friends with similar tragedies, and others in the making.

Two young bold street thugs, pants sagging, exposed underwear, endemic to loss of pride and low self-esteem count a roll of collected bills. Unphased by my presence, they flag down a potential customer. A driver stops in the middle of Avenue D, rap music blasting profanities and that despicable n..ga in sync with honking cars delaying traffic for a vial of crack cocaine; all done within eyeshot of the Fort Pierce Police substation.

I wonder if they have finished high school—lost interest and dropped out or a bad attitude got them both kicked out. I doubt either give a damn about the hardships civil rights crusaders endured during my generation. Our fights for racial justice made it possible for him to have a quality education. I watch young brothers not in school, hanging out, content just pushing dope. Undaunted by the inevitable impending doom and jail time it will surely bring. Too many glamorize the thug life in desperate need of mentoring so they can learn how to be responsible and respectable young men.

We are too consumed by self-interest. We must espouse the "each one, teach one" concept to pass along the knowledge we have acquired. No longer can we blame the white man solely for ills in our community. Whites are generally neither interested nor will they save us; we must save ourselves. We are a resilient people who rose up after emancipation. Our forefathers walked away from the plantation ragged, uneducated and free. We walked away with an uncertain future, rather than accepting the slave master's trappings of a new deal back on the plantation. In spite of enduring suffering we have an innovatively rich and vibrant cultural heritage that is an integral part of the American cultural fabric.

Why do so many blacks care so little about our communities anymore? Why have we lost our activism? The fight for equality is never over. We must not sit quietly by while others establish businesses in our communities. At the end of the day these business owners take their profits out of the community and invest it elsewhere.

We must not waver from teaching a code of ethics to our youth and to each other. As the white store manager stated, "Education is power." Jesse, a childhood friend, neighbor and schoolmate, never got past the 9th grade during our unsettled school years transitioning into integration. Smart and free-spirited Jesse and many like him faced their demise during a hostile time in our country's turbulent history of racial intolerance. Violence, riots, school fights, suspensions and expulsions were endured on a regular basis. Labeled troublemakers, without established programs to transition back into school, many were neglected and fell prey to a life of crime, imprisonment and death on the mean streets of Fort Pierce.

Almost at the end of my tour on the home stretch I spot familiar classmates, Johnny, Beanie, Squirrel Nut, Sneaky Pea, Albert and others who are hanging out on a bench sharing bottles of Thunderbird wine. Their bloodshot eyes and depressed faces look beyond reproach. They are slumped in a drunken stupor of wasted lives; all victims of the rocky transition from segregation to desegregation to integration and the subsequent racial unrest in St. Lucie County's public schools.

I imagine what stories from school all can tell. Perhaps they are faded memories and shattered dreams lost in a bottle of wine. Invisible men lost in this promised land of opportunity. I wonder whether any will recognize me now. Or maybe I should naively avoid saying hello, years removed from their lives I'll hardly be recognizable. I keep walking, thinking it will be too self-serving. I just can't stop—too many flashbacks of my past life intersecting theirs. I'm the lucky one.

A causal connection exists from their downward spiral and those years of racial indifference. These schoolmates and others were kicked out or quit, hardly tracked for follow-up and reentry they remain forgotten. An uncaring school board and faculty, racial insensitivity, and the absence of educational resources basically ensured their fate. Reentry didn't happen. Many carry an intractable degree of anger, rejection, disappointment, resentment born out every day on the mean streets.

What is troubling are remnants of the past—invisible forgotten people of my school years wandering aimlessly, carrying heavy burdens of emotional and psychological scars.

As a society, we're quick to test the veracity of their stories, ready to beat them down and regard them as excuses for victimization. In numerous major cities across America and my home Atlanta,

Georgia, so-called "Black Mecca— The City too Busy to Hate," I am saddened to see the homeless, mostly black men panhandling on city streets primarily due to an economic downturn. In a city of over 5 million, one can easily become invisible. I discovered as an addiction counselor in Atlanta, clients on my caseload share similar patterns of decline in the desegregation era with my buddies and classmates. With the coordinated efforts of Dr. King Field General and Hosea Williams inspirational messages and client testimonies sparked the birth of this book and its companion publication soon to follow.[3]

Volunteering for Hosea Williams' Feed the Hungry and Homeless Programs on regular holidays one can witness over 15,000 homeless, mostly black men, gather at Fulton County Stadium. The sheer numbers are incomprehensible and shock the consciousness of human dignity.

Several brothers were sitting at a table finishing a hot meal and struggling with an employment application as I was serving meals. "I don't know what they asking man . . . I quit school . . . I was angry at the system of integration . . . back then them white teachers didn't give a damn." A brother says. "You got to write your experience," a brother added. "What experience?" another asks. Julian and Edmond recognized me approaching. I'd been their counselor in a treatment program three months earlier, surprisingly neither had relapsed.

The struggle that day was employment opportunities. Neither of them had had success due to their lack of education. "I quit school angry at white teachers, Edmond tells me. I was smart but it didn't matter to them anyway so I quit. I was angry." "Me too brother, I kept getting suspended for fighting . . . you know crackers got under my skin." I regret it too but how can a homeless man get a job now worrying about how to get a meal every day? I get drunk."

I believe that there's a direct correlation between the many homeless brothers and sisters now invisible on the streets and the

---

[3] I was surprised and appreciative when Reverend Hosea Williams, civil rights icon, minister, scientist, businessman and politician, responded to my invitation to address those facing addiction and mental health challenges.

turbulent efforts during the 60s to integrate schools. Many suffered traumatic racial experiences in the era of desegregation. Underlying factors are consistent today—anger from the past and lack of education contribute to low self-esteem and self-hatred that inevitably lead to drug addiction, crime and becoming victims of violence.

What must we do to help heal lingering psychological and emotional wounds of our brothers and sisters left behind after the advent of school desegregation? We must resolve to revisit the past and aid those who are suffering from PTSD. Those of us who have successful careers can attest that education is the cornerstone to an empowerment that is life transforming. *Education is in fact the key to positive change.*

Our people have been left behind in disproportionate numbers. We can't afford to devalue the importance of education. The trappings of street-life have ruined my childhood friends who are seemingly lost beyond reproach. Yet they look back and say, "I shouldn't have given up . . . they wanted me to quit. . . I wish I kept fighting. My life would be different."

Lest we not forget the great strives against insurmountable odds our ancestors endured. These are exemplary success stories. Captured in Africa, many retained their cultural identity, consciously rejected slavery and remained free of a slave mentality. Millions survived the Middle Passage to North America and the diaspora as slaves. They had a brief moment of optimism during Reconstruction until Jim Crow took hold and turned their lives upside down with segregation and violence. Yet with great sacrifice and a thirst for knowledge to succeed in a new world through education our ancestors did rise up.

This book is dedicated to invisible classmates who are overlooked, marginalized, doomed to failure by the ill-prepared St. Lucie County school system. The fight for equality and a quality education isn't over. Education for sure is the great equalizer. We must aid those who continue to fall victim to the streets through poverty, socio-economic hardships and systemic racism, as the powers that push back on our significant gains through civil rights legislation. Those of us who made sacrifices and now reap the benefits of school integration must not give in to complacency. We must not turn our backs ever again, rather we must ignite a fire in the less fortunate hearts and minds to give them hope and to show them the value of a righteous struggle.

Chapter 1

BUSTER BROWNS

"Ahh! Help me! Somebody help me!" I awaken to screams from a familiar voice. I jumped into action knocking on Mama and Daddy's bedroom door. "Wake up! I hear Mr. Jesus (Spanish name pronounced hay-zoos) screaming." At the age of five I see things. Mama says it's my imagination, as if a magic wand summons images of white horses, clowns, angels, and people moving about in my bedroom keeping me company at night. "Go back to bed . . . it's just your imagination!" Daddy yells back.

"Despierta cada uno!" "Wake up everyone!" Jesus has a way of waking up the neighborhood like clockwork early on Saturday mornings. Within a short time moving into a quaint three-bedroom duplex apartment on Avenue E neighbors get to know this peculiar Mexican by his signature wake-up call. My bedroom has a window with a view of everything moving outside. Jesus sits on the steps of his trailer with a terrible hangover cursing no one. Daddy say Jesus gets this way after some woman steals his hard-earned money after a Friday night out drinking. It seems Jesus never gets it right with women.

Jesus is polite and kind to all the neighborhood kids. He is a migrant worker with a lot of troubles who I catch sadly crying, hitting the bottle, and drowning in his sorrows. Mama warns me to stay away but I'm inquisitively drawn in, listening to his troubles in broken English. Across the street is a sanctified church of some variety. Some days and especially Sunday mornings getting ready for Sunday school at our church, I watch Jesus from my window. "Hello pretty senorita!" He tips his cowboy hat at every passing lady entering church.

The syncopated drumbeats, tambourines, and amplified guitars blast as the congregation shouts and claps in time to the rhythm. Jesus quickly taps his cowboy boots in flamenco dance steps. The drumbeats get me hyped too, and I start jumping up and down on my bed. Like Jesus, I stomp and dance on the floor like the holy ghost got into me, until Daddy threatens to lay some leather on my behind if I don't stop.

Sirens are getting louder now, and flashing red lights illuminate off my bedroom walls. "Charles wake up!" I hear Mama's voice. "There's a fire outside!" I see smoke from my window billowing upwards as flames engulf Jesus' trailer next to our apartment. "Stay inside!" Daddy yells, as Gail, Regina and I look out my window for a better view. Mama grabs my baby sister Sheryl and they go outside with Daddy to investigate. Policemen hurry about keeping people back as firefighters break open the trailer door with hatchets and douse the flames. Neighbors gather and many are crying. Mama too is crying as Daddy comforts her. A stretcher brings out Jesus under a bloody wrapped sheet with his stiffly bent arms poking upwards like he was trying hard to get out. The cries get louder seeing Jesus this way and I cry too. Daddy hears neighbors tell police that a jealous man who was angry at Jesus over a woman set his trailer on fire.

I'm unable to get back to sleep. Early that morning I go outside to look at Jesus's badly torched trailer and cry some more. Jesus is dead. Who would do such a thing? Afterwards, as I play outside Mama watches me like a hawk.

There was always excitement at every turn in my neighborhood when I lived in Fort Pierce the Sunrise City. We lived in a segregated community known as Lincoln Park on the Treasure Coast in south Florida. Lincoln Park was like a small island surrounded by a vast ocean of white people; like a speck of small black insignificant matter. Fifteenth Street where I lived is on the periphery of Avenue D, the main strip, a prosperous black business district. The strip flourishes with barber shops, restaurants, pool halls, nightclubs, a theatre and pharmacy, furniture stores, funeral homes, a newspaper company, five and dime stores, and a host of other black businesses. Black people are constantly on the move with somewhere to go; everyone's anxious to get there in a hurry accompanied by the sounds of sirens and occasional gunfire. Tractor trailers speed past our home day and night, hauling tons of oranges and grapefruits, kicking up clouds of dust on dirt roads on their way to citrus processing and packaging plants. I watch and listen, marveling at all the excitement I see.

Charles and Margaret out for a night of Entertainment in one of many black businesses In Fort Pierce Lincoln Park community. Circa,1951. (Courtesy of Hurst family archives).

Sylvester or "Slobber Mouth," my neighborhood buddy, has a gift of gab. His grandmother owns a kindergarten where I attend and where she brags about Slobber Mouth every chance she gets. "Slob!" "Sista Mammie comes by to see ya . . . show ha what ya know!" Slobber's nauseating voice tells jokes and makes a room comes alive with laughter. On rainy days during playtime, instead of taking a nap, Sylvester entertain his parents' guests and us kindergartners. We laugh so hard some children wet their pants.

His parents are friends with my family. Slob's a natural born dribbler, with a rather large gaping mouth that hangs open as the constant flow of thick oozing spit drips out. Sometimes a fly lands on his blubber lips and sticks like a Venus flytrap. Sylvester's hyper-verbal action has no shame in his game. Nor is he embarrassed dribbling. The more he talks, the more he slobs. Into his teens he entertains us with a barrage of dirty dozen jokes about "yo Mama." And Slob's mother doesn't seem embarrassed, always ready with an ample supply of clean shirts on hand.

In the early 60's Fort Pierce is a medium-sized town of about 32,000 residents with a significant degree of black and educated progressive professionals with no effective political power base during Jim Crow segregation. My parents worked as common laborers. Mama gave up her dream and left nursing school to care for her ailing mother. Daddy as a longshoreman traveled up and down the eastern coast of Florida loading and emptying ships. It was a good job, long hours for a married man, his wages far less than that of whites. Daddy detested discrimination in his pay, and he couldn't conceal his hatred for racial inequality. In World War II while serving in France, the French treated him equally only to return home mistreated as a second-class citizen. "I'm a man . . . I demand being treated like one!" he says to Mama many times. I sit listening not quite understanding. It was during this time in my young life that Daddy began to lose jobs as he continued speaking his mind against America's great contradiction—freedom and justice for all.

Working for S&M Packing Company he joined the American Federation of Labor Citrus Workers Union. He help organize younger black men to speak up and out against wage disparity and mistreatment. On other jobs he tried to organize blacks, yet his robust activities had no impact against institutional racism. Singled out a troublemaker repeatedly fired from jobs in attempts to organize black workers. Daddy held meetings with angry men in our living room. "Whites have colored folks locked down with their laws," Daddy says to friends visiting. "Little we can do to change . . . unless we organize." It was during this time at a young age that I realized that there was something bad about white people because Daddy and his friends said it a lot.

My father in center ground foot on fruit box with cigar a Citrus Workers Union member and organizer circa, 1954 (Courtesy of Hurst family archives).

One day Daddy came home, pacing angrily. "I almost got arrested . . . this cracker gets in front of me to pay his gas bill . . . like I'm nobody. I ask him to move . . . he did . . . but I went off," Daddy said to Mama as he continued to pace. Daddy most days came home with distressful stories about some white problem. I watched him angrily slam doors after being fired from another job after arguing with his white boss.

Daddy gambled and as he lost jobs his gambling inevitably increased. This proved tenuous because bills go unpaid and arguments at home increase. I run to my room and hide. Mama discovers Daddy's gambling spot at the Nassau camp (a camp for Bahamian and Jamaican migrant guest workers). When he returns home an argument starts and he pushes Mama onto the bed. I pick up my red rocking chair and threaten, "Don't you hit my Mama!" He looks at me apologetically and leaves the house. I learn later that Daddy was seeing a doctor for depression. His refusal to bow down contently to an unjust system and unsteady work to support his growing family was taking its toll.

Mr. Albert Stone, a successful entrepreneur and funeral home director owned the Lincoln Theatre, restaurants, sundae shop and other thriving businesses including the Lincoln Cab Company. News spread that Mr. Stone needed ten reliable and trustworthy men with a strong moral character to drive for his company. Daddy's name was passed around, and hired to drive and was given a steady salary which improved his mood.

On weekends, Daddy invites his buddies over for card games to unwind and lay burdens down while Mama's at work. It was a way black folks found creative ways to be themselves when not under the grip of segregation. There's much excitement and I peak and listen through the kitchen door outside. Although Daddy rarely drinks, after a few beers he and his buddies stop the card game to talk of racial injustices. How some nasty disrespectful cracker cops beat and almost kill a black man in his jail cell; how quick cops put a blackjack upside the heads of defenseless drunken black men.[4]

---

[4] Strips of woven leather around many small iron balls into a flexible Billy Club—this officer's issued weapon can inflict deadly injury.

"A white cop tried to hit me." Daddy was standing near his cab late one night on Avenue D, when a white cop asks him about the whereabouts of a black man. Daddy knew him but wouldn't tell and didn't answer quickly enough. The cop rises up to strike as other black men gather around. Daddy takes the cop's blackjack away. The cop realized he's at a disadvantage and drives away. I discover a blackjack tucked away in Daddy's dresser drawer. I swing it forcefully into my palm feeling the force of its use upside a defenseless black man's head. I listen and I begin to worry about Daddy as much as he and his friends worry most weekends.

I'm one sickly accident-prone joker. "Just hurt me!"Seems it's written into a bull's-eye pinned to my chest. Accidents await me at every turn. Routine visits to Fort Pierce Memorial Hospital's emergency room for severe cuts and bruises from slips and falls; a fishbone caught in my throat; pieces of gravel lodged in an ear and nose; stitches in the upper lip after falling head first from a tree onto a broken bottle. Anemic with a heart murmur and a poor appetite, I cause my family headaches.

Exploring Grandma's new style washer-wringer machine after warnings, I keep playfully sticking my hand between the two wooden rollers. The wringers pull my arm up to my elbow making a snapping sound. I cry out in excruciating pain, arriving at the emergency room hollering at the top of my lungs. My arm looks like a big balloon and throbs in great pain. Doctors know my parents from routine visits. The orderlies wheel me over to the "colored section" I spend a night or wait again until some white doctor shows up. Each time I go to Fort Pierce Memorial Hospital I leave asking questions: "Mama why does the doctor take so long?" "Why we wait in this little crampy room?" "Why white boys go the other way?" My parents never hid the truths with untruths as I quickly began to understand why my Daddy stood up to white folks. When I get older and I am frequenting the hospital with another injury I see other colored children who are lying on the same scratched and peeling green bunk beds with badly worn lumpy and stinking mattresses I had laid on. I realized that nothing had changed.

As any inquisitive child of six would do, I internalize what I have heard and come to believe that black lives mean little or nothing. Black folks lose their lives for the sake of first saving a white one. "No matter how much pain black people suffer in the emergency room you conceal your anger . . . even though you expect a white doctor to see you after he finishes with a white patient," Mama said. I remember what grandma said although we live just two blocks away from the hospital, we're on colored folk's time different from whites.

Several weeks in a cast, I re-break my arm jumping from my tree house when a limb holding me snaps in two. Mama can't afford risking another medical bill to have my arm reset. Overtime the bone in my elbow fuses and slightly twists, limiting motion. Seldom allowed outside with friends, I must hold my oldest sister Gail's hand whenever we go for accident prevention. I feel like a pet on a lease being yanked along.

Getting outside in the sun is out of the question. Being anemic with a poor appetite causes a decrease in energy, lessening my interest in leaving the nest for the outdoors. With a poor appetite, cornbread and water is all I like and crave for. I shrink like a dried-up prune. After losing fifteen pounds below normal weight, Doctor Clem C. Benton, Fort Pierce's only black physician, intervenes and prescribes vitamins and a high-calorie diet. Soon thereafter Mama's resorts to force feeding and gives me a quick spanking if I leave one morsel of food on my plate.[5]

Gail behaves older and more mature than her nine years. She is smart and had started first grade at the age of four. Before she had turned nine, she had a pronounced gray streak near her left temple and was often mistaken as being older. She developed a greater

---

[5] Zora Neal Hurston, American author, anthropologist, filmmaker, folklorist, civil rights advocate who live, taught at Lincoln Park Academy, and was buried in Fort Pierce fell on hard times. Dr. Benton let her live rent free in one of his homes knowing the importance of her work as an artist. This black luminary respected by white business community helped in 1930's established Fort Pierce Memorial Hospital. A Federal Building in Fort Pierce is named in his honor. As a child, I have fond memories of his visits when I was in the segregated section of the hospital, and of my visits to his Eighth Street Doctor's office.

level of maturity because of that gray streak. It gets her good-intentioned comments from adult neighbors who called her the "little old lady." Children's teasing doesn't seem to bother her either. I'm attached to Gail's constant supervision aware of any attention she receives. Strategies are devised for Gail to say how yummy her vegetables are. "I want some peas!"

Over the summer Gail yells out. I quickly reply with pleasure, "I want some too!" mimicking her. I'm rewarded with books and toys.

Grandma steps in and my appetite significantly improves. Considering Grandma is part of a united front of force feeding, she stuffs vegetables down my throat. As my appetite increases, Mama rewards me with a pair of "black and white" Buster Brown shoes to wear to Sunday school. I gain meat on my gangly bones with Dr. Benton's vitamins, check-ups and weigh-ins.

Daddy buys me a pair of brown Buster Browns and later a two toned brown and white pair after my eating improves. I love my Buster Browns sometimes sleeping with them on my feet all night. After playing outside acting sporty and scuffing my favorite shoes Daddy spit shines them to make them look new. Every chance I get outside, I show them off to friends and neighbors. "Boy I'm on top of the world!"

A friendly new family from Georgia moves in the neighborhood. I hit it off with John Wesley right away. John Wesley's two sisters, Marie and especially the oldest Hattie Mae, have the prettiest smiles. Her smile incased with dimples showing pearly whites makes me crave her attention.

I'm obsessed with seeing Hattie Mae's smile every day. I can't keep my eyes off her. I'm hooked in ways I can't imagine.

My mind runs wild with angels, the Three Musketeers or a big white horse in my bedroom. I bang on Mama and Daddy's bedroom door at night for witnesses, but they won't investigate anymore. Confined to my room, to ease the boredom Mama buys more books for me to read. She takes time assisting with my proficiency. When she misses a chance reading to my sisters and at bedtime, in my little red rocking chair I read the same Dr. Seuss series, Little Gingerbread Man, Little Black Sambo and Tar Baby (Black Sambo and Tar Baby later become racially offensive to others) over and over. I watch my favorites: "It's Howdy Doody Time," "Cannonball," and "Wagon Train" on one of the only three TV channels available at that time.

Sometimes I sneak outside running like a greyhound to Hattie Mae's house. I want Hattie Mae for a girlfriend. I have a crush on her that can't wait, and everyone knows it. I strut around with my Buster Browns doing crazy things to get her attention. But Hattie Mae just laughs. Sometimes Gail lets me roam freely and I lie on my back mannishly sneaking peaks under Hattie Mae's dress as she and Gail play hopscotch and jackstones.

One afternoon, I notice Hattie Mae walking past our apartment heading to the corner store. I excitedly bolt, thinking it's a good time to show off my new two-toned Buster Browns. I run into the street into the path of a car. All I remember seeing is a silver grill bumper. The car grill hits my head, chest, plows over my leg and screeches to a stop. I awaken from unconsciousness, again in the segregated section on a funky green hospital bunk bed. Mama's crying and Daddy's worried as several white men in white jackets perch over me with red eyes staring into mine with a flash light.

I notice one of my Buster Brown shoes missing. After hearing frantic beeps from a car horn Mama sees it go up in the air. The doctor says I'm lucky to be alive. The driver barely missed running over my entire body, escaping by the grace of God with a concussion, bruised ribs and a broken leg. I lay in traction—leg hoisted up in a cast in the stinky colored section of Fort Pierce Memorial Hospital.

For a week I sleep on a rather hard bunk bed. I meet this funny guy, Curtis Hudgeon in for appendectomy surgery. He always smiles and cracks jokes. We become good friends and celebrate my seventh birthday together with ice cream and cake. Daddy brings my badly smashed left shoe home. My Buster Browns were never replaced. I never chased behind Hattie Mae again, perhaps knocked to my senses.[6]

---

[6] Several years later, I came home from Pepper Park Beach after meeting Curtis there turn on the television to the news and sadly discovered Curtis Hudgeon had drowned.

Here I am in my favorite pair of Buster Browns with my mother Margaret, and sister Regina in her Kodak moment. (Courtesy of Hurst family archives).

Chapter 2

A CRISIS AT HOME

How can you be grateful for some explainable circumstances? I am listening but not quite understanding Grandma's message, something about a prophetic sign from God saying I'm special. Some things do happen for reasons beyond your comprehension but like the old proverb that says a cat has nine lives. I could have been killed by that big car with its shiny chrome grill. Grandma says God allowed me to escape death surviving another scare.

I don't understand the crampy conditions of a segregated hospital. I know my own bed feels better than a bunk bed with a hard mattress. I want to go home. Sometime after Mama and Daddy visit, Slob and John Wesley come with their parents. To have Curtis and Slob joking helps to kill boredom and my wanting to go home. The white nurses and everyone else cracks up laughing at Slob's dribbling while telling jokes. And I laugh so hard gripping the edge of the bed. I almost fall out and hurt my leg at the same time.

Grandma comes and prays at bedside with members of Mount Olive Baptist where we attend church. After the course of all my mishaps, I become convinced I'm special and God's looking out for me. Immediately upon my release, arrangements are made for a tranquil and rural environment free of speeding vehicles. Grandma's home on Tenth Street provides serenity in contrast to our busy neighborhood.

Daddy's cab buddies, Chris Powell whom he calls "loaf of bread" and Marion Parker, come by often with my favorite snacks to satisfy my appetite and lift my spirits. Marion, a big gregarious man with a loud booming laugh tells funny jokes. I crack up laughing. Confined to bed in pain with a broken leg, bruised ribs and splitting headaches from a concussion, there's little to do and no television to watch at Grandma's house.

One day Marion brings an interesting book to read entitled, "The Illustrated Encyclopedia of Animal Life." A section had stories about Africa's wildlife and limited commentary of its people, their cultures and kingdoms with colorful pictures and maps. I spend most of my days recovering reading fascinating stories about Africa and its vivid wildlife. I can't put it down. People in the book look like me. It was not that I haven't seen black people in books before, but on "Tarzan" black people were portrayed as uncivilized.

Mama and Daddy kept a collection of reading material on the coffee table and throughout the house. Sepia magazine that chronicles black achievements; the Fort Pierce Chronicle, a black-owned and operated newspaper addressing our community's concerns and many literary works of authors like Richard Wright's Native Son, Ralph Ellison's Invisible Man and Zora Neal Hurston's Their Eyes Were Watching God. Hurston had lived in Fort Pierce years earlier and she is buried here.

I have no understanding of Africa other than seeing Tarzan on television with Africans holding spears running around in the jungle half-naked chasing white people. The encyclopedia sparks my interest in Africa. I lay in bed fantasizing about being in Africa. The book indelibly gives me a new vision. It fashioned my love of Africa in a positive light and rid my confusion from the negative depictions in episodes of "Tarzan." The book shapes my understanding about what it means to be black, and what I hoped to become. The book helped my understanding and connection to Africa and it becomes the catalyst to my enlightenment. I develop at a young age an African-centered consciousness.

I split time living between Grandma's and home. Doctor Benton finally removed the cast and I stumble over myself walking to gain strength in my boney atrophied leg.

Mama gets angry about Daddy's gambling and arguments ensue over unpaid bills. Sometimes he doesn't come home after work. Mama knows his gambling spots and she goes to get him from under a shade tree or out at someone's house. Other time she dispatches at Lincoln cabs Chris Powell his taxi buddy. Chris goes out to the Nassau Camp and urges Daddy to come home. When Daddy returns sometimes subtle arguments get loud followed by a kiss and make up.

Daddy smokes the best Cuban cigars (some say the only black man smoking cigars during those years), sometimes unlit dangling from his mouth. Mama says it helps to relax him when he's immersed in deep thought. There are increasing signs of irritability once he arrives home from work. Once mimicking Daddy with an unlit stogie poking out from my mouth he goes into a rage and kicks me. At a time of episodic bouts of anger, depression and mood swings, our family goes through hard times watching Daddy unleash residues of anger from the effects of chronic job firings he labels mistreatment. "I'm not gonna bite my lip to a disrespectful cracker!" he'd say sadly and then apologize, "I'm sorry son; I don't know what got into me." Immediately he'd lift me into his arms as I cry.

Spending time together with Daddy.
(Courtesy of Hurst family archives).

28

Some days Daddy comes home on a break and loads me and my sisters on a dispatch call to an area of the city for a pickup. Sometime he takes us riding across tickle tummy hill. We sit up front and he's smiling, biting down on his unlit stogie while customers talk about what good manners we have. Daddy provides the ultimate professionalism, having etiquette down to a science. Little old ladies would rather wait for their "sweet Charlie" (the name Charlie sticks throughout his life) than have another driver dispatched to their residence. A regular cadre of maids brags how handsome a man Daddy is, dapperly dresser, and the most reliable and popular cabbie in town. But beneath his smiles and candor, Daddy's cloaked in unpredictability.

Daddy saved enough money to buy a car which he converted into a cab. He selects his own hours to work and makes a comfortable living to support his family. At that time, cab transportation in Fort Pierce's black community is at a premium. Sometimes Daddy brings home a cigar box and coin holder worn around his waist filled with coins which he empties onto the dinner table. He made lots of money because black business is booming during Jim Crow segregation.

Mama and Daddy love reading, sitting and discussing world events. Mama is very civic minded and an active member in several community organizations. Together they often sit over dinner discussing politics and civil rights issues, especially the mistreatment of black folks in our segregated lives. Daddy love baseball, especially the Baltimore Orioles, and some days his buddies come over to watch games on television or listen to them on the radio.

Education means a lot to my parents. At bedtime Mama read to us and Daddy too, if he's not completely exhausted from work. Mama finished high school at Lincoln Park Academy in the top of her class with a year of nursing school in New York, subsequently returning home to care for her ill mother. Daddy received his early education up to 7th grade in a one-room structure. The makeshift school seated 30 children in Wrightsville, Georgia, a rural farming community. To further his education, he hitch-hiked rides 20-miles into Dublin, sometimes on the back of hay wagons. With determination Daddy got his high school diploma.

My father, Charles Lewis Hurst at age 19 looking dapper. (Courtesy of Hurst family archives).

My beloved mother Margaret Anne Jay at age 18 looking beautiful as ever. (Courtesy of Hurst family archives).

Fort Pierce's stifling employment opportunities for blacks during segregation cause mounting frustration in Daddy who is supporting a growing family. Although I become familiar with more than occasional arguments, one morning I awaken to a shouting match more intense than ever. Mama and Daddy are in each other's faces and then I see Daddy push Mama onto their bed. Almost 7 years old at the time, I go into a protective mode. "You better not hit my Mama!" I screamed, grabbing my red rocking chair, threatening to hit him with it. Embarrassment and shame thwart and eclipse his anger. Standing there a moment looking down at me, he apologetically leaves vowing never again to let it happen. And he keeps his promise, although the arguments never cease.

Mama warns my sisters and me to cautiously stay our distance. But how can you resist a father's infectious hugs and smiles? When Daddy comes home, he usually greeted us with a surprise, candy or some other scrumptious delicious goodies. The most distinguishing thing Mama likes about Daddy is his self-pride and penchant for cleanliness, unmatched. A serious cut to the chase type who has no patience for gossip. I have vivid memories of a father refusing to let an unjust system break him down have its reprisals and setbacks; a black man that confronts and retaliates against a white man is bound to lose in a court of law.

After numerous job losses, Daddy has become quite cunning in residual retaliation. I was not too young to remember the things linked to Daddy's anger. A white repairman came to clean out our backed-up cesspool leaking raw sewage and emitting noxious odors to the disgust of neighbors. The repairman stands in the backyard examining the cesspool exuding an air of arrogance in racial undertones. "Y'all people really can mess up things." Daddy put him in his place. "What people are you referring to?" The white man stutters. "Ah I meant . . ." Daddy cut in. "I know what you mean . . . Negro shit clogs more than white shit . . . where you get that damn lie from?" The white man turns ruby red gazing downwards. "Sorry mister . . . I meant nothing by it." "Then get to work," Daddy snaps leaving the repairman scratching his head, dumbfounded.

It seems Daddy sees no need to abandon his principals when racial innuendoes seep into his personal and private life. A persistent encyclopedia salesman comes knocking at the door. He calls Mama "gal" although she has since given her name. I in later years get clarity to this story. Daddy jumps from the sofa and charges, "You address my wife properly cracker or take your business elsewhere!" "Yes sir . . . yes sir," the man says. "Sorry ma'am." "If you want our business take it to the back door!" The white man complies, and Daddy orders our first collection of encyclopedias.

One day an arrogant white man shows up unexpectedly selling an insurance policy. Daddy's quick to put him in his place. "If you want my money bring it to the back door. You're on my side of town now." I sit watching the white man not fully understanding until later years. Red face miserably put in such a humiliating spot taking orders from a Negro. The salesman like money doesn't outwardly complain drops his head (as a Negro is required to do) slowly walks around to the backdoor. Daddy lets him in with a cunning smile. The salesman sits nervously ruffling through papers with sales jargon then quickly leaves. He must have understood that he was taking the brunt of Daddy's retaliation against the oppressive and unjust system he represents. He never showed his face at our front door or back door again. I remember at this young age worrying about Daddy's behavior.

Sometimes Daddy stayed home until Gail and I come home from school and then he leaves for work. Owning his own cab, he gets to set when and how many hours he works and then pays a percentage of his earnings to Mr. Stone, the owner of Lincoln Cab Company. One day my sisters Gail and Regina are watching television waiting for Daddy to come home. He enters in a somber mood and tells Mama he might be in trouble and it has something to do with a white man. Daddy's anxiously pacing in the living room continually peeping through the curtains. "Go to your rooms," Mama insists. We drag along reluctantly. Something is wrong. I peep through my cracked bedroom door, listening.

Daddy was taking two maids home from work, when a white man flags Daddy demanding he be taken home first. Daddy refused. The white man's drunk and rudely curses and make threats. "I won't tolerate your language in front of my customers," Daddy addresses the inebriated and belligerent white man. As the man persists, Daddy pulls over to the curb demanding he get out. The man refuses and yells, "Kiss my ass n....r." "I ain't goin anywhere!" Daddy drags the man out of his cab as he yells stinging racial epithets and obscenities a second time. Daddy obliges him with one of his size ten wing tips to his rear end. The elderly maid is shaken never having witnessed a black man assault a white man in any such manner, fearing the white man will retaliate with the police. Daddy leaves the man lying on the ground groaning, cursing, "I'll get you n....r." Daddy had indeed confronted and retaliated against a white man and he knew his chances didn't look good.

That evening Officer Bill Ellis a friend of our family, and Gail's godfather arrives. He is one of four black officers on the Fort Pierce police force who are only allowed to arrest black citizens. Officer Ellis (in earlier years the four were known as the "Black Messiahs" patrolling the Lincoln Park community in what was once a bread truck) comes to warn Daddy of a warrant taken out for his arrest. "For the safety of your family turn yourself in Charles," Ellis says, or they will come arrest you." "Let them come . . . I'll be waiting," Daddy replies seriously.[7]

Officer Ellis leaves unable to convince Daddy to turn himself in.

Later that night as I watch "It's Howdy Doody Time" on television, cops come with lights flashing in front of our home. Mama rushes us all into her bedroom; once again I crack the door with Gail to watch. I never knew until later about Daddy's growing impatience with Jim Crow laws and struggles that endured since his youth and now are his personal demons.

Daddy stood watch peeping through the curtains with gun in hand. Waiting outside with lights flashing is the brutal and racist Fort Pierce Police Department known for cracking black skulls with billyclubs. "Come out with your hands up!" A call out comes through a bullhorn. Mama can see cops milling about outside, guns drawn on the ready. When Officer Ellis returns to the door, he's accompanied by white cops to deliver the warrant. Daddy had finally yielded to Mama's pleas to leave, for our safety was long gone.

---

[7] On July 17, 1966, Willie B. Ellis became the first Fort Pierce police officer killed in the line of duty. His death became instrumental in opening the conversation about race and how the city of Fort Pierce needed to change. Officer Ellis was promoted posthumously to Sergeant. A Fort Pierce Police Department Substation is dedicated to his memory on Avenue D—the strip.

Chapter 3

A SCENTILLA OF HOPE

Daddy sends Chris "Loaf-ah-Bread" Powell to tell Mama he'll pick up his check at Lincoln Cabs. He'll send her money, get work done to his car and leave for Baltimore, Maryland before the police find him. No plans of returning, pleading with Mama to come, but she doesn't want to leave my sick Grandma behind. By the mid-1960s I am living regularly with Grandma with supervision from the streets almost nonexistent. On weekends, I shoot marbles, climb trees, and dig caves to hideout with buddies to keep me busy. Sometimes I play hours on hot narrow dirt roads that become even dustier after a vehicle passes by at slow speeds.

I spend a lot of time with buddies in wooded areas across the street where neighbors claim the original Fort, named after union officer Kendrick Pierce, brother of President Franklin Pierce exist. We dig caves in the area where I find artifacts of pieces of arrowheads and pieces of decayed and crystallized wood which might have belonged to the old fort.

Almost a stone's throw away a panoramic view of the Atlantic Ocean looms majestically as the picturesque backdrop to our daily activities. Even Grandma's yard provides a scenic view—like a prophetic Garden of Eden. All around are small patches of lush gardens filled with different vegetables. A canopy of mango and orange trees with an array of mouth-watering cane, guavas, bananas, avocados and wild berries separates our yard from our neighbors' yards. According to my family history, Grandpa Ollie Jay, a man of industrious wit, energy, and zest for life had a green thumb—a master of planting and gardening. Grandpa was the first to rise each morning saying, "Wake up and make something out of your day!"

Somehow Grandma believed Grandpa passed his wit on to me since I like planting in south Florida's rich sticky black muck soil that smells like something crawled in a hole and died. We're blessed because muck soil causes seeds to germinate and sprout in less time than most soils. And muck attracts bait that grows the size of your pinky, which is ideal for fishing.

The woods surrounding our neighborhood are inhabited by possum, rabbits, armadillos, squirrels, raccoons, skunks, turtles, bats, snakes, numerous species of insects and a wide variety of tropical birds. This intriguing environment sustains in me a new found happiness for the outdoors. With so much to discover, I make friends rather easily. We climb and build tree houses and dig underground tunnels in the white porous sand. We live the day off wild fruit and berries. Roasting robins we shot with our BB guns and sling shots and hide out from noisy tell-tell girls.

After weeks at Grandma's, something attracts my attention I haven't noticed before. A kind of eeriness creeps through the neighborhood bringing unwanted attention to the imminent gloom and doom in man's mortality. It appears some days and most weekends and dampens the peace and tranquility of the neighborhood and its residents. The Grim Reaper makes his rounds creeping around, noticeably interrupting our lives, clearing the streets of playful kids, stopping cars, silencing boisterous conversations, and demanding respect for the dead from a visibly sedated and captive audience. All activities cease, all eyes watch as time stands still. For these moments, I keep reminding myself how valuable life must be as I watch the big black Hearse Cadillac leads a funeral procession past our house on Tenth Street and Avenue H and dead ends into Pine Grove Cemetery.

Grandma loves weaving horrific ghost stories about the dead in the graveyard striking fear in me and my siblings as we hang to every word till late at night on the weekends. I get up enough nerve to venture and see if I can spot a ghost during daylight hours, at least to check it out.

One Sunday after church, I gather some buddies and follow the last car of a funeral procession on our bikes. We watch a funeral proceeding on the edge of Pine Grove Cemetery. Black family members crying as the casket lowers. "Why is this side of Pine Grove Cemetery so weedy and sandy and the other side neat with grass and paved hills?" I ask. "Cause that side is white . . . that's Riverview Memorial Park cemetery, Jimmy interjects. "It's not the same cemetery?" I ask perplexed, looking far in the distance at neatly manicured graves and a sectional wrought iron fence facing the scenic Atlantic Ocean. "But I thought . . ." "I know what you thought," Jimmy's Brother George chimes in. "Gramps say colored folks don't have enough money to keep a graveyard like that." "They gonna put a fence up in the back too." "Look over there," Lorenzo says pointing. Several iron posts are imbedded in the soil. "They tryin ta keep us out." "We ain't good enough you know," Sherman proclaims. "Never say that!" "We are good enough!" I recoil angrily.[8]

"You know crackers don't want us buried near um," Sherman continues. In the distance a Cadillac hearse rolls along leading the funeral procession down the hill. We cross over unpaved Tenth Street which cuts through the cemeteries, keeping the black and white sections apart. We gawk at somber white faces exiting sleek expensive limousines, while a few of them glimpse over at us a short distance away with quizzical stares as if saying, how dare you n.gg..s invade our privacy. "Two separate graveyards." I keep repeating. "How can we harm white people if they already dead?" I muse disgustedly. No one answers. I play around with this question in my head while watching the white funeral. Whites have a problem—a serious problem cause nothing's wrong with us. Two images one black the other white burying their beloved dead causes me to delve deeper triggering more probing questions. And I realize there's something sinister about segregation even after you die.

My first year at Francis K. Sweet Elementary is tough; fights

---

[8] Jimmy and George Roberts, buddies are younger brothers of famous painter, Livingston "Castro" Roberts. Lorenzo Burkett neighborhood buddy with great potential died young from complications of a gunshot wound. Sherman Atkins neighbor and friend died young from a gunshot.

going to school and fights coming home. "Bet you won't knock this stick off my shoulder!" "Bet you won't cross this line!" These threats lead to a black eye today and a bloody nose the next day, but I fight back. The "new kid on the block" initiation period goes unabated for a while. "Who can I turn to for help?" All but a few of my friends have fathers. All have an older brother at home who spends time giving advice and provides boxing techniques. I certainly can't ask Grandma! Battle weary, one day I finally do. Grandma says in her soft but stern Geechee voice, "Scaldee, (my nickname as a baby. I looked scalded with red facial birthmarks and scattered freckles) sick or not . . . don't you ever come runnin home cryin to me . . . these youngins ain't never gonna stop knockin you down till you get your face out the dirt and fight back!" "If you don't face um you gonna always be the worst kind of loser . . . one eaten up by shame . . . or a switch will be waitin for you . . . just stop by that bush and pick a good size one before you get here." I wipe blood from a busted and swollen lip unashamed. I keep bullies off my back, never lose a battle, and never bring my burdens home again.[9]

One day, I get into an argument with a tight buddy James Edwards who lives on Tenth Street and Avenue H in Cisco Quarters. He and his younger brother Eddie Joe are into a game of marbles. Hardly anyone in the neighborhood has a marble collection like me, so crown me the marble king. Most days no one stands a chance winning. Eddie loses some of his marbles earlier. James loses all his collection including his lucky toy marble. We argue, and he

---

[9] Geechee is a name from the Gullah people of West Africa. They settled primarily in South Carolina and have retained much of their West African roots. They are referred to as freshwater Geechees, inland and coastal plains and saltwater Geechees and Geechees of the Sea Islands who speak a unique Creole English. They were enslaved Africans who were brought primarily to America for their knowledge of rice planting. A comprehensive account of the Gullahs and rice planting can be found in Daniel Littlefield's *Rice and Slaves Ethnicity and the Slave Trade in Colonial South Carolina*. Reprint edition (University of Illinois Press, 1991), pp.76 and 113.

pushes me down, snatches my bag of marbles and runs. I promise to get even.[10]

All the Edwards brothers including sisters are tall and strong amazons. I know I don't stand a fighting chance. I lay in wait for James behind a row of a Bobby William's Grandma's hedges with a broom stick to whack him good. James passes to visit his Grandparents nearby. I jump from behind the hedges and bushwhack him, ramming the broomstick into his stomach. As James rolls about gasping for air, I laugh bragging, "Gotcha. I told you so!" James angrily gets up lurching forward and the chase is on. "I'm gonna kick your ass!" "You can't catch me!" I brag.

James with jackrabbit speed chases me down near my front yard as I yell out to Grandma. James' swing misses my cheek, I throw a counter punch to his stomach from which he buckles over into a slight grunt slowing him down; a perfect opportunity to pounce and tackle him to the ground. Instead, intimidated by his size, I run like a scared rabbit towards Grandma's with James on my heels. Through the screen door Grandma watches both of us huffing and puffing bent over in the front yard. "Oh no you don't . . . you better fight cause you ain't comin in this house till you fight your battles." I know if I don't fight James, the worst-case scenario is breaking off switches until she approves of one. I don't want to give her that opportunity.

The thought of being awakened from sleep, dragged out of bed for a whipping moves me to take on James. "Ya betta sock um good Scaldee. A burst of confidence builds as Grandma and neighbors watch two buddies go at it. James can smack me good, instead chokes me lightly. Too scared of Grandma's whippings instead of giving in, I fake a faint. Being anemic, I often faint and Grandma hollers, "Let him go!" "You both win!" "Cause you friends . . . shake hands and make up." James' good nature saves me from a shellacking. I come to realize

---

[10] James and Eddie Joe Edwards my childhood buddies; James became a prize fighter in the heavyweight division in Fort Lauderdale, Florida. Eddie Joe, high school teammate, All-American attended University of Miami. First-round draft pick, third overall pick of the 1977 NFL draft played twelve seasons with the Cincinnati Bengals.

fighting is part of normalcy growing up, facing your challenges without fear.

Every fight afterwards, I grow in confidence and stronger in my convictions. Proudly stand my ground ready to fight the bullies, and most often they back down. Eventually a truce is welcomed—bullies don't like a good fight from a skinny, sickly, timid boy who'll never quit. At school I exude unwavering pride. I deal with teasing, dare anyone who lays hands on me will face a tenacious fighter unleashing anger and who'll never give up.

Mama gets a steady job at General Development Corporation in Port St. Lucie, an unincorporated suburban enclave of Fort Pierce, some 30 miles south of the city limits. New home construction is happening quickly; thousands of retired white northerners trek annually to the area escaping winter snow for sunny skies, golf courses, shuffle board, fishing and sun bathing on the sandy beaches of the Treasure Coast. With these migrations south on U.S. Highway #1 and I-95 Yankees bring kids, extravagant lifestyles and appetites in pursuit of a social status only white privilege can offer. There migrations bring a demand for domestic labor provided by blacks. As new homeowners settle in, so do the masked marauders of Port St. Lucie Templar Knights of the Ku Klux Klan. I hope to see a Klan member but I never do nor do I hear any reports of insurgent Klan members reveling in hoods and regalia. I hear stories from Mama and her co-worker friends who drop by, and I worry and pray for her safety everyday because she may face one without a mask.

Between work, PTA meetings, helping with homework, church, lodge and club meetings, Mama has little time for herself. My sisters hang out after school at Grandma's until she gets off work. What little space carved out for me is quickly invaded by noisy pretentious sisters bickering over petty issues. All of Grandma's goodies— savoring homemade biscuits, delicious baked delights, and my favorite store-bought apple strudels are devoured. A bit spoiled and selfish, I'm in no mood for sharing. I had been the center of Grandmas' attention until their arrival.

There are few amenities of any comfort at grandma's house. I don't do much complaining, and gradually adjust exploring rural living all around me. Tensions mount between my sisters' complaints of discomforts and inconveniences. It isn't long before ensuing arguments over the lack of hot water, bed space, a mirror, hair pomade, a pair of scissors and the likes; just girl issues. My finicky sisters are having difficulty getting along. What few amenities Grandma has at home, Gail and Regina exploit in games comparing Grandma's antique beds, wicker sofas, tables and items to their circle of friends' stylish furniture in our neighborhood.

There are games like the "haves and have-nots." Grandma's money is tight so snacks aren't like being at Mama's house. Playing imaginary games, eating our favorite foods or snacks does little to ease our cravings, but we're never hungry without food. Grandma knows how to stretch a meal, rustle up bowls of potato and onion soup with a piece of cornbread to subdue our complaining until Mama brings home groceries. We live under siege but not under conditions like some neighbors below the poverty line.

Common laborers who live in the Cisco Quarter's apartments nearby live off meager earnings from the tomato fields and orange groves and at least have running water and electricity. I'm astutely aware not to be embarrassed about our modest conditions. Although whatever explanation Grandma gives never gives me any real satisfaction. She has primal instincts and believes in making a way out of no way. She can get the ultimate wear out of every pot, pan and utensil. Grandma has these old slavery time customs passed down through generations. Survival skills ingeniously ingrained in the souls of black folks, too personal and not readily relinquished even with the possibility of modern accommodations.

Grandma is accustomed to primitive contraptions like heating irons that are warmed by the fire to press clothes. Kerosene lamps, and an old durable wood burning stove full of soot that cooks slowly but efficiently and never breaks down; a galvanized steel tub used for bathing and washing clothes with a scrub board; a cast iron kettle for boiling clothes and making soap from animal fat and lye. Grandma puts little value in new items; too stubborn to change even if she could afford them. We get by without electricity and a bathroom for months. A hurricane months earlier demolished her outhouse only to be replaced for months by a bucket—a "slop-jar."

Witty on her feet, Grandma can maneuver around any visitor's request with an excuse for not using our slop-jar. Before my buddies dare ask embarrassed, I just say, "Maann if ya got to go ya better run home fast." "My Grandma don't like anybody pissin on her toilet seat!" A supply of kerosene fuel lamps gives light to darkness and relieves some of my fear of the dark shadows I see always lurking throughout the old house. Grandma believes Grandpa's spirit looms near as a beacon of hope and security for us. "Don't you start that worryin about nothing Scaldee," she says affectionately. "Ain't nothin to fear in this old house . . .Grandpa looks after us." I wasn't so sure. I see shadowy figures, I suspect, of Grandpa and dead relatives duck, shift, move stealth-like through our house watching me.

Before I was born, Grandpa Ollie died of a heart attack while whipping Aunt Ruth at the foot of my bed. Some nights I awaken to footsteps and see a shadow of a human figure at my feet. Must be Grandma looking after us. The old wooden shotgun house that sits on concrete cinder blocks has seen better days. It's badly in need of repairs with broken windows, pealing exterior paint, leaning badly to the right from past hurricanes that could still blow it to smithereens.

Forced into retirement from backbreaking work in the tomato fields, Grandma keeps a ledger of her meager earnings of old wrinkled bills, silver dollars and coins in several large mason jars tucked away near her bed. She stretches her social security check to pay monthly bills and buy food. Like everyone else, she gets government commodities consisting of canned meats, peanut butter, beans, rice, butter, cheese and other dry goods to supplement our meals. Grandma lives a purpose-driven life with God as the centerpiece in it.

Grandma provides a source of comfort and inspiration that fuels my growing sense of awareness and confidence. But it's explorations in the wild lush outdoors I discover silence, a sense of peace to ponder over my thoughts, my insecurities, my very existence. It's during these silent moments when I try shutting out the harsh reality of being poor. Over time I confront inescapable truths exposing more truths, and I hear the indiscreet people's mouths whispering, spreading gossip. I'm no longer able to hide our secret from neighbors' ears and eyes. And when the whispering gossipers laugh behind my back—my naivety drastically changes. I realize if we're poor, we aren't like some families in Cisco Quarters "dirt po, more po, can't afford the other "o" in poor." Being above dirt po isn't necessarily mentioned in your face. Yet, poor's not a despicable word not unpalatable but it is not something to tease anyone about.

I grapple over these burdensome experiences. Poverty and its equivalency is the outcome of an oppressed people in Jim Crow segregation. With segregation black folks live unashamed in mixed neighborhoods of haves and have-nots, professional and unprofessional. Grandma proudly convinces me we're still blessed. Grandma's sense of humor about how she survived the Great Depression keeps me hopeful. She never concedes to poverty. Always deflating it with reconciling words, "We ain't poor . . . just blessed…. waiting on God's salvation, hallelujah!" I suppose her belief system is a way to cope, stay sane and grounded. Just like black folks have always done during hard times.

When my sisters spend the night, Grandma in her witty way keeps things lively, entertaining us with jokes about the huge flying cockroaches or Florida palmetto bugs coming out at night to play. "Y'all sit still cause time for us to make room for our cousins." Cockroaches gather inside on hot summer nights attracted by the light from kerosene lamps. As if equipped with radar they fly around our living room looking for a landing, zoom down, get inside our pajamas. We laugh so hard at each other screaming, shouting, jumping, and rolling around on the floor like being moved by the holy ghost shaking the roaches loose.

Grandma has fun grinning through a toothless smile swiping at a flying cockroach. Cherry screams while rolling around on the floor with a roach crawling down her back. We all join laughing so hard until our stomachs start cramping. Laughing probably confused these critters to scurry about for dear life and land on us. We scream and holler at Cherry who is not so lucky when a roach gets smashed in her pajamas and another in Grandma's hands.

Some hot and humid nights, big cockroaches come in through cracks, searching for water. These palmetto bugs get in my bed and interrupt my sleep, emitting an awful defensive skunk-like odor at the end of a fly swatter. Spraying and killing is never enough because the sweetness of fallen fruit in the yard and light through cracks in the old house attract them inside. The old house keeps you alert and on your toes.

I slowly learn Grandma's ways. A stickler for cleanliness, she harasses me and anyone else about washing hands before and after meals, even if I dash outside reentering in a split second. She passes her compulsion on to me to this today. "Scalldee! You better not go to bed smelling like a meal tonight or you gonna get a visit from the roach patrol!" Forgetting, I pay the price when I sneak a piece of squirrel nut candy and fall asleep with a sweet sticky film on my lips. The next morning, I awaken with swollen lips from roach bites. After "once bitten, twice shy," I no longer like hiding my face, shying away from blunt of blubber lip jokes at school. I get the message.

Besides pestering roaches, Grandma sets rat and mice traps before bedtime. And some of these vermin seem to have gotten comfortably domesticated—even territorial. Some nights entering my bedroom with a lamp I might spot a rat in a corner. The vermin just sit there guarding its territory, watching me as if saying, "I ain't goin nowhere buddy." Like I'm the stranger invading *his* home. I stomp and make noise—these rats sit like pets and seldom scurry away. Like telling me, "That's all you got?" Big ones too, keep returning to the same corner. One night a rat brings a friend and they both sit watching me. I get angry, set traps and kill them both. We're poor all right, yet somehow refusing to allow it to cripple me psychologically and emotionally.

Living near woods in a mosquito-controlled district breeds humongous ones. Sometimes rain produces infestation so bad that it forces everyone to stay mostly inside until the spray man in his truck comes to fumigate the area with a DDT insecticide. The fumes seep through cracks and broken windows. Grandma with Sonny

Boy underfoot have covered food items from contamination. My sisters and I sneak outside with other kids playing tag in thick odorless white clouds with zero visibility. Rural impoverished areas of the city is where much spraying is done. Many residents get sick, but struggling poor and powerless people worry more about survival than the illness spraying can potentially cause.[11]

Some weekends Grandma needs time to herself. We spend nights at Naomi Jordan's or Marion Quillette's home—Mama's friends and lodge sisters have children who are our friends. Sometimes a cab takes us there. One night my sisters and I spend the night at the home of another one of Mama's lodge sisters. Inside is this shining grey casket on a pedestal sitting in the middle of the living room. A dead man is lying inside after a wake earlier that night. My sisters were too sleepy to notice. I can't sleep all night, needing to urinate so badly but too scared to get out of bed.

The casket remains open. I can see part of the man's head lying there with his arms crossed. A hallway bathroom is just by the casket. Not able to hold it much longer, I tiptoe slowly down the hall keeping my eyes on the man lying in that casket. As I get near his face it begins to glow. His eyes seem to open and his arms move away from his chest. Scared to death, I almost wet my pajamas running down the hall. In fact, I tinkle on myself, too embarrassed to scream and wake everyone. I get underneath the bed, stay there dozing until almost daybreak. I take a peek down the hall and see that the casket is closed now, wishing it had been sooner. I dash to the bathroom so relieved I almost scream. I look at the casket and realize the moon glow and blowing tree branches casting a shadow did the trick. Fear can make you delirious and play tricks on your mind.

---

[11] By 1972, DDT is banned after test results indicate exposure causes cancer and other health risks to humans, endangers wildlife and compromises the environment. Several neighbors die suspiciously of cancer. Rumors swirl around the neighborhood that DDT is the most likely culprit. During the prevailing hostile racial climate, the powerless people did not have the financial means nor the legal recourse to fight against the manufacturers of DDT and other noxious chemicals. Compounding these problems was a judicial system that discriminates.

When it rains, we're in trouble. We get buckets to catch the leaks from holes in the tin roof, and afterwards the teasing begins: "Maann y'all house got so many leaks in the roof when it rains . . . y'all walk around inside with umbrellas." Y'all house lean to one side so bad you can't stand straight." "Defend the spirit within you . . . you are special . . . they don't understand," Grandma says more than enough times. No, I don't really understand. What do I being special have to do with being poor? I learn staying at Grandma's house is a test of pride and humility.

Mama brings used clothes home belonging to a son of her white employer before the school year. Rather than throw any away, she insists they get put to good use. I pick through almost new expensive styles of pin-stripe shirts, and the no iron needed khaki pants. More clothes than I ever wear. I decide to do acts of charity. I gather my old clothes in a box with these almost new expensive hand-me-downs. I don't want to be first in the neighborhood wearing paddy-boy clothes. My buddies are happy wearing and not caring where they come from. Some so "po" unexposed to styles to know what white boys wear. Clothes aren't an issue for me. Daddy never misses sending money replacing school and summer clothes I outgrow.

I keep some newer white boy's iconic polo knitted shirts and Izod socks to wear with my penny loafers. I wear a Texan style string tie and pants large enough to grow into. I'm one of the better dressers at school, having two choices of clothing—preppie-studious and a faddish look.

My teachers approve with pleasant comments and smiles. No one ever teases. You can't tease style when you're looking good. But the irony is teachers expect much more from those dressed for success. Even appearances can be deceptive. I'm just as poor, but I pay attention to what I wear unlike some classmates who come to school sleepy, dirty and smelly, wearing yesterday's clothes, unable to disguise it even if they want to. It's upsetting clothes can create symbols of success and divisions between the haves and the have-nots.

A "dirt po" family from a rural part of Georgia moves to Tenth

Street and Avenue H into the Cisco Quarters low rent apartments. Like Grandma's shot gun home, Cisco Quarters is one of the oldest structures in the neighborhood. The residents are mostly transient seasonal migrant workers or common laborers who move on with the end of the harvest season. John Philyaw watches his two sisters and eight brothers play in the dirt yard. Everyone walks around barefoot on dirt roads. The Philyaws are "dirt po." None of John's siblings ever wears shoes since they hardly have enough cloths, and some younger brothers wear their sisters' dresses. Others play in the dirt, naked. John's mother Ms. Lula Bell moved to Florida after John's father unable to find work abandoned them. John likes to say his father didn't shirk his responsibility. "My Daddy left desperate . . . can't find no work . . . he's comin back." John and I have something in common— father abandonment.

Ms. Lula Bell comes and goes a lot in search of work. John, his sisters and some brothers haven't gone to school in a year. His mother settles down with temporary work in the tomato fields. It saddens me seeing John sitting on the steps waving as I walk by on my way to school.

Lula Bell loves eating corn starch and always keeps a box of it on hand. When she runs out and can't afford any, John digs out clay from the red Georgia dirt shipped to South Florida to cover potholes after a hard rain. Mae Bell eats it regularly. Sometimes John, his sisters and brothers eat it to kill hunger pains. It moves me emotionally. I never thought it possible eating dirt.

John's quick-witted—when you get him to talk, but around anyone else he withdraws into silence. I believe he's embarrassed by the abject poverty he can't escape. Teasing behind his back comes with being "dirt po." It hurts me watching his mother alone, struggling and John a slow reader, smart but unable to attend school. I want to do something about it. At first, I sneak some hand-me-downs to him. I tell John, "No more dresses on your brothers." I go home and tell Mama we must help. My sisters find good dresses hardly worn for John's two sisters. Mama purchases a few outfits for the little ones. Her white employer thinks it's a good idea and has several nieces and nephews become contributors. Mama gets her club and organization members involved to get the older children school records from Georgia. Help John and his older siblings get in school, pay daycare fees for the little ones until Lue Bell gets on her feet. Lue Bell can't thank everyone enough. John unfortunately failed 4th grade caused by moving too often. The idea of helping a family in need makes me feel good inside, realizing our sacrifices aren't uncommon. It's what black folks do all the time—look out for one another.

Doing a good deed, I learn humility caught in the rapture of that moment. Out of it, I see over days and weeks my buddy John blossom talking more and smiling, something he rarely does. I make sense of Grandma's peculiar statements, like "Invoke the spirit within you, special child."

Most weekends other neighborhood boys challenge us to a game of sandlot football. Our neighborhood plays Avenue F boys. On the final play of the game, John makes a tackle on the five-yard line preventing a touchdown. The game ends on that final play. The F boys are sore losers and the boy tackled on the final drive yells out, "John! Yawl so po, yo mama eat dirt to make a meal!" The F boys erupt in laughter. John calmly smiles. "Yawl so po yawl can't afford the o and r in poor." The F boys crack up in spasms laughing. John short and muscular for his age confides in me he's grown accustomed to these types of jokes. I never see him get mad or fight anyone. He's tough enough to take any joker on. Such a rare moment, John smiles I misinterpret, fools me; I burst out laughing when the jokes get funnier.

The F Street boys know we're tight, and I burst out laughing more. As if my laughing justifies it being alright. I stand alone. No one else on our team laughs. Suddenly, John body slams me to the hard ground. Everyone goes silent. "Who's laughing now?" He yells out standing over me. Tears build in his eyes because I hurt and deceive my friend. Even neighborhood girls on the sidelines cheering our team to victory are silent. I lie there on the ground in agonizing back pain embarrassed, ashamed how arrogant I've become. I fail to recognize the essence of John's display of silence, his smiling not to dignify their teasing or retaliate in anyway. As I, too, over the years learn to deflect teasing. I lose what pride I have and in the absence of it, slip and lose what humility I thought I have gained. I betray a friend who believes in me. I vow I'll never laugh at another humiliating joke towards anyone again.

I have plagiocephaly or flathead syndrome and suffer the pain of being teased, but learn to ignore it. I have learned not to dignify giving anyone power in their own self-aggrandizing entertainment at my expense. One of the reasons I believe Grandma says I'm special is to insulate me with self-pride, immunize me from life's cruelties—those words spoken to hurt me.[12]

I learn unabashedly those that tease are self-haters with poor self-images. My condition doesn't affect my ability to think and be loved by others. I know those that seek to humiliate are blind in ignorance and their insecurities will eventually be exposed. And it mostly happens in classroom, scholastically outdoing jokers I get the chance to see how vulnerable they are. I never once revert to shaming even them. John too learns how to cope by shutting out humiliating jokes. I should have known better.

One day after school Daddy calls. As usual we all get a chance to talk on the phone. Unlike my sisters, I never show much enthusiasm. Over the years, I grow numb and uncomfortable talking to him and at times avoid Daddy altogether. I come to terms with him moving from Baltimore to Rochester, New York with jobs at Kodak Film Company and later Xerox Corporation earning far better wages than any here in the segregated South. His not returning home was a foregone conclusion.

Daddy keeps pleading with Mama, even sends money for us all to come up. Mama vows never to uproot us from Grandma, leaving

---

[12] Plagiocephaly or craniosynostosis is a common correctable condition. In medical terms the coronal or lambdoid sutures closes which leads to the flattening of one side of the head. It can be congenital (present at birth) or for me, lying on one side during infancy caused it. It can be dangerous and cause severe pressure inside the skull, which I miraculously never developed. With Grandma's support, and her proud and determined way, she protected me. I refused to allow the teasing to affect me either emotionally or psychologically, I became stronger. Nor did it affect my mental acuity. All praise is due to almighty God.

her alone. He usually calls on weekends after sending money via Western Union. "Hi son. I'm coming home to visit." I drop the phone not knowing what to say. Since he sounds quite sure of himself, I believe it. It's 1961, I haven't seen him in almost two years, but he said it before, and I've learned not to get my hopes up. This time seems different. But days before his arrival he disappoints me once again. As years pass, I try not to dwell on it. Especially when Mama gets upset about something to do with Daddy leaving, or about feeling stuck and giving up her dream of becoming a nurse like her big sister, Aunt Alberta. Daddy just keeps making promises he can't keep. I keep hoping he stops saying it because I stop believing it.

A year after I come to live with Grandma, she becomes very ill and, for convenience, Mama gives up the apartment on Avenue F to care for her. I remember my sisters talking excitedly about Daddy's arrival. I'm sitting alone in the kitchen eating a piece of hoecake watching Grandma cook as sparks dance and flicker from the wooden stove's kindling. I close my eyes and imagine those sparks are a sign of hope; Daddy will come rescue us for a better place and life. Within days of his expected arrival, he phones with a change of plans. He can't come but sends his love. No further explanation.

Once again, the inevitable happens: he makes another promise. Where is he when a growing boy needs his father the most? There are too many unfulfilled promises. The sparks of hope I imagine coming from Grandma's wooden stove become just a glimmer. There's no numbness this time, just familiar anguish in the depths of my soul. I must release it. I'm feeling vulnerable and confused. I don't know how to purge myself of these emotions. I don't understand why I even feel what I'm feeling. Surprised at the anger that has laid dormant inside of me for so long. I hate Daddy but love him just the same. I pray he'll regret not coming to visit. Hoping that something bad will happen to us that will get his attention and change his mind. And the manifestation of these tormenting thoughts strike, tell me with resounding effects— be careful what you wish for.

In September 1961, Hurricane Carla sweeps torrential rains across Florida. Our old house takes a pounding before we can recover. Then Hurricane Hattie blows 100 mph winds in October, destroying residential and commercial properties, ravaging crops, and uprooting thousands of citrus trees. Each time Daddy plans another visit it is abruptly interrupted by a hurricane. Like a tag-team match, before we can recover, within three years Alma, Flora, Ginny, and a tropical depression of 125 mph winds causes our old weather-battered house to lean even more.

Hattie's winds are unrelenting, snapping limbs from our tall Australian pines. There's mass flooding outside. Locomotive whistling winds loosen nails, causing our tin roof to rattle and window panes to vibrate. I dash around getting extra buckets as rain drips through the roof's openings. Flying tree branches scrape across the tin making piercing noises as if the old house is crying out for help. "Pray Scaldee . . . ask for forgiveness . . . ask God to take it back," Grandma says. I go to Grandma's room and kneel beside her bed and together we pray. As the old house shakes and rumbles, I ask God to take back, something bad happening to us so Daddy can come. I wonder if I'm being punished, unforgiven by God's wrath because of my selfish thinking.

By late August 1964, Hurricane Cleo strikes the Atlantic Coast of Florida, moving northerly with powerful winds reaching over 110 mph. Daddy cancels another visit. Earlier in the day, some neighbors come over and help Grandma and me reinforce loose windows panes with tape on the side of the house that dramatically leans, and we fill buckets of water. Advisory hurricane warnings blast all morning from Grandma's old wooden radio. All we can do is wait it out and pray for the best.

Grandma's calm and seemingly unnerved by the imminent danger of Hurricane Cleo's winds building momentum as it sweeps up the Treasure Coast. She tells stories of how the rickety old battered shotgun house has survived the worst of storms. With optimistic resolve, Grandma can humor the dead and calm the stubborn nonbelievers with a prayer and a miracle story. "We all gonna trust in the Lord," she says. "He bought us this far . . . he's in control." At that moment I realize why the old house leans so badly to the right. On that side of the house there are fewer trees to absorb the thrashing winds.

My Grandmother's old shotgun house lean to the right on cinder blocks with two very tall Australian Pines in front yard withstand many years of hurricanes circa, 1946. (Courtesy of Hurst family archives).

By early evening the skies darken as Cleo moves up the coast. I peer through a crack from my boarded bedroom window at the pitch-black sky. Lying in bed, I listen to the siren roaring loud warnings across the city from a huge weather tower in the distance. The whistling winds blow large objects across the yard banging against the house, causing it to shake and tremble on its brick cinder blocks. Heavy rain falls onto the tin roof with ear piercing noise as rain leaks through the roof like sprinklers.

We place pots throughout the house to catch water, but previously undiscovered leaks allow more water to seep into the old house. Large limbs from our Australian pines snap all around the house as the angry gale winds twirl mangoes and oranges off the trees and throw them against the house. The tin roof makes syncopated explosive sounds. Lying still in my bedroom in the light of my flickering kerosene lamp I listen to the whistling winds making eerie sounds. I'm scared to death. I pray that God takes back the evil things I'd hoped for about Daddy years ago, because the hurricanes keep coming each time he doesn't. Throughout the night Cleo won't let us sleep, and when morning comes there's blown roof shingles, trees limbs, debris, damaged houses, downed power lines and electrical outages throughout the city.

We're spared with no major damage. But living a few blocks from the Atlantic Ocean creates massive flooding. Rescue workers canoe Grandma and me to a designated fallout shelter at Lincoln Park Academy gymnasium. For several nights we live there on mats until the water recedes. The rescue team canoes us back home. I see water moccasins and rats swimming in the water through the woods. Rats are the least of our worries; Grandma remembered to set traps for those that get inside for shelter on higher ground. Families further south have much larger worries of alligators, taking shelter inside homes and on roof tops.

Surveying neighboring homes, I see that everyone survives with damage mostly from flying debris and tree limbs. A huge fallen limb smashed in a portion of our tin roof, but God answered our prayers—the old battered house withstands another hurricane. Hurricane Cleo doesn't take a soul. But before we can breathe easily Hurricane Dora is spotted, then Gladys, Hilda and Isabelle, all bringing heavy rains causing structural damage throughout the city in the span of several months. I still pray, asking forgiveness, hoping that another hurricane not overtake us and that Daddy will come home. Now if God can just give another sign, a glimmer of hope that our lives will get back to normal I'll be satisfied. After much prayer another hurricane season passes. I think my prayer is answered because the old house survives and I'm no longer ashamed how it looks.

Chapter 4

LICKIN STICK

Whoever say a little pain never hurt any one? Maybe pain is good to get your mind thinking how to behave. Or you got to hurt before you heal, but you never really heal when pain keeps hurting you or someone else. Teachers have every kind of excuse justifying why it got to hurt. How does one justify what constitutes a spanking and when it is necessary? Corporal punishment is the great equalizer for behavioral modification—to change your ways. A good old-fashioned spanking gets you straightened out in a hurry. The duality of teaching and disciplining pupils is frequently expected from teachers in our community. Teaching in my youth is thought of as a noble profession. And with corporal punishment comes great latitude dishing out pain. Parents expect teachers will help develop good character traits in their child's behavior to move the race forward into new dimensions of prosperity. Every teacher uses corporal punishment, either to conform, intimidate or motivate pupils.

By today's standards, corporal punishment amounts to child abuse. As a youth, I don't quite understand why a minor incident in the classroom moves the teachers to take me to the front of the class for a spanking. While for others it's just a simple timeout. On any given day, I can be confined to a corner of the room in a 15-minute timeout standing on one leg facing the wall. Other times a large cardboard box in front of class keeps the bold, brave and daring secluded from class stimulation. I avoid these types of discipline, but others unwilling to yield to structure find themselves isolated for some time. Punishment causes many distractions away from effective teaching. I sit at my desk distracted by whimpering noises, and pleading cries from a trouble-maker needing to be freed from a cardboard box. Only the teacher has the power to decide. A child daring to leave without permission knows that the next step brings greater punishment at the principal's office. "The box," as we call it, is a calculative technique, cruel and impassionate with effective results by reducing visual stimulation for the child. As the box eliminates attention your eyes can't see from the child's disruptive behavior, an attention seeker in a box can no longer get to fuel and channel his or her acts through classroom laughter. It works every time. Within a half hour boredom sets in—you'll be pleading to change your ways, crying, and promising to cooperate.

Anyone who enters a cardboard box is made an example of so others won't try anything else. The brave are subject to such corporal alternatives as knuckle bashings with the ruler or standing in a corner quietly facing a wall. If you defiantly reject the alternatives your rump belongs to Principal James A. McNeil's paddle or strap. Notwithstanding the whipping you'll surely get from your parents. Black teachers still exhort academic excellence with exemplary regularity yet the harsh punitive treatment in pursuit of achieving success has its setbacks. Invidious discrimination, its limitations and all its equivalencies in pursuit of higher achievement no doubt provoke black teachers' frustrations. We hear our teachers complain but hardly realize why. As students we don't understand that the school board is responsible for our inferior and inadequate school supplies. Dedicated teachers channel their hard-earned money on basics: chalk, erasers, crayons, maps, pencils and rulers when funding falls desperately short.

Fort Pierce's progressive thinking blacks in the early 1900's campaigned long and hard against the racist school district to educate their children. The momentous results of their efforts brought forth meager returns. The first school was a small tin storage shed on Eighth Street, hardly an environment suitable for educating eager black children who had been denied for generations access to free education. The primitive unnamed structure demonstrated how difficult the struggle for racial equality was in the St. Lucie County district steeped in the laws of Jim Crow segregation.

In 1906, an old Army-like barracks was donated to the black community. Before 1920, the black community pooled its resources and the school moved to Thirteenth Street and Means Court providing classes up to the 8th grade. Without funding from the school district, mothers sold 10-cent sandwiches and raised enough money to erect an outdoor basketball court. Volunteers fenced in the outdoor court and sold tickets to fund school expansion. Parents wooed highly regarded Principal James Espy from a better paying job in Georgia. With parental assistance Espy persuaded the school district to build a black high school. Parents pledged $1600 and within one term ended up almost doubling that amount. Within one year, a proud and encouraged black community raised enough money to expand and the first black high school Lincoln Park Academy was built south of Palatka, Florida.

Once Lincoln Park Annex, one of four rows of outdated naval barracks donated to blacks to become Means Court Elementary where I completed my first through fourth grade. Photo taken for 1947 Lincoln Park Academy, Moon yearbook. (Courtesy of Hurst family archives).

In 1928, Lincoln Park Academy became an accredited senior school. What distinguishes Lincoln Park Academy in Fort Pierce to this day is that it is an elite academic school of excellence, due to the efforts of Espy. The principal's high academic standards insisted on degreed teachers. This was a luxury for black schools considering that at the time not a single accredited black high school existed in Florida. What's so egregious, only eighteen black students attended 12th grade in the entire state.[13]

I started the 1st grade one block from my home at Means Court Elementary on Thirteenth Street (its four wooden structures have endured many storms and remain in their original state), the original site of Lincoln Park Annex, Edna Sheppard proudly tells her class. Means Court as the first black elementary school has a rich history in St. Lucie County. I didn't see the importance in those first years, but as I pass through each year, I hear the stories teachers so proudly tell. I come to understand its historical relevance. Each teacher tells us, "Let's us not forget the hardships our ancestors endure, and the impact education has on our lives." I cherish these moments in our history throughout my early school years, how the right to an education empowers powerless people.

Here I am in first grade looking studious.
(Courtesy of the author).

---

[13] Lincoln Park Academy had the distinction of being one of four accredited black schools' in Florida. Students trek far north as Palatka to New Smyrna and far south as Delray Beach and across the state from Tampa to attend high school at Lincoln Park Academy. *Audria V. Moore, "Treasure Coast Black Heritage," 1996, pp. 35-43.*

Starting school in the early 1960s, "Whites Only-Colored only" signs are few but remain the last vestiges of Jim Crow segregation as it winds down. I have few interactions with whites doing business in and beyond my neighborhood borders. I sense something disturbingly different in my encounters with whites—skin color is the standard bearer for egregious laws of racial separation. I had learned much from Grandma's tours and talks while grocery shopping on the streets of Fort Pierce. Racial segregation affects the psyche, how one feels, thinks and sees himself or herself. Like any inquisitive young mind, I wanted to know why was it so? And more so, what was the root cause of it? And why can't I swim, drink, eat, sit in accommodations available to whites? More and more questions followed and Grandma was eager to satisfy my appetite for asking.

I develop a heart murmur coupled with anemia. I feel weak, faint and have a poor appetite that accompanies these conditions. I have problems concentrating; daydreaming, thinking of my Daddy spills over into class. My 2nd grade teacher, Ms. Millie Miller is a strict, autocratic and punitive disciplinarian. She rules her classroom with imprudence. Miller informs Mama that I'm day dreaming and not completing class assignments. She expects answers when your name is called, and you better have one or else.

If you don't deliver for lack of attentiveness, you get the ruler across the knuckles. If you don't do your homework, you better have a legitimate written excuse, or you get sore knuckles. One day, Miller catches me daydreaming. She insists I answer a question from the textbook my class is reading. I don't respond at all, not knowing the answer. Miller thinks I'm ignoring her. "Kenneth comes to the front of the class right now!" "Hold out your hand . . . make a fist." She angrily strikes cutting into my knuckles with the edge of her ruler. Short choppy strikes tear open skin and draw blood. This is how boys are handled. Girls are spared with a flat angle on their palms. Five to ten hard strikes are standard—get the job done. I dare cry and angrily return to my seat.

Miller has a way throwing erasers at anyone who dares to talk while she writes lessons on the chalk board. I get struck across the head with her eraser with chalk dust powdering my hair and face. I'm caught daydreaming again, snap out of it embarrassedly, surprised at the sound of her voice: "Kenneth you don't hear me calling you!" Classmates giggle and I'm seething with anger. I never complain to Mama, all part of disciplining in the realm of acceptable standards. But oh, if parents only knew!

Ms. Miller loves oatmeal cookies. She sends one of her pet girls who sit in the front row to a store across the street on Means Court. The cookies are a penny each that Miller loves to devour. Miller was Mamas' teacher at Lincoln Park Academy. The teacher had the nickname "Ole Gate Mouth" because her mouth was so wide. Of course, I never tell anyone, afraid of the consequences if she finds out I know. At quiet time, she sits at her desk easily stuffing whole cookies into her wide mouth. I raise my head from the desk to sneak-a-peak. I get caught giggling at her tossing cookies down her big mouth. At this moment I refuse to ever let her strike me again for such a minor infraction. "Kenneth, come to the front now!" "No!" "Come and get you punishment now!" "No!" I keep repeating. Finally, Miller, short and husky, drags me screaming out of the classroom.

I'm about to see "Dr. Do Right," Principal James A. McNeil's name his wide flexible strap. The kind barbers use to sharpen shaving razors. McNeil lets me off easy with 3 licks, only because I turned in my homework.

Feeling sick, I return to school with unfinished homework. Again, I refuse to let Miller crack my knuckles. This time McNeil, a soft-spoken man stands in the doorway of his office watching Miller drag me inside. He looks down at me through black-rimmed glasses, walks over to his desk and opens a lower drawer. "Well, son you can't seem to get enough whippings ah?" "Let me see." He measures his paddle and says, "You got the doctor before, let's try my 'licking stick' this time." He pulls out a wide wooden paddle. My heart thumps fast and furiously standing there with my head bowed. "You said 'no' to Ms. Miller . . . that's being sassy . . . bend over, hold on to that chair tight . . . it'll be over before you know it." I get five licks, maybe more. I lose count, each producing a yell from intense pain. My butts on fire—it's electric!

Miller stands watch at the office door, smiles and pats me on the back, as if regretting it more than I. "Get back to class son and be obedient," McNeil says as his secretary hands me a note to give to Mama about my whipping. I wobble back to class on weak rubbery legs and a sore behind with Miller in tow. A faculty member monitoring the class gives me a smile, as if Miller did the right thing. Not a pin drops after a whipping. All eyes are on me as I embarrassingly try hard not to sit where it hurts the most.

I tear up Principal McNeil's note on my way home, so Mama won't find out. At a PTA meeting, Miller says to Mama, "Did you get the note about Kenneth's spanking for disobedience?" Mama follows up with another spanking. Miller, I believe, is mean spirited. I hate her loud intimidating voice. The way she slams her pointer against a desk to get the class's attention making everyone nervous. Because of my illness with anemia, I fall asleep and I get behind in my grades. Although a controversial teacher by any standards, later I realize that Bernice Miller is as dedicated as any teacher working within the limitations of segregation. Her methods of discipline are meant to push and get the best out her students. She and others are true visionaries. I'm certain as I look back at her consistent comments on my report cards about my progress, expressing similar sentiments to all the parents: "Kenneth must study harder and prepare himself well to face challenges of a new day waiting."

Because of my anemia of chronic dizziness and fainting, I fall behind in math and reading. With Mama's insistence that I do extra homework, and Miller's patience eventually providing support, I make commendable improvements. Over the course of my four years at Means Court Elementary, Mama's and other parents' involvement in PTA help develop strategies for improving the quality of education and learning environment. Parents and teachers take collections helping to buy much needed supplies. Each month, a teacher will implement a committee and designate parents to write letters to the school board, addressing classroom deficiencies. Mama sometimes spearheads a list of demands which are reinforced and validated with the signatures of concerned black citizens. Through their progressive efforts, a gradual shift of responsiveness by the school board netted significant improvements however fall far short of what's rightfully needed in a segregated school system.

Segregation often places almost impenetrable barriers between teacher and student, given that the black community is employed primarily low paying jobs mostly from seasonal migrant work. As a result, the teachers' messages do get lost. Some students come to school sleepy, hungry and unable to concentrate because of little or no food, and parental guidance is at a disadvantage. Aptitude tests allow some teachers to whimsically place students according to their ability in one of three makeshift group models: Smartest in the front rows, average in the middle rows, and slowest in the last rows. With overcrowded classrooms, teachers often move away from rigid daily lesson plans and get creative. A "Pet System" is in place. A student must complete all class assignments, homework must be turned in on time and good grades must be achieved. Good grades and conduct without corporeal punishment gets you a seat in the front rows. Group one consists of pets, mostly girls—all knowing; hardly ever out of favor, spoiled, and rarely called on. Teachers' assistance goes to those lagging academically, are rarely moved to the front of the class. I never reach the front rows, but stay in the middle until after 4th grade. That's a titillating story worth mentioning.

By 1964, I attend, Francis K. Sweet Elementary, a modern school in comparison to Means Court. Ms. Barbara Scott like Miller has a despicable way of disciplining the class. An entire classroom disruption is a ten-minute timeout in silence; a talking violation results in you standing facing the wall; a second talking violation the same day results in facing the wall and standing on one leg. Students known for repeated disruptive behavior face two options: take a timeout in a large cardboard box in isolation or get familiar with Principal Calhoun's licking stick. Scott uses a ruler as corporal punishment, but rarely and hardly causes injury. Scott has a more sinister way of maintaining order with hot sauce in a box under her desk. A threat of hot sauce however extreme is the ultimate measure Scott has yet to use to discipline and control.

One day, Scott gets hit by a flying paper jet. She's quick to accuse.

Tank my friend is no saint, has a reputation for sassing when false accusations are hurled at him. "Robert, did you throw it?" "Yes." "Come here now!" Tank decides to take his medicine. Tank often misses several days a week and comes late. "Calm down and stay focused," I keep saying to him. Short, stocky built like a spark plug with fire power, Tank, no bully, has a short fuse with a chip on his shoulder for whatever reason. Tank sits mostly quiet. Scott knows he's unprepared and often embarrassingly seeks answers to questions he doesn't know. "Why can't you get it right?" "You're not dumb!" "Why bother coming!" Scott cracks. Tank gives some farfetched answer that draws giggles. Tank, typically silent, retaliates. "You ain't smart either!" "Who yah foolin!" Scott shudders from a stinging blow and loud giggles. "Come stand here on one leg and face the wall right now Robert!" Tank readily obliges like it isn't anything. It rattles and demoralizes Scott, because, in the process, Tank enjoys making fun and faces at her. Over time, even Principal Calhoun's licking stick can't do the trick; Tank always returns smiling and making fun behind Scott's back.

Tank and I become objects of Scott's frustrations most days. Still weak from anemia and a heart murmur, still occasionally fainting in class, I'm an object of bullying. As I sit attentively, bullies nearby team up and commence an onslaught of popping upside my head. I turn to catch one and then someone else pops me from another direction. "Ms. Scott make them stop!" I yell, angry and frustrated. She's impervious, inattentive, and doesn't listen to accusations. Bullying starts with her back turned, writing assignments on the chalkboard. And often instantly, I'm the culprit caught retaliating, standing over a bully punching as he innocently looks on. I'm defenseless and accused of being the class disrupter. I take my timeouts against the wall. I dare run home crying like a sissy. I have no choice but defend myself.

I'm Scotts' goat. All I can do is whine. No matter what comes out of my mouth I'm indefensible. Throughout the year bullying continues some days. I can hardly concentrate on my assignments, and when my grades fall for the term, Mama takes notice. Under pressure, finally, I break down and reveal the cause. Mama arranges a parent-teacher conference to address my concerns with Scott and Principal F. D. Calhoun. Scott is insensitive and accusatory and doesn't waver, casting me as an instigator. Admitting is never an option as Mama explains, Scott is indifferent and refuses to listen to the root cause. Calhoun sits idly by neutral, listens and admits that the situation should be handled differently in the future. But Scott firmly stands her ground. She asserts that she has caught me on numerous occasions swinging at a student. Then out of the blue she accuses me of talking back, that daydreaming not illnesses are the cause of my poor grades.

"He daydreams," Mama says emphatically, "That much is true. He made good grades daydreaming last year." Mama can't understand why now such a drastic turn for the worse. "Kenneth loves school . . . hasn't missed a day," Mama adds. After the conference, Scott distances herself with ambivalence for my concerns. The head popping continues, and my anger builds to a tipping point after Tank mysteriously disappears for a couple of days.

One day Tank returns to school after a 2-day absence, a stinging blow shakes me out of a daydream. Dudley Adderly points to Jack sitting at a desk on my right. I spring up ready to swing, catch myself thinking about trouble. Surprisingly Scott notices but says nothing, continue to write on the board. "I'm gonna getcha . . .wait and see," Jack says smiling just as school let out. "Kenny, you can't let um keep doin it man," Tank says. "I'll get um one day," I say reluctantly. "No. You gonna get him after class this day, buddy." "What?" I slump low in my seat to a thumping heart out of rhythm, in fear. Tank tells Jack that I want a piece of him after school to stir it up. Classmates tag along through the Pine Grove Cemetery trail where most fights are held going home. "Ohhh ohhh, you gonna get your butt beat," everyone yells at me.

I walk with Tank home. Right behind us is Jack smiling assuredly since he's about to chalk up a butt whipping on one more chump. Tank yells, "Right here!" We stop in a sandy part of the graveyard. Jack yells, "I'm gonna kick your sickly ass." A crowd gathers, cheering wildly in my corner. Tank leans over my shoulder, "Don't worry, ain't no double-teaming." With that said, I gain confidence.

"Kick his ass Jack." His buddies egg him on. "I bet you want step across this line," Jack says. I step across it. Jack looks a bit timid at his buddies, surprised. My heart no longer was racing in torrid thumping. Just calmness knowing Tank's on my side.

Facing Jack within inches, I see reluctance and fear in his eyes. He reaches down and puts a twig on his shoulder. "I betcha won't knock this off." I, without hesitation, knock it off ready to do battle. His lips quiver scared until his buddy cheers dissipate, turning against him into laughter. "What's wrong Jack? You scared?" Jack bows down, walks away with his entourage ashamed. Tank puts his arm around my shoulders smiling, "You won . . . you see they're the real chumps."

I meet Robert "Tank" Williams in the summer of 1963, sneaking around in my backyard craving sugar cane, avocadoes and guavas. Neighbors get into the habit of taking mostly oranges and mangoes, any fruit really, when it falls on the ground. We don't mind folks we know and never think of it as stealing, just satisfying their sweet tooth. I'll chase off a few boys I dislike. Tank comes off cool, polite and apologetic all in one sound bite. It makes me hesitate how I should handle him. "Hey man, who told you to cut our cane?" I ask knowing the answer already. His machete gets my attention, but it's how he responds impresses me more. "Sorry, I shouldn't have, but I can't help myself." "So, it's you I've seen here sneaking around, chopping our cane . . . stealing avocadoes too." "I don't care much for those . . . my brother does . . . I like cane . . . I'm sorry." My tone mid-range elevated; his soft voice assured, unwavering in a cool demeanor. "Who are you?" I ask inquisitively. Tank weeks earlier moved into a big white 2-story house across the street. Men and women are in and out all times of day and night with live music playing. "Do you like music?" He asks, deflecting attention away from himself. "My uncle got a band . . . you should come by and hear them play." Of course, I love music, but Grandma warned me earlier on not to go there. "That white house is the devil's workshop, she says. Tank surely wasn't the devil, and Grandma just doesn't understand.

The Lone Wolf Club really is a band. Young members in their

mid-twenties wear black vests or jackets emblazoned with the band's name and a hollering lone wolf on the back. Tank lives with his uncle Zuba and the band's members in a communal setting. Zuba, the band's leader plays bass; Everett on drums; Renaldo cool and quiet on guitar; Teddy always primping his doo, on organ; Melvin on sax, a lady's man and Skinny, lead singer, really isn't skinny at all but a bit more towards hefty. Tank resembles his uncle in stature and quiet disposition. Zuba's a shrewd no nonsense bandleader and manager with little patience for jive during rehearsal times. I like how he handles business like a busy bumble bee buzzing around. He collects rent from the members and as a tailor designs and sews their costumes. When Zuba speaks, he gets respect from the members—and they listen.

The Lone Wolf Club is a road band Zuba spends hours on, arranging songs and dance routines and the band's stage presence. The band has a repertoire of songs from James Brown, Jackie Wilson and Sam Cooke. All members wear greasy processed hairstyles called conks. Their ladies come over before hitting the road on touring gigs with a bag of Red Devil lye and Vaseline for touchups. All day the house stinks of lye poured onto peeled raw potatoes and eggs and turns into a gooey brownish-yellowish concoction. I sit with Tank and John watching as each member waits their turn killing time and boredom playing cards and gambling. Their ladies stir this stinky stuff with a wooden spoon in a big jar until it becomes jellylike ready to apply. Members groan and complain as when applied the lye puts their scalps on fire. Finally, Vaseline massaged into the hair and scalp stops the burning and shampooing and cool water rinsing brings relief. Members put on black do rags tied around the sides to retain flatness and style with a bouffant-type James Brown do.

The band's wild rehearsals have visitors dancing to loud amplified guitars and organ riffs. Skinny does the splits and slides his feet and pirouettes James Brown and Jackie Wilson personified, with the showmanship of Cab Calloway's floppy hair thing. The house turns into a nightclub, as people drop in and out partying and drinking beer and liquor and getting high. I sit by a living room window relishing it all one moment, the next moment thinking about Grandma showing up with a switch.

After a session, the band takes thirty. Tank leads me upstairs and we listen at a bedroom door to ladies screaming in ecstasy. We peep through a partially shut door and see two ladies with Melvin naked in the same bed. Another time a long-legged lady lying on bed throwing a kiss to another. It was a happy time of a short-lived summer when my curiosity fades and I wonder after Grandma's warnings that something truly sinister is happening in that house.

Tank sometimes disappears for days. I ask Zuba where I can find him. "He'll be back in a day or two. Why?" He says guarded. "I Just want to know," I reply. Tank's always uptight when I ask where he has been. So, I stop asking. His moody spells mean trouble for Ms. Scott. Normally poised and silent, he has something deep on his mind, so I give him space. After a square meal of lunch, he's back to his usual self. Word spreads that I stand up to Jack which ends the head popping from others. I settle down and focus on my school work while Tank goes into a fog teasing Scott with playful innuendos as the class breaks out into laughter. Scott becomes incensed with anger but not at Tank. "Stop it, stop it now!" I grow resentful of her pointing at me, "Kenneth! Are you a part of it? I dare you to laugh!" "Robert gets up here now!" Tank stands before her in front of the class. His head proudly held back and his barrel chest poked out, as everyone looks in complete silence. She scrounges around inside her desk drawer and pulls out a bottle of hot sauce. "What's she gonna do?" someone asks in suspense. "Don't know," another says curiously. "Shake this bottle of hot sauce into your mouth until I tell you to stop." Tank does what he's told. "Now swallow it!" Tank does it with ease as the class watches in shock and awe. Scott recoils surprised and snatches the bottle from his hand. Tank licks his chops and with typical swagger returns to his seat, eyes blood-shot, but still smiling.

One morning Tank says, "I'm gonna get that heifer." "You gonna get the licking stick," I say hoping to discourage him. Tank wasn't hearing it. "Look how she treats you . . . I don't like her . . . she ain't a good teacher," he says. I see a troubled buddy. Scott's anger escalates while Tank suppresses his. I come to realize we're quite similar. I feel an upsurge of anger when someone teases. I learn to suppress and control it, but is that a good thing?

"Good morning," Scott says smiling as she walks into a quiet classroom, and proceeds to sit at her desk. Suddenly in a loud resounding shrill, she bolts upwards reaching back and grimacing in pain. The class is startled. She pulls out something from her rear-end. "Who put these tacks on my chair?" No one knows, but I have an idea who. Tank's devilish smile tips off Scott who thinks he is the culprit. All eyes shift first focusing on Tank and then on Scott. I sit quietly unfazed as the class becomes a chatter box of who did it. "Kenneth, did you . . . you know . . . tell me now!" She speaks waiting. "I didn't and I don't know," I say with a smug grin. "Alright then, Robert did you do it?" "Yes!" he says smiling with pleasure as the class ooed.

Scott paces while contemplating the serious nature of the matter, considering how to handle it. The class waits silently in suspense as Scott looks perplexed, embarrassed by Tank's humiliating joke. "Silence!" she yells. The class shifts into sudden stillness. "Come here Robert . . . this being a serious matter I'll deal with you, not Mr. Calhoun." Tank my tight buddy never backs down and takes his punishment. Scott this time reaches beneath her desk and opens a box and pulls out a whole bottle as Tank watches smiling. "I want you to drink this entire bottle," she demands. Tank takes the bottle of hot sauce and turns it upside down drinking its entire contents to Scott's amazement. Tank this time hands her the bottle and with his usual grin and swagger and puffed out chest heads back to his seat. His eyes are red hot tearing up to an outpouring of cheers and oohs. "The whole bottled!!" the class yells in unison. Tank feeling no pain sits down and brags, "I love hot sauce . . . hope you'll give me more!" The class erupts in laughter. Scott's shoulders slump in frustration and leaves the class defeated. Tank's bound to get a taste of Principal Calhoun's lickin stick.

Walking home with classmates laughing and joking about the incident, Tank never says a word. He's in trouble and everyone suspects his days are numbered in Scotts' class. A few days go by without Tank walking with me to school. One morning I stop by and the big white house is vacant. A neighbor shares a rumor the Lone Wolf Club's band's bus crashed off a cliff on the Smokey Mountains of Tennessee killing several members. "What about Tank?" I ask. "Don't know," the man says. No one knows for sure. Days later another rumor surfaces that Tank's being abused and was taken away and to my disappointment and grief, I never see him again.

I welcome spring's outdoor activities. Inside a hot classroom I have tendencies to get weak and faint. The class practice styling colorful ribbons around a May Day pole. The Brooks brothers, Donald and Matthew are always friendly. After Tank disappears, Matthew take leave of his senses in playful silliness. "Hey sick boy with that flat head." I jerk around not expecting him to stoop to name calling. Anger builds and intensifies. I smack him in his open mouth about to filter out syllables into despicable teasing words and draw blood from his upper lip. Mathew is surprised by this new aggression and retreats whimpering to older brother Donald. Classmates gather, girls yell out, "Fight! Get um Kenny!" Donald approaches as Matthew musters up nerves to talk more trash. "I'm gonna kick your ass just wait!" Donald assures me. "Do it now, you don't have to wait," I say urging him on. Donald in disbelief never witnessed such intensity in me. Scott comes over and Matthew points to his busted lip, proof I started it. Joycelyn, Bookecia and Marilyn, come to my defense, but Scott isn't in the mood. We both go see Principal Calhoun and hope with a stroke of luck we might avoid his lickin stick. It appears I get an adrenalin surge of energy, feeling more energetic than I've ever felt before. Maybe it's the Cheerios, but then I remember Grandma saying, "just wait a week or two when the Geritol kicks in you gonna feel it."

Geritol for anemia iron deficiency couldn't have come at a better time, boosting my appetite. I gain considerable weight on my skinny frame, eating vegetables that I never liked before. I'm riding high on a surge of confidence and energy. The punch must have convinced Calhoun, what Scott had said at Mama's conference about me behaviorally. A Geritol surge of energy got me carried away. "I'm sorry. It's the medicine my Grandma put me on." I try to explain what caused me to do it. Calhoun, a principal of few words and a quick swing of the paddle, rebuffs such an excuse as nonsense. In fact, he laughs. What matters is that I hit Matthew first. His swollen busted lip is proof. Matthew looks on indulging himself with a self-gratifying smirk. I try explaining desperately. I no longer can concentrate on class work. Teasing about my head doesn't matter to Calhoun. What matters most— right then and now is his flashing paddle quickly asking Matthew to bend over. His smirk fades into fright as Calhoun administered five licks in quick succession to both of our behinds.

When I receive my report card, I failed 5th grade. I feel my heart murmur flutters and skip beats hearing happy girls and boys all around whooping it up sharing good news. Feeling faint and dizzy, I fall to the floor. I awaken to Joycelyn shaking me to my senses. I vaguely hear someone's voice yell out excitedly, "Kenny you alright . . . you get promoted? I did!" All I feel is emptiness, hurt and shame. How can she do this to me? My grades are marginal at best, by Mama's standards although not failing. If only mama listen to my complaining Mrs. Scott allowed bias and subjectivity to come into her decision mama subsequent challenged but to no avail. In an impromptu conference with Mama, Mr. Calhoun stands firm in supporting his teacher's decision. I vow no one will take advantage of me ever again.

Chapter 5

GET BACK

I live around successful neighbors and business owners in my segregated world. Boatwright Saloon, Richardson's T.V. Repair, Docks and Ryal's grocery stores and Fat's Restaurant all own business on Avenue D. Mr. Fat and Ms. Sister, both affectionately named, live next door. Most mornings before I leave for school, I sneak a peek from my bedroom window at Mr. Fat kissing his wife before leaving to open his business. Each time on their porch, Ms. Sister adjusts his suspenders and rubs his big tummy like a crystal ball. She puts her arms around him for a kiss as his tummy gets in the way. I laugh at her struggling to get a kiss. He laughs and bends over making it easier.

I admire how they never argue, are always happy and in love. I think of Daddy's absence and withdraw into my thoughts. Mr. Fat, a jolly man, always wears dark suits and likes to tease me as I head out to school. "Put some sense in that noggin today boy . . . don't let it drain out before you get home," he'd say laughing. "Do something special for someone today," he adds with a jovial spirit. He's a neighbor with a kind heart who I enjoy and love listening to; his stories how colored folks got over in hard times keep me focused. "We survived and are still surviving, just like cockroaches, can't kill us off," he'd say laughing.

One summer morning Mr. Fat died and day by day Ms. Sister falls apart. Mama tries helping her run the business on Avenue D. Without Mr. Fat in her life, the business overwhelms her and she never fully recovers. Mama and the neighbors' emotional support isn't enough. In a short time, she loses her mind heartbroken and her home falls into a state of decay. Walking the streets barefooted mumbling incoherently to herself until she gives up the spirit. Mr. Fat and Ms. Sister leave a deadening imprint on my spirit for quite some time.

In the summer of 1964, Daddy ships from Rochester, NY three Schwinn 3-Speed English racer bicycles. Gail's is blue, Regina's is pink, and mine is burgundy; Sheryl just a baby got a tricycle. The bikes are weird looking with sleek frames and puny tires, more expensive than the usual bikes and triple fast, they are the envy of every child in the neighborhood.

Life's changing—abolishing segregation as I know it is a hot continuous topic in the news. But I don't see integration in my neighborhood. I closely watch and ask Mama or Grandma each time about something I don't understand. When Congress abolished Jim Crow segregation in 1964it was just the law, not in the hearts and minds of most white folks. Mama is active in the community and she treads into new areas of the city that were previously off limits to blacks. Mama challenged the new law to prove blacks aren't second-class citizens. "They don't want us eating at Woolworths . . . don't like us shopping downtown . . . that's all changing now," she says.

Months pass until Chicago, Philadelphia and Watts race riots send shock waves into inner-city ghettoes across America. Protests and racial unrest appear everywhere. In Fort Pierce, riots breakout at the Greyhound Station on U.S. Highway #1 when a black man refuses to move from a once all-white seating area.

My eyes stay glued to television, and I watch politicians shift their focus from the Vietnam War to the domestic crisis at home. My mind is ever evolving as I listen to visiting friends of family and neighbors speak about social change affecting our city. Still within my isolated world, I hardly witness anything out of the ordinary. I see no evidence how laws might be bringing change as I have little or no contact with whites.

During that hot summer, everyone was talking about change. "Gotta have a new outlook for colored folks," Grandma keep saying. Mama talks to our neighbors the Burkett's in the backyard. "We're going to Pepper Park, white folks beach," Ms. Joanne says. "It's time for a change. We like Frederick Douglass Beach but let's see if the law works," Mr. Willie Lee suggests.

We all pack into the Burkett's panel Chevrolet station wagon like sardines; Mr. Willie Lee and Ms. Joanne, Lorenzo and Diane Burkett, Mama, Regina, Cherry and me. Pepper Park, a white beach is quite a departure from unkept Frederick Douglass Beach's landscape of uncut grass, sandy spurs and Jellyfish infestations the Fort Pierce City of Parks and Recreations care little about. And the dreaded biting sand flies are ever present at our beach for too long, but we have grown accustomed to the city government's neglect. Smoke fills the camping areas and the smell of barbeque makes me hungry. Pepper Park has modern pits, tables, restrooms and shower stalls. Even a portion of the beach is reserved as a nudist camp, which is fenced off with bamboo and matted straw for privacy against the public's eye. I watch a nudist enter clothed and he gives an evil eye when we exit the car. "Stay together y'all, Willie Lee says. I don't want to show out and go to jail out here."

Mama and Joanne sit on towels and watch Cherry play near the shoreline. Lorenzo and I stand on a sand dune high above, watching a sailboat in the distance. A cluster of blacks already splash in the cool turquoise water of the Atlantic Ocean's Treasure Coast swimming off by themselves. Red ropes attached to red buoyant balls extend from the shoreline far out into the water. One side appears sectioned off for blacks and the other for whites. I watch baffled. "Whites are restricting this public beach too," I say to Lorenzo. "No, Daddy says it's integration, can't you see? We at the white beach now." Lorenzo doesn't get my point. In my upbringing and experiences with Grandma downtown, my suspicions are heightened in the midst of white people. I study a few blacks among the majority of white beachgoers separated by a rope. I conclude that rope is intended to keep blacks and whites separated.

The turquoise water looks inviting. We're reluctant to get in until a black girl in a one-piece swimsuit runs by. We're excited, but before making a splash, Lorenzo and I bolt for the restroom. "Where ya boys think ya goin?" a pot-bellied old white man with pealing sun-baked skin grins, blocking our path. "To the bathroom," I answer, stepping around him. He grabs at my arm. I sidestep and move away. I smell alcohol on his breath. "What that you say boy? This bathroom ain't for coloreds," he snarls. "It is today and we goin," I retort. "My Daddy says everything is integrated. If you don't believe me, there he is over there." Lorenzo points to Willie Lee standing on a sand dune curiously watching a short distance away. Lorenzo, more outspoken than I, taunts him. "Ask my Daddy. You scared?" Willie Lee watches admiring our bravery. "Everybody knows this beach is integrated now," I say proudly. So, leave us alone." The old man looks over briefly at Willie Lee, a burly muscular man over six feet tall, shakes his head, grunts three times and walks away.

Regina and Diane splash away with two other black girls they meet. The cool refreshing aqua blue water is a relief from the hot scorching Florida sun. Lorenzo and I go frolicking near the rope barrier. "Let's see if I get a reaction." Willie Lee, assertive and confident swims under the rope barrier where whites splash and play. Lorenzo and I follow suit, submerged in a game of tag and resurfacing on the opposite side. We repeat this feat several times, and I emerge wiping the salty water from my eyes to the sound of loud whistle blowing. A dirty blond-haired teenager with a crew cut posted as a lifeguard stands next to us, surrounded by a group of white onlookers.

"Hey! What you're doing! Don't you hear my whistle? You can't swim on this side of the rope! Get back to your side where you belong!" His voice is loud and firm. I clear my ears of water unable to catch what he said. I suppose my puzzling look draws him closer. "Hey boy! You on the wrong side of the ball and rope," he growls. "We're not moving. . . this beach is integrated," Willie Lee bellows. The white life guard agrees but insists that the other side remains for blacks. "Get back!" he demands. "This beach is integrated so we can swim where we want to," Lorenzo and I reply swimming away and ignoring him.[14]

---

[14] Parks and Recreation of Fort Pierce soon thereafter removed the floating balls and ropes. Perhaps doing our little part contributed to abolishing one of Fort Pierce's few remaining symbols of Jim Crow segregation.

The lifeguard is flustered by our defiance even more when whites gather to protest. "You all don't understand." "No, you don't understand!" Willie Lee cuts in, explaining the 1964 Civil Rights Act that firmly states that Jim Crow segregation is abolished. The lifeguard puzzled by our actions, retreats to confer with a group of white men nearby who assure that we are safe. But the lifeguard takes it personally. "Mister, I'm just doing my job. I don't want trouble." He is perplexed and nervous. "If you don't start any, there won't be any," Willie Lee adds.

A sparse group of blacks come splashing over to join us on the other side. The lifeguard throws up his hands, signaling frustration to white onlookers watching uneasily. "Well, why can't you do something!" a few whites bark. Others grumble, wading to shore where others are gathering. Suddenly a group on shore curses and screams and points at us. The ruff tides make what is said mostly inaudible, but I can only imagine from their anger and resentment they're shouting racial slurs.

The lifeguard, embarrassed by the ordeal, turns sharply towards Willie Lee and whispers, "These people on shore are angry. I can't stop them. You better get back for your own good." By now we're a black wave of solidarity, splashing in excitement while a few brave whites take a stand and join our side. "I'm sorry you have to go through this," a white man and his wife say. "Welcome," Willie says smiling.

Although I fear the worst, it feels like winds of change have awakened the sleeping giant in us. But the spunky lifeguard wasn't done yet. "You better get back or I'll get the police!" he warns, yelling through a bullhorn. By now our confidence and defiance soars, which triggers more obscenities hurled at us by hecklers on the shoreline. "We ain't moving," some young black boys and girls yell repeatedly in unison. Mama, Joanne and Cherry watch intensely from the shoreline with black and white women.

Hecklers wave down a state trooper cruising through the park and a hush falls over our celebration. Fear and uncertainty fall upon us. Within minutes the hecklers and sunbathers encircle the trooper and shout out their demands. We stand in solidarity, black and white watching as the trooper struggles to quiet this riotous crowd. "What if we go to jail?" a man turns to ask Willie Lee as we grow impatient. "We got rights. That trooper can't do a damn thing," Willie Lee answers. I embrace the idea we might go to jail. I envision a scene of black boys and girls singing freedom songs in a Birmingham jail and think it can't be that bad. "You're not breaking the law, you are making history," a white couple says standing nearby. For once, I see sincerity in their eyes and it makes me smile victoriously.

Lorenzo, Diane and Regina are splashing around like it's our last dip at Pepper Park. Within minutes another state trooper appears. They huddle together high on a sand dune away from the rowdy crowd. The troopers are indecisive and gesture slightly. In their final moments they come to a consensus—we have rights. The troopers know it, and the angry crowd knows it too. I feel amazed at such a time in my young life blacks no longer tolerate anything less.

Jim Crow segregation in 1964 is finally dead, awakening black folks to act according to new civil rights legislation against discrimination in public places. To the dismay of angry sunbathers, one trooper grabs the bullhorn, "Alright, break it up! Move along! This is a public beach for all!" His resonating message disperses defeated hecklers. "Praise God! All glory be to God almighty!" come many shouts in jubilation. We stay splashing about watching old timers, many perhaps for the last time longing for this day, and give their blessings.

We laugh and joke awaiting the conductor to elevate the north draw bridge to let a ship pass under. Diane and Regina relive moments a white girl plays splash games with them. "Her Daddy pulls her away, but she keeps coming back," Dianne says excitedly. "He quit trying," Regina adds. Mama looks out over the Atlantic Ocean and smiles proudly. "Aren't you proud of them?" she says to Joanne. "Yes, I am. They got spunk standing up for what's right." Silence sweeps over our excitement into one of reflection. For in our young lives it was an invigorating experience on the beach which we try comprehending. Our parents know with certainty the incident, in some way, will impact our lives in the coming years.

Chapter 6

BLUE-EYED DEVIL

Most Saturday mornings Lorenzo, James and Eddie Joe Edwards and I shoot marbles on a narrow dirt road in front of my house. I win all their marbles and James crowns me Marble King of the week just as a familiar voice rants in the distance. Sister Rose, a light-skinned mysterious bible thumping crusader, approaches us. Neighbors call her a prophet, even angel-like. Sinners see her none other than the devil himself in disguise. Others say she's crazy—too fanatical with her face close to yours doing her fire and brimstone preaching. Grandma just calls her Sister Rose, a good friend preaching the gospel for Jesus.

Always in a hurry, Sister Rose wears her signature long black flowing dress. She has long flowing curly black hair under a wide-brimmed black felt hat and in her hand a Moses-like staff that gives her a biblical appearance. She pauses momentarily to swipe her staff at a few dogs barking at her heels. Dogs don't seem to like her. Some days she stands out on this big empty lot across from my home attracting subdued passersby. Few neighbors have the courage to be visible. She prophesizes singling out sinners to come forth and get saved. "God ordained me to preach the gospel so heathens may be saved!" she says in a raspy growling voice. She randomly selects a sinner's house. Anyone refusing her entry, she'll stand in their yard preaching loudly while shaking her bible towards heaven.

A winehead staggers past, heading towards Sister Rose unable to elude her. In a tangential way of quoting scriptures, she preaches at him in rapid fire. "Liquor and whore-mongering means victory for Satan. You better let it go and get right with Jesus or die and go to hell!" she growls. "I'm tryin ma'am. I'm tryin." The man staggers away. As we shoot marbles, neighbors in Cisco Quarters make a mad dash inside.

We're scurrying about picking up marbles as she stands over us. "Hello boys." Wipes glistening sweat beading up on her brow from the stinging hot sun. "Boys, are you saved in the Holy Spirit, baptized in the name of Jesus, accepted Jesus Christ as your savior?" Looks at James, Eddie Joe, Lorenzo then me. "Ah, no ma'am," Lorenzo replies shyly as Eddie Joe laughs and James runs off. "Well you boys better get right with Jesus. Satan gonna get cha!!" she shouts, pointing her finger.

"Is Sister Jay in?" I nod. It's early for Saturday morning bible study with Grandma before I can sneak off. Grandma calls me. "Kenny! Lorenzo! Come here this minute!" When Grandma doesn't use my nickname, I'm on alert. "You're doing work of the devil not the righteous up in that tree house," Grandma says. Sister Rose sits grinning appreciatively. We're bewildered by Grandma's question. "Don't play ignorant," she continues. Lorenzo's mouth droops and he stares blankly as we stand mute. Sister Rose caught us spying on Tatterman. Sister Rose delivers her weekly sinners report to Grandma.

We'd been hiding out in an abandoned tree house watching through binoculars as Tatterman takes women in the woods and makes out, near our underground dugout. Tatterman sells potatoes around town. Women, even married ones, are attracted to his charm and contagious smile rather than to his truck of potatoes and other vegetables. Tall, muscularly built with charcoal black skin, Tatterman is the ladies' Masai warrior. He turns lady customers into his suitors. Every evening he brings different women out into the woods. Sister Rose, I suspect, must have noticed our shadows up high stretching out onto Eighth Street when the sun is at its peak and Tatterman and his suitors appear.

"That Tatterman is a fornicator, a sinner going to hell!" Sister Rose shouts. I don't know what fornicator means, but I have my ideas the way Grandma and Sister Rose imply. "The ways of a man and woman are sacred in marriage and the eyes of God," Grandma says in her usual whisper. "Amen! Glory be to God!" Sister Rose seconds it. Sister Rose has been on to Tatterman for quite some time. But being confronted by her doesn't seem to deter Tatterman nor the women from his routine.

Grandma doesn't want our minds tainted by Tatterman's behavior. She opens her bible to read a few verses, rebuking Tatterman's sinful acts and asks God to forgive us. Sister Rose's eyes pierce through Lorenzo's restrained grin, and suddenly springs up from her seat. She grips Lorenzo's forehead, squeezing it. "Release! Release! Release! The devil out this boy's mind in the name of Jesus!" Sister Rose is sure to tell Lorenzo's mother. Grandma sure to read and explain bible verses for my sin. I miss a few Sundays working in the fields to attend Wednesday evening bible study at church. Grandma won't have it any other way.

I was dragging my way to bible study when a peculiar young lady gets my attention. Lidia Thompson, a neighbor and once a prostitute dressed in a long flowing white dress with matching headscarf. A group of younger girls dressed similarly gather around her outside a Sanctified Church. "Hi Kenny! You don't recognize me now do you?" she smiles. I'm surprised, seeing such a drastic change. "Are you saved?" "No, she ain't saved," the young girls say giggling, rushing off inside to the thumping sounds of bass, drums and my cousin Otis's squealing electric guitar. It seems to me rock 'n roll rather than gospel.

Lidia made a valiant conversion to the Nation of Islam in prison. I know little of her faith, only what the news media likes to falsely label as hate. Malcolm X and Cassius Clay, my heroes, changed their names and joined the Nation.

I take notice of Lidia's calm and peaceful demeanor. No longer wearing revealing short dresses and eye-catching skin-tight pants, Lidia was looking regal. She notices interest in my eyes and invites me out to a meeting with Mama's approval. "If it helps blacks, what little I know does, I'm for it," Mama confirms. "I think you'll enjoy Minister Leonard X. He's changing how so-called Negroes think of themselves," Lidia says.

The following Saturday a black Lincoln Continental rolls into the driveway followed by another car with several women, including Lidia, all in headscarves. Sister Gloria, the minister's wife steps out the inwardly opening suicide doors thanking Mama for allowing me to attend. "We need more like you," she says with conviction. At eleven years of age I don't know any Muslim Temples or have any Muslim contacts in Fort Pierce. Minister X and his entourage come from Miami's Liberty City, fishing for converts, in search of lost souls. Ex-convicts, the down and out, bums, drunks, those of ill-repute, it doesn't matter. As the minister's cars roll away from my front yard, Ms. Dottie, a neighbor resting under our shady mango tree, looks up at Mama heading back inside. "Hey Margaret! That's ah nice lookin fella come by. Don't trust um though, if ain't wearin a mustache, that for white men. Ah colored man aught ta have hair on his upper lip. Without it he luk like ah sissy."

The meeting arouses excitement, an urgent need to question I can't readily find a soul to get answers. I contain it with Grandma's cautious reminder not to yield to a dogmatic approach: "You're Christian. Don't judge, follow your heart to the truth. God's calling you regardless from what ministry." I keep an open mind. My thoughts are contrary to her beliefs. In some way I am drawn by the aura of Minister Leonard X even more to his strong character, like Daddy's. I want to know what caused Lidia to drastically change.

Before the Saturday meeting I try recruiting James, Eddie Joe, and Lorenzo. I tell them that the minister has something important to say about black folks. All had gone to church and such a meeting will ruin a day at the beach. "You crazy goin with those people."

We roll up to a small rundown cinder block building isolated in a weedy field off U.S. Highway #1. The building and windows are riddled with bullet holes and spent shell casings lay scattered about. A reminder we might be trespassers and somebody's target practice. A gaping hole in the roof makes for needed ventilation as overcast clouds darken above us blotting out the stinging sun. "Why we're having a meeting at this old dump?" I ask Lidia once we exit the car. "We have to, our people not ready to listen to what the Minister gonna say."

Several men dressed in dark suits stand guard at the entrance. My heart pounds at their secretiveness. A huge man in charge of security advises me to empty my pockets and briskly pats down the outer layers of my suit. I intently grimace and stare disapproving. "It's for everyone's safety little brother," the man says. I'm thinking, safety from what? He's patting outer layers of my clothing while he's exposing a gun in an arm holster. What kind of message needs protection with guns? Did someone want Leonard X killed? I wrestle with my thoughts, assuring myself that it's a good thing that Minister Leonard helps blacks.

The excitement before arrival is replaced with apprehension. A meager group of five men and six women with several small children sit on rickety old rusting chairs, waiting. Not a single boy my age is in attendance. Lidia waving me over to come sit near her perks me up. Leonard X walks up front in a slow methodical gait like a man in deep thought. Any doubt about what I'm going to witness disappears. Looking out among the few of us, his once piercing smile doesn't hide his disappointment when he sees the dismal turnout.

"Assalamu alaikum!" Gloria, his wife, Lidia and a few women and men reply in unison: "Wa alaikum assalaam!" "All praise is due to Allah—(God) the lord and cherisher, sustainer of the world." His face is now stern and focused. Sweat beads on his upper lip, my thoughts harken back to Ms. Dottie's comments as he wipes with a handkerchief— his lip without a mustache does give an effeminate appearance.

We gather here today to speak of the so-called lost Negro in North America! How the so-called Negro wants to be like his slave master! We know him as that blue eyed-devil! With every provocative statement, loud salutations follow in rhythmic cadence. "Teach Minister Leonard!" "Tell it!"

I'm leaning forward gripping the edge of my chair, listening intensely. Clinging to every word, I am no longer concerned with no hair on his upper lip, I shout my approvals too. Standing erect, his voice elevates and fills with intensity to a fever pitch.

Brothers and sisters, we must depart our ways from this devil! The so-called Negro loves this blue-eyed devil more than he loves himself . . . more than he loves swine! And you know the Negro loves despicable swine! The so-called Negro would rather give up his businesses for the sake of integration! Do we have any so-called Negro business leaders here today to explain? No! Why not? I visited Avenue D! I see your black-owned businesses. The theater, drug store, restaurants, gas station, your newspaper company, even your night clubs, juke joints and others! The so-called Negro would rather give it all up for integration? When the so-called Negro gives up all his businesses that blue-eyed devil gonna move right on in and steal your power! Of course! The so-called Negro's happy to give it away . . . happy to integrate . . . sit next to that blue-eyed devil. That's right! Steal the so-called Negro power to control his community! That despicable thing doesn't want to integrate with the so-called Negro! That despicable thing doesn't even want to live around the so-called Negro! Just try and move next to that devil! Wake up brothers . . . so called Negroes wake up! We gonna be tricked with integration! The so-called Negro rather worship an image of a white Jesus! Yes! That's right! Just ask the so-called Negro to take down that blue-eyed devil in his church and put a black Jesus up! Paint a Jesus in his own image! He hates his blackness so much you'll have a fight on your hands! Oh yes! The so-called Negro would rather worship Jesus in the image of his blue-eyed oppressors. Isn't that's right? You think whites will put up a black image of Jesus? Need I answer that for you?

The voices in the audience elevate. "Noooo!!"

When the so-called Negro comes into enlightenment, he will see the truth. Right? We know Jesus is a black man. Right? What does the bible say? The so-called Negro is trained to believe whatever that white devil does is good! But asked the so-called Negro what he thinks about his fellow brother! Oh yes! The so-called Negro will tell you something negative! That's right! The so-called Negro doesn't trust his brother the black man! Long as the so-called Negro rather stay ignorant not read and improve himself! The so-called Negro will never tire of pleasing his slave-master! Open your eyes black man! You better wake up before it's too late and know thyself! The so-called Negro rather intoxicate his mind with mischief, stealing, gambling, drinking, drugs, killing each other. Self-destruction, just what that white devil wants you to do rather than educate your mind! That's right! Anything to keep the so-called Negro ignorant of truth . . . the original man! That blue-eyed devil despises enlightened black men and all people of color who speak the truth! That despicable devil fears a black man with knowledge of self! That despicable devil wants to keep our true history from the minds of our still enslaved brothers and sisters, the so-called Negro not here listening today! Ain't that something! These so-called Negroes better wake up! Wake up now! Before it's too late! That's why we got to learn our own history! That blue-eyed devil not gonna enlighten you or teach you about your glorious past! Oh, that devil might tell you about slavery and try to humiliate you and make you feel ashamed. They keep you thinking that's all your history while they twist it and serve it to you in their textbooks and conceal what you need to hear out! That's right, they conceal, and they hide the 'real truth' from you! That's right, because you're ashamed of your blackness and ashamed of Africa! Shame of your wooly hair! Your big gorgeous lips and nose! You ashamed because you don't know, the so-called Negro don't want to know, wants to remain in ignorance. That's right! The white man likes you blind to exploit you, to keep true history from the minds of people of color the world over! Not speak the truth! Those blue-eyed devils dare not want you to hear it! That despicable devil fears a black man with knowledge of self! That's right! If you offer to give the so-called Negro knowledge about his true self, before he believes you, he questions, he doubts, he becomes scared! He first wants to know what the white man thinks! That's why I can't get a decent building to speak to you! That's right! That's why the so so-called Negro not here listening today. Ain't that something! Not one! I ask for available space to rent and meet, but the so-called Negro wants to know what the white man thinks! That's right! Think the police might come! Let them come so-called Negro! If we had used your businesses, we won't worry about the police! No! You didn't offer your businesses so-called Negro! Because we're here in this rundown joint! And I don't see no trespassing signs! The so-called Negro better wake up! Before it's too late! That's why the so-called Negro better learn about his glorious past! Better learn about Africa! Love Africa! Why you think that blue-eyed devil stole Africa! That's right! We gonna run um out of Africa brothers and sisters! Run um out! Because the black man is God!"

Mesmerized by the audacity of his boldness. Minister Leonard X went on and on, untiring with so much fervor until the sun broke through ominous clouds bringing light from a gloomy room over the large gaping hole in the roof onto Minister Leonard X's glistening face and upper lip with no mustache. It is only now that I realize I have spent hours listening. When he finished my mind's transfixed in thought, not remembering when and how I got inside his car. Rolling up to my driveway, my thoughts are busy playing catch up, trying to retain what I heard. "I hope what I said in some way helps you understand what's needed of you. Please join us again," Minister Leonard X's voice is somber and calm. His message was quite a departure, unlike any Reverend Cliffin's rambunctious sermons.

That night as I try to sleep, my restless mind analyzes parts of Minister Leonard X's speech, unable to forget parts that impress me the most. Understanding clearly now what I'm hungry for—knowing thyself is power no one can ever change. No one can ever define you. Inspired, eager to read more, curious to know whether some of what he so profoundly says will present itself in my first year of integration.

Chapter 7

THE WHITE MAN'S BURDEN

"Pickin green maytas by the piece yawl! Ten cents a basket, gonna need 20 mo wirkers today!" a man yells out. "Pickin red ripe steak tomatoes at $7 by the day folks. I need least nine mo strong men!" another competitor yells. "Come on. . . you're tall for twelve. They might hire you," Gail says in her typical bossy way. I just listen. In the fall of '66, I seized an opportunity to work and take on responsibility buying my own clothes for the upcoming school year. Mama's taste of pin-stripe shirts and permanent-press pants no longer appeals to me. I want hip fashions. "You can use money Daddy sends me for bills. I'll buy my own clothes," I say proudly. Mama laughs. I'm out to make my own money and buy what I like. A challenge I welcome.

Gail gains experience picking tomatoes last summer with neighbor contractors, Henry and his wife Odessa Melton. With more than enough crews, Gail can't go with the Melton's this time. So, we awaken to Grandma's Big Ben clock each morning at 4:30 a.m., and walk three blocks with our packed lunch to a migrant loading zone at the Lincoln Theater's parking lot on Avenue D. "Remember, you stick to me. Don't say a word, you understand?" Gail puts her serious face on which is most times. "Remember don't say a word. I'll do all the talking."

Old school buses painted in an array of colors with black contractor names like Snow, Howard, Campbell, Melton, Coe and others artistically painted roll in and out. Noisy men and women joust for positions in front of the buses. Some stand on the periphery smoking, sipping coffee, and even huddling up passing bottles of wine. "Come on boy!" "Lets' see if we can get hired." Gail grabs my hand and yanks me towards several empty buses. I dread standing in line waiting to get picked. For three consecutive weekends, I'm yet to get picked and I'm tired of rejection having to return home while Gail gets hired. I'm feeling lucky this morning though. I come up with an idea. I stand on my toes to look taller and to look a little older. As we gather around crowds of workers, a contractor, short sooty black man with a goatee, deep sunken eyes and a growl in his voice urges everyone to form the usual line against the bus. "Da white man here dis mornin." And oldhead who sips his coffee whispers this rarity to no one in particular.

The planter dressed in casual wear stands watching. Many migrant workers who are seasonably aged, tired and abused shuffle slowly in line against the bus. "I need 20 mo strong good workers today, piece work!" the sooty black man yells again. The Planter walks by inspecting each worker from head to toe, never saying a word, points out each person onto the bus. I'm between a drunk barely able to stand and an old and bushy headed man shabbily dressed. The white man stares briefly at the three of us. He signals the bushy headed man on the bus. "Boy, ya too young, cain't let ya go, and you," singling to the other drunk, "Go home and get some sleep." "Mister please, please, let my brother go, he can work. He's strong, and he's a good worker!" Gail pleads as she sticks her head out the bus window. The Planter looks over at his contractor. "Grady what ya think? He too young boss?" I stand arching up higher on my toes, angry not because of rejection but because Gail is begging this white man. I envision a scornful scene of plantation owner at an auction in the *Master of Falconhurst* novel choosing his slaves. "Please sir let him go. I promise he's a good worker," Gail continues. The Planter unconvincingly nods his head. "Ok. I'll take my chances. You better not prove me wrong boy." He signals me onto the bus.

As we roll away, a man and women knock on the bus door. Grady stops. "We got room for one mo." "I can't go without my wife," the man says. Grady slyly look over at me. My heart thumps rapidly. "Boy ya lucky dis mornin or I best git ya seat fa betta wirkers iffin not fa the white man." "Sorry just got one seat left." Grady continues. The man in disbelief takes a quick peek inside at me, pulls back dejectedly, standing there with his wife as Grady rolls off. A sense of guilt comes over me. That man and his wife needed work more than I do.

It takes at least two hours to reach our destination in some unforgiving small town. I sit next to an elderly unkempt man realizing why everyone passed his seat. The smell of yesterday's liquor and sweat makes a stench so sickening I can barely breathe. As the bus rolls along most people sleep, some with lively chatter that keeps Grady alert. I contemplate Grandma's' last words to me as I was leaving home: "Hard work makes a man out of you. By end of the day you earn it." Unable to sleep, I listen to tired harden faces chat about making a meager living finally dosing off. At sunrise we reach Immokalee (meaning "my home" in the Seminole language), a small agricultural town considered America's tomato capital. Tomato fields blanket the land farther than the eye can see. Not a shade tree in sight.

Dew's still on the tomato plants as we begin to pick tomatoes to place in our wire baskets. Grady, the straw boss, pulls me aside, "You look strong ah nuff ta lug fa des old women. If ya ain't, ya will be fo da day is ova," he says, cutting a silly grin. Two old hags, a snuff dipper and the other with a rotten toothed smile. A look of uncertainty sweeps my face. "Ya betta keep up wit us sonny. Us can show pick!" I realize what a difficult position I got myself into.

Throughout early morning, I lug two full baskets of green tomatoes dozens of times over to the roadside, dumping them into a large plastic vat or cardboard box. Before noon the sun is scorching hot. Carrying both baskets starts to feel like a 100-pound dumbbell in each hand. The two old women fill the next two baskets faster than I can empty them. Hot and exhausted, I can't go any further and ask for a break. "Boy you cain't stop. Us wirk this way. You break we git Grady ova here!" the snuff dipper snaps, looks over at me, spits and a wad lands on my shoe. As if she is commenting on my audacity, and convince myself she's the sensible one.

I dread limiting two old women's potential earnings and Grady riding me. There must be a better way. My intuition when I first met Grady had told me that there was trouble on the horizon. Grady, a short pudgy man, has a Napoleon complex with an intense anger that he ratchets up and unleashes on taller men. Some oldheads say he's the second coming in the white man's image. His hitch man to serve and please.

During the morning, Grady viciously ridicules and threatens weaker workers. By noon my arms are aching and dripping with sweat. I have no hat to ward off the stinging sun. "Lunchtime!" Grady, the straw boss yells. News gets back to him that I'm complaining. As I walk in the direction of the bus with other workers, he yells, "Hey ya little n..ga!" I never stoop low and answer to that despicable word. I keep walking, ignoring the straw boss's obscenities. He catches up to me. "Boy what da hell wrong wit ya? Ya don't hear me callin ya?" "I don't give you power answering to that word." "Listen ta this little n..ga!" he laughs. "I answer to. Kenny." "Well, I be damned! Ah young smart ass too!" "Leave that young jitterbug alone Grady. Pick on somebody ya own size." Older seasoned workers laugh and tease. Grady hardens and thrives on the attention.

All eyes shift away from me to the relieved chatter lunchtime brings to tired workers. "Them ladies good wirkers. Stop ya complainin. If ya cain't keep up git your ass on da bus ya undastand?" I say nothing as he walks away.

I join young brothers eating lunch on the shady side of the bus. Most are young, muscular school dropouts, in their late teens and early twenties accustomed to back-breaking work. Bets are made who can lug and earn most by the end of the day, running with their baskets across rows to collect 20-cents per basket. Split the profits with workers on each return. "Hey Jit! Don't pay Grady no mine. That n..ga crazys," a brother about eighteen says with others in agreement. "We went through it too. Until he sees you a good worker," another says. "It's Grady's way initiating the new." I sit listening, absorbing it all, their talk about money, girls and cars. "You too quiet Jit!" "You gotta give Grady piece of ya mind," another interjects. "Yeah, he like that," yet another says, "cause that white man ah ride um, if he doesn't ride us." Curious, I ask, "Do you'll go to school?" "Hell no, we quit," a young brother says with all seemingly in agreement. "Why?" "Money. We got needs," yet another chimes in. All with a look I often see in my buddies, and I suppose, in some ways in me—a doggedly need for material things synonymous with depravity and the poor. All quit school between the ages of 14 and16, they laugh and joke with the desire of dollar bills in their eyes. I sit listening as the scent of tomatoes and pesticide kill my ordinarily hearty appetite, so I'm up for nothing more than a soft drink and a snack.

"Wirk time people. It's hard but fair. Ya cain't make no money eatin. Let's git ta work!" A recognizable loud baritone voice jolts me to my senses and a rush of anxiety clings to my stomach.

I dreaded the thought having to lug more tomatoes. Rosie, an old man taps me on the shoulder. I had observed him at the loading zone sipping a bottle of cheap wine. He sits down behind me shaking like a leaf in need of a drink. His nappy hair is almost completely white, his clothes in tatters and a foul body odor permeates the air around us. He looks at me, smiling, "Young man listen. You'll do better pickin maytas. That white man's n….ga gonna ride ya til he fire ya. You be alright." It's of little comfort, yet worth keeping to heart. I feel rejuvenated, grab two baskets not knowing what to expect. What's certain is the same two old women are without a lugger. The day gets hotter and the pace faster. Gail thinks it's best I quit lugging for these old inconsiderate women. I have something to prove, I'm no quitter. But I'm being unrealistic. I'll wind up with a hernia lifting too many heavy baskets. I hope someone comes to my rescue. I quickly discover in empty eyes and numb weathered faces complete silence whenever Grady, the straw boss, appears—a server of retribution on the powerless.

I have a pocket full of dimes that I can't wait to count by the end of day. My arms and back are sore. Sweating, dehydrated and tired out from the afternoons' scorching sun, but determined to get through the remainder of the day. "So ya decide ta pick, ya cain't handle it. Thought ya a man. Just a young punk like da rest!" Grady yells angrily. The wisdom of Rosie's words rings true. Picking tomatoes is not for the weary; backbreaking work requires hours of standing and bending until your back aches. You get on your knees some to ease the back pain until it hurts again. The arsenical pesticides get in your clothes, pores and causes skin rashes. My fingers cramp from pulling tomatoes from the vines and without gloves the morning dew and pesticide on the leaves cause my fingers to burn and when dry itches. I seek relief from a water boy carrying his bucket. Expect a refreshing drink, I am disappointed when I sip the distasteful sulfuric water that smells like rotten eggs. I cringe having to drink from the same germ-filled cup that wineheads with nasty hacking coughs use.

Up ahead, a group of men and women chat and laugh to get through the hot day. One lugger, a young brother, smiles and tries to rap but Gail isn't flattered all day her eyes never sparkle nor does she smiles. She admirably handles the young brother's advances quite well. There're no one my age, so I blend in, listening and laughing at jokes told by nasty old men entertaining themselves to get through the day. A sudden hush falls over the workers followed by clouds of dust sweeping across the field. "Here comes da white man!" someone blurts.

A cloud of dust settles on everyone. A white truck rolls up with a large CB antenna on the rear. The planter, a lanky man, gets out as laughter and playfulness cease. Whenever the white planter enters a field, his eyes are shielded with mirror shades that give him an intimidating presence of the unseeing, yet all-watching eyes. Grady walks over to the planter's truck. A group of old men near me whisper, "There goes the straw boss, the white man's flunky." They share this common belief. "Overseer" on the plantation seems appropriately deserving of this label for Grady.

Grady leans into the window of the truck grinning. After a quick chat, Grady and the planter look over in my direction. My heart kicks fast in double time as I feel them watching me. I've fallen behind, even after Grady sent a man to help catch me up. Tired of picking, hands sore from lugging my own baskets instead of the women, I'm about to give up. The planter approaches with Grady on his heels, bends and pulls back vines with fast erratic moments. I'm concededly spent but give a half-hearted last-ditch effort.

There's utter silence with the exception of rustling vines from workers picking vigorously in the planter's presence. Suddenly, the planter straightens up, walks over, bends inches from my face, takes off his shades exposing tired red eyes, and says calmly, "You leavin good maytas behind. Too many. I cain't tolerate losin money like this." He straightens up, towering over me as I stand arms folded in perceptible stubbornness. Grady watches him closely. "You understand?" "Yessa boss, I ah stay on him boss. Like white on rice."

Onlookers half-pick watching the planter speed away, kicking more dust off to another nearby field of workers. Grady rips into me. "Boy ya makin me look bad. My job hard enuf, ain't gonna cut ya no mo slack. No one cain help ya now. Ya on ya own!" An upsurge of determination comes over me. In times of trouble, Grandma's words reverberate resolutely, I embrace them, and in times of need they give me strength and peace. "You, my Grandchild will find a way. When you want a better way." It's like I'm reborn again. "It's ok, I can handle it," I say calmly. Grady gives a perplexed grimace, shakes his head and walks away.

Grady hardly let up, calls me unforgiving names, and only after several men he calls his best workers and a few elderly ladies appease him with potato pie, and Gail's pleas, does he retreat only to return refueled with more toxic words. "Ya young sorry n..ga!" Stings me almost to tears, pushes and rides me like a horse in the Kentucky Derby.

We break for the day as the sun descends in the distance. I follow a tired haggard bunch to the bus on the roadside. Workers laugh and joke half-heartedly in relief after a long arduous day. Everyone quietly counts their earnings. I have $15 worth of dimes. More than I ever imagined earning but far less than others. It's my consolation from Grady's relentless abuse. I proudly don't let him defeat me. I keep working and winning. On the bus back home, sleep is a remedy for the tired and weary. We reach Fort Pierce's loading zone after 7:00 pm, the normal time of arrival in the life of seasonal migrant workers.

Gail thinks I should stay home protecting me from Grady's abuse is too much work. Grandma convinced her of my unerring determination. "Let him go. Scaldee mind made up." I somehow psyche myself out of my senses with a joyous feeling thinking about all those dimes in my pocket. Earning my own money is rewarding.

With some earnings, I purchase a straw hat and gloves to cushion my swollen blistering hands. Grandma gives Gail and me pork and beans cans with punctured holes to drink from, secured with strings to attach to my belt. She rubs my sore hands and arms with ointment before bedtime, and with encouraging words, I sleep well. I awaken the next morning invigorated, even against Grady's nastiness.

The planter doesn't show for the lineup. Yet, Gail insists we go back into the eye of evil with some of her girlfriends and we do. Standing in line once again tip-toeing to fake my height, Grady with his typical toxic tone spots me leaning against his bus. "What the hell. Ya ain't gettin ya sorry young ass on my bus again!" I'm not floored with shame in my resoluteness now, and Gail with friends allowed to return can't rescue me this time. But a tall burly middle-aged woman in a headscarf intercedes. "Grady! Give um another chance. Let um pick with me. You know he did ok yestidy," she says. "Knaw, I ain't gon be sponsible fur him ta day. I cain't git enuf good wirkers as it is!" There's a scarcity of workers. Planters are offering 20 cents a basket, a special markup due to their concern that the tomatoes may rot on the vines from an impending rainstorm. Grady can't find a descent crew, so he is forced to use worn out older workers. I'm turned down but relieved to return home and get some sleep. A cunning reprieve at the conspiring hands of the women in head scarves wasn't meant to be. Instead an old man sneaked me onto the bus. The old bushy gray-haired Rosie who stinks something awful conceals me next to him in a rear seat.

Grady doesn't discover me until we reach Immokalee, and begins to furiously making idle threats. "Ya walk home fo I let cha wirk, the white man don wan cha comin back!" He adamantly says. His insolent words become a smoke screen as the women with headscarves intercede once again, "Grady let him work. He's betta off in the field. I'll think of something to tell that white man."

Early morning dew lingering on vines penetrates my gloves. Before noon, the weather man announces from a transistor radio another hot scorching day. I thank and applaud the old man and women's efforts contriving against a scoundrel like Grady—it's a blessing in disguise.

All morning, I severe ties with two complaining old women. I vigorously pick, mustering enough energy to lug and dump my own tomatoes in a large vat of water on the roadside. Feeling energized I skillfully pick with efficiency like never before, but still lag a safe distance behind the others. I swing my baskets of tomatoes masterfully and less laboriously across every row to the roadside and spot the white man watching from his truck a short distance away. His head turns and stares behind mirrored shades, I suppose critiquing my work. Perhaps even eyeing the burly women in headscarves I pick next to. Maybe Grady has convinced the planter that I'm doing a decent job. During the morning, Grady makes his rounds, seldom checking my work. When he does, he leaves with a compliment: "Good job, keep it up." The old man Rosie's advice pays off: First, part vines in tomato beds from the top down, then lift and check beneath. This proves beneficial. Exuding confidence after lunch, I let my guard down and start to lag noticeably falling further behind. Even after Rosie and his buddies' warnings, I can't catch up.

I stand up and notice Grady and the white man still watching. The planter gets out of his truck, voice blaring up towards Grady, hands gesturing animatedly as they approach. Both stand watching over me as I bend over, nervously picking unenthusiastically. The planter moves in closer, breathing laboriously in my face. I jump back. He takes off his mirrored shades, turns away and checks behind me. Once again, he stands inches from my face. "Listen boy, you doin fair right now but keep up. Grady should da left you back in town. Leave one good mayta on a vine, you be sittin on the bus, neva come back in my fields. Get ta work and catch up."

I feel compelled to let him know that I have a name, but sitting all alone on a bus is too much to bear. And Grady, I suspect, must have put a pleasant bug in the white man's' ear to warrant a second chance.

"Waterboy!" I yell watching him run, earning his keep in the scorching Florida sun, as he meanders through rows of thirsty workers. Water is premium relief to fertilizer particles irritating a throat. As the hot sun descends in a cloudless blue sky, two rows over Rosie and his two buddies share a fifth of Thunderbird wine. Suddenly a familiar silence signals the planter is approaching once more. Bookie, one of Rosie's buddies, shoves the bottle down his loose-fitting pants' pocket. Rosie and his buddies fall behind, to the white man's displeasure. He walks moving in and out of the trenches digging through vines towards Rosie and his buddies picking together. "Hey!" he yells frantically in the direction of the men. "What da hell yawl been doin? !You boys leavin dam good maytas. Git ova here!" The two grab their baskets, Bookie looking noticeably drunk, falls down into a seizure, his body jerking in reflexive movements. The planter's cherry red sun baked face lights up. "Hey Grady! Git ova here quick!"

Workers gather around Bookie lying between rows, eyes rolled back into his head, arms and legs jerking and twitching as spit forms at the corners of his mouth. The scarfed lady calls a water boy over, wets a handkerchief and wipes Bookie's face, fanning him with her straw hat. Bookie lies there wheezing and snoring laboriously. Minutes later he awakens with a puzzled stare. "Hey everybody, we got a field to pick! Git back to wirk!" the planter yells. As Bookie is helped off the ground, the planter spots a wine bottle protruding from his pocket. "So that's why I can't get no damn maytas picked! These men are drunk! You two git on da damn bus!" "We good workers, please mister," the tallest says with a nervous chuckle. But the white man's not buying it. "I want um on the bus!" "Don't beg!" Rosie interrupts. "Never beg! Where's your dignity!" Rosie exerts himself in a way the planter takes notice of but can't turn back in need of sacrificial lambs. Finally, I suppose my lagging behind set it all in motion.

"Anybody else caught with a bottle, I'll dock ya pay too. Yabe finished wirkin for me!" the planter says leaving. Grady comes over, stands a moment in pomposity and arrogance watching Rosie watch his two buddies crawl about defeatedly on their knees searching through vines for neglected tomatoes. "Ain't no need ta pick none now, git up and go ta da bus!" he laughs, full of himself. Looking spent and defeated, Rosie's buddies stagger across rows of tomatoes onto the bus. I'm numb.

Grady does not consider Bookie's seizure nor conveys a hint of compassion. It becomes evident migrant workers are devalued pawns. That white man doesn't give a damn about humanity, only production and crop yields. "All right folks listen good, no mo time fur lollygagging around! We gon finish this field fo knock off time!" Grady says. The planter sits in his truck with a conspicuously intimidating presence, a reminder, behind mirrored shades, that he's the sentinel on watch.

As morning progresses, Grady reveals a meaner more sinister side randomly singling out workers with disparaging statements, "n..ga ya pikin too slow. My Grandma kin pick fasta than you!" Like a joke all in presence of the white man but no one laughs. His helpless victims are defenseless in silent disgust. I watch silently too, at Grady as the epitome of ineptitude and betrayal. His egotistical self-absorbing mannerisms are to please the white man at the expense of irreparably harming his own people.

I become so entangled in my frustration seeing the insurmountable hardships powerless black folks face. I somehow, in my mind, become obsessed by what I witness is helpless gullibility of black folk with little or no education. I write then as I write now, little short vignettes late into the night of these things I encounter. Throughout my seasonal work, I write, and I began to truly believe the importance of an education.

Just before lunchtime, I seek refuge in Rosie's company. We're partnered off as I continue lugging my own tomatoes, praying to survive another day but fall behind again. In an adjoining field a plane flies over, circles twice as if suspended in indecision. The pilot playfully circles once more, nose dives then levels off descending unusually low in our direction. I notice a sinister smile on the pilot's face as he zooms so low everyone ducks as a cool breeze sweeps over us followed by a heavy mist of pesticide. The pilot circles and nose dives once again, descending even lower releasing a second spraying. Workers grumble, and my suspicions are true—crop dusting is the norm, but you never get used to.

"Why does this happen?" "No one complains." I question Rosie. "No need complainin, that's what always happen. Why complain? Nobody can do nothin. That white man show ain't.

"You better cover up." "Grady no one git on the bus...best stay in this field...it be clear in no time!" "Yessa boss!" Grady replies. Workers accustomed to such practices protest passively by covering their heads and faces with clothing. I look for Gail as a thin film of milky white liquid falls from the sky covering my clothing. Gail and a group of women escapeagainst the bus. I'm deep in center of the field. "Why didn't that white man warn us?" "Why should he?" "He's in money business not people business,"Rosie says. "It's gotta be laws against this!" I say incensed. "What law. We ain't got power to change it." No one can give another straight forward answer as the planter and his henchman, Grady sit comfortably in the air-condition truck watching.[15]

My eyes, nose and throat burn, irritated by pesticide. Water brings some relief. As I catch up, Rosie on the opposite row falls further behind. "All right old man git on the bus!" Grady yells from the truck. Unwavering, Rosie doesn't say a word and walks, with his head held high, to the bus. "Damn it ya n..gas! Yawl makin me look bad out here!" I get up off my knees and lash out. Relinquish anger for that day and the day before. "Is n....r the only word in your vocabulary?!" "We got names!" "You act like ah n....r...you ah traitor to your race for that white man!" "What ya say boy?" "You heard me!" A mixture of silence and laughter sweeps across the rows. "Kenny please, don't talk back!" Gail cries out afraid for me. Grady looks stunningly surprised as the white man approaches.

"What's goin on here Grady?" "Oh! I'll take care of it boss." "No!

---

[15] No enforceable laws with bite exist for seasonal and migrant laborers against deplorable inhumane working conditions. I experienced my share of threats and intimidation working in torrential rain, severe heat, frigid temperatures, and a crop duster raining down pesticides. The Fair Labor Act of 1966 guaranteed only minimum wage protection, it failed to eradicate discrimination, verbal abuse, poor sanitation, health risk and cheating the poor out of fair wages.

Tell me what goin on right now!" Grady squirm nervously. "It ain't nothin boss, he wirkin too slow, complainin bout crop spraying irritates." The planter pulls his shades from his reddened eyes and sun baked face, looks over at me momentarily and turns towards the workers. "Listen up yawl!" "I got money invested in this crop and depend on yawl doin good work. I pay ya'll damn good money, special price now 30-cents ah basket by da piece. Ah storm ah comin. I gotta have this field picked by evenin dammit!" Not a bit of excitement results from his desperate words, only tired, worn powerless black faces. He turns back towards me standing there: "And you! Git on the bus. I had enough of ya complainin and sloppy work!"

Heading towards the bus, I overhear a dangerous and inexcusable Freudian slip by the planter. "I pay yawl nig, uh, I mean I pay yawl good money to do da work. Grady keep an eye on um and push um good." I watch the planter head towards his truck as Grady looks shamefully at me, knowing, I suppose, that I overhear the forbidden slip. He turns and walks away unable to hold his gaze nor say another word. Perhaps it finally occurs to Grady, in the white man's mind, he's a n..ga of little importance too, a burden just like the rest of us.

I get on the bus as Rosie and his buddies smile. "Welcome aboard," he says. "I like how you handle yourself out there just then." We talk until it's time to go home. Rosie once a married man, college educated and owner of a successful laundry business was taken down by his alcoholism and adultery. "I be first to admit I'm an educated fool, weakness for women, I lose the love of my life, everything."

Rosie spent ten years chasing the season up and down the East Coast from Florida to upstate New York. Hard labor and cheap wine makes him a shadow of his former self. "The bottle helps ease the pain of rejection and abandonment from a beautiful wife and kids." A tormented winehead still retains his dignity and spirit. Rosie smiles as I sit near him. "You know young man, I'm at the end of my days. Not much I can say or do can make a difference now." "We' ain't valued for our work. When you get old like me you get put out to pasture." His voice tapers off eclipsed by a group of old women in the background singing a melody that provides answers to their suffering with a prophetic message:

Glory, glory, hallelujah
When I lay my burden down.
Glory, glory, hallelujah
I'm going home to Jesus
When I lay my burden down.

"Yes siree, neva met a planter giva damn bout workers. Need us but don't giva a damn bout us, we the white man's burden. Yes indeed!"

I understand from Rosie's life in a cruel system that depends on exploiting migrant labor. I too am like those who are becoming a beast of burden carrying the planter's heavy load. I see Grandma toiling in tomato fields overworked, underpaid until she succumbs to illness. Bits and pieces of paper I find, she painstakingly scribbled on while in the tomato fields to keep track of her meager earnings.

On our way back home, Rosie's stench doesn't bother me as much as before. I become accustomed to his stench from yesterday and even from days before: body odor and waste matter, and noxious fertilizers and pesticides mixed with sweat. I become one of the white man's burden.

During the remainder of the summer, I stay away from piece work where earnings are greater but the work is harder. Although day work (means by the hour) slaving at 8 dollars a day is not so hard but earning less. I gain a work ethic, earn my keep. I accomplish my goal buying stylish clothes I like for the upcoming school year.

At 12, I'm affected by migrant worker exploitation and mistreatment in Fort Pierce agricultural driven economy. It validates for me what Rosie has said, his revelation that white planters select among us the ignorant conspicuous self-hating souls to act as their intermediaries. Grady enforces the planter's will like an overseer, pushing and slave-driving the cheap labor for big profits.

Chapter 8

SEPARATE AND UNEQUAL

We sit quietly awaiting the return of Ms. Florene Robinson, who's off on a short recess, probably to the ladies room. It's a hot day and everyone is sweating profusely as we return from the playground. Our classroom, always hot and stuffy in the summer, today is like an oven. There's no air conditioning and everyone is restless, talking and laughing in an orderly fashion. No one dares horse play in Ms. Robinson's class. No one dares take advantage of her absence. We don't dare mess up our bragging rights—the best teacher at Francis K. Sweet Elementary! Not even on the last day of school.

I sit impatiently watching the long hand of the clock on the wall not move fast enough to end our school year. Ms. Robinson's always conscious of the time. "Where is she?" someone asks. "Why on the final day of school?" Finally, I hear sounds of swift moving heels rushing down the hallway. She enters apologetically, looking elegant as ever. Robinson is every bit of splendor, poised and articulate—a natural born beauty queen. Never raises her soft voice; hardly lifts a finger to get our attention. Smiling, her eyes set aglow, move up and down rows landing on us as if she's our mother sadly being separated from her children. She releases a breath of air and pauses a moment, leaving us in suspense. She holds a piece of paper in her hand and begins to read what sounds like the memorable U. S. Supreme Court's ruling in the 1954 landmark case, *Brown v. Board of Education of Topeka Kansas:*

To separate black children from others of similar age and qualifications solely because of their race generates a feeling of inferiority as to their status in the community that may affect their hearts and minds in a way never to be undone . . . we conclude that, in the field of public education, the doctrine of separate but equal has no place... Separate educational facilities are inherently unequal.

In 1963, only 12,000 of the 3 million black school-aged children in the South attend integrated schools. None of the schools were integrated in Saint Lucie County, Fort Pierce. Twelve years after the passage of *Brown v Board of Education*, Saint Lucie County Public School Board members along with other staunch southern segregationists remain defiant as ever to maintain a segregated educational system. As civil rights organizations apply pressure and President Johnson passes the 1964 Civil Rights Act only a few black Children attend Fort Pierce public schools and Joh Carroll Catholic School at the beginning of my 1966 school year.

Florene Robinson a brilliant teacher and historian instill in young minds dignity and racial pride with stories of black heroes. Taught girls and boys etiquette (good manners), how to cook basic foods, types of stitches how to do for self, and those lacking personal hygiene skills. (Courtesy of Hurst family archives).

Everyone looks bewildered, mouths agape while listening attentively and clinging to every word, as Ms. Robinson deliberately enunciates every syllable to make her point. Ms. Robinson maintains her professional demeanor as she looks out at the class. She smiles and her mouth quivers. A small tear forms and trickles down her cheek. Her small fingers tremble as they grip the sheet of paper. Her voice cracks happily as she imagines what will be possible for her students, more than she could have ever hoped for in her lifetime.

"Some of you will integrate a white junior high school next term. I want to know what you think about what I read. I want to hear what's on your minds. How you feel about it." There's complete silence. Then questions come rapid fire: "What does integrate mean?" "Why do Negroes have to integrate?" "White people don't like us, ain't gonna like us anyway." "What's wrong with Negro schools?" "Yeah!" "My Mama says they won't come to ours." "It's not fair!" Finally, an opening comes. "Do we have Negro teachers to help us over there?" I ask. "Will you come teach Ms. Robinson?" So many questions to answer and she does her best.

Weeks earlier before Ms. Robinson says her goodbyes, letters are sent home for parents' signatures. Few parents approve of sending their children to St. Lucie Junior High. I'm one of a few classmates stirring parents' hopes and aspiration—not my own. I'm like others naturally curious whether it's a good decision to integrate.

The majority of black parents are apprehensive. "I don't want my child exposed to racial insults and violence. To be in isolation with no support, to be experimental guinea pigs for verbal and physical abuse," a neighbor tells Mama. I don't know what to expect. But I watch enough news of angry whites hurling racial insults, throwing rocks and bottles at blacks entering their schools to know I'm not welcome. "Those of you integrating will make history," Ms. Robinson says. "With integration we will establish new friends," she continues. Our own schools and communities will never be the same again isn't enough to calm my anxiety.

Ms. Robinson, standing poised before her class, is interrupted. "Ms. Robinson, but I don't know anybody white!" a girl says emphatically triggers laughter. "We don't either!" the class responds in unison. The girl's declaration speaks volumes of truth about separation in the South. Ms. Robinson finishes answering our questions, realizes the gravity of our discomfort will be challenging and our lives will be changed forever. "I enjoy having each of you. I love you all, and always will. Do your best and you will succeed; may God bless you all." That is the last thing I remember Ms. Robinson says before the bell rings ending the 1966 school year.

Mama on occasion does some domestic work for an oil tycoon's relative. Helen drops off Mama with her two sons, Victor 11 and Carl 12, my age, in the car. Sometimes with Helen's car idling in our yard, a lengthy conversation ensues. Helen without hesitation turns down Mama's offers to come inside, insists she's in a hurry while Victor and Carl eagerly await her permission to get out of the car. We laugh and joke, keeping our distance on opposite sides. I ask Helen if they can sometimes come over. Both listen to their Mother's deflating excuses. Not once does she make a counter offer to invite me. A peculiar feeling comes over me that moment. I get a sense I'm different and each encounter afterwards seems superficial to me. With heightened awareness I know that my skin's the barrier that separates us.

Some mornings I curiously watch Helen roll up in our yard. My sisters also watch Helen smile as she leaves. "Mama, does Ms. Helen smile like that when you're working?" Gail asks one morning. "Not much, but she's nice. I guess that's how Ms. Helen calms her nerves, she never drives through Negro neighborhoods," Mama adds. The more I watch Helen, the more I come to understand that whites are guilt ridden and just not comfortable around Negroes. But of course, that's their problem.

In my own encounters with whites and what I overhear and learn, impacts how I see them and explains why I have a bitter distrust for all white people. Although I am growing up in a Christian family and have been taught to love all people regardless, I find it hard to reconcile my feelings. I suppose it comes from encounters with my own people who are powerlessness and express their ambivalence. I become keenly interested in trying to rationalize their struggles. In the downtrodden there's always struggle, and in struggle there can be strength. Some are able to extract some optimism. So, as I listen to neighbors from different sides of life (many in Cisco Quarters), I become keenly aware of my own struggles and I'm angry. And the restrictive and distinct racial barriers cast by a dominant white society and how I must maneuver through it my next school year increase my bitterness and my resolve.

A gathering after services at Mount Olive Baptist Church. Front row left Regina and Sheryl. Back row Gail and I. (Courtesy of the Hurst family Archives).

I know early on my parents see the inquisitive side of me wanting to know why things are as they are. I languish over a point of view stuck on why. Blessed with a family willing to let me ask questions and debate is encouraging. Amid the struggle for racial equality in the late 1960s and the civil rights gains, my parents want my sisters and me to get a quality education through integration mama says is the way.

Mama is especially concerned about me, and I think the neighborhood boys in general. She has witnessed some of my friends' low self-esteem and negative self-images, and their declining interest in school. I believe this explains her desire to expose her children to different cultures by way of desegregation, to open our eyes and our minds. Mama never lets us forget that segregation cheats our race out of opportunities to grow. Until St. Lucie County's school system invests equal funds for a quality education in our neighborhoods, she decides we'll be attending integrated schools.

Each night our family gathers in front of the television to watch NBC Nightly News with anchors Chet Huntley and David Brinkley. It's always been Daddy's favorite television program. Mama and Daddy enjoyed discussing social and civil rights issues, especially politics and the electoral process. Since Daddy's departure, it has become a family ritual. Civil rights issues take center stage in our family and Grandma likes watching quietly, smiling with an "amen" each time Chet and David discuss civil rights struggles. Since the March on Washington in 1963 and King's memorable "I Have a Dream" speech, she optimistically absorbs every bit of news on racial equality. "Coloreds are protesting with dignity," she says. With the passage of new civil rights legislation in her golden years, Grandma is glued to the TV. And she's pleased. Grandma keeps with the old Negro saying: "God may be late, but he's always right on time!"

The winds of change in desegregation policies sweep across the airwaves of America. One evening while eating dinner, Mama calls me into the living room. "I think you want to see this. They're talking about your new school." St. Lucie County School Board, twelve years after the passage of the Civil Rights Act, will open its doors to black students. The board remains in absolute defiance of the Civil Rights Act, and allows only three schools to integrate: Dan McCarty High, St. Lucie Junior High and Fort Pierce Elementary, all in white neighborhoods.

The board implements a "school choice plan" for my 1966-67 school year. The school board's purpose and intent is to not bus white children, to keep them in their own neighborhood schools and to protect the status quo. Mama looks rather resentful at the board's decision. She wants my younger sisters, Regina and Sheryl, to attend integrated schools without incident.

Florida counties throughout the years have successfully used "school choice plan" tactics to prevent an influx of black enrollment at white schools. This tactic violates the 1964 Civil Rights Act. Before I become fully cognizant of segregation's crippling effects, I listen to Mama engage lodge sisters Naomi Jordan and Marian Quillette in debates. I listen from outside with my ear to the screen door until Mama shoos me away.

The Zenith Club provide meals, clothing and sponsor financial aid and scholarships to needy college bound students. Back row on left, my mother, Margaret Hurst, fifth from left in glasses friend Marion Quillette, second row on right friend Naomi Jordan. (Courtesy of Hurst family archives).

At church I listen to my pastor R.F. Cliffin, president of our local NAACP, address civil rights issues in his sermons. Our insurance agents P. J. Wallace and Walter Butler, the church's deacon, talk about civil rights as do the men at Cureton's Barbershop where I get my hair cut. I hear heated debates on racial inequality while I wait in

Dr. Clem C. Benton's office: "Negroes in this town always talkin . . . little action and no demands," an old man says. I come to realize that this meant hardly any real change happens without demanding it, which is consistent with passed civil rights legislation. As Frederick Douglass proclaimed: "Nothing concedes power without a demand."

There is enough sophisticated black leadership at the local level, but what's needed is a clearer objective. We need a movement to boycott white businesses and get a foothold in changing the deeply entrenched white controlled political system. We need elected officials to advocate for us. We are further marginalized without enough strong progressive leadership. Fort Pierce needs to desegregate on all levels. Whites certainly see no genuine (without court mandated) need to initiate integrating institutions until blacks take a more pronounced radical step. I listen to the educated and uneducated and it occurs to me that whites are just as content as we are moving along slowly by their standards. This is confusing to me as blacks aren't content to move slowly according to the conversations in barbershops and among the lodge ladies that comes over to see Grandma.

As I prepare to integrate St. Lucie Junior High, it's clear black leadership in Fort Pierce has yet to coalesce into a strong and effective front. However, black leadership, teachers and some whites aren't fooled by the board's "school choice" strategy for the coming school year. They see it for what it is, an ill-conceived illusion, an affront to integration. Throughout Jim Crow segregation, Florida's school boards are compelled to shield so-called impressionable angelic white children from sitting next to inferior black children. Implementing "school choice" provides that shield beyond the scope of the Civil Rights Act of 1964.

The issue of desegregating the system has become for whites an inescapable beast of burden. As I ponder over the upcoming year, my anxiety builds. I realize how important my situation is. Many friends' and classmates' parents prefer their child to remain in segregated schools rather than moving to integrate. This thinking comes from years of deeply engrained distrust of an insensitive white school board.

Notwithstanding, in some instances "school choice" backfires. A few Florida counties successfully gain through integration a majority black student enrollment, making the headlines. Fort Pierce's branch of the NAACP and other national civil rights organizations increasingly gain ground in the fight for desegregation. Yet a consensus remains settled across white America: "We ain't ready to open the floodgates for you n.....s yet!"

There are news accounts that teachers will prepare for racial sensitivity classes. I wonder what good that will do. A few weeks before school, at the end of a long hot summer working in the fields, I surmise much as I view the protesting and rioting on the news. I see angry whites and I know that here whites will hate seeing us crossing over their forbidden boundary lines. How will I fit in? I know there'll be challenges. I watch the news media as it plays on my emotions. "The First Black Students to Integrate a White High School." "The First Black Chief of Police." "The First Black Congressman." "The First Black Army General." By the late 60s these announcements gain tremendous popularity. Soon governmental entities endorse these subliminal and superficial anthems of black progress. Progress such as this originates primarily from the northern states stirring up mostly southern masses into the belief that black people are rapidly making big strides integrating into mainstream America. Soon to be realized dreams create lapses—take our eyes off the prize and away from the masses of poor blacks, a farce of tokenism and trickery at its finest.

The token black achievements trigger white disdain and fear. I overhear a white lady in an A&P grocery store say to a clerk: "Give Negroes too much too fast, they'll never be satisfied until they get more." Yet, this so-called token black success, however gratifying, ties into the perceived criminal element of our community. "Black commits murder." "Black raped." "Black robbed . . . etc." Bamboozled and scrutinized, we awaken to the harsh reality of being demonized, which heightens white fears and translates into more racial hatred and bias.

As a child, I remember seeing a young, suave and handsome Doctor Benton strutting down the segregated hallways of Fort Pierce Memorial Hospital. Well respected by whites, he works tirelessly serving the entire black community in his upstairs office on Eighth Street. I take note of it because Mama subscribes to popular black magazines that chronicle candid believable stories of black success. Stories I read written by African-American writers are more credible, free of suspicion from biased slants that appear in the white press. I read black propaganda that fuels the fire. Black leaders like Malcolm X and Stokely Carmichael criticize the manipulated and hand-picked Negro success stories and urge for inclusion not tokenism. "The white man means to appease us, keep us content, letting in a few happy Negroes." This becomes Malcolm X's mantra.

Mama's skilled at picking our brains with probing questions; she does it religiously after coming home from work. It's an unavoidable interrogation. "How was your day at school?" "What good things did you all discuss in class?" She enjoys listening to us express ourselves, be it trivial or matters of concern. A week before our first day of the new school year, she calls us near: "This day is what I pray and work hard for . . . no longer will America ignore you . . . I want my children to get a quality education. I want you all to get to know whites, all races."

How does an expected minority and arguably ill-prepared Negro student transition into an integrated school atmosphere? Familiarity with segregated schools was a precursor to our salvation, protection and peace of mind. One thing I was certain of was that Grandma prepared me well for these harsh realities: "Colored folk ain't known nothin but struggle." Grandma never allows me ever to forget. "Struggle is good if you makin progress," she keeps reminding me through dentures. I know about struggle, how to survive all right, that's how I earned my thick skin.

I feel a sense of invincibility having received from Florence Robinson blessed messages of encouragement. Having few pleasant encounters with whites, I'm cautiously optimistic integration won't be too difficult a challenge. Some days I can't shake off doubting. Can I compete? Make good grades? Win respect from my soon to be white counterparts? I have no answers to questions ruminating in my head. My thoughts drift to a scene from "Branded," a western starring Chuck Connors. He plays a Civil War soldier who was court marshaled for cowardice. His sword broken and his uniform stripped of its insignias, he comes home despised, hated by locals, and branded a traitor to his country. The opening scene always shows the fort gate shutting behind him and the closing words: "Wherever you go for the rest of your life, you must prove, you're a man." I wonder if I am tough enough. I suspect I'll eventually get into a fight, but I can face the inevitable challenge of competing scholastically with whites.

"Child, you don't hear me calling you!" Her startling voice rings in my ears as her heavy hands almost shake the life out of me. "No." My mind's a thousand miles away. "My Lord, you look burdened by something!" Grandma says staring over rimmed eyeglasses, wiping snap pea stains on her apron. "I'm worried about school with marching, rioting and fighting that I see on television. White people must really hate us." "Scaldee, white folks gonna always despise us, we got so much God-given talent. And they know it, we just ain't tapped into it all yet, right now we just a thorn in their side."

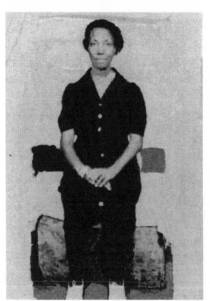

Viola Clary Wright Jay, born in 1889, 24 years removed from slavery.
(Courtesy of Hurst family archives).

Grandma's enlightening words of wisdom in her Gullah dialect of African origin bring me comfort. She lures me into her kitchen and insists I wash my hands. We sit snapping peas together, talking—not a pot-watcher (In earlier years, I loved watching her cook and stir goodies in pots on a wooden stove) on this day, just a willing participant. "Scaldee, don't look back yet. You ah new generation of redeemers. Life gonna be a lot better for you. Better than my life. You don't want ever go back through segregation."

Grandma's words reverberate truths. "Make a way out of no way," she always believes. Some enduring hardships attending segregated schools are deeply engrained in my psyche, hardly imaginable. At 12 years of age, I want to always look back. Too many unforgettable things—good and bad memories I just can't shake off. Memories imprinted in the annals of my consciousness I can't forget even if I want to. As I write, the formidable years of segregation evoke flashes of titillating memories. Daddy trying to make an honest living comes home with bursts of anger. Complaints of getting revenge from some disrespectful cracker. Whites make more money driving, restricting black cabbies from picking up whites in the white sections of town. Daddy sometimes drops Gail and me off to school. He complains after a downpour creates muddy pot holes that mess up his cab while the white residential roads are paved. Having fought for his country in World War II and not having experienced discrimination from the French, Daddy does get angry. He smiles a lot, but underneath that smile I remember a man on the edge of outrage unwilling to swallow his pride. Anger gets him in trouble keeping jobs as he confronts disrespectful white men. Daddy can't stomach bowing down at a time when whites expect black men to do just that. I'm proud to say that Daddy was always industrious, finding a way to support us, even if it comes from gambling.

After Daddy leaves for Baltimore, my sister Gail and I walk a block on dusty dirt roads, like most black children do, to school every morning. When it rains some days, cars splash mud and water out of potholes onto our clothes and shoes. On hot dry days, we eat dust blown by cars and trucks along the way. I realize afterwards what makes Daddy so angry.

Although the Civil Rights Movement is at its embryonic stage in Fort Pierce, our consciousness is elevated to deal with the good ole boy system. As I prepare to challenge segregated public schools, blacks are slowly challenging segregation in other public places. I imagine with little retaliation either by loss of job, threat, harassment or life.

Fort Pierce, unlike many towns in the South, had white residents with a higher degree of tolerance. Even in education, to some degree, they build Lincoln Park Academy almost identical with equal or more expenditures than the white Dan McCarty High School. However, Means Court Elementary is far from your typical school. The school board spent money to build a new white elementary school, while ours consists of four long decrepit wooden buildings donated believed to have been used as World War II amphibious naval training barracks. The buildings offer first through fourth grades. Schools for blacks are a world of invisibility—an island unto themselves. Little or no influence in their own education and hardly the focal point of a school board that buys into the equation of "separate but equal" education, black schools are seriously lacking. Fort Pierce's racist school board history were no different than other Florida Counties giving the bare minimum to educating blacks.

During my first four years at Means Court, whatever supplies the school board discards we inherit, which amounts to the white schools' junk. Outdated and badly worn and torn books, desks and furniture covered in graffiti marred with poetic racial epithets. Discarded school supplies kept in separate buildings designated "For Colored Pupils." While white schools receive much of the boards' budget allocated for new supplies, we get very little.

Mama gets tidbits of insider information from neighborhood teachers, Elizabeth Espy and Gustarva Hussain who have connections with caring white teachers. Black teachers for all practical purposes often reach into their pocketbooks to buy pencils, chalk, crayons and notebook paper. I overhear Hussain lamenting about when a quality education will come over the horizon.

One day while riding with Mama and a family friend, I don't realize that there's a white school no more than a mile from our home. Fort Pierce Elementary is a wooden structure, beautifully built with large intimidating columns in front and a well-kept lawn with endless rows of neatly manicured flowers and hedges. Its playground shows off modern equipment that dots the landscape. I ask if we can stop a moment to look, but Mama believes a white police officer cruising in the area might spot us and arrest us for trespassing. Mama's always cautious about taking chances and rightly so. Well-assembled manufactured metal equipment with bright shiny colorful fixtures protrudes from the ground. Our playground, in contrast, has old dilapidated seesaw and merry-go-round made of wood, rusting monkey bars badly worn beyond their day. Disappointedly, staring out the window, I resent how lucky white kids must feel having such a playground. Had we stopped and tried our luck, we'd surely stand out like flies in buttermilk.

Children have fun on playground of Lincoln Park Academy circa, 1920. Notice the same barracks later relocated to Means Court. Starting school term during the 60's students play on similar rusty monkey bars and sliding board, broken swings, wooden see-saw and marry-go-round quite inferior to nearby playground at an all-white Fort Pierce Elementary. (© Courtesy of St. Lucie County Historical Museum).

Throughout my childhood there are reminders that it felt wrong to be in contact with white people. Living at Grandma's some Saturdays, I hooked up with Jesse Hawkins and Calvin Barnes to explore the outer perimeters of our neighborhood after making a few bucks hustling soda bottles and shining shoes. We sneak off across the tracks to the downtown businesses on Second Street to gaze at items in window displays. We laugh and joke, imagining being rich and buying whatever we want. The stores and streets are usually crowded with white patrons and a few clusters of black folks. We take note how store managers suspiciously watch our antics. Calvin's digging this nice popcorn shirt in a display window when a young white man comes outside, "You guys move along if you don't plan to buy anything." "We might," Jesse replies, smiling. "I doubt you have allowances." "What's that?" Calvin asks. "Shut up man!" Jesse snaps, surprised Calvin doesn't know. "I'm sure you don't have money at your age (Jesse's 13, Calvin and I are 12), you guys too young hangin round here. I don't want no trouble." "We not causing any," I interrupt. "And I don't want any, so move!" he adds. We give a nasty stare down and move along.

I spot a stylish blue crystal Bulova watch on window display at Sweets Jewelers. We're gathering around the collection chattering noisily as a pompous old lady turns up her nose and grunts as she steps inside. She gestures to the manager Rosalee Arnold, who I recognize. She is busy with a customer and turns her attention to a younger man. Both glare at us a moment until the man hastens outside: "You boys need to leave. You're annoying my mother. Go away before I call the police!" he insists angrily. "We ain't doin nothin to yo mother." Calvin replies in his usual coy demeanor. "We ain't said a word to her," Jesse adds. "She wants to look at the display and you boys blocking her view," the man says firmly. His contentious mother smirks at us from behind the window, but never asks us to move. "There ain't no law against lookin!" I interject. "There's one against loitering and you don't have money," he laughs. "Damn well can't afford these watches so move along!" Ms. Arnold is finishing up with a customer and steps outside. "Wait a minute!" "I know (I come to look with Mama on occasion) the mother of one of these boys, what's the problem?" "Somebody needs to teach um manners. Go back where they belong!" "Where is that?" Jesse smiles, cloaking his grin in sarcasm as his eyes redden. I sense an upsurge of anger. "The Negro section, where else!" the man's seriousness fades into laughter. "It's ok. (Ms. Arnold asks for my name) "Kenny and his friends are ok." She motions and diverts his attention back inside.[16]

Within minutes (we learned that a nearby business owner across the street calling Sheriff's Office about a disturbance) a Deputy Sheriff rolls up to the curb. "Where you boys heading?" "Why? I'm tired of answering that question," Jesse snaps. "Boy, don't get smart with me!" "We're heading home," I say to avoid trouble. "Good, go back to your side of town. I don't want no problems from you boys." The ordeal rattles my senses with wicked thoughts. Where do I fit in? After all, Jesse and I are soon to integrate a white school. As we trek back across the tracks, I notice a vein in Jesse's neck pulsating and he's grinding his teeth. We keep pace with superficial chatter. All the while listening to Calvin repeat somberly: "Man what's wrong with white people?" What little excitement and optimism I have about integration quickly fizzles.

In my thought process there is something sinisterly injurious to white folks' peace and tranquilly in the presence of black folks. We are interlopers in our own country—like pestilent vermin, despised, hated and shunned. We venture downtown, testing the powers of our imagination at first. I leave wanting affirmation that our humanity is just as good as theirs. I wanted to see, hear and watch white people in my presence give positive reactions. I wanted validation what I already know by age 7 that blacks are a despised and hated race.

Whenever I'm confused, I confide in Grandma, who is deep in her own spiritual realm. And I often think of my influential teachers like Ms. Edna Sheppard, Ms. M.J. Thomas, Ms. Lois Finn and Ms. Florene Robinson, who all garner respect in our community. All have

---

[16] Ms. Rosalee Arnold is one of few white business owners and managers to allow blacks to take merchandise home on lay-away accounts. My blue crystal Bulova watch my mother later purchased from Sweets Jewelers would soon for me stir up school accusations.

been blessed with healing powers to teach. In the 60s, our teachers have an aura of invincibility and they can do no wrong. Teaching is a noble profession that the black community reveres and trusts Teachers are arteries through which information flows into our homes and communities. Finn reminds her students, "You are the ears and voice of our community, our beacons of hope, our instruments of social and academic change that will bring a new day." They're qualified, dedicated, highly motivated teachers, eager to teach under seemingly insurmountable odds, under the crippling effects of Jim Crow laws. The teachers' patience is tested daily, but somehow they persevere. Many students come to school from the poorest of the poor—uneducated, unskilled, domestic and migrant working-class families, some sleepy, hungry, in yesterdays' smelly dirty clothes.

When you haven't eaten a full meal since yesterday's lunch, how can you concentrate on class work? Once the hunger pangs set in, somebody's bound to get irritable and disruptive. Before mid-morning, there's much intense stimulation. I witness frustration on the teachers' faces each day. They are frustrated by the shortage of textbooks, school supplies and light bulbs to read by. And sometimes a teacher's frustrations gets misguided unintentionally toward some students.

I continue suffering with anemia coupled with a poor appetite which tends to accompany this condition. Immediately after Daddy leaves for Baltimore, my ability to stay focused and complete my assignments has been affected. Some days I have problems concentrating, instead I am spending too much time daydreaming in class. I realize how much I miss Daddy. From the outward appearance his absence appears to cause a burden, but this is unjustified—Daddy maintains his financial obligation to his family.

Each month teachers initiate committees, designating parents to write letters to the school board addressing classroom deficiencies. Sometimes Mama spearheads the parents list of demands, but their efforts continues to bring about very little change.

By 1963, after President Kennedy's assassination and his civil rights bill fails to pass in Congress, racial equality remains the preeminent issue for blacks in America. Nothing seems to matter more than the race question. Black pupils in St. Lucie County still use old, outdated books and supplies from white schools. Hand-me-down textbooks are filled with graffiti and pages filled with racial epithets of hate deliberately marked up and meticulously torn out to prevent blacks from reading and completing assignments. Worn out desks and tables are vandalized with carved graffiti of hate poetry; a daily reminder why I am hated. I already knew the answer.

While on the playground, a faculty member comes running, literally crying "President Kennedy has been assassinated!" My 4th grade teacher, Ms. Lois Fenn suddenly breaks down in tears, so do we for our beloved teacher, not really understanding. A president's assassination is an unprecedented event to comprehend for a young mind. We sit in class quietly around a transistor radio listening to breaking news. School abruptly lets out early for the day. Later in the evening, my eyes are glued to CBS anchorman Walter Cronkite making a deliberate announcement choking on his grief: "President Kennedy died 1p.m. central standard time." It changes black folks' lives forever.

Racial progress in Fort Pierce is moving slowly, although segregation in public accommodations linger. President Lyndon Johnson inherits Kennedys' civil rights bill and pushes it through Congress into law in 1964.

Ms. Lois Fenn, tall, slender and gregarious teacher with a beautiful smile, enjoys taking a few moments on Monday mornings before class to discuss his or her weekend experiences. Her question is never directed at any specific pupil, rather she glances over the class, expecting volunteers. I excitedly raise my hand, eager to share with the class an experience I have had over the weekend. Fort Pierce's slowly changing, although the last vestiges of segregation in public accommodations stubbornly lingers.

One Friday night, Mama decides that my sisters and I should go integrate (our first visit) the Sunrise Theatre on Second Street downtown. We climb the metal stairway's fire escape in back leading to the exit door that reads "Colored Only." A tall wiry white man stands at the door's entrance. "Tickets are 50 cents," he says unenthusiastically. We go to the balcony, notoriously known as the

"Crow's Nest" or "N....r Heaven;" names I despise.

No indignant attitude occurs from white ushers when we enter the back door and sit in the balcony. A few blacks gather around an attendant's portable concession stand in the corner where we buy popcorn, snowballs and candy. A movie with a mixture of romanticism and comedy has the white audience in an uproar. On my way to my seat, I stand at the railing a moment watching white cozy couples below, laughing it up. Not a hint of laughter in the "Crow's Nest" above.

I sit near my sisters staring at the movie screen displaying familiar lily-white faces. The upper balcony is small and cramped with a rank scent of daily body odor and stale cigarette smoke rising from below. The balcony section isn't filled this night. Ten or more people sit quietly watching a rather boring movie under the suspicious eyes of ushers. Not a single sound of laughter. I imagine that the majority of blacks would rather stave off humiliation and patronize the Lincoln Theatre in our own community instead.

I remember what Grandma and Mama's lodge members says that "being Separate sho ain't equal" without freedom to sit and go where you please. Not an utterance from those seated around me. Just numb wordless expressionless black faces staring at the movie screen. I wonder if their thoughts are similar to mine. When the usher leaves his conspicuous seat,a man gets up, silently walks over to the balcony railing, looks down momentarily then empties his box of popcorn onto whites below and leavesout the backdoor exit, the way he came in. A few blacks in the balcony laugh defiantly, which Grandma says is the younger generation rising up.

As a child during the Jim Crow era whenever downtown, I can only imagine what it's like inside from similar excitement on display.
(© Courtesy of Koblegard family archives, 1947).

The Cherokee Lodge, Fort Pierce headquarters of the Eastern Star, one of several organizations my grandmother devoted her time and efforts in pursuit to help uplift our people in the Lincoln Park community. I got to hear fiery debates by visiting lodge members on racial injustices help shape my racial pride and cultural awareness. (© Courtesy of the author).

The defiance of that black man arouses in me, as it did in him, a feeling of satisfaction. Raining down popcorn on the white crowd below was the object of the man's frustrations with an unjust system. "I think the man threw the popcorn because it's not funny at all being treated different," I say to the class. Ms. Fenn, having listened to my story, looks at me with an approving seriousness. Some mornings, I'm admonish for unenthusiastically rising slow to pledge allegiance to the flag. I watch documentaries with grandma on my hero, Cassius Clay (Muhammad Ali) stand against racist U.S. governmental foreign policies. His religious beliefs are vilified by white America false and unfair views of The Nation of Islam as a sect of hate. Clay has a charismatic way of telling it like it is; in your face rhetoric leaves an indelible impression about racial inequality in America. Grandma's stern intent is to expose me to historical events, mold and shape my character so that I am consciously aware and prepared to deal with a new dawn.

A chubby church lady friend of Grandma's come visit and engages in an impassioned conversation about America. This gets my attention: "The American flag means something better for whites . . . less for coloreds . . . our children stand, pledge allegiance too in school . . .but we don't get liberty and justice like whites . . . why stand?" "What she mean by that Grandma?" I ask. "Colored folks stand up proud for the flag . . . but our government treats us different." I often hear some of Mamas' Eastern Star Lodge members say: "Negroes are separate and sho nuff ain't equal!" I believed it. Something's wrong about always using worn out hand-me-down books with racial epithets. Racial inequality is a preeminent fixture on my consciousness.

I begin to question the meaning of "with liberty and justice for all." Anticipating that stanza, walking to school, repeating it over in my mind is difficult to reconcile. Standing in class, reciting these words I know are untruths.

"All rise and pledge your allegiance to the flag," Ms. Fenn announced as she always does every morning. I have an awful time standing and saying, "With liberty and justice for all." Words of lies, Grandma and Mama explain with such depth and clarity are contradictions. Yet, I suppose Ms. Fenn ignore me is her way of understanding my thoughts from the encounter at the movies. I was certain to experience more social injustices at a pivotal time in my young life. America has yet to live up to its true creed.

At the beginning of 6th grade, some teachers like Fenn and Robinson have a creative makeshift aptitude test, and students are placed in a three-tiered learning model that reflects their scholastic ability like the earlier years. The smartest sit in front rows, average in middle, and slowest in last. She provides much individual assistance to the middle-and lower-tiers, and those falling behind. Congratulating and recognizing those with improvements move to appropriate rows does much to motivate students. The "Pet System" is still in place for some teachers that caters to their favorites by completing all assignments and homework with good grades and overall conduct. It seems biased, but it compels, motivates and encourages all to work harder and make it to the front of the class in a seat with the highest recognition. Rarely does a pet get called upon; they're in the "all knowing" group one. Teachers do spoil their pet pupils who are, by the way, still mostly girls.

Not until Ms. Fenn's class do I reach the front row. By then I'm confident, keenly aware of who I am and what's expected of me in a changing world. I know being separate isn't equal.

Chapter 9

REAL TRUTH

"Help!" "Another one drops, shaking like a leaf!" "It's too hot!" a woman yells. A man dies and maybe another will. July in South Florida is the most dreaded month of summer. Hardly a breeze blows to moderate the intensity of the scorching sun. Heat waves so stifling I gasp to breathe. Fruit groves and vegetable fields are unbearable to work in. I witness another old man, the second in a day, fall down between the tomato rows and suffer a heat stroke or a seizure. If it were not for the woman with ice in her cooler, he might have died like the other in the middle of nowhere.

Wineheads are the first to fall from dehydration into shakes (delirium tremens), not eating, refusing to pick until a sip of Thunderbird wine touches their parched lips. And the heat makes tempers flare. Which makes straw bosses (overseers) ornery, mirroring the same madness again and again but at a higher level. "Pickum close Jitterbug!"

"Ya gotta bin yo back Jit! Git unda them mayta vines good!" I hate tomato fields, but vow to make enough to buy my own school clothes. Pressure is on me and I'm determined. I avoid piecework on unbearably hot days. Although my earnings are greater by the day at $8 for eight hours of work. Conditions are just as harsh in day work although straw bosses don't harass you as much. Harsh conditions keep me graciously humble respecting the back-breaking strain endured by seasonal migrant workers. Through my experience, I acquire a good work ethic being in the thick of it.

Before summer's end, I manage to save about $200 to buy school clothes and supplies.

Whether picking tomatoes, cucumbers, bell peppers, oranges or grapefruits, I experience how the need for money manipulates and makes poor people cheat—swiping another's basket to fill up for an extra dime; pick a worker's row to fill a basket; steal a lunch to refuel and battle the sun. This will never be my life.

Rosie's revelations, I clearly see, are the torments of a migrant's life. And more often than not, cruelty of white farm owners manipulates the most gullible, self-absorbed intimidating Negro straw bosses to humiliate powerless people. Tadpole is like that. He's short, muscular, barrel-chested with beady eyes sunken into a protruding forehead. What he lacks in height, he makes up in attitude. He isn't above reproach, has a quick temper with a calculating smile and an appetite for pretty women. But in the fields, his smile vanishes. His eyes widen with excitement and he changes into a man obsessed with getting attention and self-aggrandizing.

Tadpole stalks and harasses to feel important, and it has a way of sneaking up on you when you least expect it. When the white man comes around in his truck, Tadpole's little beady eyes dilate. What a pity seeing him run around nervously, stuttering to please, "I-I-Um on-on-um boss! Got-got um pickin um close!"

One morning the planter walks to the edge of the field and yells out orders. "Now Tad, keep um out here long as yir can even if it's gonna rain! I gotta git this section picked . . . I want um picked close! Git um out thir fo rain cause um to burse and rot when the sun comes out!" he yells. "Yessum! Yessum boss!" I-I-I'm on um like they stole something!" "Auh right, yawl heard the man! Git back workin!" The planter sits in his truck for a moment watching Tadpole do his thing, and then drives off to another section.

A slight drizzle turns into a heavy downpour as the sun recedes into the darkening clouds. Soon the rows between tomato beds become unbearably muddy from the intense downpour. We dash for shelter on the bus. After an hour, the rain lightens and a rainbow brings forth radiant colors. Then the white man reappears, "Tad! What the hell! I wan um in the field workin now!" He steps into the doorway of the bus and removes a cowboy hat from his head, which touches the ceiling. He stands well over six feet in an intimidating presence with a weathered and rustic face, big ears too large for his small head and a tubby stomach sticks out like a cartoon character.

"They wa-wa-won't work in-in the mud boss," Tadpole says in a submissive stutter. "Well, I pay ya tar keep um in my fields!" he fumes. It seems an eternity has passed before he finally notices our presence as if we're nobodies—invisible. "You people I wan yawl out in da fields pickin! That what I pay ya fir! Ya hir me! Move!" His Florida cracker twang elevates as his squinting eyes survey the faceless workers.

The planter keeps wiping a large reddened grotesque cancerous-looking bump on his nose with a handkerchief, then exits the bus. "Yawl best get back to work!" Tadpole snaps, turns silence into grumbling. No one moves, and I see a look of indecision and fear in the eyes of older workers until one short gray-haired man speaks. "Tadpole, you and that white man can go to hell! I ain't moving! We no work in Texas this way," Hector says in broken English. "Yeah, that white man crazy . . . we ain't nobody slaves!" a little old quiet lady adds. "I got bills and two wives to please, gonna be mad if I don't come home with money, but I ain't pickin in the rain!" a younger man adds comic relief and laughter.

I take note at their courage and sacrifice. At times, I carry a pad and pen in my back pocket, scribbling down my thoughts, noting the vignettes I observe in the fields. Each day laborers play out intriguing scenes I want to capture. Something about migrant workers, the era of segregation, and the similar conditions of slavery intrigue me. Especially at a time when I'm reading books about slavery and plantation life. Tadpole's ways remind me of an overseer's mentality on a plantation, doing the white man's bidding.

"No want trouble señor. Just feed family," Hector says. Hector comes to Fort Pierce in the pickin season with his wife and three children who all move into Mr. Fat and Ms. Sister's condemned home. No electricity or running water; they get by using kerosene lamps and an outdoor grill. Squatters, perhaps illegal immigrants too, violating the law.

Mama lets Hector fill buckets of water from our faucet. We do what we can to make them feel at home as neighbors. Hector's a nice man struggling to survive like everyone else. Tomas, the older son, who is my age, teaches me how to make enchiladas. Hector laughs and smiles a lot, reminds me of Jesus, the nice man I knew as a child.

When the sun doesn't pierce through a canopy of dark ominous clouds—we didn't get off the bus! A bus of Negroes from America, the Caribbean, a Mexican and his wife, and a drunken white man down on his luck stand our ground. As Tadpole rolls off with the bus, the planter rants and raves, threatening not to hire us again. "Tad knows yawl faces!" the planter yells back angrily, driving off. We're united. The planter's surprised by our unexpected reactions, which makes him eat his words. We are a vulnerable people when labor is in demand to move a product but not in this instance we stood our ground and made our point. Time is money—to white farmers and citrus owners, it's no different. Tadpole, his usual aggravated self, can wait to see us Monday morning.

I come to understand in 1966 that a little old gray-haired man had had enough. I read about Cesar Chavez, a Mexican civil rights activist, who had founded a United Farm Workers Union to organize over 50,000 farm workers against discrimination in California and Florida. But in 1966, the UFW has no bite, and no real legislative laws are passed against planter abuse.

I hear nothing of any laws in Florida. Yet, I feel a part of the migrant plight for survival; complaints and rising voices challenge inhumane working conditions, low wages and windfall profits for citrus growers.

Mama suggests that Gail and I relax during the remaining days of summer before school. I dig up worms from our bait bed out back, get my bamboo pole and go fishing. Go one last time to the nearly abandoned Fredrick Douglass Beach after integration laws are passed. Walking along the sand dunes, I watch seaweeds wash up on the shoreline as I move about avoiding overgrown weeds and sandy spurs. It occurs to me the poisonous stings of jelly fish and integration finally give reason for blacks to move quickly away. Now in a new era, blacks make progressive steps integrating Pepper Park Beach, which we had protested at a few years back. Now we're abandoning our own beach—what a shame.

Lidia is elegantly dressed in a royal blue long dress with a neatly wrapped white hijab (headscarf). Although she's nine years older than me, mature, wise, more self-assured in her present life than her past of prostitution, I like her in a secret way. She stands majestically in front of my cousin Otis' Outler Sanctified Church in the neighborhood. Young girls admire her neatly wrapped scarf similar to theirs, defined in my eyes as a crown of beauty. The scarf replaces and becomes now a religious symbol distinguishing her beauty like a mane of hair that speaks to stylish individualistic taste for solicitous attention.

Hands clap and feet stomp to the African syncopated rhythms of the drums and tambourines. The beat runs through our veins as Cousin Otis plays his electric guitar just like Bo Diddley did, making his guitar holler. I peep inside and watch pretty women dressed in long flowing dresses and head wraps, clapping and singing. I dreamed about being in his Sanctified Church playing a bass guitar. I believe it is the reason cousin Otis encourages me to join.

Minister Leonard X of the Nation of Islam is back, probing neighborhoods for misguided souls. It takes some coaxing to get a few neighborhood buddies away from an afternoon game of hard nose sandlot football. But George and Jimmie, Lorenzo, Jinx , Pookie and brother Peewee do a better job bribing me to buy moon pies and sodas before they agree to come along.

Passersby gather in Bamboo Park on Seventh Street across from Moore's meandering creek that separates the black district from downtown's white business district. Several Muslim men and women from Liberty City (one section where Miami's black community lives) are setting up tables with Islamic-themed literature, books, newspapers, pamphlets, cassette tapes and bean pies as a few stray folks curiously gather. I'm excitedly encouraged by Minister Leonard X's persistence and dedication, trying to bring attention to a worthy cause.

"Assalaamu alaikum, Brother Kenny. Pleased to see you again," the Minister says as he extends a firm handshake to us all. Minister Leonard X hands everyone a Muhammad Speaks newspaper and give me cassette tapes and other literature for my indulgence and for inviting friends. "Why you set up on this side of town?" I ask. "Why not? I notice so-called Negroes regularly walk this route to shop at the white man's businesses. Perhaps I can get them spending some money with us too," he smiles. "Makes sense to me," Jimmie says in his usual entrepreneurial spirit, thumbing through a pamphlet. "I like makin money too, gonna start me a business sellin somethin." "Good young brother. We're about selling goods doing for self too, but today it's educational, knowing thyself 'real-truth' we're selling today."

The minister explains that so-called Negroes spend more money on foolishness rather than investing wisely. "We need to establish more businesses for our people. "If we can reach a few in this park, why not? Who's gonna integrate a white school this year?" Minister Leonard X asks. All my buddies point to me. "Brother Kenny, do you think that 'blue-eyed devil' wants to integrate schools in your neighborhoods?" "I don't think so," I say unknowingly. "If I went and get called a n..ga, I'll fight and get kicked out," Pookie and Peewee replies. "You must learn to fight with your mind not your fist little brothers." "What you mean by blue-eyed devil?" Jinx asks curiously. The minister and a few of his followers smile. "The oppressor, the white man." Peewee, the youngest, looks puzzled. "This government is run by racist white men who want to keep us complacent, hold us back from advancing. Brother Kenny, I'm told you read and love your history, speak and learn truth they hate to hear. Wherever that blue-eye devil goes, the minister quips, he wants to rule, corrupt and destroy nations of color. Look at Asia, India, South America and Africa. We must continue to wake up and rise up." he continues.[17]

Minister Leonard X has Pookie and Lorenzo, unlikely readers,

---

[17] Kenny "Pookie" Knowles and brother Michael "Peewee" Knowles, childhood buddies, neighbors with gregarious personalities, misguided, didn't finish high school, fell prey to the streets. Both did stints in prison and died young.

utterly confused, and Jinx, not much a history buff as I am, a little lost. Jimmie and George have had more exposure living in Connecticut, they're familiar with black Muslims and respond favorably. They are accustomed to hearing their older brother Livingston say, "We must do for self, don't depend on the white man."

"My Grandma say if white people stop Negroes from grocery shopping she'll survive off her garden." The minister laughs, in fact everyone does, after George tells how many gardens Ms. Gertrude has.

The minister addresses a few bystanders purchasing materials displayed on the table. I notice Lidia no longer smiling. Several sisters have her reeling under pressure to avoid pitfalls of the devil. I overhear them say: "Sister Lidia, we know you're alone, you gotta be strong, read the Koran, pray, and minister to lost sisters out here." After their advice, Lidia cheers up, no longer looking troubled or confused. I wonder if she's following her heart or has yet to discover if it is really committed.

A short distance away, the white vendor with his parrot stares as bystanders applaud the minister, who is addressing a growing number of onlookers. A police officer leaves the station across the street. He pulls his cruiser slowly over to the curb, rolls a window down listens and watches. "Oh, don't worry. This is a public park and we have every right . . .the police are familiar with the Nation of Islam in Miami. Very soon they'll be familiar with us in Fort Pierce too," the minister says assuredly handing out literature, as onlookers smile nervously due to such boldness.

His audience watches as the minister points in the direction of the cruiser, taunting the police officer. "You see he knows so-called Negros in Fort Pierce don't put their tax dollars to good use, don't enjoy all the amenities of taxpayer citizens have every right to be here and speak out in this very public park." The officer must have got his message of dissent, and pulls away burning rubber.

Aside from my father, I had never witnessed a black man handle himself with such confidence, addressing the issues of blacks. I'm impressed with Minister Leonard X, and a few new committed sisters and brothers in attendance to the Nation's doctrine. Only a few believers remain, as those uncommitted walk away enlightened, knowing the validity of his message is indisputably on point—the white man still has his foot on their necks.

Some weekends I stay away from the grind of picking something in the fields. Our neighbor Ms. Gertrude has several gardens in our and neighbors' yards. Her gardening has a message: utilize every inch of unproductive land. The Roberts' family consists of Livingston "Castro" Roberts, the eldest, a daughter Gertrude (named after Grandmother), and brothers Frances, George and Jimmy, my buddies. I help George and Jimmy swing grub hoes turning up soil and clearing weeds, as well as fertilizing the soil and watering plants. I miss out on the summer fun. I'm too tired for fun activities after early mornings and afternoons laboring in the Florida sun. Ms. Gertrude is robust and strong-willed as she turns a half acre in our yard into one of her prized lush gardens. At end of day, well-prepped soil yields the fruits of her labor.

Jimmy and George don't dare neglected their garden duties. Ms. Gertrude can be pleasantly snappy. I jump in and help grub untapped rich mucky soil in our yard—vegetables spring up quickly. George and Jimmy are smart, industrious and obedient grandsons. I often watch in awe as Ms. Gertrude the boss orders them about without dissent, question or hesitation—just a "yes ma'am."

Jimmy and George come down south from Hartford, Connecticut with many experiences far beyond the average school boy. We immediately hit it off because of shared interests in reading, exchanging books and talking about life. The strangest and most morbid things we enjoy doing is playing in the graveyard. We identify names and discuss with imagination what the deceased were like when alive. I exploit what I learn from Grandma, a freshwater Geechee and share it with my friends. Gifts of money, charms and toys, favorite plates and silverware, a variety of items with sentimental value are placed on the graves. To make the deceased's afterlife pleasant, far from the hellacious suffering endured here in America. Grandma says leaving gifts to the dead goes back to slavery, an African tradition.

Pinegrove Cemetery's a reflection of time, names, stories and events we reflect on when honoring the dead. Since I help the Shaw brothers dig graves, I become comfortable among the deceased. Sometimes we play games challenging each other's bravery lying still on graves until dark and beyond, and see who'll break in fear with some wild claim of seeing a ghost. My idea of "invoking spirits" of our ancestors is the way Grandma tells her stories.

Someone claims to see a spirit's face rise-up from a tomb. On some foggy nights, we break and run for home, frightened having seen an image of a man, woman, and child moving through the cemetery.

There's much to discover in my neighborhood and much wisdom if you listen. For this intrigue, I listen to elders, and to those who have prestige in my community. Grandma has given me a ravenous appetite for their stories of life.

Many neighborhood buddies migrate to the back porch of Ms. Gertrude's big two-story house just to watch Livingston "Castro" Roberts paint. Castro teaches through doing, that you learn to paint through imagination. Castro paints with speed and artistry and turns out picturesque landscapes to sell on the highways. "This is who I am. Everyone has a creative side," Castro proclaims. "Use it, do what you love. Mr. Charlie downtown won't give you a job use your imagination and make one." We sit, listen, and sometimes if he allows us, which is often, gather some framing boards and nails to help his brother Frances while Castro paints, stains and adds the final touches before heading off to sell his paintings.

It's Saturday morning, before the first week of school. Jimmie comes by to wake me out of a good sleep. Jimmie's excited about a small family circus set up in Bamboo Park. Jimmie likes playing jokes and I'm mostly a sucker for them. I'm unconvinced, since Minister Leonard X plans to spend his last Saturday afternoon selling Muslim materials in the park before leaving. Jimmie makes a bet for my favorite Orange Crush soda to come along and see.[18]

---

[18] Livingston "Castro" Roberts, landscape artist and a masterful spinner of motivational narratives. He captures and inspires young minds to use their imagination to get their hustle on. We neighborhood youth treasured Castro's (nicknamed because of his Fidel Castro beard) advice—we sell

I know If Jimmie loses, as consolation, he'll make a desperate bet, one that not only he but many older black folks claim. I believe their claims are untrue, yet rumors abound: in the park a white vendor with peacocks, teaches his parrot vulgar, offensive and utterly annoying words. Jimmy claims that the parrot squeals frantically in his cage when blacks appear: "N....r stealing! N....r stealing!" Jimmie places a bet on the parrot. I suspect that if there's no circus, I'll buy him a soda if the parrot squeals that word I hate.

There are no tents, nothing resembling a circus other than an elephant and a small mobile camping trailer. We get a closer look and I touch the elephant, and out of nowhere a tall gangling drunken white man with reddened eyes yells waving a liquor bottle. "What da hell yawl little n.g.s doin ova hir messin wit my elephant!" "You a n....r cause a n....r is low down nasty act like you!" I say. "All we did is touch him!" "You little smart ass! I'll kill you!" "Let's go Kenny!" Jimmie grabs my arm as I jerk away. Anger builds, no white person ever called me n....r before. "Come on Kenny, let's go now!"

The white man smiles, then suddenly runs and picks up a sharp pointed metal rod used to poke and move his elephant. "I'll kill you! I'll kill you!" He charges. I pick up a loose chain lying on the ground and swing it around toward him. I hold him off for a moment, but he measures my swings as I back away. He finds an opening and thrusts the rod into my stomach causing me to cringe and buckle in pain. I strike him lightly with the chain on his wrist, enough to stop his momentum. "I'm gonna kill you little n...r!" He puts up another charge thrusting the rod towards me. Jimmie rushes in and grabs my arm and yanks me away as the rod barely misses my chest. "Come on Kenny! You bleedin! Run!" I drop the chain and run.

---

newspapers, bottles, lemonade and we shine shoes. I'm inclined to groom my work ethic and independence. Castro with Alfred Hair, Harold Newton, James Gibson and Roy McClendon are first of todays' 26 landscape painters. Later, the painters are famously known as "The Highwaymen."They traveled the highways selling paintings from the trunks of their cars. Roberts, a stickler for detail, is considered one of the most important and influential of the highwaymen artists. The artistry in his paintings are brilliantly illustrated. See Gary Monroe's, *The Highwaymen, Florida's African-American Landscape Painters,* 2001.

My heart's pounding fast. We stop at the edge of the park since the white man doesn't give chase. My T-shirt is bloody from a nasty gash on my stomach as blood oozes out. I feel no pain from the intensity of what happened. "You wait! I'll be back with my brother, and he's gonna kick your ass!" I hear the white man's voice fade in the background, laughing as he yells back, "He betta bring his gun!" "If Yawl n....rs can afford one!"

I don't have an older brother, but Jimmie knows his brother Frances is just the person for back up. I'm in pain come to think of it. It's a hot sunny morning and as we walk the bleeding won't stop. "Why don't we go to the police?" Jimmie pleads as we pass the station. "What they gonna do? He'll lie, he's white and who you think they'll believe?" Jimmie thinks a moment, hearing enough stories of injustices in Connecticut. "I'm gonna kill him," I keep repeating angrily. "Then why don't you go get stitched up?" Jimmie reasoned. The hospital's less than a block away. Years of being injury prone, a doctor or a nurse might recognize me and contact Mama. "My Mama can't afford another hospital bill." Jimmie's confused and keeps quiet as we walk in haste trying to keep up with my troubled mind.

"Shot guuun...shoot um fo he run now!" Junior Walker's blasting from Mamas' RCA Victor record player when I arrive home. Gail and Regina are on the front porch. The screen door out back is unlocked, so I sneak into the kitchen. Grandma's in the living room dozing off. She'll raise a holy fuss catching my sisters dancing the boogaloo and jerk. I sneak into the bathroom as Junior Walker wails: "Shot guuun!" A shot gun will do just fine, it's what I need, thinking hard and desperate.

I wash out the gash with cold water to stop the bleeding. Flesh hangs open and I suspect it needs stitches. I clean and dress it with peroxide and an ointment, and then wrap it with gauze and tape from the medicine cabinet. My head throbs from fear and rage gnaws in my brain, my eyes redden, and a tear trickles down my cheek. I look in the mirror and a lethal imagination fills my head with evil, ruminating thoughts of vengeance.

I'll get Grandma's pistol and kill him. But where does she keep it? I'll get a knife. But will I get close enough? I'll get gas and burn his trailer down with him in it. But how will I do it? And what if I get caught? I'll get an older tuff guy to kill him. But what if he gets caught and tells? Hours pass as I continue seething, trying to make sense of it all. My mind plays back the incident over and over, every detail until I suddenly come to my senses. I've been numb about Daddy's absence all these years, just a singular thought—Mama is a good mother and you left her alone. And now I'm alone without you to turn to. I'll deal with it alone, get my revenge in a new integrated school and unleash my anger. I won't be defeated.

Whenever there are difficult decisions to reconcile between anger, fear and reality, my pigeons always calm me. But somehow my thoughts of retaliation rattle them into a nervous stir. So, I talk to them and feed them, and we both feed off each other's energy, and they feel safe, and I feel reassured.

My pigeons are a relaxing diversion to release pinned up anger and a way to escape from my troubles. (©Courtesy of the author).

Later in the night, I sit at my desk in my bedroom and begin to read Message to the Black Man in America. Unable to concentrate, I hear the white man's laughter echoing in my head. Anger I manage to control consumes my thoughts, so I rewind, playing back the incident in the park. In the gloom and doom of it comes provoking thoughts: are all whites blue-eyed devils? At least the vendor in the park doesn't seem to be. Is it as the minister describes, all about power and control? Is the white man's elixir to feel all powerful reign superior over people of color? I have many questions. I begin reading passages in my book, and I come to believe that not until the so-called Negroes have true knowledge of self through our own history, real freedom, justice and equality will never be.

The black man in North America must purge the yoke of mental slavery and self-hatred. I hear and see it time and again. We wallow in self-hate and we inflict it against each other. This is what holds us back. And it occurs to me that this confirms what Minister Leonard X means by real-truth. Only when we rise up, self-actualize (reach our full potential) through our own efforts as a people, will our condition change. Resolve sweeps over me and I no longer want to retaliate against my enemy. I read late into the night until the bulb begins to flicker. Tiring, I close my eyes and slip into darkness.

Chapter 10

IMPETUS FOR CHANGE

Silence sweeps across nervous faces of chattering students as our school bus creeps south on Thirteenth Street to Sunrise Boulevard in the heart of white middle-class neighborhoods. As the bus crawls along, I admire Spanish and Mediterranean-style homes with nicely manicured lawns. Although I can't see them, I know that there are swimming pools in their carefully tended backyards. Our first day of reckoning arrives to face the unknown—the unspeakable truth—we deserve a quality education.

I sit quietly staring at the sanitized white neighborhoods imagine someday I too can have a nice home and yard like the privileged white families. We are now traveling in areas that we wouldn't have dared to get caught walking through before integration. Now integration makes it possible to bus minorities to white schools not whites to black schools. Imagine that.

I picked at my stomach that began to itch and had festered a little. I had done a good job concealing but not taking care of it. The thought of what happen days ago set me into a state of anger. I realize the scar I will have to live with for a while will be the object of my anger.

The superintendent of schools Ben L. Bryan is busy at work calming parents' fears. He gives assurances that the teachers are prepared, well informed to handle disturbances, instructed to keep their eyes and ears open for trouble. In meetings with teachers, Bryan reinforces the school board's obligations to every student. He believes many of the problems can best be solved with the understanding that every child must be equally helped to learn as much as possible.

Mama retains her typical positive self-assuring forecast before departing for work. "Gail, Kenny and Regina be successful today, stay positive." While Mama shows no signs of worry, Grandma approaches the matter cautiously. "Don't let them cause you to lose your temper or else you give them power to win. Keep your heads up high." She closes with Psalms 23:23, her favorite prayer.

I ponder over the wisdom in Grandma's words. She lived most of her life on the cutting edge of caution with expectations and dictates from white people. Now it's my turn, by way of integration. In her eyes I see pride, which reminds me of the ole civil rights protest song:

"I ain't gonna let no body turn me around
Turn me around, turn me around
I'm ain't gonna let no body turn me around
I'm gonna keep on ah walkin', keep on ah talkin'
gonna build a brand-new world...'

In a reflective moment, I won't let anything stand in my way. As the bus creeps along quietly, I imagine my arrival at school will replay what staunch Alabama segregationist Governor George Wallace did. How he stood in the doorway of the University of Alabama denying black students entry. I envision the same as what Arkansas Governor Orval Faubus did when he sent the National Guard to block enrollment of nine black students into Little Rock Central High. Who can forget that!

Everyone is quiet, reflective, staring out the windows. I anticipate as in Alabama and Arkansas angry mobs of whites holding placards, hanging black dolls in effigy in efforts to prevent our entry.

Ms. Ellis our driver rolls into the bus zone bringing it to a stop. White teachers awaiting our arrival wave enthusiastically. As black students leave the buses, a crowd of curious white onlookers stare blankly. An eerie feeling comes over me watching a group of noisy white boys laughing and pointing at us. "Good luck! Hope you'll have a great day at school." Ms. Ellis opens the door to a crowd of noisy white students. Several teachers order them to disburse. As I exit the bus, two boys shot birds (symbol meaning to kiss their asses) with their fingers. We have no idea what it means. One young white teacher greets us with a big smile. "Welcome students, welcome to St. Lucie Junior High School!" Two black teachers who are standing off by themselves are bombarded with questions from eager black students. To my dismay, there are only two black teachers out of 56 white teachers. Both look as alienated and lost as we do.

Teachers assign monitors to give instructions for those needing directions to homeroom classes. Recognizing a few teachers' faces from an abbreviated orientation the day before, I make my way to homeroom behind a small group. Someone yells, "N.....s go home! We don't want you here!" A short middle-aged balding teacher walking with a group ahead of me turns abruptly in the direction of the voices. Several white boys, standing on the periphery of the loading zone, laugh. "Which one of you said that?" he asks. The boys bolt down a corridor and scatter in all directions never breaking stride. They're out of sight before he dares to chase them.

"Come along, don't pay that any mind. Oops I'll have the janitor get that up." He looks at graffiti on the sidewalk. Someone with white chalk meticulously wrote: "N.....s go back to Africa!" Underneath is the drawing of a happy black face colored in with black crayon with big white lips, eyes and nose.

During the first week of school upon our arrival or departure racial epithets appear daily on the sidewalks. Quickly as it's removed, culprits somehow clandestinely strike again. Then suddenly it ceased. Partly because Mr. Mullins threatens suspensions to anyone caught smearing school property with graffiti. We began to retaliate against those behind it.

Each day begins with corridors filled with chaos. Hundreds of loud chattering students are barely able to maneuver past each other. "Fight! Fight!" someone screams, pointing in the direction of a corridor. Overcrowded conditions force black and white students to come in contact for the first time. Accidental bumping triggers a domino effect of fights we use as retaliation. Teachers can't maneuver through crowds fast enough to stop them. As quickly as a fight is broken up another erupts.

While meeting with a few buddies, the first tardy bell rings frantically.

I push my way through a crowd of laughter emanating from my homeroom. I pause momentarily to listen, to get a sense of security to lessen my apprehension. It seems like a happy class, so I quietly enter feeling confident that everything is going to be all right. I sit at a desk in the middle of the classroom with hopes of going unnoticed—as invisible as possible. The class suddenly goes silent. I look up and a majority of whites giggle, looking at me as they suddenly move away like Moses parting the Red Sea. I'm the only black in class.

Before I can determine what's going on, a white boy sitting in an adjacent desk gets up. "I'm not sitting next to you!" He moves to the other side of the classroom to roars of laughter. Stunned, I look at our teacher, expecting guidance, a response of some sort, but there's none. This tall skinny blond with pale skin and bushy eyebrows watches timidly. She just sits frozen with her mouth agape, speechless as a few other blacks enter and experience the same reaction.

I'm one of five blacks in a class of about 30 whites. It occurs to me we're intended recipients of attention and laughter. One by one each white student in proximity to a black student follows suit. It's a game of musical chairs that continues until every seat on the periphery of the room is occupied, as if we're contagious. Hoping to show solidarity, I move next to the four blacks seated in the middle of the class. We sit waiting for our homeroom teacher's instructions to rescue us. Expecting something, anything to divert attention away from us. Instead, she remains quietly flustered, anxiously gripping the edge of her desk.

The charade lasts what seems an eternity, as we sit in shock surrounded by empty chairs. "All right class! Order! Order!" The nervous tone of her voice lacks confidence. She introduces herself timidly as Ms. Nancy Colcord. "I will not tolerate this nonsense!" Her voice elevates and gains confidence. The class continues in playful chatter. "I said silence! Silence!" Colcord strikes a pointer against her desk. A cracking sound abruptly brings about a hush and stillness into somber faces as she takes charge of her class.

The only black girl among us starts tapping her fingers on the desktop. Her eyes water as she makes an angry face at Colcord. We sit waiting impatiently, seething with anger beyond comprehension. Colcord's face reddens as she becomes more visibly shaken by anger and urgency on our faces. "Young man, you and the rest of class will be assigned a seat tomorrow, or you will see the principal, do you understand!" Finally, she snaps out of her fog into a voice of reason.

"I don't sit next to Negroes!" a boy responds defiantly with sarcasm that provokes an outburst of laughter from his peers. "You will in my class, you understand me!" "Yes ma'am," the boy says as the bell rings and homeroom ends. I'm overwhelmed with anger.

Traumatized by a display of prejudice, I sit glued to the seat, humiliated but refusing defeat. I want to lash out and smack that white boy, but I thought of Grandma's words: "Don't let them cause you to lose your temper or else you will give them power over you and they will win." I slump back into my desk, realizing I have Colcord for homeroom and first period math. Two of the other blacks are gone. Colcord cautiously approaches and whispers in my ear and to the others, "I'm sorry. I take full responsibility for their behavior." She promises it won't happen again and she'll do what she can to make our experience comfortable and welcomed. She speaks with compassion, but her words give little consolation, watching intensely as others enter first period and take their seats away from me and my black classmates.

I will always admire Nancy Colcord desire to overcome prejudices for cultural sensitivity when others refused. (Courtesy of the author).

Ms. Colcord immediately takes charge of the class on the next day as she assigns all students to their respective seats. Although I anxiously await similar incidents, none surfaces on the magnitude it did on my first day in homeroom. Throughout the year, she lives up to her promise. Before the year's end, Colcord waves me up to her desk. "Kenneth, I'd like you to know you've been an inspiration to me, you've helped me to reflect on my prejudices and change." She was grateful having me in her class. She gives me a signed school yearbook photo of herself with kind words on the back. I return the same. It becomes an impressive heartfelt moment; other whites I hope will reach a similar awakening in years to come.

Overcrowded classrooms present serious problems for everyone. Racial tension sparked by integration let the lid off Pandora's box in ways unimaginable by teachers and administrators. Blacks and whites mingling for the first time on crowded breezeways (open areas) present serious incidents too difficult to manage by either faculty members or monitors. Blacks make up less than 20 percent of the school's total population of 800 students. We succeed by sticking together on issues that matter most—our pride and dignity.

Walking down congested hallways, the moment I look into a white face eyes shift away. Some retain a friendly smile which makes me feel hopeful. Yet, I can feel the stares and I can hear whispers. I inadvertently touch a white girl on a congested hallway, she looks at me angrily and jerks away. I grow accustomed to hearing others scream, aroused by false accusations towards some black student: "Oh! He touched me! He touched me!" I'm become increasingly aware integration brings much drama from white girls' exaggerated responses intended to draw attention to themselves.

A rumor spreads quickly that whites are attempting to ambush black students on their way to class. We start walking to class in groups and give black girls added protection. Teachers patrol breezeways as monitors assist those still unfamiliar with classrooms and keep watchful eyes for erupting fights. Many are surprised by our assertiveness unlike the passivity of a generation before us: "Just letting you know, you hit me I'm gonna hit back."

Heading to class, I unintentionally bump into a white girl. We momentarily stare at one another. I expect a scornful look, instead she smiles and we both awkwardly apologize. She has big emerald green eyes. As I walk to my next class I discover that we are both in Ms. Kluppleburg's English class. Suzanne, a shy pretty Jewish girl with a friendly smile, proceeds to walk with me to class, totally oblivious of the head turns and whispers. I consciously put space between us in an attempt to avoid trouble, but she keeps apace. We hasten to class together, animatedly walking and conversing until I recognize the familiar silence followed by whispers sweeping over the room.

Throughout the early weeks of school, Suzanne's under tremendous pressure from her peers. She receives threatening hate letters taped on her desk and most of her friends disassociate themselves from her. The cafeteria is already racially polarized—I wouldn't dare sit next to her. She's labeled a Jew "n....r lover." Despite my discomfort, we continue sitting next to each other in class under the watchful eyes of others. We usually exchange trivial talk, and I look forward to every Monday hearing about her weekend excursions horseback riding, camping, sunbathing by the pool, water skiing or some trip out of town. Finally, Suzanne admits feeling guilty sharing her experiences; she realizes how much discrimination and poverty limits variety in my leisure opportunities.

I never anticipate such sincerity in someone white like Suzanne. We continued on occasions walking to English class together. And I discovered her father was once a New York trial lawyer who defended blacks in civil rights cases. Our enriching conversations broaden my horizon. It gives me a new perspective that there are some whites who share in our fight for freedom and equality.

One afternoon during gym I almost get into a fight. Todd, a white boy pitching deliberately out of frustration, throws the soft ball directly at me, attempting to steal base. He laughs when I dive to the ground as the ball barely misses hitting me in the head. Since the beginning of school, it becomes apparent Todd doesn't like blacks. He wants no part playing on the same team with blacks. He doesn't take advice well from black players and moves away when one stands near. After reaching base, I immediately run towards him. Before I reach him and swing, Coach Valentine, a tall burly olive-skinned man, orders me to stop. "He threw the ball at me coach!" Todd denies it. "Ask any of them!" pointing to two black boys I haven't met, confirming and siding with me. Coach is at a loss what to do until two white boys also confirmed my point. He orders us both to run four laps around the field. I go into a defense mode. "Why do I have to run when he started it?" "You were about to fight if I hadn't stopped you." I lap Todd several times while he whines. After a half-hearted lap, he refuses to run any further. Coach gives in to his complaining without hesitation, as I run sucking hot air, stunned by the break he gets. Todd with a sly smile cunningly shoots me a bird on his way to the locker room.

I go into Coach Valentine's office as he sits unaware of my presence, looking at some papers on his desk. "Coach?" "What are you doing in here?" My entry's unannounced. "Why do I have to run all my laps and he doesn't?" I'm assertive, expecting an explanation. "That's my decision not yours. Now get out of here. Take a shower and get ready for class!" he barks. "Coach, that's not fair." I whine, unmoved. "Boy don't you ever again question my authority!" I let him know Todd's errant throw was deliberately intended to take my head off and he deserves to be punished. My refusal to leave and my petulant knack for demanding answers to what I believe are injustices, get me into deeper trouble.

Coach must sense in me a contemptuous little brat. A black boy ardently confronting authority is a new and uncomfortable experience. Coach Valentine lashes out, writing me up as argumentative and disrespectful. At his behest, I again find myself visiting the dean's office.

Dean Jack Brennan's hell-bent on convincing me that I have become a troublemaker. "You need to show some gratitude being here, or else you're headed for trouble," he says, before giving me a pass to my next class.

I'm undeterred with the conviction to bring attention to incidents whenever I feel devalued and mistreated. Even if a teacher doesn't like it, I plan to bring truth to power. I'm convinced that Coach Valentine might have allowed his prejudices to interfere with how he mishandled the situation. I believe it caused poor judgment in his decision making. Perhaps, the coach feels uncomfortable solving disputes between races, but I know he shouldn't have allowed Todd off the hook. It's inequitable and unfair disputes like this that brew racial conflicts.

Through my experiences I'm evolving, moving forward with a sense of purpose. I have new found confidence and I exert it through enlightenment—of who I am and what I hope to become. All through segregated schools I was timid, quiet, introverted, and avoided calling attention to myself because of my health conditions. Desegregation sparks a new beginning, assertiveness with poised outspokenness as I grow stronger and conscious through my readings. I discover none of this sits well with white authority.

There's limited access to recreation in my community. One small inferior recreational facility serves the entire black community. No swimming pools, little adequate space for indoor or outdoor activities. I'm reminded of a deteriorating drive-in theatre owned by whites now abandoned once we frequented reinforces my reality that segregation makes it possible to make the best of what you own.

Seldom do whites and blacks mingle in public places or in social activities. Most whites still cling to old ways that reinforce racial prejudice in public accommodations. Only Jackie Caynon, a so-called token black city commissioner enters the political arena. Elected in 1967, he does his best. Somehow with little political clout he allocates funds in the Lincoln Park community. Whites are accommodating to a lesser degree, long as we never encroach upon their comfort zones in pursuit of what is rightly ours. Without much strong leadership, we remain mostly a passive people never truly rocking the boat, for now.[19]

One morning walking into class, I see that Suzanne has moved

---

[19] Jackie Caynon, a building contractor by trade in 1967 became the first black elected official in St. Lucie County. He served as St. Lucie County City Commissioner until 1978 with distinction. In his second term he served as Mayor of Fort Pierce, pro tem. *Treasure Coast Black Heritage,* Jacks, Moore, Hudson 1996. p. 47.

two rows over into a desk closer to several white girls who once despised her. She offers no explanation, perhaps having been cautioned because of the trouble it is causing. After several weeks, the ostracization she experiences becomes too great. She keeps her conversations and association with me to a secret minimum. I understand, and I hold no animosity. It's the system, not her. The system in the midst of change can rebel all it wants. No longer can it ignore us. Rather we will confront and address our concerns. Forced integration can be unwelcoming. Change is happening and no one can do anything to stop it.

Sometimes numerous fights erupt throughout the day in hallways and classrooms. On my way to fifth period, a few of my buddies from Francis K. Sweet observe a group of white boys accost a petite black girl, pushing her face into a water fountain. She's no match in her efforts fighting back. I yell out to the boys as she curses and swings, her face wet and eyeglasses twisted on her face. We chase the boys unsuccessfully as they scatter in all directions. We arrive back at the scene. "Those crackers say this fountain is for whites only! I told them well, this black girl's gonna drink some water from it today!" she proudly proclaims, victoriously defiant.

We hear more rumors that a band of whites is roaming the halls looking to intimidate us in the old Jim Crow ways, to restrict and confine our use of certain water fountains on campus. Some whites have the audacity to demand blacks move off walkways whenever someone white passes, and to carry their books when asked and complain about using shower stalls after we do. We rattle whites out their comfort zones and we keep moving forward.

I get a crazy notion and walk alone through a designated area of a breezeway, where rednecks say blacks will be attacked without a pass. I discover these types of scare tactics are nothing more than bluffs.

Those whites are so outwardly against integration that they are blind to our resolve. We have an urgent need to take ownership of white privilege; to get a piece of the pie. We have manifest destiny for equality on our side. Most of us are poor, tough and street wise, full of jive and vibrato that whites have never encountered. We have nothing to lose and everything to gain.

At the end of each day, buses line the loading zone to carry us back into our segregated communities. Noisy students hang out windows, yelling good byes to new black friends. Some sit silently, while others laugh sharing jokes and stories about new school experiences. On the eve of my inaugural integration week, Mama, Grandma, my sisters and I gather around the television. We listen to a reporter's concern about racial incidents in the schools. Throughout Florida's counties there's school chaos—fights, suspensions, reporters trivializing its historic significance and more.

In my first week, black students face a multitude of controversial suspensions and parents take their complaints to the lily-white school administration. The superintendent and rank and file members have little or no voice of reason.

I'm not surprised that many of my classmates' parents chose not to allow their children to integrate. More than 75 percent of St. Lucie County's black student population remains at segregated schools in opposition to integration. Not because of racial reasons, but because of a history of unfairness practiced by a white school board that alienates black parents. They rather not cater to whites in opposition to integration. The board doesn't devise a school transitioning plan nor establishes any dialogue with black parents who are legitimately concerned.

The board purposefully casts a cloud of indignation and disrespect by deliberately devising an impartial "school choice plan" or "open enrollment" program to deter greater number of blacks from attending white schools. Aside from this plan, the board perpetuates a myth that blacks are more content to remain at inferior schools than to integrate, thereby anticipating that whites will gladly remain at their own. The school board underestimates the desire for change in blacks. No longer do we desire holding on to badges and institutions of segregation. We're elevating our consciousness towards racial equality and justice. The school board's dubious school choice plan is short lived and eventually backfires.

In 1966, Fort Pierce, like all southern cities, experiences a rocky transition into integrating schools and public accommodations. My neighbors and black populous in general have their consciousness raised as we witness pursuit of new civil rights legislation with fervor of activism on a national level. Until school desegregation, nothing catastrophic shocks the consciousness of our community leaders towards any significant social activism movement. Seemingly, we're content eating and shopping at a few select restaurants and chain stores that are willing to tolerate our patronage.

Small town Fort Pierce in the 1960s is unyielding to part ways from white southern traditions. Rather it takes lethargic steps to change. I embrace this new challenge of change through activism. I often lie in bed and ponder over the long enduring hardships of my ancestors. I vow to do my little part to make change possible wherever and whenever I sense my rights are being violated.

Chapter 11

CULTURE SHOCK

Being out of your familiar surroundings is like being a fish out of water—you struggle, trying to breathe life in a new world. At some point in your experiences you realize it's now time to fit in or else get swallowed up by the big fish. Integration was like that big fish and it was called assimilation. I know my people suffer from corrosive self-hatred and lack of cultural identity, that we have been robbed of our humanity in a system of chattel slavery, yet we are now moving forward.

I didn't realize how much division there is among whites themselves. I discover white racial distinctions—one class pitted against the other. Who fits where on the social status totem pole? You have hippies with peace symbols, hip huggers and sandals; surfers with loose-fitting jeans and T-shirts; swampers of swampland in jeans, camouflage hunting caps; agricultural farmers known as "ag boys" with "Future Farmers of America" emblems on their jackets and a rebel flag on their caps; and preppy conformist conservative types with crew-cuts, bouffant hairstyles and dull fashions when compared to the styles worn by members of the liberal counter culture. This is how whites sort themselves out. Blacks aren't part of this white social paradigm, but if they were, they'd be on the lowest rung.

Swirling rumors at school reveal that whites think blacks are lepers, the untouchables. Blacks in our community are considered 'guinea pigs,' symbols used for our experimental leap into integration. Racial attitudes—those of blacks and whites are slow to change. Whenever I encounter hippies in the corridors, they typically offer a peace sign with their fingers. I move with optimism, trying to fit into something positive at my own pace.

When I tune into the news, I'm keenly interested in civil unrest and movements throughout America. Before my first integrated school year ends, Chicago and Detroit go up in a blaze of racial frustrations, just as riots in Florida, New York, California, Michigan, Mississippi, Ohio, Alabama and others have done before.

I'm in awe how black people unleash pent up frustrations and rage. They literally burn down Watts in Los Angeles causing 34 deaths and costing millions of dollars in destroyed property. I'm glued to the TV, flipping between ABC, CBS, and NBC, the only national networks available at that time. I catch old footage of documentaries on protest and civil unrest as James Meredith, the first black in 1962 to integrate the University of Mississippi. I cringe as Governor George Wallace stands in the doorway of the University of Alabama in a symbolic gesture to bar integration. With his bold racist statement *"Segregation now, segregation tomorrow, segregation forever"* delivering a very clear message to all southern blacks and whites.

I, too, am part of the hippie counter culture, and I'm proudly black and very enlightened. I'm against, and quick to point out, inconsistencies in racial inequality. Whites may say I'm militant or radical and that I don't fit into white society's label "sixties baby boomers." I'm rebellious but not a spoiled brat. I have been against black authority in some ways but not against family values in ways of whites and the privileged. In my own segregated world, I don't know any blacks proscribe to or fit into that definition.

Brent is from a wealthy family. I meet him on the basketball court and I see that he is in dire need of his parents' love and attention. "Dude, my parents are always traveling on business, don't give a damn about me, come home and I'm ignored. I'm supposed to be obedient? I hate them!" I'm blown away with his logic. I'd never heard such a thing from blacks, but I hear it often from whites. Rebellious Brent doesn't fit the image of his banker father who is probably grooming his son to walk in his footsteps. Brent's outside the mainstream image. He refuses to bow to his father's autocratic demands to dress conservatively and conduct himself like a choirboy.

I'm in culture shock when I encounter whites who don't conform to the stereotypes we have of them. We are more familiar with the diehards holding onto their beloved southern tradition with urgency and fear. Brent is empathetic to our cause, but not quite willing to step into the spotlight once he's targeted with a rain of "n....r lover" epithets. Never will I push the issue. He must do so of his own free will, a conscious decision to stand up for justice.

Like Brent, some whites gradually shift from their old beliefs and initiate conversations on race. I am hopeful. I envision that we all must participate in trying to effect change. While there's much we all must partake, if integration will succeed or school is as ever like the first day of integration polarized as ever.

There aren't easy answers to these racially divisive matters. I didn't ever want to force the race issue in a white school, although as I mature and come into awareness it is the likely decision I must reach. As days and weeks pass, I have concluded someday I must force it. More and more we are overlooked—invisible to the blinded eyes of white classmates and instructors. It is only when faced with some school infraction, and mostly against whites, are we no longer invisible. Rather, we are quickly singled out and summarily dealt with.

I play on the school's Blue Devils basketball team. We are playing against the Hurricanes, and Joey, a white teammate, rarely passes the ball when I'm open. Only after our coach yells to run a play to get me open does he pass it to me for a shot. We get into an argument over it after losing a game. I ask him, "You got a problem passing me the ball?" To my surprise he says, "Yes. My father says you Negro guys take too many shots." Surprised, "Why does he thinks that? Most of my shots go in, yours don't." Joey doesn't answer. Why does his father say this? Was it jealousy, hatred or am I overreacting? Basketball's a team sport, it's not about selfish play. I suppose Joey's lackluster game isn't as good as mine, and his father doesn't like a black kid out shining his son.

St. Lucie Junior High 1967 Blue Devils intramural team. Back row left, me and Chris Benjamin also teammate and nephew of baseball coach Albert "Baylock" Benjamin.

There's a one-sided malady of culture shock for blacks. Our frustrations run deep in reaction to the administration's pandering. "You must initiate friendships and fit in." Blacks' response: "Hell no!" For guinea pigs we did not experience culture difference at black schools and now you want us alone to fit in—isolated in a sea of whites. You can't force acceptance to a white school's culture and traditions without considering the value of our culture. We're not willing to abandon our culture for the sake of integration. Imagine how white students would react if they were expected to sacrifice their culture in a black school that had only black traditions!

Each day crowdedness spills over into racial hostilities, sparking teacher resignations at St. Lucie Junior High. In the midst of confusion comes "Rat Day." It's a popular rite of passage for freshmen aspiring for acceptance. This campus tradition is for newcomers to stake out a place of identity.

Leading up to Rat Day, eighth and ninth graders share their old experiences. "At first it's fun until I got angry. I was about to cry doing crazy things all day," a chubby acne-faced white boy says. I am totally against what I was about to subject myself to. "It about school spirit," he says. I wasn't about being the brunt of juniors and seniors jokes, and humiliated by their exploits for fun and jest.

The majority of 137 blacks out of 847 students are suspicious of the hidden dangers Rat Day might pose. Rumors spread like wildfire. Whites don't want blacks participating, so they'll subject us to slave-like degrading acts. We are cautious.

Freshmen must distinguish themselves in tattered old clothes. My reason against participating is how my buddies Beanie and Johnny will react. They'll see me wearing tattered old clothes I don't ever wear unlike the clothes they wear to school every day. Beanie and Johnny are so "po" they're below the rank of "poor" so to speak.

Beanie is very conscious of his tattered look and Johnny mainly gets teased daily wearing high-water pants above his ankles. I won't ever poke fun at them. Many black and some white schoolmates are at the poverty level. I remain humble in the presence of the less fortunate—I'm a little better off. At such a time, I want to instill pride in Beanie and Johnny. Believing in my parents' saying, "You might be poor in what you have, but you don't have to act like it." To dress poorly, since I would never do so except in this instance, is arrogance flying in their faces. I chose not to wear raggedy clothing nor participate in Rat Day.

I convince Ronnie, a buddy, not to participate. On the morning of Rat Day, to make a statement, I put on my light blue and white striped Ban-Lon knitted shirt and white bell bottom pants and penny loafers. "I ain't wearing white pants to get dirty acting like a damn fool for no stupid freshman tradition." Ronnie is into hip fashions, so he too dresses up instead of down. He wears flared blue jeans, a striped pressed shirt and vest and white converse tennis shoes. "We lookin fly," Ronnie says. "That's the point, we untouchables ain't participating," I add.

The announcement comes over the intercom after homeroom. "It's Rat Day! Enjoy yourselves!" Everyone briskly runs out into the corridors. Upperclassmen immediately start pranks on willing freshmen. I make my way to first period where a grinning stout upperclassman with flaming red hair approaches me, "Hey you!

Aren't you a freshman? I want you to bark like a dog!" he demands. "You crazy? I'm not participating." "It's your first year, it's in the school spirit. Better get used to doing what we say!" He protests. "I won't participate in this stupid crap!" The white boy shrugs and walks away.

The majority of poor blacks from migrant working families don't participate. They're as insightful about the matter as I. Most middle-class blacks dress down in tattered clothes and join in. "Why ain't you dressed like us? We're having fun!" I maneuver my way to class and watch those blacks of middle class families give credibility to faculty urgings to ignore dissenters.

"You set a bad example. It's all in good spirit and cheer, our school tradition," I get admonished by a petite teacher with thick bifocals. I wasn't giving in. St. Lucie Junior High isn't my school if I don't feel welcomed.

Some blacks do whatever it takes to fit in, anything asked to benefit and keep whites comfortable in our presence. I suppose that accommodating becomes the operative word. What I observe weaving through chaotic crowds of laughter between classes doesn't give attention to our needs.

White teachers poke fun, laughing into spasms at several black boys crawling on all fours barking and at the shocking scene of a black boy twisting like a girl. Demeaning gimmicks. I wonder if some blacks realize that they are providing whites with a much-needed minstrel comedy hour.

I come across a scene and curiously stop to watch. A skinny timid white freshman girl is compliant to the commands of a black girl. She smiles, licking her chops as if saying, "Oh how I long for this day!" The white girl eagerly jumping hopscotch on the sidewalk while yelling out: "I love eating watermelon and chitlins!" She repeats it over and over.

What really gets my attention in the chaos is a white upperclassman who has a chubby black freshman in glasses with a dog leash around his neck doing jumping jacks on command. The white student then throws a pencil like a bone as the freshman gives chase, barking as he fetches it. I shake my head as if I don't see it. The freshman returns with the pencil, totally oblivious to the white boy's friends enjoying every minute of it. "Good tricks rat!" The white boy pats him on the back, pleased with his doggy tricks and walks away laughing with his buddies.

"Hey man, why do you let that white boy make you act like a fool!" I blurt. "Ah man, I'm just having fun, why do you take it so serious?" Sporting a wide smile, he's clearly caught up in the excitement. "Did you hear about making blacks act like slaves?" His eyes get beady, processing what I say. "No man, I didn't hear anything like that." Undeterred, he hastily runs off seeking to be mistreated in another dog and pony show.

I try to comprehend what I'm feeling. Am I being too serious? What makes someone think all is fun and games when the intention of a provocateur may be an act of denigration? How can you not be aware and unnerved by it all? How can one not think simulating the scenario of a dog chasing a bone as orchestrated by whites is not self-deprecating and demeaning? How can one not realize that behind this charade is ill-will or evil intent? I envision purpose at this historic time of integration. Rat Day is a pretext for the administration to notice how black freshmen are eager to assimilate. My moral compass speaks to me—I shouldn't play and paddle in shallow triviality. I refuse to play along for a few smiles and a pat on the back. I refuse to feel dehumanized, demoralized and mocked.

Freshmen wearing a "rat hat" and two others put in ridiculous positions
by an upper-class (ninth grade) girl student during Rat Day.

In between classes on this day, teachers are lenient on lateness. The tardy bell's just a formality ignored. Everyone wants to see Rat Day in its finest hour. Clusters of students jam the hallways at every turn, watching some rat freshman do his thing. All for the sake of good ole school spirit. As the school day comes to a close, no one seems to laugh anymore. Participants have grown weary and their enthusiasm weens. Everyone has had enough, or have they?

As I am walking down the hallways, I spot something right before my eyes. "Giddy up, ride um cowboy!" Lawrence Russ, a black ninth grader, sits on the back of a white boy on all fours as the boy makes sounds like a spooked horse. The scene ignites protest from a flock of whites. "Hey! Get off him!" "You can't do that!" Several monitors rush over in their defense. "Get off that young man!" "What's wrong? I'm having fun like everybody else...I get it. You can't stand what you see? Ah ha!" Lawrence is a jokester but no fool, a serious brother. His words spoke volumes—white teachers couldn't handle a white boy in a submissive position.

"Enough for Rat Day!" a teacher adds. Some black freshmen non-participants emerge. Arthur Lamar, Felix Newkirk, Marion Sikes, Robert Adderly, Oscar Offord, Terry Miller, Ronnie Briggs and I, all assertive 7th graders and conscious warriors. We become antagonistic, monitoring rumors of slave acts. We disrupt white upperclassmen subjecting blacks to acts we consider offensive. "You didn't stop it when a black boy had a leash around his neck," I protest. "Yeah, you looked away smiling," Felix interjects. Not one white teacher answers, slithering away quietly.

Plainly an issue of unfairness—a willing white participant comfortable on all fours making horse sounds. White superiority diminishes when the black student asserts his dominance atop the white student on all fours. All day between classes sullen-faced blacks run around in tattered clothes doing all kinds of humiliating acts. By the end of the day many quit, awaken out of a fog into reality. An outbreak of fights occurs because overly zealous whites are unable to determine which blacks are participants in old worn out clothes from those wearing them out of necessity. Rat Day is a theatrical exposition of absurdity.

I establish good relationships with my homeroom teacher, Nancy Colcord and the dean of students, Jack Brennan. Aside from them, hardly any teacher or administrator gives consistent expressions of encouragement since my arrival on campus. It feels like I'm unwelcome and invisible as ever but it doesn't matter. No one can stop me from getting a quality education. Do white people think we can't sense when we aren't wanted? Are we too sensitive? Have we developed from our historical hardships keen radar to detect the slightest hint of racial and social injustice?

I need to let my guard down a bit, but I can't because Grandma primed me to be conscious and proud of my race. Crossing over, giving a little of yourself expecting to get a little back. I won't assimilate, giving up all of myself. I can't witness a single injustice and let it go without consequences. I remain suspicious, questioning myself many times. Is assimilation really integration? Reality starkly reminds me as I return home each day from school, passing through slum-neglected neighborhoods that it is not.

In 1968 a new hip television series "Mod Squad" captivates hearts and minds of young black and white viewers. Clarence Williams III, a black star, becomes our salvation. Sidney Poitier was among the first black actors to provide positive role models for blacks on the silver screen. Images of blacks on television are generally relegated to demeaning characters, prancing around like buffoons, uttering "Yessum and nawsum."

At age seven, I innocently watch Tarzan, amazed at the action and adventure. Having digested much of Marion Parker's *Africa and its Animal Kingdom* book, something curious troubles me about that movie. Consciously more aware, I dissect the scenes. I ask myself how Tarzan, a white man, can be king of an African jungle? How can he possess so much power in a vast continent like Africa, when he was born elsewhere? How can Africans continue to get easily manipulated by so-called great white hunters and colonizers? Practically every scene portrays Africans as mindless, uncivilized heathens. In contrast, Tarzan performs invincible acts, swinging from vines and eluding and defeating spear-throwing warrior tribes. His acts of killing ferocious lions are viewed as heroic feats.

"Tarzan," in my opinion, is the most racist program ever. Very early in my youth by reading enlightening black books watching racist movies like Tarzan I learned never to watch again.

Finally in 1964, when Congress passed the Civil Rights Act did Bill Cosby become the first black actor to co-star in a drama series on television. (In 1956 Nat King Cole hosted his own variety show) "Civil rights protest marches finally put Hollywood's feet to the fire. It is nice seeing blacks in positive roles for a change," Mama says. Cosby teams up with Robert Culp, the former plays a Rhodes scholar, who doesn't drink or smoke and is multilingual. He poses as Culp's personal trainer. Culp, on the other hand, plays a negative character—drinker, smoker and womanizer. Indeed, the Civil Rights Movement plays its part piercing the moral and social conscience of Hollywood's directors and producers who portray negative images of blacks on the big screen and on TV. Hollywood directors and writers were careful not to offend black socially conscious and white sympathetic liberals whites. The rating were high because of black viewership were probably enough of the market to worry about appeasing us.

Cosby paved the way for Greg Morris on "Mission Impossible" and Don Mitchell on "Ironside," who play strong black characters with intelligence. In 1968, "Julia" premiered with actress Diahann Carroll in the lead role of a nurse, and Ruby Dee in "Peyton Place" portrayed a neurosurgeon's wife who was politically outspoken.

Clarence Williams III portrayal as Linc on "Mod Squad" helps to booster every black's racial pride. Linc doesn't act like a buffoon, rather he is hip and articulate in decision-making situations. And he's the coolest member of a cast that includes Julie and Pete, his two hip white detective partners. The strong silent laid-back type sporting a mean Afro, dark sunglasses and tight bellbottoms— blacks can relate. All my homeboys take time off hanging out to catch another episode as Hollywood appeals to blacks. We are becoming increasingly proud of our blackness.

"Mod Squad" helps to change racial attitudes at school. Blacks and whites imitate the latest hip fashions worn by the program's cast. Psychedelic print blouses, vest and hip hugger bellbottoms become the fabric symbol of the hippie movement. The low-cut hip huggers become popular among some blacks. I discover the pants are cut short at the inseam or crotch which fit low on waistlines exposes navels and tummies. For the administration hip huggers immediately become problematic with whites boldly defying school strict dress code are often sent home. I quickly trash them.

Ronnie and I have social studies class together. He is a funny hyped brother with a twisted sense of humor and we hang tuff together pretty tight. White girls pass in the corridors shaking their little flat pancake butts in hip huggers, with navels showing just above wide leather belts with peace sign buckles. Ronnie yell out, "Skinnn is innnn!" They turn and smile at us.

At 14 years of age and packed tight like sardines in the corridors boys get sexually aroused pressing up against girls. On one occasion, I deliberately risk touching this white girl's unusually round butt—a new discovery. She looks back at me with a nervous smile. I'm a little embarrassed and quickly apologize, not knowing how she might react. I don't want to cause a riot with her screaming, "This n....r feeling my butt!"

Bumping into someone is routine. No one ever notices because the breezeways (open areas) are overcrowded. On another occasion, I inadvertently touch a white girl's butt and she doesn't look back. I touch her again intentionally and she whispers something to her girlfriends. They all look back at me, giggling. I start telling other boys about my little escapade, a new experience. Those two girls must enjoy spreading word to their friends too, because each time I touch her she does nothing but smile.

Changing classes each period, white girls seem as determined, innovative and deliberate as we are. Their abrupt stops cause Ronnie, Beanie and Johnny to bump into them from behind. The breezeways are so crowded that they obstruct the teacher's view. One ugly white girl with bushy eyebrows and a pointed nose like Pinocchio grabs my hand and puts it on her butt, then turns around giggling back at me with dingy yellow teeth. I almost scream.

Beanie named us "Booty Snatchers" because no one catches us. Inevitably some of us must have touched the wrong white girl's butt.

Rumors flare through the school's intercom system in all the classrooms: "Anyone caught making deliberate uninvited physical contact in the corridors faces suspension."

More monitors appear between classes. One old hawk-eyed white teacher watches every black boy nearing a white girl. We're kept under surveillance as suspects, so it seems, for the entire year. "I'm watching you boys, keep your hands to yourself now!" monitors say as we pass. No one ever gets caught. We keep doing it because white girls like it.

A faction of white boys complains that white girls are getting too close to black boys. I become friendly with a few, especially Susan, a tall slender blonde who sits next to me in math class. When we bumped into each other in the corridor she or I strike up a conversation. I'm comfortable chatting with her since, over time, integration allows some whites to let their guard down. Even I let my guard down somewhat. Susan usually taps my arm with an urgent need to chat about something. She has a beautiful smile and I think she likes me.

On breezeways out in the open, I'm conscious of what others might think. It doesn't seem to bother Susan at all. I'm not interested in white girls, although interracial dating is very much out in the open with couples holding hands to the disapproving eye of students and faculty. Brothers Harrison and Coleman Freeman are high profile, prancing up and down the corridors during lunch break. I suppose sisters are threatened by white competition and rightly so. This is a time when hip huggers are the new fashion craze on campus. The brothers are really getting hyped looking below the waistline and white boys too. But there lies the problem. The low cut at the waistline and inseam appear especially design for whites with little room for black butts at all. I'm no connoisseur of a girl's tush, but I notice most white girls butts are flat appear to sit on their back— butts are either flat at and below the waistline or curve out far below the waistline then sag or droop; while most sisters butts curve out at the waistline. When a sister wearing hip huggers exposes every bit of her curvaceous round onion butt brothers began to take notice of the detail in those hip huggers. Pushing through a crowd one day, a black girl stops to flirt and busts her inseam. "These pants don't fit right for a sister," she says disgustedly. "I wear um for you brothers and now ya'll chase behind white girls flat asses." I give her my smelly T-shirt out of my gym basket to cover her gorgeous round onion butt and convince her that belief will never be true.

After a month wearing hip huggers rubbing painfully against my crotch, I put them in their rightful place—the garbage can, and sisters do the same. I think most brothers and sisters gradually catch on—if you are hip—hip huggers are designed for low waistlines and flat butts.

Eugene "Junior" Boatwright lives in the neighborhood and hails from one of the few middle-class families whose parents own several profitable businesses and rental properties. Junior is smart and articulate, but he is freehearted with money. While attending Means Court Elementary, Junior lines his pockets with quarters from his mother's Coke machines, causing quite a stir when he tosses quarters away in the playground. Junior earns the name Robin Hood, giving to the less fortunate. Teachers threaten to send him home for his acts of charity. He stashes coins outdoors underneath our classroom, which sits on cinder blocks. When our teacher isn't looking, he tosses coins in the air in the playground and we scramble like chickens getting them.

Junior has a taste for fashion as we enter junior high. Our taste for stylish clothes emerges. While I work hard earning my keep in tomato, cucumber and bell pepper fields, his parents give him an allowance to buy whatever he likes. I can earn $7 a day for eight hours of work in the late 60s, which is decent money then; or work all day earning at least $15 or more, getting a dime a basket. And if I lug baskets for old ladies, I have better earnings and get muscles too.

Junior convinces me I can earn more working less for his father. I obviously like the idea. I need cash to keep up with the latest fashion trends. Junior's father is a fruit contractor who often gives us extra money for filling large tubs (bins of oranges, tangerines or grapefruits). When I don't make as much picking, he goes into his father's cash box and gives me a little extra. "Don't worry about it. I do it all the time. He won't miss a thing, here's 50 dollars for you and 100 dollars for me." I never complain.

Every Saturday after work, Junior and I are regulars at Richard's Fashions, several blocks from where we live. One of the few Jewish businesses in our community with a line of hip young men's fashions. Richard is hip to us and knows the difference between quality fashions and fades. He lets us establish credit, take shirts, pants, anything to wear while paying on it.

Into my second year of integration, Richard's smile fades into paranoia. I walk in, speak and he doesn't notice. He's staring out the window at passing cars as if something's about to happen. "Are you all right?" "I'm fine, just thinking." I brush it aside and go to the young men's section like a child in a candy store.

On one occasion I interrupt an argument between Richard and two black men in Army uniforms. Heading for the door, one with dark-tinted shades points a finger. "Don't give me that shit maann with that fake smile, all you care about is our money!" "Come on man we're on leave. It ain't worth it and the cops." The other brother grabs his friend by the arm. "What it is soul brother?" (Sixties street slang greeting) "I'm cool," I say as they exit the store.

"What's that all about?" I ask. "I don't know, maybe I'm culture shocked." "Me too, at school," I reply. "I never thought I'd offend soldiers. "All I say, I know you're proud fighting for your country." Richard looked perplexed. Times are changing, and change has caught up to him. Black militancy displays an impatience for change and it's encroaching on his busy little clothing store.

Richard's eyes are gloomy watching through a window at a crowd briskly passing by. "I support integration and civil rights, why are they angry at me?" He's solemn now. I couldn't answer for the soldiers, only for myself. "Their anger ain't about you, it's about the system that lifts you up and keeps us down. You profit from what we don't." Richard's dazed by my comment. "You're smart. I never thought you'd speak like that," he says in a restrained voice. "It's a lot you haven't heard me say, at least not yet." I leave him with a quizzical stare, as if concerned about me that his store credit might be in jeopardy. I'm evolving consciously, further beyond his or my own culture shock.

A loud noise leads me to the Busy Bee pool room next to Richard's, a place where gamblers, hustlers, pimps and pool sharks hang out, honing their skills. I stand near the doorway, peering inside. A heated debate goes on. "Whitey thinks brother's gon fight his wars, we so blind, our minds shackle in chains dying for what?" "Eat in a white diner . . .walk downtown without being harassed, come home still be call ah n..ga?" "Hell no, I ain't goin back!" "For what!" The black soldier I encounter in Richard's says, "That honky next door needs to lay off that patriotic bullshit!" "Honkies in the Army mo racist than civilians, we might go AWOL!" the other says.

There's a revolution taking hold in the minds of black people. Richard sees opposition in blacks will lead to reprisals he can't afford. So, I watch as he plays along, and I see fear set deep into his eyes. His status in our community comes into question, trivialized by a sudden radicalization of young black men in his midst. He's perceived part and parcel of the problem. He's the common enemy, part of a racist system that puts Richard into culture shock.

"My business days are numbered," he says. He never expects militancy or change to come so quickly. "It's happening everywhere," I remind him. "We're tired of waiting for change Richard." I suppose he expect change to come to Fort Pierce in the unforeseeable future, slow as molasses as it always has everywhere in America. But now with intensity and urgency we can't wait any longer. A veil of paranoia transforms Richard's sense of humor into fear.

Experiencing school integration shocks the consciousness of every child, black and white. How can it not? We're making history, pursuing Dr. King's vision and making it a reality. Some mornings at the bus stop we young brothers get into heated discussions about the movement. "Yeah man, we gonna keep on pushing, like Curtis Mayfield says, the train ah comin we won't need no ticket we just get on board." "Ain't no turnin back now!"

"What yawl excited about? I hope it's homework!" Carrie Ellis our bus driver says to a roar of laughter on our way to school. "You boys and girls got courage when you chose to integrate when others refused. Stay positive. Wake up white folks and make um think."

I proudly strut around campus, holding my head high. No white will get me riled up and distracted from why I'm here. I see a similar cockiness in every black student I pass; a seriousness having something to prove. Hollywood is moving away from caricatures like Stepin Fetchit and Rochester as well as roles of maids and shoeshine boys. It appears Hollywood is more attuned to positive black imagery as blacks move into a new paradigm of bold hip ways of expression. Several whites find our straightforwardness, confidence and bodacious attitudes offensive and threatening. No longer are we a passive and submissive generation, we assert our rights— we're here and we have a voice!

In classrooms, social clubs and activities we assert ourselves not to be outdone. Many resistant whites go into protectionist modes of thinking. We quickly realize assimilating isn't so simple. We have an obligation to step up and make changes, to break down old stereotypes with social activism even in its crudest variety. One such incident snowballs unexpectedly from mean-spiritedness into something positive.

Pickles, a 6'5" 250-lb behemoth ninth grade redneck has a thriving reputation bullying smaller boys. Pickles doesn't realize some in his sixth period gym class have had enough. We count on imposing brothers like Malachai Bacon, who is equal to Pickles in stature, strength and athleticism to bother. Malachai is put on standby. "We can handle him," Ron tells Malachai. "We gonna psyche him out," Malachai laughs. "Ok. I got your back, so pray he don't get you first."

Ron and I have sixth period gym together. To beat the mad rush for premium space, we arrive minutes early waiting for a rowdy crowd of ninth graders to shower and clear out of the locker room. We routinely watch Pickles gasping for air, dead last on his final lap. Ron laughs this time. Pickles looks over. "You damn boys betta not be standing out here tomorrow, I'm gonna kick yir asses!" "I got your boy swinging!" Ron says giggling, grabbing his crotch and shaking it at Pickles. "How you gonna catch us?" I muse. Pickles bends over gasping for air and then gets a burst of energy and straightens up. "I don't like yawl standin here watchin me run, I'm gonna get ya." he warns in southern twang with a menacing stare. "We're really scared!" I laugh, taunting him. Pickles stares hard at us, barely able to carry his tired body into the locker room.

Pickles get increasingly frustrated at Coach King teasing his blimp-like movements. We're targeted as Pickles' whipping boys, unaware of what we're up against. Blacks are in the minority on campus, so our survival instincts kick into a protectionist mode whenever we're at school. Suspecting that trouble is imminently lurking, we move about in groups. We see Pickles on the breezeways, and Beanie one of the best "playing the dozens," starts jawing. "Hey Pickles! You big sorry doofus!" "You mad cause yo mammy ain't got enough milk in her tits for you to suck!" "Pickles you so ugly when yo mammy had you she kept looking at you sayin be somebody else please!" "You big sorry dumb baby Huey!" Ron adds. We laugh as he goes red-faced. Pickles and his buddies have never heard anyone play the dirty-dozen think we lost our minds.

All week Pickles puts up weak and unsuccessful chases through crushing crowds of students. Towering over everyone, he's noticeable, a slow giveaway. Hall monitors admonish, yell and scream, trying with little success to slow us down. Each day a few black freshmen join in the teasing. Pickles is astonished, frustrated by this kind of bombardment he's never faced before. A brother yells, "Pickles! You big sorry dill Pickle!" Pickles turns to react. Someone else yells from another direction, "You big lard butt! Yo mammy took Geritol when she had you!" Pickles gives chase, determined to catch someone, anyone, but it is impossible.

In our usual spot, we're outside the locker room leaning against the wall watching Pickles laboring for the home stretch. "Run! You big sorry joker!" "That's the best you can do!" "We still here standing, chump!" "Whatcha gonna do about it!" "Yo mammy disowned yo sorry ass!" Pickles shoulders slump as he lumbers into the locker room.

We jawed and jive every chance we get. Pickles face and scalp redden through his crew cut, reluctant to look our way. "Guys please! Please! Stop it! I get your point!" We get the scoop from a black ninth grader that Pickles told his buddies: "These black guys don't let up. I don't like their funny game of teasing about your mama." Pickles sees us approaching, panics and veers in another direction. I say to Ron teasingly, "Pickles is avoiding us, he's no longer having fun."

One day before PE we don't see Pickles laboring into the home stretch dead last. "Let's see if he's inside," Ron says. A few ninth graders hastily dress, late for sixth period. Pickles comes out of the shower wrapped in a tower, unexpectedly spots us watching him, and cringes. He approaches cautiously and whispers, "Ok, Ok, please not here around these guys." We're slightly captivated by this gesture. "I'm apologizing to yah," he whispers. "Please don't teasin me again. I won't botha yawl anymore." "Ok?" We reply amusedly. Pickles concedes to a truce, realizing he's been outsmarted.

Pickles underestimates our gaming tenacity—selling wolf tickets, shucking and jiving, doing the dozens that black boys do to humiliate each other on the streets makes us stuff. We underestimate his temperament, he never once calls anyone a n....r. Pickles maintains the pride he stood to lose and so do we. After all, what he bargained for and got was a taste of black culture shock.

I'm shocked seeing white boys who are 13- and 14-years old smoke cigarettes, dip snuff and chew tobacco in bathrooms. Pot and Quaaludes (a barbiturate) are white boys' introductory drugs of choice. The few black boys I know who smoke do it undercover, out of the public's eye. "How long you been smoking?" I ask a white boy puffing on a Marlboro. "Since 7 or 8, my parents couldn't stop me. They let me do it now." With integration comes the drug scene, a new encounter across the tracks. Blacks dealing and negotiating goes on in crowded bathrooms. Marijuana is the hors d'oeuvres to cocaine, amphetamines and LSD, a smorgasbord of choices.

The drug culture on campus comes by open invitation. First the hit, then the taste, followed by the snort. A euphoric sensation gradual shifts our "eyes on the prize" away from a quality education. Integration unwillingly brings an unwelcome guest with an ominous warning: *Soon I'll come in dark gloomy places of despair and wreak havoc on vulnerable people stripped of knowledge and cultural identity and leave them to a life of dependency, self destruction and death.*

Drug use and sexual promiscuity, according to Fort Pierce medical auxiliary personnel, contribute to teen pregnancy on campus. White girls conceal their pregnancies, hardly noticeable until reported to the administration, which prompts the school board to establish a "Teen Alert" program targeting ninth graders. Classes are offered about anatomy, physiology and reproduction. The school board thinks it will suppress the spread of venereal diseases. It is no more than a scare tactic that has little effect.

Classmates of the redneck and preppy variety disappear unnoticed until rumors swirl about their withdrawal from school. "What happened to Dawn?" I ask a reliable source. "She got pregnant, maann, she's a goner." White girls suddenly reappear after short absences amid rumors of abortions—a despicable word in the black community. White boys locker room jokes bear out the truth: white families have the financial means to make a pregnancy go away. Such a hidden procedure comes into the open as black girls discover the means to end a pregnancy.

To assimilate is to fit in where you can get in, but only if it's to my liking. The administration keeps a heightened awareness to racial conflicts in its student body. This phenomenon isn't new. Civility on campus is tantamount to a principal and his administrators' careers that are beholden to a school board's policies and public trust.

I watch a conservatively dressed white girl become tense as a black boy sits near her. I imagine that she too suffers from some derivative culture shock. When we sit on benches or stand in lunchroom lines next to whites mingling in their cliquish circles we stir up small chatter. The conversations taper off as whites become increasingly uncomfortable as they inch closer to the unknown— fearful of opening a door to discovery.

I hear outcries from blacks and I hear praise from good intentioned whites. The administration doesn't understand, never envisioned and is incapable of adapting even if it wants to. Black youth's intractable anger festers from isolation, from poverty and from the absence of opportunities. I can't detach my life experiences or my feelings and leave them at the door before entering school is impossible. I see greater numbers of brothers and sisters lagging academically, lost and frustrated in an insensitive white school system. It stands to reason that they feel left out. Blacks are invisible— untouchable. What continues to emerge, as I move about campus over the days that turn into years, is that the structural assimilation of blacks into the dominant white culture requires us to sacrifice our own culture. Its substantive value is lost in the hallways of our integrated institutions.

As social psychologists envision—integration and assimilation put the spotlight on us. This paradigm shifts and crosses over and puts white culture central stage. After two years at St. Lucie Junior High, I see integration as a smokescreen with little benefit. My token white friendships are on a part-time basis, only at school. Most whites rather feel comfortable with conforming non-threatening blacks.

Whites go about doing their thing and blacks do theirs. We're in a laboratory of social change—we're white folks' experimental guinea pigs! As more blacks cross over the tracks, discover new cultural encounters, and are exposed to amenities deprived of during segregation too long, their eyes are opened. We have new first edition books without graffiti and bigotry, access to quality supplies and new and different ways of thinking, saying and doing things. The more I hear the word assimilation the more I understand the importance of holding steadfast to my cultural belief system. I have questionable optimism and my experiences from Jim Crow segregation have me holding on to unresolved complex issues that are minimized and overlooked—anger and rage. I rap with brothers and see that we share feelings that rest just below the surface in wait.

In class, I listen to the teacher lecture about all that is identifiable in her white world. I am deeply frustrated when I hear the questions she poses to the class, oftentimes ignoring the black students who are interested in joining the discussion. We're required to know the subject matter without asking any questions. It's frustrating that anything black of comparable value is never mentioned. I stay in my thoughts, deflecting any urge to burst out in opposition.

I look around the class, studying dull eyes in sullen empty black faces. Many come to school with cocky street sophistication—

bodacious attitudes accompanied by a swagger that exudes, "Yeah, I got style, I'm bad, and you better know it!" "Get used to it!" Bold and self-assured are qualities rarely portrayed by blacks on television, causing shock and awe among our white counterparts. I and others become survivalists equipped with coping mechanisms, and we start to exact attention to *our needs* as we are absorbed further into a paradigm of assimilation and inclusion.

One Saturday, I sit in the waiting room of Dr. Benton's office awaiting my annual physical. A group of elderly men engage in a heated debate why blacks never challenge eating at Woolworths on Orange Avenue. The men get quiet when Dr. Benton enters. "Interesting," he says. "You like to know my opinion?" he asks. The men nod affirmatively. "We're afraid to challenge Jim Crow." Dr. Benton understands Woolworths isn't excited about integration doesn't expect their management to remind us of 1964 Civil Rights Act and invite us to come inside, Never!

There's no better time in history I'd rather be born than during the great revolutionary protests for racial equality in America. Two years after the Civil Rights Act of 1964, I challenge Grandma to sit and eat at Woolworths' counter. Reluctantly at first, hampered throughout her life by Jim Crow segregation, I proudly sit and eat fries, a burger and a shake while Grandma sips a shake through her dentures, smiling proudly while receiving commendable service.

My eyes wide open with pride follow Dr. Benton's lead, exercising my rights every chance I get. I test public accommodations never frequented by generations of black folks before. I make conscious efforts to do my small part. White businesses that want my money must treat me with respect.

Chapter 12

ANGER AND BEYOND

"Get it all out! Say what you feel if it makes you feel better!" Carrie Ellis looks through her big rear-view mirror at two girls sitting together talking. A licensed barber by trade, civil rights activist in her own right, Ms. Ellis has a canny way of encouraging students to open up to release tension. She realizes that our lives being transformed by integration has historic significance. The softness of her voice calms and relaxes my nerves on the short trip back home. "Girl, I got three days for whippin her behind, she called me a n..ga!" One girl in pigtails says to another laughing. "Well that might be funny now, says the other, you got suspended and the white girl didn't." "What your Mama and Daddy gonna do when they find out?" Carrie asks. "Beat that ass!" someone yells out. "Oops! Sorry Ms. Ellis!" "What do you do if your teacher calls you a n..ga?" "I'll report her to the principal." "What if your parents tell the principal and nothin happens?" the girl replies. "They'll have to suspend me for speaking out under those circumstances," Ellis muses. "Well, happen to a girl in my class!" "A teacher used that word?" "My God!"

Rumors stifle the air around Nedra Jenkins' teacher each morning after calling her a n..ga, Nedra corrects her pronunciation and then politely and cunningly says it again. Only after Nedra's rigorous objections to members of the administration does the name calling cease. But the harm has already been done.

I sit quietly listening to boisterous chatter from several boys in the rear of the bus, bragging about eluding teachers after whipping up on some white boys after a fight. I get no racial epithets hurled at me, although I struggle to control my anger to whispers and slighted remarks from white classmates. I stare out the window seeing nicely manicured lawns flash by in a white neighborhood. My mind drifts to another place and time, as sharp bolts of intermittent pain gnaw at my stomach. Caked blood soaks through the taped bandage weeks removed from the spearing incident, miraculously free from infection without professional medical care. Without stitches I can't avoid aggravating my wound during gym, so it takes longer to heal. The incident creeps back into my consciousness, rewinding each scene as I search for answers. Anguished over the fact that I wasn't the right age, size or strength to defend myself, nor managed to recruit anyone to help.

My need for revenge is fueled by hate towards white people. I can't shut it out. The white man in the park leaves a mark on my stomach, and a disturbing scar on my consciousness. Coupled with racial tension magnified at school, I have persistent questions that I can't block out: Why am I hated? Why such hatred drives a man to try and kill me for touching an elephant? All, I believe, is revenge and retaliation.

Grandma's earliest stories living in Jim Crow segregation and my own sporadic experiences reinforce hate. Neither she nor my parents raised me to hate. I can't shut out Grandma's words of truth that keep reverberating in my mind: "Don't let them get the best of you, you give them power and they will win!" Even for Mama's sake I promise to maintain some semblance of civility and control, as difficult as it is.

With many black suspensions and expulsions for carrying knives, fighting and unruly behavior, black enrollment falls to below 200 before the end of the first semester. Inescapable racial tensions have a smothering effect on me. An occasional friendly white smile is gratifying one moment, a cold unfriendly stare reminds me not to get too comfortable. In a hostile climate, I avoid initiating conversations with whites as much as possible because most are neither friendly nor responsive.

No one likes being ignored under any circumstances, so one day

I decide to assert myself with the hope of breaking through social and racial barriers. Before class each morning, I get with other black boys for a game of 21 on the basketball court. Many white boys play before we arrive by bus. I expect some classmates who play together during PE and on intramural teams will join in a full court game. We take the court, but most leave angrily without saying a word as others gradually follow. I interpret their actions as follows: they're not getting a grade to play with blacks before class so why play?

Over time two friendlier white boys, Jock Ivey and Mike Hogan, join our teams. As we get comfortable around each other, I ask them both, "Why you risk name calling that might get you beaten up?" Jock gets quiet a moment as he looks seriously at me. "My parents admire Dr. King, what he's doing for Negroes. They taught me not to hate and to learn to get along." Surprised by his revelation, I admire his candor. Although skeptical of Jock's revelation, if he does make it through our first year with that attitude it will help make King's dream of equality a reality.

Jock and Mike put their words into action, developing good friendships and gaining popularity with many blacks on campus. I can't break through Jock or Mike's circle of friends. When I strike up conversations they deliberately change the subject to talk about some jive topic I know nothing about. With Jock or Mike around I insert a topic, letting them know I'm intelligently reaching out again. Jock stumbles over himself apologizing for their behavior. "They can go to hell! I don't need them to like me," I say to Jock. Jock and Mike remain cordial friends throughout school. But a racial climate of tension prevents friendships from fully blossoming beyond school.

Mealtime at St. Lucie Junior High is the most segregated hour of the day—my "happy hour." Time to hangout, unwind with friends, escape the madness and enjoy a good hot meal. We laugh, joke about getting into fights with white boys, talk about sports and gossip about a new girl we like. The cooks (black and white) laugh and joke and give us a little extra to hit the spot. Black cooks bring recipes from segregated schools and incorporate tasty soul food recipes into the menu. Many days a delicious hot soulful meal keeps my mind away from trouble. Can you imagine white people under any condition not having black cooks in their kitchen?

Whites take the majority of tables in the cafeteria while blacks carve out a small section in a corner. With the overcrowded student body bursting at the seams, Principal Jesse Mullins minimizes the chaos by arranging two meal sessions. Teachers monitor against unruliness and fighting—we eat in a hurry and leave the cafeteria. Congestion and an outbreak of violence will be difficult to contain by an already shortage of full-time teachers who are on strike.

Mullins believes that the seating arrangement among blacks is visibly divisive and obviously doesn't portray the image he wants for his school. Mullins wants news coverage to show positive portrayals of race-mixing as a way to bolster his school's credibility. This political strategy can make him and his faculty look good on the evening news. However, he's keenly aware that altering our seating arrangement can possibly incite an explosive situation and result in bad publicity.

During meals, I sit and marvel at white teachers stumbling over themselves spying on us. I imagine they must see us as happy little "picaninnies" during mealtime. We laugh but keep our conversations mostly to a whisper. Not able to hear what we're laughing about until some joker explodes, drawing attention and causing the monitors to get nervous. They suspect we're plotting a disturbance. Paranoia runs deep when blacks eat together.

This monitor I call Ms. Polly with flaming red hair, granny glasses and a high-pitched voice, is vigilant in trying to promote her ideas of racial equality. She gives pep talks about fitting in: "I must remind you of the importance of getting to know your peers. You must start sitting with white girls and boys over there. Ok?" she says with a wide phony grin. "Why should we eat with those who prefer not to eat with us?" I ask politely. She's always polite. I keep my cool as others are about to snap. "How many times we got to tell you, we ain't goin over there!" a brother adds with the approval of others. "Well!" she murmurs, and briskly walks away. I sense Ms. Polly thinks impoverished blacks from across the tracks should be afraid to stand together and challenge her authority. Perhaps she thinks approaching us in the cafeteria appeals to a more primal side of our growling hungry stomachs. Maybe she even thinks that deprived black bellies are amenable to her persuasion. Breakfast and lunch are the only wholesome meals many will eat. I dare say we have lapsed memories pandering to their fears and discomforts about us. We are willing to challenge them without appeasing them.

It's puzzling watching some white teachers prance around, supposedly with enlightened minds afraid and ready to rebuff blacks at the slightest violation of a school rule. I can't envision anyone feeling comfortable after being called n...r during mealtime. It seems ridiculous that any one of us would enjoy ourselves sitting among whites who might prefer we don't for the sake of superficially integrating their group.

Whenever blacks do receive invitations from a few whites making good on an offer, others leave in opposition. Sometimes the scene erupts into Fights. Blacks in the minority can sit by ourselves bravely and hopeful minded. Whites that do invite blacks to their tables more frequently will surely get ridiculed as "n. . . r lovers." The school's monitors contrive to establish friendly relationships, desperately trying to adhere to Mullins' scheme of integrating the cafeteria. But "window dressing" the real issue is the real problem; pretending that everything is racially copasetic.

School officials blindly believe that real integration is in progress. Without first addressing the root cause—engrained racism from traditional stereotypical beliefs persists. Suffice to say, I'll never agree to any teacher who insists that I jump around and play the role of a "Stepin Fetchit," smiling, scratching, buckdancing and shuffling to get along at an all-white table. Nor will I sit passively by, waiting, hoping and expecting social change. It will come in time or else I'll raise hell to gain my equality.

There are blacks commit themselves to violence. Others as I, share visions, making personal promises to beloved teachers like Florene Robinson, Lois Fenn, and our families that we will work hard to put our best foot forward. It doesn't mean we'll take part in appeasing whites or put band-aids over real problems of racial prejudice that we'll face. We in numbers will do it our way for the next three years. In the wisdom embodied in Florence Robinson's prophetic words, "Your presence and commitment, your bond, sticks together and things will change for the better."

There's a crisis of overcrowding in St. Lucie County's schools. During PE, 171 boys squeezing into a small locker room, doing acrobatic movements to get into one of the twelve showers is an exercise in futility—a horse race. After a hot and sweaty day, tensions already run high, provoking an occasional fight after a losing race to a shower. Blacks number about 20 out of 171 boys. We carve out a corner of the locker room for ourselves. We work as a team, getting in and out of the showers holding each one until the last person has showered. It works to our advantage, because we notice early on that most whites are reluctant to enter a shower without expecting a fight.

Tom has a habit of watching blacks shower. I catch him sneaking peeks. Word spreads that he's a faggot. It takes days to figure out that he doesn't like using showers after blacks. Tom prefers to wait and use one after a white has finished. To avoid conflict, he and some larger boys get their kicks bullying smaller timid white boys to take showers after them. Tom and his gang delay other whites from showering, singing the lyrics to a popular Beatles tune, "We all live in ah yellow submarine." Many are repeatedly late for class. A group of frightened white boys gets enough courage to complain to PE Coach Valentine about their repeated lateness to class. The coach ordinarily watches for problems, and gets irritated when so many wet boys are bumping into him asking questions. Impatiently he makes a mad dash to his office to hide out.

One day Malachi Brown, a freshman Gator football player, decides to put a stop to it. Tall and muscular like a Mandingo warrior, Malachi's a cool brother always in control, always smiling, giving the appearance of a non-threatening "Happy Negro." When he steps into the circular open area of the showers, there isn't one for him. He selects one reserved for Tom and his boys, who abruptly stop singing. Tom and his boys with mouths gaping, watch dumbfounded. "Hey Malachi, I'm saving that shower for someone," Tom says with confidence. Malachi keeps showering, smiling and showing his pearly whites. Tom repeats his reminder, as other boys yell out in agreement. Malachi keep showering as he ignores them all.

Tom is also a freshman and outweighs Malachi, equal in height, but not nearly as muscular as Malachi. "Malachi, did you not hear what I just said? Move! That shower is for my buddies only!" "And if I don't, will you come over here to do something about it?" Malachi's permanent smile evaporates like the warm water on his ebony skin, as he leans over into Tom's face. Tom is motionless, in bewilderment as is everyone else who is watching. In the stillness only the sound of steamy running water makes a droning sound. "Ok man," Tom blurts out softly, backing away defeated. Fear sets deep in his eyes like there's nothing he can say or do about it. Tom throws his towel, not out of frustration but out of embarrassment, and sits on the bench where it lands, as his boys try to cheer him up. The damage has been done.

I'm leaning against a wall on the breezeway before the bell rings for class one morning, jiving with Jessie Hawkins and Ron Briggs, two hood buddies. Someone hits my shoulder. I turn, a chubby petite black girl in fourth period English, Mitzi Evans, stands next to me with a frightened look. "Hi Kenny, see that white boy in the plaid shirt? Can you stop him from messing with me? He sits behind me in third period and pulls my hair and says 'Negroes stink.'" She speaks in a soft voice. Jesse, Ron and I agrees to jack him up, but Mitzi proudly says "No. Just scare him, an apology would be nice." Mitzi's a smart girl who thinks that this white boy sitting behind her may retaliate or make threats. We agree to rattle him with a "stare down" tactic, which is used on the streets when we're about to kick some ass, and psyche him out. We stake this white boy out, following him every chance we get until he notices our staring. We keep it up on breezeways between classes, waiting for him to break. In a short while he rubbernecks nervously to see where we are. As paranoia sets in, Jessie wants to jump. "No. Let's play it cool so we don't get in any trouble. We'll follow him around for two days until he snaps," I say.

Within two days, he breaks down. "Everywhere I go, you guys follow! Did I do something wrong? Please, please stop staring at me! Leave me alone!" He clearly is rattled, so we work the final snare. "See those boys over there," Mitzi says, pointing at us. "They want you to have this." Looking confident and reassured, she hands the boy our note. The white boy nervously opens it and reads: "White boy, we gonna rotate kicking your ass every day you put your cracker hands on Mitzi!" We await her report the next day. Mitzi comes over smiling. "He's sorry now, wanna know what he can do to make it up to me." "Treat you to lunch for one week!" Ronnie laughs. "No. I can't accept that," Mitzi resists. "I just want him to apologize." We agree to let it go at that. She thanks us for helping her out. We share a laughing moment together for the importance of looking out for one another at a white school.

We all think Mitzi let the white boy off too easily. One day Jesse sees him leaving class and making the mistake of going into a bathroom stall to take a crap. We decide to have some fun. Jessie and Ron stand watch at the door. Finally, he comes out startled. "You forgot about your ass wiping today didn't you?" I'm bluffing to see how he reacts. "What I do man? What I do?" "You think blacks stink, don't you?" "I apologized; I don't pull her hair anymore." "No. But you shamed her." "What you gonna do Kenny? It's your fight or else I will," Jessie says itching to fight. Realizing he's not getting jumped, he gathers himself and walks up in my face. "Come off it man! Get a grip!" "So, what you gonna do?" His confidence builds. I'm surprised he's called my bluff. Ron and Jesse egg me on. I can't back down. Before he cracks his mouth, I pop him in it. "That's for calling her a sink Negro!" Then again, pop! "That's for pulling her hair!" Standing an inch taller and rail thin, I underestimate his "Ag boy's strength. He pins me against the wall, and I catch a hard-grazing right on the chin. He's cock strong but his reflexes are slow. I sidestep and catch him with a left on his nose as it drips blood. "Get him Ken!" Ron yells. "Ya betta not let that white boy kick yo ass!" Jessie laughs, realizing the white boy is testy and capable of it. We tussle a moment as I punch him in the stomach. He throws a wild punch that misses and I counter with a blow to his stomach, taking the wind and the fight out of him. Ron is guarding the door and yells out, "Somebody's coming!" We rush out onto the corridor mixing in with a small crowd of students, leaving the gagging white boy bent over. I make it to my next class trembling. "Are you alright?" a classmate asks. "I'm cool." But I'm really not. Uncontrollable rage building inside of me scares me. Someday I'm going to get hurt or hurt someone else.

My sisters, Gail's in tenth grade at Dan McCarty High and Regina at Fort Pierce Elementary, are making good grades, adjusting well with fewer black students in attendance and fewer racial incidents. I put less emphasis on studying. "Kenny, I expect your grades to get better, you can do better than this . . ." Mama pauses in mid-sentence, adjusts her reading glasses to review my report card. "Mama, I got mostly Bs," I say whining.

Report card reviews can be scary with Mama meticulously going over every letter grade, jotting down notes on the subjects that need improvement. She believes in establishing communication with teachers early in the year. And if necessary, she writes a personal note with assurances and suggestions for improvements. I get stuck with extra homework.

"What about your conduct? You got good grades, but how are you adjusting?" She pauses over coffee. "Don't worry, I'm doing ok." I'm sneaky and my conduct is suspect. Mama interrogates like a detective, even like a psychologist, to get inside my head trying to find out where I am emotionally ever since I was in grade school.

Mama's every bit a dreamer as Dr. King. She believes that racial equality is worth every bit of the struggle. In her wisdom, she understands adjusting to an all-white school takes time. Nothing can be more of a relief than to let your guard down, relax and not worry. I'm not optimistic and I lose patience fast. I escape a few suspensions for my conduct. I'm lucky.

Neighbors are telling Mama: "I ain't lettin my child be no guinea pig at a white school!" Most black parents think the few of us crossing over are experiments in abuse. Anticipating humiliating incidents, we're gladly run with open arms back to all-black segregated Lincoln Park Academy. Mama never thought of going backward she was taking her children into forward progress. I have thoughts of betrayal because all my buddies are enrolled at Lincoln

Park Academy. I must answer some unsettling questions: "No! Attending a white school doesn't make me better than you. No, just being around white people all day doesn't make me act and talk white. No! I don't plan on being an Oreo cookie."

During sixth period, Ms. Garin teaches social studies at St. Lucie Junior High and she sometimes cuts out newspaper articles to use in her class discussions. Since I read the newspaper daily, I'm familiar with the hot topics on her desk. She avoids opportunities to discuss articles on school integration and the most controversial topics describing blacks as socially and culturally disadvantaged. Garin goes out of her way to discuss city government issues, which is out of character to leave out social issues. I sit quietly during my first year, absorbing it all, as white teachers are trying to stay calm. My stomach churns in response to the rigid teachers who avoid racial issues. I listen to privileged white attitudes brought out in gossipy topics. "It's so unfair that the city government wants to allow my neighbor to extend his parking lot." "My father sits on an advisory board and there are ordinances…" On and on it goes. Black classmates listen impatiently as this foreign chatter flies over our heads.

On rare occasions a racial topic sneaks into a class discussion, which creates obvious discomfort for our teachers. They all do a quick tap dance shift away and dare to recognize our raised hands. I suppose there's fear of candidly exposing personal feelings and beliefs. Such moments help us to better understand each other; to grapple with our fears, beliefs and racial stereotypes in hopes we will derive at cultural sensitivity.

One day I get frustrated after Garin finally cuts out an article on school integration. A white girl naively believes forced integration threatens her way of life. "I think it's so unfair for them to come over here. We have to wait in long lines to eat lunch, dress out for P.E., shower." "Ooh, that's so awful sweetie. It has been difficult with inadequate space here." Garin sugar coats over the real issue, obscuring reality. Many more will come, and it's time you accept that fact and adapt. This is what should have been said. Disgusted, I finally lash out interrupting that crap, "We deserve a better education just like you. We're here to make some changes around here."

Garin anticipates my occasional outbursts, and diverts and side-steps instead of examining my point: "All right class, let's move on to the topic at hand." A few socially conscious whites become increasing interested in knowing about our problems. "Ms. Garin, can we spend some time before class talking about racial problems in school?" The Jewish girl who happens to blurt this out causes some grumbling. "It's about time!" "Can we bring in our own news clippings?" I suggest. Before I go further, "Kenneth! You are disrupting my class!"

At first, Garin appears timid, opening dialogue from a willing and integrated class. She should have seized that moment and nurtured new understanding from a black perspective. I suppose her reluctance epitomizes the ambivalence and frustrations of a pending teachers' strike. I discover that our school board suggested cultural sensitivity workshops, but our white teachers are ill-prepared on the subject. Class after class they retreat from dealing with we—invisibles exposes their weaknesses. Such an embarrassment and the threat of ineffectiveness looms over all of us.

Some high-strung blacks are problematic. In each class I become increasingly opinionated in my commentary. Garin, because of her insensitivity, takes my actions as intimidating and threatening rather than delving and probing into why I speak up and out. What does occur, to my dismay, is a "U" for unsatisfactory on my report card in all categories pertaining to citizenship (behavior, adjustment, effort and attitude). I have a bad attitude according to Garin because I question her. I'm taught at home through family debates to question and participate in discussions and I do so in class because I want to bring attention to racial issues.

Mama writes a note questioning what I specifically do wrong. Garin writes: "Kenneth interrupts class and has difficulty controlling his anger." Mama can't afford taking time off work for a conference on the matter. She previously addressed my attitude with other teachers. She stops me one morning as I'm about to leave for school. "Ms. Garin mentioned that if you interrupt class again, she'll report you, and they'll put a board on your butt with my permission. Or I'll come out and do it myself. You don't want me taking off work for that!"

I explain blacks are overlooked and devalued, and it causes me to become frustrated and angry. "She won't recognize my hand," I plead. "You must understand white teachers have problems too. It takes time, so in the meantime keep your mouth shut and do your work! Dammit!"

With few black teachers and faculty to offer support, fights and suspensions are common. Accidental bumps happen frequently. A white boy bumps into me, I go berserk and I punch him in the nose. "Why you hit me man!" His nose bleeds as I swing once again. I don't recognize Joseph, a curly haired boy from my sixth period PE class. One of only a few white boys are brave enough to risk being called "n….r lover" and welcome me to junior high. "Why me man? I thought we're friends!" he repeats, choking teary-eyed. "I'm sorry. I'm so angry," I say ashamedly, walking away. Fear was in his eyes and he must have seen the rage in mine.

"Hey Kenny, that's how you do it, you knock the hell out that cracker!" Montee, a headhunter (to punch someone without reason) yells braggingly. "Give me some skin!" Blacks and whites pass by shaking their heads disapprovingly.

Rage beyond anger is a liability I can't shake off. Angry outbursts towards my sisters is alienating me from my family. Mama worries about my erratic mood and behavior suspects that television and newspaper accounts of racial unrest must be contributing to it. Day after day, I am a lit fuse ready to explode any time someone ticks me off.

One day I'm called upon, an unexpectedly rare opportunity to answer a question. Unprepared, I blurt out the wrong answer. White boys sitting behind me snicker. "Man! He's dumb, just like the rest of um!" I turn thinking it's Ricky, a blond redneck and his boys. "You got a problem?" he states grinning. The others strain to control their laughter. "I'll see you after class," I whisper to him. I wait patiently for days and finally catch him in a bathroom, smoking. There is a mixture of blacks and whites congregating and he's without his buddies. I call him out: "Ricky, I'm gonna kick your ass!" Suddenly a teacher bolts in to catch a few boys smoking. The bathroom, notorious for fights, is under surveillance so we clear out. Ricky escapes, and I have time to calm down.

I'm normally quiet in class unless I have something I need to get off my chest. But I get snappy with Ms. Colcord and she requests a conference, curious whether anything is disturbing me. Mama reaches out, but I keep giving superficial reasons for my behavior. Finally, I take her suggestion and sign up for little league baseball. Something—anything to take the edge off.

When I'm not playing baseball, I join intramural football and basketball teams at school. On the football field, rage appears during practices that evolves into a shoving match with a white player, simply because he delivers a clean tackle when I catch a pass. Coach Burleson benches me for poor sportsmanship. I must get a hold of myself emotionally if I'm to survive the school year in a system, I believe, that expects blacks to fail.

After fifth period one afternoon, I hear, just ahead of me, a familiar clicking sound of metal taps from the heels of cowboy boots striking the sidewalk. I look up at Brad maneuvering through a crowd, dressed like the Dallas Cowboys full-back Walt Garrison on a popular Skoal commercial. He has a piece of Skoal smokeless tobacco stuffed between his cheeks and gums, the favorite of most rednecks. Brad's left jaw looks swollen as he bends over and spits into a flowerbed sitting off the sidewalk. His sun baked skin and rugged features from farming make him look older than he is. Brad's alone without his flunky buddies close by to intimidate and help bolster his bully reputation. Most everyone outside his circle of friends wants to kick his cocky ass.

Brad runs slow as molasses and has powder puff hands that miss every pass. He likes playing quarterback during third period P.E. Jessie gets angry and snatches the ball out of his hands and takes over as quarterback. Jessie's athletic, a star infielder who can play any position on our summer league baseball team. Brad is funny and easy going, but unpredictable when angry. Jessie steps up to him: "You play receiver today, so let us see what you got." Jessie throws a pass that goes through Brad's hands, striking his head. "Mannnn! You the most uncoordinated white boy out here!" Jesse takes a word out of white boys' vocabulary. Everyone cracks up.

Coach Burleson watches and laughs. Brad pulls a tantrum whenever things doesn't go his way, and he does again as he heads for the sidelines. He pouts with a few of his redneck buddies in pursuit.

Coach Burleson confronts Brad with a tongue lashing. "Son, why do I go through this with you every day?" Brad sits on the sidelines ignoring coach. "Because I don't like being around Negroes!" he snaps. "I'm not asking you to like Negroes, I'm asking you to cooperate, to get along if you plan to pass my class!"

Brad's defiant as ever and refuses to dress out for P.E. as the rest of class sweats in the heat. Every day Brad and his buddies sit on the sidelines laughing, whispering, and cracking jokes. Brad disguises his humor when he says some guys, and I pay close attention, listening carefully to his peculiar jokes about intellect: "When do an armadillo know it's safe to cross a highway? He won't. Like some people he's too dumb to know what coming ahead. What do you tell a coon who counts to 7 and...?" "Brad was making fun of blacks," I say to Jesse. "He ain't worth it man!" A sandy headed white boy warns, standing nearby. Jesse picks up a rock, waits for the right moment and strikes Brad on the arm. "He's a jerk man. Ignore him, he's nothin but white trash!" Surprised by this new revelation, not expecting this term to be used against Brad, deserves a laugh. But I don't like the humor. I see it in the same negative light we use n....r against each other. The negative connotations both offend. I detest that word. All the pain and misery it has caused since our ancestors arrived on the shores of Jamestown, Virginia.

Whites degrade each other with "white trash" and come to our defense? I'm curious why he calls Brad white trash. "He's poor, so what gives him the right to dislike you? He needs to shut the hell up!" the boy says. "So, am I black trash?" The white boy looks perplexed. "No. I mean he gets discriminated by whites like you too," he adds. Simply put, his distinction surprisingly mean, Brad's poor just as much as most blacks are. Brad in comparison to white upper and middle class status words has no bite, no relevance. He is viewed as of lesser social status therefore like most blacks. Brad takes heat just like blacks by his own. I come to realize whites are just as twisted hating each other as we are.

So, here we are meeting each other on the breezeway. I give Brad a "stare down" tactic. Tough, brazen, cool under pressure, Brad is unfazed. He turns, passes by me as he spits a wad of tobacco juice at me that misses. "What ya gonna do about it?" he smirks. I go berserk and punch him in the face. As we're about to go at each other, two burly white male teachers snatch us up from behind as we're kicking and screaming. We get a trip to Jack Brennan's office, the dean of students. Brennan, a big man with bushy eyebrows and mustache, bends down in our faces with a refresher course on the consequences of fighting. "Do you like it here Kenneth?" "It's ok," I say dishonestly, avoiding his eyes. "Do you like it here Brad?" Brad looks up. "Yes." "If you boys plan to remain at this school, you better get along. I got a crowded school with enough problems."

For days Brad doesn't show up for PE. Coach Valentine discovers during roll call that Brad's parents withdrew him from school. A small but increasing number of white parents are withdrawing their children from public schools as they flee integration. As racial incidents increase, private schools spring up in St. Lucie County and the surrounding counties. Even some black parents, fearing the worst, transfer their children to other county schools that don't have a history of racial incidents.

I constantly feel enraged and its intensity scares me. I don't want to be labeled a fighter, which is what I have become known as to the principal and dean. Mama reminds me that with patience comes maturity and with silence comes growth. At thirteen, I have little patience. Mama doesn't know that my anger lies with white people was caused by that man in the park.

The Panthers piles into the back of Coach Albert "Baylock" Benjamin's old rickety pickup truck, one weekend after a little league baseball game in Hope Sound, Florida for the 46-mile trek home. Fifteen boys cram into the back of the truck. Older teammates intimidate the younger smaller ones as prime targets of horseplay. Teasing turns into heated arguments that escalate to near fights. I dread these long trips home. I'm not the smallest nor the youngest, no longer sickly and weak. Normally, I'm quiet and introverted around teammates, and then unexpectedly come out of my shell in defense of timid teammates succumbing to physical abuse. The older boys play the "head game" mercilessly, popping the young defenseless boys on their heads. I get targeted under the cover of darkness. Someone tees off upside my head. I immediately go into a rage. All the humiliating years of enduring teasing, I had never once retaliated. Grandma's wisdom teaches me well: "Don't let teasing make you angry, it gives them power over you, causes more pain. Ignoring kills their spirit and makes you stronger."

For too long I have suppressed my anger. Older now, I unleash it with a vengeance. Not for the sake of name calling, but to challenge anyone thinking I'm weak and won't fight back. Rage surges and overwhelms me emotionally and I'm ready to fight like a rabid animal. Persistent teasing about my plagiocephaly has taught me to cope. I vow that no chump is ever going to pop me upside my head again without a fight. I go after the jokesters: Henry "Goose" Mims, Kenny Mills, Leroy Woody and Chris Benjamin. All overwhelm me from every angle, direction, every turn. With the truck moving I can't keep balance with little space. My reaction time is slow. I'm a sitting duck at a circus shooting gallery. I see stars from their onslaught and hear laughter after every lick.

"Coach! Coach! Make um stop!" Raymond "Booty" Gandy cries out until Baylock pulls over. I push the oldest and strongest, Chris, Coach Baylock's nephew, rather than his co-conspirators. Surprised, Chris a ninth grader he and I both know that I don't stand a chance. It doesn't matter. I'm enraged. My pride and peace of mind are at stake. Chris bows up his chest, our eyes meet and he's ready to pounce just as Baylock intervenes. "What's this all about? "Y'all teammates. Stop horse playing back there before someone falls off!" Chris doesn't see fear in my fiery eyes, only glowing intensity with nothing to lose. No one ever tees off on my head again.

One of the earlier championship Pony League teams. Top row on left: Coach Albert "Baylock" Benjamin, teammates Jo Jo Osborne, Charles Johnson, unknown player, Robert Birks, Harold Bentley, Coach Wesley Dixon. Front row: First three unknown, Donald Brooks, coach Baylock nephew, Chris Benjamin, Henry Mims, Coach Emanuel Green missing. (Courtesy of Wesley Dixon).

School is the perfect playground to unleash anger. I roam around campus with a group of project boys who are just as angry. In defiance of school rules, we call ourselves "headhunters." We roam breezeways looking for a quick fight. Our firebrand activity is the "head game" tactic brought over from black schools. We target rednecks sporting short military-style crew cuts. Someone yells, "Hey honky!" as we're walking behind, and when he looks back one of us circle around pops him upside his head. He turns again to look, another pop! Repeatedly unleashing an onslaught of pop, pop, pop! From every angle the victim's head reddens and he becomes enraged with defenseless anger. Doing crazy herky-jerky moves, he breaks free running and howling like a wolf in the night.

Anger causes me to act outside my true self. I plot, scheme, waste time and energy rather than focus on schoolwork. With vengeful obsessions, I mistakenly enter a bathroom on an isolated corridor known as a redneck hangout. I find myself staring into the eyes of four boys with greased back ducktails, like James Dean portraying a defiant guy in the movie, "Rebel Without a Cause." Ag boys are known to dislike blacks. All wear blue club jackets with "Future Farmers for America" emblazoned on the back and some with a small rebel flag.

The Ag boys mostly hang out on the isolated F-wing corridor of the technical and mechanical labs. Two wear pointed cowboy boots, jeans with big western buckles and a wad of snuff or tobacco lodged between their lips and cheek. I enter with an air of caution. Our eyes lock, sizing each other up. Two are using two of the three latrines. Two others stand over the sink restyling their greasy slick backed ducktails. It's too late to break for the door. I hesitate a moment. To retreat gives the impression I'm afraid and it will backfire later. I walk slowly past the two who are staring in the mirror, watching my back as their laughter ceases into silence. Entering a stall is a risky move that would make me vulnerable to a gang-style attack. I cautiously gather myself and go to the middle latrine between the two and relieve myself. A bold tenacious move considering I am breaking one established black code: "Never enter the enemy's bathroom alone without protection in numbers." My mind races with paranoid thoughts of a frontal and rear attack. My heart pounds with a smothering rush of adrenaline. Everything's blurry as the walls close in. I sweat and become dizzy, feeling faint as laughter echoes and reverberates off the walls. I nervously spin around with a clenched fist, expecting a fight. "Come on you motha f..kas, you want a piece of me!" "Y'all ain't bad, come on!" I yell like a fool. Bathroom walls look much smaller as the boys stand in silence, staring. "What the hell is wrong with you rat? (school term for 7th graders) You gone crazy or just having a bad day?" All are ninth graders leave laughing, as I stand alone and embarrassed.

I gasp for breath, I'm hyper-ventilating in my own stupidity, slumped over the sink and feeling faint. I throw cold water over my sweaty face, trying to calm myself down and return to my senses. In the mirror, I see a disturbing image of myself staring back with undeniable rage. I'm frightened by it since it is causing serious mood swings, impulsiveness, erratic behavior and it exposes me to risky situations.

Arriving at St. Lucie Junior High, I had hoped to be judged on character and individual merit alone. I never expected that fighting my way through school would accomplish anything.

Expectations for black assimilation into white traditions contributes to racial tensions and exacerbates my anger. The administration puts more time and energy into assimilation, and less time into exploring the reasons for racial tensions. Blacks are seeking administration support, and a few whites have our concerns at heart. Aside from Principal Mullins, few white faculty members listen. Concern, I suppose is accountability—good local news and reports to Housing Education and Welfare (HEW) for federal aid rather than real social change is something but clearly not enough. Urging blacks to initiate white friendships is overemphasized. With 1,300 students, next year, St. Lucie Junior High School's population is expected to swell past 1,671, with a shortage of teachers.

The idea of walking lockstep to a sanitized version of how an integrated student body should behave is insulting. In my displeasure, I have no desire to condition myself in such a manner. Since our arrival, there are no welcoming committees or any transitioning programs. Only sidewalks and bathrooms filled with racial graffiti. Our administration hardly listens to real black concerns about adapting to an unwelcoming environment. A few good "black poster child" images are displayed to news cameras to promote a good integration story.

In class I'm angry how we're marginalized. I don't want to know anything else unique to white culture. I feel invisible sitting among my white peers. My GPA spirals downward. I become more and more emotionally unraveled, not academically inclined as before. Simple mistakes I make on assignments gets me increasingly irritable. I cringe with anxiety, embarrassed each time a black classmate reads poorly, misses assignments or gives wrong answers. Rumors spread that white teachers inflate their reports unfavorably to the school board on black academic and social progress; stereotyping will magnify black failures which advances the myth that whites are academically and socially superior.

I suppose, we're expected to sit idle, since we don't know what else to do. We act civilly, not reacting to subtle giggles and snickers by our white peers, but this only adds fuel to my anger. I'm convinced that court ordered integration will never change the hearts and minds of white people until they first change the defect that's within them.

Sometimes vindication comes unexpectedly. I lay in wait, knowing that it's just a matter of time before my chance arrives. And it does come when Kenny Mills lets arrogance gets in his best teasing about my head. I can handle it; I have the power, he doesn't. But when he plays the dirty dozen, it gives me an excuse for vengeance lying dormant—waiting subconsciously. Not for some jive classroom remark directed at me, but for what I believe he took part in teeing off on my head a week earlier that night returning home from a baseball game.[20]

Kenny's a popular teammate, good all-round baseball player but a jokester and slightly immature. I believe he hoped to impress older and influential teammates Chris Benjamin and Leroy Woody teeing off on my head than younger teammates. His part in the "head game" becomes my redirected revenge.

During PE in the locker room, I punch him in the mouth, swinging wildly. He retreats, and we both damage wire locker baskets. While in Ms. Colcord's class, I said his answer was incomplete. I don't appreciate his "Yo Mama" joke and I become enraged with a flashback of "head popping" in the back of Baylock's truck.

The incident and minor damage to school property earns two Kennys' trip to the dean's office. "Hurst, not you again," Jack Brennan says disgustedly. Instead of facing suspension, we get a lecture on school rules. Brennan is a fair Dean, Brad a white boy I got into trouble received similar warnings. Towering over us, "You

---

[20] Kenny Mills, Pastor, community activist and founder of The Soul Saving Bible Station reached the Pinnacle of his ministry by establishing programs designed to build character, cultural awareness, and meet the educational needs of inner-city youth of Fort Pierce.

boys speak intelligently, don't waste time on such trivial matters. Don't waste two days of study hall. Bring your books," Brennan says towering over us. I'm lucky. I dodge another bullet.

Black students have need for recognition, to be heard, get our point across. Too often, we're labeled angry militants. We're invisible slipping into cracks and crevices or into a Vail of alienation. I witness it during arrivals of "new guinea pig" even among assimilated blacks for class recognition—a "turning against the other."

Dean Jack Brennan a burly Big Ten football player see potential in me as black suspensions soar disproportionately.

When three academically competitive classmates, in this instance, Larry Lee, Kenny Mills and I so desperately want to be heard. After much waving our hands, Ms. Colcord finally recognizes me over Larry later turns into an argument was counter-productive to our level of consciousness. The troubling thing that sets me off is Larry has an engaging personality was totally out of character, get lure into Kenny joke and jump to his defense. I jump out of my seat and challenge Larry not Kenny Mills toe to toe until Ms. Colcord intervenes. Larry's a class act and we later apologize, and exchange school photos, as does Colcord as a gesture of kindness evident to our upbringing.[21]

I enter class to snickering classmates pointing to some coward hastily scribbling "n....r lover" on the chalkboard. Lola Cox enters seconds later and rushes over to erase the harm already done. The class is in complete silence. "So, what you gonna do about it Ms. Cox?" I say, looking sternly into her eyes. "Yeah Ms. Cox. If you ain't we will!" black classmates say in agreement, waiting for her response. She hesitates to think how to handle it. Normally, she takes charge of her class. "I need to know who did this. I won't tolerate such language!" she says, speaking softly but with authority. "I promise there will be

consequences. You will be punished!" Cox is one of a few white teachers who is sensitive to the needs of her black students. The next day she announces that the culprit has been caught and has received a three-day suspension. She refuses to give a name. Later, rumors fly that a white girl in an adjacent classroom knows the culprit. I join a few black classmates looking for her, but we can't find the girl. We wait three days and discover who missed three consecutive days of class. It's Ricky, the joker I almost fight. He gets the stare down tactic until I catch him in the bathroom alone. I step to his face, snarling. "So, you hate Ms. Cox because she cares about blacks' ah?" "What!" I explode into a barrage of punches to his face and stomach. He screams like a little girl. "Don't beat me up man! Don't. I'm sorry. I didn't mean it!" I anticipate he'll put up a decent fight, but he doesn't.

For years blacks have struggled to deconstruct the myths around the passivity of previous generations. The exaggerated images of Negroes shuffling, skinning and grinning obediently have been the prevalent stereotype on movie screens. Generations of whites have accepted and expected such demeaning characteristics in their domestic servants. I suppose upon our arrival, whites expected to

---

[21] Larry Lee, businessman, owner of State Farm insurance agency came into prominence elected into the State of Florida House of Representatives serving from 2012 to 2018, in the 84th district which includes St. Lucie County.

dish out their aggressions and we'll respond passively, without ever fighting back. It doesn't matter that Ms. Cox is white. I must defend her on principle for her courage. She admits changing her prejudices and ill-will, and vowed defending what she believes as unfair treatment against blacks. After punching Ricky, his face reddens and his pimples burst and bleed. "Speak another bad word to Ms. Cox and it'll be worse." His eyes widen in fear. I must look like a raging lunatic.

Sometimes during quiet moments, I think of Daddy, how Jim Crow segregation generated so much anger in him. Seven years have passed since I last saw him. My memories are fading. When Daddy calls regularly, I don't know what to say anymore. I say anything. The more Mama and her friends tell me about Daddy, the more I sense we're alike with his pride standing up against Jim Crow. Doing what black men do, suppress anger to cope and keep jobs to support families. Son of a strict Baptist minister in Wrightsville, Georgia, Daddy a dapper dresser was known for flaunting his pride around disapproving whites. Brutally beating the taunting son of a prominent white family in revenge almost ends up with the lynching of his brother Clinton, who was left for dead. Daddy escaped shots from an unknown white gunman, car chases and hiding out in the attics of relatives' homes to evade sheriffs while hearing threats coming from below. "If Charles and Hubert didn't enlist in the US Army, crackers was gonna kill um both." Charles got so angry in those days; we were afraid for his life," Aunt Georgia says.

The more I learn and compare my similarities to Daddy, the more uneasy and scared I become. I don't want to end up as he, driven to a state of depression. My conduct at school is surely being mentioned, I suppose. Grandma's the only one I can confide in. In her late 70s, she has endured much under Jim Crow, yet maintains an unyielding faith in God. I have never known Grandma to languish in hatred or encourage it. "Leave it to God's redeeming mercy, colored folks will overcome white folks' evil ways," she often says.

I can listen to Grandma all day, foretelling God's will to man's wrongdoings against his fellow man. At school, I grow impatient waiting on God to do something about it. One day the sweet smell of candied yams lures me into the kitchen. Grandma pulls out a tray of hot biscuits and she shifts around on her bowed legs. She notices me watching her. "Scaldee? I kin see somethin heavy on ya mind," she declares. Whatever I hide from Mama, years of wisdom and a keen eye in the spiritual realm, Grandma will detect a soul in trouble. Like good old times during our pot-watching days, I haven't opened up to Grandma in a long time. She moves around the kitchen as I pour out my soul to her. "White people don't want us…don't like us…teachers ignore us…Mama want me to sit, say and do nothin about it." Grandma speaks with a soft soothing prophetic voice in her Gullah or Geechee dialect opening doors to understanding. Her poetic words, always thought-provoking, have for me a kind of vindication full of optimism in the old axiom: "You must reap what you sow." "Scaldee, colored folk are rising up now, aint gonna take that mess no more. White folk don't wanna bow down to God and answer for their evil ways. Integration changes things."

I don't feel comfortable sharing with Grandma what I have felt over the course of months— uncontrollable rage. How it manifests into recurrent nightmares. In my dreams, I'm unable to elude a red-eyed grotesque looking white man endlessly chasing me with an iron poker throughout a park while a host of onlookers with no faces cheer and laugh. Finally, he catches up after I trip and fall. Standing over me, he lunges with his rod just as I awaken. I always awaken in time frighten before he thrusts it into my stomach.

Other times, I have a terrible dream of an incident I witnessed. During the summer of 1962 Grandma took me to see the annual Sandy Shoes Parade on Orange Avenue. The last event, culminating seven days of rodeo, square dances, beauty contests, food, children's activities, floats, Color Guards, Shriners, marching bands and all its pageantry, is for whites only. Jim Crow laws not yet abolished, so whites get "front row seats," while blacks stand behind them.

To avoid nasty inconveniences and hassles, blacks get a better view either by sitting or standing on the hoods of cars. Under Grandma's watchful eye, I, along with other boys, climb trees to get an even better view. The last event is Hundreds of "cracker cowboys" on horseback from Fort Pierce's Cattleman's Association (many from Okeechobee traditionally follow after the Sandy Shoes Parade) create a stir. Cowboys ride horses, shoot guns in the air, do rope and horse tricks in their cracker tradition. Clowns following in the rear dress in colorful outfits while others toss candies from floats, which is the highlight of the parade.[22]

A clown shoveling horse manure yells out, "N.....s gets back!" Black children push toward the front, hoping to get a few candies left by white kids. An overly zealous black boy caught up in the moment of excitement steps off the sidewalk into the street. As he bends over picking up pieces of candy, a "cracker cowboy" takes a whip from his saddle and gives him several lashes across the back. The boy's not wearing a shirt and yells out in pain as the crowd watches, many screaming in shock. As the boy struggles to his feet, another cracker on horseback takes his rope, loops it into a lariat and starts swinging overhead and around the screaming boy's waist. He ties it to the horn of his saddle and drags the boy on the hot pavement for a short distance. I watch in horror as pieces of flesh open on his back. The boy curls up in pain with the rope around his waist. He goes into convulsive kicks in shock against laughing hecklers. One white man yells, "That n....r got what he deserves!" Those "cracker cowboys" ride off leaving the boy curled up on the hot paved street.

"Let him go! Let him go now!" I hear several black men yell, pushing forward through the crowd. It's too late. What could they

---

[22] I'm a Florida cracker," an old white man once proudly said picking tomatoes. Cautious yet surprised by his revelation, I discover cracker is not necessarily a disparaging term. First cattle brought from Spain thrived in Florida over 500 years ago, long before they came to the American West. Cracker denotes a sound produced by the whips of Florida's cowboys. The sound is as loud as gunshots while herding cattle, hence the term cracker cowboys or Florida crackers. "...Cracker common to Georgia and Florida...the word comes from the skill with which stock tenders cracked their whips." *Florida the Land of Romance*, Dorothy Dodd, 1956, pp.56-57. Other accounts of Florida cracker culture, "corn cracker" applied to Daytona Beach moonshiners use of cracked corn mashed after fermentation, distilled into 'white lightening...nickname Georgia Cracker believed to evolve from the term corn cracker. *Cracker: Cracker Culture in Florida History*. Dana M. Ste. Claire, 1998 p.30. Cracker Jack and Cracker Barrel are synonymous with cracker culture.

have done anyway? A cracker cowboy has already jumped from his horse untying the boy. A few whites jeer and laughter pierces through a stunned crowd. One of the black men lifts the boy up and carries him in his arms. As the boy cries, I see blood and open flesh from welts and scrape marks lining his back and stomach. As the black man, with bulging eyes and intense facial expressions, screams with anger and fear for a doctor, he's drowned out by the hysterical black and white crowd.

No medical help comes. The men rush off with the boy, disappearing into a crowd of whites slowly and quietly stepping aside. Angry blacks gather as a heavy-set black lady yells, "That boy didn't do nothing wrong for that to happen! What yawl men gonna do about it?" Several black women grumble. Their question dissipates into muteness as the men's eyes shift downward as if the answer can be found in the soil beneath their feet. A white woman looks over, reacting to the black women. "Somebody should find a policeman and press charges!" Grandma suddenly walks up, grabs my arm and yanks me away as several white policemen appear and disperse the crowd. That white woman speaks first, then the heavy-set black woman, but the white officer appears to be disinterested.

Horseman from the Cattleman's Association strike fear in many blacks with loud snapping whips, tossing lassos, gun and rifle fire as clowns follow in the rear. Photo by The News Tribune

Walking home, listening to the angry crowd quickly changes my sadness into fury. As a people, we're truly powerless. I have nightmares haunting images of that black boy holding onto a rope, being dragged down Orange Avenue as chunks of flesh dangle from his back. At the end of my dream, a scene from the incident changes and something more horrific happens—he looks dead, extends a hand out to me to help him. I always awaken frightened, heart thumping, breathing laboriously. I imagine the boy's tormented because he never got his justice. I think about that for a long time and also think about me not getting my justice either, from the white man in the park.

Chapter 13

THE LEARNING CURVE

"Tell your mother that Ms. Hussain and I are going to a teachers' orientation and awards banquet." On a hot summer day, I was perched under a shady mango tree, sipping a soda trying to cool off. Ms. Beverly Espy and Gustarva Hussain are neighbors and veteran teachers winding down their careers. Ms. Espy substitutes when my teacher is absent, and she's a regrettable replacement for me. She tells Mama everything about me that she disapproves of. "Do you hear me?" Ms. Espy, the nosiest of neighbors asks, watching me like a hawk.

The school board's honoring Sara Douglas from our community for excellence in teaching for 35 years at segregated schools her entire career. Mama goes over to meet Beverly and Gustarva, after both returned from the banquet. What's reported sparks concern in the minds of parents and teachers alike.

Two of the guest speakers are black. The first guest speaker is the coordinator of community service programs, invited by the St. Lucie County School Board, to discuss teaching techniques and materials for the "economically and culturally deprived." The majority are white teachers who have limited or no experience with black students and are unprepared for integration in the upcoming year. Considering all the national attention created by the 1963 integration of Central High School in Little Rock, Arkansas, many white teachers now have concern.

The second speaker, a rather muscular black man, represents the Office of Economic Opportunity (OEO) and its anti-poverty program. Before delivering his topic, he pulls out a small Confederate flag and places it on a table. Standing on the podium behind a lectern, he peers down at a crowded audience of mostly white teachers. He reminds them that every community has two cities—one mainstream and the other invisible.

"This flag (rebel flag) is a symbol of the South and you're a part of the South!" he shouts. "If you wrap a cross in oil and burn it, it doesn't shake my faith, nor does a flag waved as a symbol of hatred!" As he snarls, sweat drips from his brow and forehead illuminating his dark skin. "Oh, he surely got those white folks attention alright!" Gustarva says laughing. The idea seeing this big black muscular man grimacing and holding a rebel flag must have scared the hell out of whites.

This prelude opens a topic for discussion. What's it like being an economically and culturally deprived Negro child today? The school board wants to get a jump and address the integration issue, hoping to reduce white teachers' anxieties. We expect that racial problems might be ignored by the absence of communication between teachers and students. For this reason, white teachers express feeling ill-prepared and inadequate, never having taught a "deprived" black child. Classroom problems are best solved by informed teachers understanding how to help every child learn much as possible. White teachers find themselves in the awkward position of being privileged and completely detached from the black experience.

The muscular black guest speaker points out to white teachers that they should not assume that a culturally deprived child is dumb merely because of a low IQ score. "Mental tests are based on the culture of the middle class, and because they don't know that culture we say they're dumb. They're not. What if the tests were prepared by culturally deprived students, we'd all flunk!" he adds.

His closing remarks raise brows, causing a stir of controversy among black and white teachers. "You must treat each student according to his needs. Look at the Negro as a "separate individual," his sensory perception is different. If he hasn't seen something before, how can he know?"

I realize that although black teachers do their best with what they have, receiving an inferior education is a costly one. Despite my disadvantages

I don't think of myself as part of a test tube experiment. I want to compete equally, with support and encouragement without special treatment.

The greatest educational deprivation I experience far greater than at St. Lucie Junior High happens at segregated schools, with no access to updated materials. I have noticed that shortages at a white school do not compare.

Before integration, caring, trusting and nurturing black teachers speak expansively of unity—we're all in this together. Individual attention and emotional support, even when strict, foster in every black child the importance of getting an education. Our segregated communities and many others across America, to be sure, are tightly-knit just to survive.

I get to know teachers who live in my neighborhood and I worship next to them in church on Sundays. Some had even taught Mama, and they developed a bond in the struggle for racial equality and social justice.

In September 1966, Florida teachers of the Classroom Teachers Association (CTA), including our teachers at St. Lucie Junior High, are on strike. There are walkouts and boycotts over worsening conditions, including the shortage of school funds, low salaries, inadequate materials and a shortage of teachers. A strike extends beyond my expectations. Each day as I sit in class, teachers in other classrooms walk out. I wonder anxiously before each class if my class will be next.[23]

Integration creates overcrowded conditions more severe than the school board's expectations. Only three St. Lucie County schools integrate despite the federal law: Fort Pierce Elementary, St. Lucie Junior High, and Dan McCarty High. The average classroom size exceeds 35 students, requiring classes to be held in the cafeteria. The white school board concedes to use three old wooden Lincoln Park Academy portable buildings to accommodate the overflow.

Massive teacher resignations result from overcrowding and from

---

[23] The 1967-68 school year school begins with the Federal Education Association calling for a one-day walkout of 50,000 Florida teachers. In need of art, music and PE, teachers launch campaigns to prevent new teachers from coming to take jobs in Florida. This impact prevents tourist and new industry from coming to the Sunshine State. Teachers sought $277 million in raises over a two-year period. The Florida legislature vote to grant only $79 million.

the cutbacks in federal funds due to St. Lucie County School Board's defiance to fully integrate. Shortages in textbooks barely meeting state minimum requirements aggravate the already near impossible situation. St Lucie Junior High's outdated buildings put a strain on every possible activity. Tight conditions heighten racial tensions before anyone knows what's happening.[24]

St. Lucie Schools Lacking In Specialized Teachers

Teachers 'Disappointed'

30,000 ROAR SUPPORT

Mass Resignations

Secondary Schools In FP Are Closed

FEA Says 35,000 Teachers Resign **Teachers Show Battle Fatigue**

St. Lucie Schools Expect 10.500 Pupils at Start

Industrial Arts Lagging In Fort Pierce Schools

$1,500,000 Bond Issue for School Building Validated

'Teenage Alert' Program Sought

Quality of education can no longer be understated not just for blacks anymore, but for everyone. As Malcolm X so bluntly put it: "The chickens have come home to roost."

---

[24] From the beginning days of integration all students struggled disappointedly from distracters of teacher low morale, strikes, an outdated overcrowded school lack of adequate supplies. But for the black underprivilege white teen pregnancy, venereal diseases, alcohol and drug abuse was the ultimate dose of culture shock.

Disillusioned black parents ask if integrated schools are any better than all-black schools. The board's deliberate twelve-year integration delays move blacks to embrace the long-held adage that "The chickens have come home to roost."

Black customs and traditions that we value at our schools have all but disappeared. Now here we are, intended to blend inconspicuously together with whites as federal law pushes for complete integration. It seems all a game once I step on campus.

The first thing immediately noticeable on the breezeways (open walk areas) and in the classes is that I'm ignored. Hardly any whites care to notice that I exist. I'm invisible, just as the guest speaker mentioned. There isn't much mixing or blending. Blacks and whites keep to themselves and to each other.

In classes with few blacks, every word spoken and every question answered is closely scrutinized. As days pass, I'm watched like some exotic specimen under a microscope. Eager eyes watch and cling to every syllable I pronounce. The whispers, giggles and sly remarks make many blacks feel unwelcome, particularly after a teacher's litany of defeating comments. "No. That's not quite the answer I'm looking for." "No, your answer's incomplete, not well thought out." "Your answer isn't correct...sorry." "Speak clearly. I'm not understanding what you're saying...you're having problems expressing yourself." If internalized, the humiliation can easily make one succumb to thinking he or she is dumb.

A black classmate stumbling while attempting to answer a question causes white teachers to become frustrated, avert their eyes and attention away from our basic need to compete. With jubilation, our white counter-parts outshine us.

We sit mostly in clusters by choice, only because some teachers dare to enforce mandatory seat assignments. Sitting next to black classmates provides encouragement and a protective shield. For those needing help, this seating arrangement builds confidence and comfort. We support each other with study groups to aid those falling behind.

I still struggle grasping unfamiliar math and science concepts. I learn significant periods in American history and have a little difficulty with securing a command of the English language and effective verbal skills. Junior high imposes more discipline and a rigorous mode of learning. My white middle-class teachers have high expectations for knowledge of subject matters, expediency in learning them, and efficiency at moving from one theme to another. The fact that I must get used to their rigid styles gives little opportunity to clarify my answers when incorrect.

Class exercises are demanding and challenging. I feel, as all black students do, humiliated under constant attack and scrutiny. Our weakness in some subject areas exposes us. Consequently, blacks receive another form of humiliation when teachers simply ignore us. Our frequent wrong answers lead us to be banished altogether from class discussions. This shrewd act is unlike anything I could have imagined. Despite whatever shortcomings at our segregated school, our teachers gave us individual attention and praised us with encouraging words. Black teachers inspire an interchange of ideas and spark class participation. I need to hear that to boost my confidence. In contrast, white teachers try hard to avoid blacks who answer incorrectly. If only they would take a little time to talk to us, it might help reduce our classroom jitters.

Within months of my first semester in seventh grade, standardized California Achievement and Metropolitan Achievement tests are given to measure scholastic abilities. It's about the learning curve, to see what you know. But for many blacks, rumors abound suggesting that it is really about how we measure up against whites. We're tested over and over again. It never dawns on me until Mama reviews my report card. "Do you know why the letter "R" is beside your classes? Look." She holds up my report card and goes down each subject with her finger. "It means remedial. You're behind in subjects and need to improve." I have an "R" for every subject taken but science. And science I have the letters "BGL" below grade level. "How can you get a C in gym!" "You're guaranteed an "A" in Physical Ed and a C is just for dressing out!" she says, growing angry. I try explaining how I got Cs and Bs, trying to deflect her probing. But Mama understands the corrosive nature of enduring segregation and an inferior education. Remedial grades aren't good enough. "You must do better," she laments.[25]

I suspect our scholastic abilities are tracked against whites. I'm fortunate to get decent grades considering all the racial distractions. Mama needs answers because I've always been a good student. She knows mistreatment in any way I will speak my mind. I give lame excuses that white teachers expect passivity overreact when blacks speak their minds. That is how I explain why I am punished with having to take remedial courses. Mama looks hard at me and points a finger in my face. "Don't ever lie to me with excuses. You're where you are because of what you didn't get in segregated schools. It's not all your fault." She understands that the insensitivity of white teachers who are unaccustomed to assertive black boys will cause problems. Mama don't want me to fail as I do in fifth grade.

A significant number of black students fall below the national scholastic average and whites do as well. I lack basic knowledge in some subjects just as my white counterparts do. "Don't let it get you down," Mama says. "Laws are on the Negroes" side now, at least you have up-to-date textbooks."

It comes as no surprise that whites recognize and understand words that are familiar in their culture, which places them at an advantage. Many words that are familiar to them are foreign to us, outside the scope of our experiences. This seems to align, I suppose, with the thinking of the black man from OEO. My love for reading, word recognition and comprehension places me and a significant number of my black classmates on equal footing. But others fall behind. We aren't outclassed but out socialized in our experiences and orientation to new spheres of learning. I know early on many of my neighborhood buddies are doomed, destined to fail, once doors of integration fling wide open.

Most of my neighbors are from impoverished homes, greatly

---

[25] California Achievement Test CAT) is a national standardized test founded in 1926 and introduced in 1934 designed to test student performance level in reading language arts and math. Metropolitan Achievement Test (MAT) introduced in 1932 is a standardized test to measure student progress and trends in a school district.

disadvantaged. Few have a stable family network that is interested and provides support for education. I come to integration with a sense of pride and cultural identity learned at an early age, with the belief that I'm an "African in America" already stamped firmly in my consciousness.

For many at school, academic self-fulfillment is in special need of attention. Most of my buddies have little, if any, interest in it. Jim Crow segregation put a whammy on young impoverished black boys. However, it shouldn't have to be that way, regardless of the circumstances. I believe one is predestined to succeed with support and determination, prayer and a little luck. If a flower can grow and blossom out of cow dung, even in spite of it, one can become a productive and successful citizen.

Some people believe that integration humanized blacks for the first time, as it opened up possibilities for whites to see and understand the depth that we can think, feel, hope and achieve. We could all get to see each other's weaknesses and strengths, and that no one should be judged by their color, but by the content of his or her character. I don't come to integration with an inferiority complex, so it isn't a surprise to find some ignorant whites still clinging to the idea that they're better. When I sneak a peek at their test scores, I discover mine are just as good or better.

Competing in class, your strengths and weakness become exposed. The quality of my grammar, writings even penmanship are equal to or superior to that of any white. And some can't even spell or write complete sentences.

There are moments when I come to class motivated, feeling as other blacks the pressure to prove myself in hopes of breaking down false perceptions and stereotypes. Feelings under siege, I want badly to excel and not repeat a grade again. Certainly not at the hands of a white teacher who seems to care little if I succeed or fail.

I can't help noticing one day Grandma sitting on the sofa, frowning at the television. She reacts to a news reporter interviewing a lady in front of an elementary school. The reporter hastily tries keeping up as the lady walks briskly away, leaving the school grounds yanking a young boy by the arm. She abruptly stops, turns and looks squarely into the camera and yells out, "My child ain't spending another day in this school! I'm putting him in a private school. Let'um try an integrate that!"

There are diehard whites who're hell bent on keeping things the way they were. Into my second year at junior high, a significant number of whites withdraw from St. Lucie County Schools. Yet, student numbers swell at 1,320 crammed into an outdated school building in need of more classrooms, a gym for assemblies, better stocked library, larger cafeteria, dressing rooms and shower facilities.[26]

Some white parents believe that their child's ability to learn is hindered by our presence, implying that we're too dumb to attend school with their child. They sell this propaganda to others to justify pulling their child out of our so-called integrated school. Some of my friends' behavior reinforces the belief that blacks aren't up to scratch. I think of a few of my buddies who lack discipline: Johnny and Beanie's excessive absences, their unfinished homework assignments, their inattentiveness and sleeping in class; and Sneaky Pea and Squirrel Nut's failing altogether. Sneaky Pea and Squirrel Nut are in several of my remedial classes where they both act out. It seems they display anger to hide their shame and academic weaknesses. Both test below grade level and are labeled slow learners. I squirm low in my seat, listening to Squirrel read slowly, mispronouncing and not knowing simple words. This hurts and embarrasses us both.

I know Squirrel Nut because of his ravenous appetite for the candy with the same name. Sneaky Pea, is a kleptomaniac with a small head that doesn't match his overweight body. Mr. Riles, a neighborhood storeowner, can never catch either of them stealing. Sneaky's slick and steals only small items, hiding his spoils under armpits or between his big fat thighs that rub together. "I don't like crackers staring at me. I ain't dumb, just get nervous, them white teachers don't care anyway," Squirrel says. I start a study group that gets off to a shaky start, but confident it's just a matter of time until we see results. "I'm quitting. The hell with school." I try convincing

---

[26] According to St. Lucie County School Board statistics.

Squirrel it's the wrong thing to do. I know Sneaky has other ideas too.

I struggle to measure up in my remedial subjects, facing some hard truths. What white parents say about blacks is scary. I become introspective. "Do I want to be at this white school?" "Am I a failure?" "Are whites smarter than blacks?" "Can I do better than I am doing?" I don't like doubting myself. There's no need thinking that there are no dumb whites. And I know all blacks aren't dumb either. I come to realize years of outdated books finally catches up with many blacks like me, even though we are supposedly on equal footing with whites. "It isn't your fault. It's Jim Crow segregation," Mama says. But try telling that to my snickering white classmates.

I still have unanswered questions. Through Grandma's remarkable courage and life experiences, she instills in me a gift of unshakable pride. I never thoroughly understand it until failing fifth grade. Crying, I know I shouldn't have failed and my friends know I shouldn't have. Grandma pulls me close, wipes away my tears and shakes me to attention. "Scaldee!" "Listen to me!" "Let your Mama handle it. You gotta be strong, prepare yourself for something betta to come!" She primes me with confidence, "You got to believe in yourself!" Grandma's challenge instills confidence in me. I can achieve and succeed just like anyone else.

Whenever I go through a difficult time, Grandma reminds me I'm a special child. "You got a gift. Someday you'll realize it. I see compassion in your spirit." She understands I will have to compete, not just alongside but against whites. "That's how it always been Scaldee, even in the old days colored folks try ta be betta cause they see us less than um anyhow."

The first time I have doubts, I'm smothered and hemmed in all around by a bunch of wannabe smart ass white boys. It happens when fewer blacks are in a classroom. I notice similar reactions of desperation on a few faces of my black classmates; petrified not of whites but competing alongside them. Naïve white teachers know little about our backgrounds and most care and know little about the limitations imposed by segregation. Never at our schools do I recall a black teacher, not even Barbara Scott, ridicule in a vindictive manner our ability to learn with such remarks: "Do you not get it!?" "You should have learned this material in your own schools." Without compassion, they berate us despite the reality of limited resources and inferior materials hampering our progress. When places, things and events in the world of information—in our world change so rapidly around us, it takes time for us to catch up.

I suppose I'm naïve to think teachers shouldn't point out our deficiencies without any encouragement. Don't let us be scapegoats accepting all the blame for our shortcomings. Black classmates participate—raise hands hoping to get noticed, trying to dispel racial myths and stereotypes. Still tacit discouraging signs get played out in classrooms: Blacks have little effort to learn.

In the summer of 1963, Bobby Williams comes from rural Alabama to live with his grandmother on Tenth Street and Avenue H, next door to our home. Perhaps a different outcome might have occurred for a troubled friend without proper adult guidance. Bobby spends hours caring for his grandmother. Mean and ornery at times from constant pain, she relies heavily on Bobby for almost everything. At age 13, Bobby comes and goes as he pleases after Ms. Doralene, with chronic rheumatism confined to a wheelchair, goes to bed early. Sharp as a tack with a mechanical mind, Bobby has the knack for taking lawn mowers and appliances, from junk piles, apart and getting them in working condition, sometimes to the chagrin of a neighbor who buys it back.

We have eighth grade science class together, a subject he really loves and is at the top of our class with excellent grades. Some days, we get together after school and work on science projects. Some days within minutes of getting started, Ms. Doralene starts her constant calls. "Oh Bobby, come here quickly!" Bobby leaves to rub ointment on her ailing and twisted rheumatic hands and feet. Little, if any, homework gets done.

Late in the school year, something drastically changes Bobby in a mysterious kind of way. His grade in science goes from A to C, although he continues to study at my home. Bobby was shouldering too much responsibility caring for his grandmother. A few months into the school year, his mood and behavior become increasingly erratic. Before then, Bobby was determined to succeed, possessing in science an unwavering enthusiasm. His tenacious attitude and outgoing infectious personality wins over hard liners like our science teacher, Ms. Taylor, who ordinarily never notices black students. Bobby steps into class exuding an unmatched confidence—"Watch me now!" "This Negro is smart!" Ms. Taylor's annoyed by his antics and cockiness, but she is surprisingly restrained.

Without any sign of trouble, he takes a downward spiral; reading monotonously slow, forgetting and mispronouncing words. He exhibits erratic mood swings, disrupting the class repeatedly when he blurts out wrong answers. "Please, please let me try again. I know it! I know it! I'll get it right this time. Give me another chance!" After class I pull him aside. "Bobby what's wrong? Why you act this way?" "Just leave me alone!" Disruptive white classmates once jealous of his achievement burst out in laugher. I hide my face in my hands. I'm feeling sorry that I can't figure out what's wrong with my buddy.

Ms. Taylor recognizes Bobby's declining grades and she too knows that something's wrong. In a cautious way she holds him over after class, as I watch from outside the doorway. "Bobby, are you alright?" "I'm concerned about your behavior and you're not focused and not doing well. Can I help you? I must let your parents know." "I got problems at home I got to work out." "Oh, I see, let me know if I can be of any help." Ms. Taylor's genuinely concerned.

Bobby never talks about bearing a heavy burden, taking care of his sick grandmother. When missing from outdoor activities, I ask about it, but he gets uptight, cracks a joke or changes the subject. Bobby is hiding a secret that ultimately gets the best of him.

Early one Saturday morning, I hear a noise outside. I watch from my kitchen window as Bobby kneels behind a neighbor's car. Curious to know what he's doing, I hide behind a tree watching him place one end of a piece of water hose into a neighbor's gas tank and the other end into his mouth. He siphons gas as it flows steadily from the tank onto a soaking rag and puts it over his nose. So preoccupied huffing, he doesn't notice me until I snatch the rag from his face. Bobby's high as a kite slumped against the car, looking up and smiling as his eyes roll back in his head. I am so incensed that I repeatedly slap his face, trying to wake him out of his high. "Why're you sniffing gas Bobby? You gonna kill yourself man!" His eyes glazed over and he's slurring words I can't understand. I get him to his feet and sit him under a canopy of orange trees in my yard as he falls into a slumber. Bobby huffs gas, aerosol sprays, glues and paint thinners. He picks up this habit from white boys' invitations in school restrooms. Huffing provides Bobby with an escape route from the harsh reality of caring for his grandma.

I can easily place some blame on Ms. Taylor. But is it fair? Even if I didn't know at first, were there not early telltale signs in class? After all, why should she or any one else care what happens to a troubled black boy?

Teachers are entrusted with responsibility to educate and report signs of distress. All seem insignificant in the midst of a two-year statewide teachers strike aimed to increase their pay under some horrendous teaching conditions.

Bobby drifts away, missing school. What can I or anyone do? Bobby's addiction is something I know nothing about. But what of his family? Abandoned by both parents, adopted by an ailing grandmother, he is without support. I try with indiscretion to help, but my appeals fall on deaf ears. "Bobby's not doing well in school. He gets dizzy, terrible headaches," I say, hiding the truth. "I see his teachers' letters, something wrong with that boy," Ms. Doralene shows the slightest outwardly concern.

Bobby almost gets shot siphoning gas from a man's car in Cisco Quarters. I realize I must act quickly to help my friend. I devise a scheme. He'll accompany me to my doctor's appointment near Fort Pierce Memorial Hospital, a few blocks from where we live. Bobby agrees, but a block away he gets anxious and decides to turn around. After much persuasion, I offer to buy his favorite RC Cola and chips, which calms him down. I convince him to accompany me to my appointment at the hospital. We're reproached by a suspicious white receptionist with a snarl in the waiting room. "Your name isn't in my appointment log. Where are your parents?" I ask to speak to a nurse. A nurse appears. "You don't have an appointment." "Can I see a doctor? It's important," I insist. With aggravation, she grunts and departs.

A doctor enters impatiently, stiff-lipped. "Where are your parents? You have no appointment here." "My friend needs help." Bobby is alert and stiffens up. "Maann you fool me! I'm leavin!" "He huffs gas and glues, all kinds of stuff! Can you please help him?" I plead exasperated. Bobby runs off. The doctor stands there, stuck on the formality of parental consent. "My friend's hooked, you're supposed to help him!" I scream. "How awful. Sorry I need his parents…" His words grow faint and insignificant as I walk away.

Bobby's mood swings vary from irritability to anger to crying spells. School's no longer important, coming over to study is irrelevant. Bobby goes missing for hours, even days, reappears, dirty, antsy and tired. Neighbors sense something's wrong. I finally break down and tell. "I smell it on him. It never happened until he goes to that white school. I hear about huffing on the news." "I can't do nothin with that boy. Kenny talk to him," Ms. Doralene insists. "I been talkin. He needs a doctor. Can you take him?" "Ain't got no money." Goes deaf and rolls away in her wheelchair.

I must have been naïve at different times, thinking the odor on Bobby is Ms. Doralene's rubbing ointments. I see a brilliant mind wasting away. What might the future hold in the dawn of a new era of equal opportunity? Valuing our friendship, I agonize over not having acted sooner, that I might have made a difference had I acted early on. I convince Bobby to come back to school, but his attendance is as erratic as his behavior. He sits quietly most days, idly staring into space. And when he does assert himself, he gets frustrated over his wrong answers. "Let me think. I know the answer, wait a minute!" he yells, becoming increasingly agitated. "Sorry Bobby, Ms. Taylor interjects, since you don't know, I won't allow another response." Other times subtle shiftiness in his seat is a dreadful sign of restlessness he won't remain in class at all. Before the day is over, he's gone on an impulse. Before the end of the second semester, Bobby recovers with great improvement.

In the summer of '68, my aunt Ruth and uncle Jesse visit from Cleveland, Ohio and Mama surprisingly insist I return with them without any say in the matter. She always look for opportunities to keep me busy over the summers or a way out of Fort Pierce. Constantly preaching, I need to stay away from the streets (where I began to occasionally hangout with buddies) or end up like some she help with assignments when they come over to study.

Fort Pierce goes on a street-widening mission backed by eminent domain. Doralene's home sits on the corner of Avenue H and is condemned. The city needs half of the property. Doralene and Bobby had to go. She dies after the City of Fort Pierce bulldozes their entire home and Bobby drops out of school.[27]

Some mornings waiting for the school bus, I stop Bobby in a depressed mood catching a hustle at the loading zone on Thirteenth Street. "Those crackers downtown take our home, the only home I know."

"All I know this white man tells us we have to move. My grandma got nothin...she die ...and I got nothin." Bobby, at 14, has no stable relative and is displaced from his neighborhood friends. He drops out of school and becomes homeless before I enter ninth grade.

Seeing my buddy this way is disturbing. I won't give up, but convincing him to go back to school is difficult. Some weekends, I purposely go pick fruit just to get inside Bobby's head. Get on the same contractor's bus and nag him until he gets angry. "Bobby you're too smart to quit school, why you doin this to yourself, drinkin that cheap wine?" I repeatedly say. "Naw Kenny, those crackers don't give a damn bout us. You wastin time tryin to change my mind! Leave me the hell alone about school! I ain't got ah family to take care of me like you!" Bobby now has decaying teeth and bad breath. Not knowing what to say plays on my caring nature. He gets passed about, from one distant relative to another and disappears.

I vow, even after he became addicted to wine and difficult to reach, that I would never give up on him. Thunderbird wine and

---

[27] Eminent domain gives power to a federal, state or municipal government as well as to a corporation to take private land for public use. By law, any person subject to taking must receive just compensation. To my knowledge, Ms. Doralene was not rightly compensated for the loss of her home under eminent domain.

years of sniffing poisonous fumes makes his face look beaten and much older.

Most brothers I hang with, especially Sneaky, Squirrel Nutt, Beanie and Johnny, distance themselves from my petulance reminding them to stay in school. Both barely make it through eighth grade, and are placed in special education but never attend. "We listen to you, ain't gonna change how we feel. We got shafted and ain't goin back! We angry cause them white teachers don't listen to us. Tell us next year we must go to a special class. Hell no! We ain't crazy so we quitting."[28]

I feel subtle messages of opposition in situations played out, not always in words, but actions. I look in cold eyes of the old guard, watch and read body language, hear in a voice penetrable messages from these stubborn holders of old racial stereotypes and traditions determined not to give in to change.

My distrust grows out of tacit expressions of dissent I see in white faces: "Don't expect much help from us. You want to come, now fend for yourself. We don't want you here anyway."

I try staying optimistic and determined. Cultural sensibility should be enforced but it isn't. I detest teachers' subtle and tacit ways of putting blacks on the spot. Where are the compassion and understanding when you hear, "Sorry, your answer is wrong, did your school not teach this? What don't you understand? I will not call on you again with your incomplete answers." "Are you reading what everyone else is?" This demeaning litany of criticisms arouses unsettling anger in me time and time again. My anger I hide away under lock and key.

I miss the familiarity of our black teachers' style and creativity that foster class debates. Too often our deficiencies are pointed out. Without tact or any sense of fulfilling their mission to teach all students, our teachers call us out mockingly. I observe in a few struggling black classmates that the teachers' language reinforces

---

[28] Like Bobby, Johnny and Beanie, Squirrel Nut and Sneaky Pea at a young age lack parental guidance were predisposed to lures of the streets. All quit St. Lucie Junior High by 8th grade and a truant officer visit as a deterrent, I know of any come into black neighborhoods to follow-up.

ole "black dummies" stereotypes and prejudices.

One afternoon in Ms. Garin's social studies class, I lapse into daydreaming. I suppose I do so as a formidable defense, shutting out some of deficiencies I face academically and things I don't like about integration. "Kenneth! Kenneth! Are you ignoring me?" I look up blankly as if I am awakening from visiting some enchanted place unaware how I got there. "Are you alright?" Garin asks, to an outbreak of laughter.

The reemergence of daydreaming becomes constant during classes. "Name the last two southern states to join the union." She has no idea, nor can she fathom that I have gone light years inside of myself and I know nothing about what she's asking. "Ah, I don't know." The words fall out before I realize it. Garin, I suppose, has noticed for some time my daydreaming. With the slightest hesitation, she moves on to someone else. I make a poor showing of myself. Ms. Colcord, my math teacher, soon becomes genuinely concerned about my daydreaming. Curious about what's disturbing me, she sends a note requesting a meeting with Mama. "Kenneth is daydreaming in class. He doesn't seem excited about being here. He's not taking advantage of an excellent opportunity."

Mama is disappointed that she is unable to get every syllable from her lips as she hems me into a corner of my bedroom. She's not one to lambast me proceed to do so. I explain with excuses and superficial reasons. I don't want to worry her. I come to grips with disadvantages being hurled at me over the years, not because of me but because of a system working against me. I am disillusioned knowing, as I know many others feel similarly, I am an outcast.

In English class sitting next to whites, I wonder how long must I take slights and be so sensitize to smirks and giggles. In our struggles to assimilate at school, I want to lash out every time a black classmate gives a wrong answer, because our wrong answers when compared to our white counterparts are magnified by a teacher's silly sarcastic remarks.

Oliver's an upper-middle class dirty blond white boy who isn't smart. His socio-economic status hasn't resulted in much academic achievement. His status leads him to believe, I suppose from his actions and inactions, he's better. Oliver comes to school each day dressed in jeans and wrinkled surfer T-shirts and penny loafers. His father is a realtor and his mother a lawyer. With his poor southern diction, he thrives on attention. Often eager to raise his hand, Ms. Garin obliges, despite expecting the same outcome—wrong answer. Oliver nervously freezes up, stutters and stumbles over answers. Frustrated, he hits himself upside the head, as if at any minute a right answer will spring forth.

After a black classmate mispronounces a simple word, Oliver whispers "dummy" to his friend. I spring from my seat, erupting, "You got something smart to say?! Say it to his face dumb ass!" Oliver sits quietly. "Kenneth! Quiet! I want tolerate that language! Sit down or I'll give you a slip to the office!" I can no longer take the innuendos and smart aleck remarks. "If he doesn't shut his mouth, I'll shut it for him!" "Alright, I've had enough of you! Take this slip and go to the office now!"

I personally place enormous weight on my shoulders in defense of negative comments made against black classmates. I take the pink slip. Garin accuses me of ingratitude. I walk slowly to Principal Jesse Mullins' office. I need to make a statement. I want white people to know blacks aren't beholden to an image of passivity that shouts, "Stay in your place and you won't have any problems." I need to be in control of my emotions, I suppose. I do want to at least show that blacks aren't predisposed to anger.

Mullins thankfully relinquishes his earlier threat of suspension if I show up in his office or the Deans' office again. There are too many serious infractions occurring daily for him to overreact to my appearance at his office. Under fire from the public's outcry about sporadic racial incidents, the campus is inundated with savvy reporters seeking newsworthy stories. Mullins has too much on his plate, including complaints of "foul" lodged by black parents about the disparity in numbers of black suspensions.

In spite of certain truths, I realize one must be prepared and expect a different outcome. Numbers of blacks and whites are failing miserably. And the pressures of succeeding makes me feel like a guinea pig studied under a magnifying glass, coupled with maintaining civility and patience. All this is an enormous thing to control.

With the realization of being in some remedial classes, I am motivated as are others to excel. But others are labeled slow learners, and they're noticeably behind one or two grade levels. Slow learners, black and white, are prone to frustrations and embarrassment routinely as their abilities are tracked. Black children's scores are scrutinized even more than those of their slower white counterparts. Some blacks simply shut down and become nothing more than a faceless person occupying a desk— invisible.

I meticulously review and familiarize myself with assignments before class. Before speaking, I cautiously fashion every word and phrase for the correct pronunciation and grammar to avoid an onslaught of teacher criticism. My preparation pays off surprisingly well with encouraging words. "You're correct, thank you. That's the answer I'm looking for." I get excited receiving a little praise.

Hungry for recognition we thrust ourselves involuntary in classroom debates. It is clear hardly a teacher believes we are worthy of receiving. We're mainly squashed out like a fly in the path of a fly swatter— eliminated from classroom discourse. Many blacks come away adversely, affected by the learning curves in testing. We need to improve. I consider that white teachers feel they are benefiting society by uplifting the culturally deprived and economically disadvantaged black students.

The teachers' strike continues (through eighth grade) with shortages in special education and such specialized extracurricular classes as music, art and physical education. Teachers teach out of their field and fill vacancies in subjects they're not certified to teach. How are we expected to learn with so many distractions and hardly any teachers? Teachers who continue to instruct are ostracized by their colleagues for not striking.

I'm receptive to a highly competitive challenge. If a black classmate falls behind, we all help each other to prove we can compete. I raise my hand to answer questions every chance I get for a shining moment of satisfaction. Sometimes it slips away.

The idea of thinking logically and participating in debates is a prerequisite for improving grades. To just give any answer isn't good enough. I'm careful when given the chance not blurt out any answer; it must be well thought out. I place added pressure on myself and blacks in class as we encourage each other. I'm motivated to excel. I have the need to help to advance our race. As Ms. Robinson reminds us: "We're the vision for the future."

I'm reminded of Ms. Robinson teaching her students survival skills, such as ironing, stitching, showing girls and boys how to comb their hair and how to dress appropriately; also how to take care of personal hygiene and behave like little ladies and gentlemen. We line up in single file for meals, a boy before a girl. Every boy repeatedly steps out of line to hold the cafeteria door for the next girl entering behind them. Girls sit quietly as every boy remains, standing behind their chairs until every girl is seated. All eyes are on Ms. Robinson, who is proudly seated at the head of table, awaiting her nod to be seated. Our class holds the attention of other classes that are captivated by the interplay of male and female roles. Perhaps the mannerisms and respectability are gone, but not forgotten, of those segregated years.

Our arrival to the white academia is one impression white teachers dare to teach. It is analogous to Native Americans welcoming the Mayflower landing on Plymouth Rock. The Pilgrims were outwardly gracious to establish trust and to offer their guarded support to the colonists facing their first harsh winter in the New World. Like Native Americans, blacks are cautious, yet trusting as they enter into a new world of integration. We never receive our welcoming. Pilgrims, too, deceive Native Americans with white supremacist beliefs of uncivilized heathens. Similar feelings percolate on campus as blacks and white venture into an integrated environment.

We don't arrive at white schools as the colonists did, asserting their dominance over every aspect of Native American culture. We come willingly after America's moral conscious finally awakens. Yet white America, like Columbus and the Pilgrims, lost an opportunity for understanding.

If integration is to work, it needs to abandon its white supremacist ideology. The will of an oppressed people has spoken, awakening America to change her evil ways. I fall under the learning curve again with vocabulary testing. Testing and retesting to evaluate basic elementary skill levels many blacks don't have because of an inferior education attained under Jim Crow segregation laws. I improve out of remedial classes like many others. What becomes clear, just as our parents predicted, we're truly guinea pigs in a once pristine white academic environment.

Chapter 14

SHUFFLE ALONG

There's a kind of twitch, a feminine twitch that I've noticed for a little while. It can't be true. I doubt it. "That boy can run!" "We need him on the track team!" Coach Valentine tells Coach Haley. "Track or cross country?" Haley asks. "Both," Valentine replies emphatically.

I'm always on Juniors' heels in second place. I can't ever catch up and pass him during P.E. But that twitch, I'm suspicious from rumors I hear. Now it comes together. All this time on occasions buying the same cloths we both like, as friends and neighbors we will dress alike on occasions. Now my suspicion heightens as that twitch becomes more pronounced the faster he runs.

I suppose I'm in denial, since I know all along over the summer during my visits to a neighborhood rummage store. I buy a baseball glove, Jerome gets a bat, and Junior purchases ladies' things—a wig here, lipstick there. "It's for mama," he says, but I wonder. I shut it out as nothing. But now that twitch, as I run behind him, is annoying and disappointing when I no longer suspect, but believe Junior's a homosexual.

I hear sly whispers from a few black classmates on the sidelines after finishing laps. "That sissy can run." In the know now, I can no longer dress the same as Junior. But I can't reject him either just because of this discovery. I prefer to keep it to myself.

"We got to study. We can't let these white teachers . . . some don't care and they'll fail us," Junior reasons. We have taken divergent paths, but on occasion we try to study together and

215

discuss schoolwork, teachers and school gossip. "Some of us not taking integration seriously," Junior points out. Sometimes we sit on his front porch or stand in my front yard discussing homework assignments into the night. I'm more tempted than before to ask him about his sexual preference because there is a white classmate in the same predicament. Douglas, a white boy gets lambasted each time he enters a restroom. He too has this feminine twitch about him. "You queer! Faggot!" Douglas gets it up close and personal when he finds himself trapped in a restroom stall. "Stop it! Leave him alone!" I yell, not sure why I risk helping a white boy.

Over time, I suppose defenseless Douglas brings out compassion in me from being teased in previous years and that day of teasing my friend John. I so far have kept my promise never to do it again. I have never liked hateful teasing done to anyone in any manner. "He's just a queer, that's all," white boys proclaim, puzzled by my concern for defenseless Douglas. "Thanks Kenneth, that's awful nice of you." I saw in his face a helpless need to be rescued, which brings me to my senses that Junior is gay.

Someone taps my shoulder and I turn to see it's Dan with his freckles and crimson cheeks, and Anna, a shy white girl with a chubby face. Both classmates are in third period social studies and they're looking around nervously, as if it's risky being seen with me. "Can we talk somewhere?" Dan asks. I lead them away from heavy traffic to a safe spot under a shade tree. "We admire your bravery," Dan says. "How can you stay focused . . . and your knowledge of black history . . . when Ms. Garin doesn't want to hear it?" Anna asks. "We don't think it's a distraction, she's just being mean." "Why are you telling me this now?" "We wanted to . . . but racial problems." Dan's genuine. "We welcome you. We know it's coming a little late." Both hold out their hands in an awkward moment and we shake. "This may come as a surprise, but we think there is white teacher prejudice against Negroes," Anna admits with Dan agreeing. I never expect whites to say it and know others are afraid to say it too. "We want to be supportive," Anna continues, shyly smiling. I admire their bravery, but what of the others? Why haven't they come forward? It's a Kodak moment.

There remains a faction of diehards with the air of white supremacy and privilege about them. They get up and move when I sit next to them. In the breezeways (open area), students engage every day in the endless futility of pushing, bumping and maneuvering as if we're on an obstacle course. It reminds me of my first trip to New York when we navigated the streets trying to squeeze through a crowd, avoiding eye contact and any kind of communication.

Diehards have the audacity to expect blacks to step aside when there's little room to pass. White girls expect me to give up my seat, so their friend can avoid sitting next to me. "The gall!" "How dare you!" I get from an inadvertent bump, and am expected to apologize when I didn't initiate it. I pick up on their not so subtle mannerisms suggesting that I assume a subservient position, as if I were their passive butler. We must "stay in our place" seems to be the message.

We aren't ever going to be the belittled Negroes of the Jim Crow era to satisfy the diehards' discomforts and expectations. Jim Crow is dead, but its vestiges linger as integration pushes back. In the words of folk singer Bob Dylan, "the times they are a-changin'."

Overcrowded conditions make it difficult for students to keep focused. Anger, rejection, alienation, and the need to belong lead to mounting tensions that erupt into fights. Overcrowded classes lead to the inadequate supply of textbooks. We have to share and some white classmates avoid sitting next to blacks so they don't have to share with them. I try staying focused on school work, but there's always another hurdle to jump over. Black classmates pool together in groups and share textbooks. Our congregating creates heightened suspicion. We're suspected of plotting some insurrection against whites. We hear the nervous murmurs of paranoia. "Alright boys and girls, let's not group together," which is clearly an inconsistent message with the necessity of sharing books. Blacks must not gather together; they must assimilate at all times.

Dan and Anna are few exceptions. White volunteers are ridiculed and called names. This can be the undesired consequence of reaching out. If blacks ask to share textbooks, it likely implies that sharing will be with someone white. This draws a few frowns and groans and fewer volunteers. White teachers are often left with demanding actions that inevitably lead to stupid outcomes.

One day a white girl enters science class late without her assigned textbook. Sitting next to someone you don't know to share a book can be a bit awkward and uncomfortable. If someone doesn't have a textbook because of shortages, the class rule says you must share. I overhear this disgruntled white girl say, "Wasn't for all these Negroes, we won't have to share." "You better get used to it. We're here and more are coming," I demur quickly, adjusting her reality. Of course, she claims that she doesn't mean anything by it, but sharing her textbook is a necessity. I come to realize after all that sharing with the opposite race is not a bad idea because it encourages dialogue. We may get to know one another and release some racial tension.

For a few years now I collect non-poisonous snakes, and over time my collection has multiplied into ten different species. Bennie and Johnny live in shotgun row houses near Avenue D and Beanie and I have coops of homing pigeons in our backyards. We learn from Beanie's father, a World War II veteran, how to breed and train them as carrier pigeons, to deliver messages from his house to mine and back. Quite a feat to master.

Beanie, Johnny and I have classes together. We all are tracked into remedial classes. Both barely focus on school work, I know for Beanie and Johnny because of being far behind academically, but for me the material was beneath my knowledge base. I sit on Beanie's front porch waiting for Johnny, so we can go over an English assignment that both have problems with. Beanie's parents, who are heavy drinkers, start to argue. "You, worthless piece of sh.t!" "Why don't you be a better man and take care of your responsibilities!" Beanie's mother lashes out at his father as he walks out the door. "Where you're going?" When he doesn't answer, she throws an empty wine bottle striking him on the head. Blood gushes out causing a nasty gash. Beanie's father turns expressionless and watches his wife cry. "I I I'm sorry baby. I'm sorry, but, but that boy's slow. Help him with his lesson!" He takes a dirty handkerchief and wipes blood away. "I know you don't mean it," a man of few words says in a slight stutter.

Wine gives a boost of confidence that wipes away his stutter altogether. "I can't help him," he continues, "I don't have much schooling. If that boy don buckle down at that white school, they gonna shuffle him along in a special class." We sit staring at him as he slowly walks to a corner juke joint on Tenth and D. Beanie turns away from his mother who is drunkenly crying in the open doorway. "I don't ever wanna be like him," Beanie says shamefully.

"I form a study group. Don't you wanna get promoted?" I asked. Beanie's more than Johnny willing to study, ready to polish his study habits with purpose. Johnny will follow Beanie's insistence in anything he does because Johnny feels indebted to do so. It's because one day, a miraculous life altering event changes Johnny into overbearing gratitude for Beanie.

It happens at the Superior Fertilizer Company. We wait until late evenings when the sun goes down to walk a mile along railroad tracks near the Atlantic Ocean. We gain entry, sneaking past a security post and the watchful eyes of a security guard, into an industrial plant and hide until it gets dark. We wait until closing, then climb silos half-filled with fertilizer where pigeons sleep and nest, tucked away high up in lofts. We quietly climb three stories to the top lofts which is an enormously dangerous task. We're too young and foolish to appreciate the risk.

We're skilled catching pigeons. It takes not being afraid of heights and having patience with the steady numbness of nerves to hold onto the small ledges like a careful mountain climber. You must calculate every move and remain extremely quiet while climbing in the darkness. Flashlights are out of the question, so we depend on a street lamp outside. The slightest noise can spook hundreds of pigeons in a confined area, sending them flying frantically in tight spaces. Their dangerous beaks and sharp claws can cause serious injuries. We come prepared with pillow cases with the eyes cut out that we put over our heads to protect our faces against a colony of spooked pigeons protecting their young when predator hawks are near. We use our bare hands to better grip the ledges, made slippery by the pigeon droppings.

Nesting pigeons protecting their young will swarm down and ram their beaks into you. At this critical moment you must not panic, holding onto a ledge for dear life with one hand while warding off pigeons pecking at your face, hands, and body with the other. It's like a scene from the Hitchcock movie, *The Birds*. So, we take many risks, clinging dangerously to the edge of small ledges to keep our balance.

One night several pigeons swarm down upon Johnny, pecking away at his fingers. Swinging to keep them away, his foot slips off the narrow ledge. He loses his grip and falls several stories into tons of fertilizer below. Johnny lands on his feet, but the impact of the fall causes the porous fertilizer to become like a giant sink hole and Johnny slowly sinks. Johnny screams for help as soft unsettling fertilizer acts like quicksand, gradually swallowing him up to his waist. I cling to a corner ledge of the silo, watching from high above frozen, frightened and helpless as Johnny cries out. "Help me Beanie! Please help me. I don wanna die!" Like a skilled mountain climber, Beanie moves hastily below, risking his own life to save his buddy as pigeons are swarming and pecking away at him. With fertilizer up to Johnny's' chest, Beanie extends his leg far enough for Johnny to reach and pull himself free. Reaching the edge of the silo completely panic-stricken, Johnny holds tightly against a beam and cries gratefully. Beanie reached Johnny in the nick of time saving him from a suffocating death.

That incident in the summer of 1967 is why Johnny has infinite gratitude to Beanie for saving his life and will do anything for him. That summer night ended our pigeon ventures forever. That summer also had a lingering sadness for me when Hot-Rod and Bow-legs, my two neighbors, drowned. It's often said that "tragedy lurks at your front door." Whether this is certain or not, a Cadillac hearse passes by my house often as it heads for the graveyard. I had become familiar with death, digging graves, burying the dead and losing a neighbor most summers. The Grim Reaper dwells at Taylor Creek just a short distance beyond the graveyard. For decades, its tempting emerald green and opulent waters have taken hundreds of victims. Most panic and drown when surprised by a submerged docile sea cow (manatee) swims underfoot, feeding on sea lilies and algae.

Johnny is a follower, while Beanie is assertive and an attention-seeker. Both are in eighth grade and both repeat two grades. I proceed with caution, as I can relate to their situation and I don't want to arouse their sensitivity about being detained."Beanie, if you don't get Johnny over to study he's gonna fail." "I know, we both gonna fail," Beanie replies. "He comin, if he ain't lost his books." Beanie laughs. Some days after school, we study on Beanie's front porch, and other times on a bench in my backyard under shady orange trees. Beanie has a gambler's itch influenced by his older brother Teddy, a dropout wannabe street hustler. When Teddy comes by flashing wads of money and jewelry from gambling—off Beanie goes.

Our study group is always erratic, hardly productive and once Bobby shows up, who I haven't seen in days, dirty, smelly, high on some kind of inhalants that distract him and nothing gets done.

I often pass Ms. Wright's, a lodge friend of Grandma's, on my way to Sunday School. She likes to keep abreast of my progress at "that white school," she says. "Sonny, you be serious bout ya lesson cause them whites spectin ya ta fail anyhow. Don't want ya there anyway. It's ya right now, be serious or they gonna shuffle ya along." I asked what she meant. "Child move ya to a dummy class, course Sister Jay tells me you ain't dumb by no means, but some prejudice white may wanna prove ya is. Course I know and you know they wrong." She smiles and spits out snuff juice from her lower lip.

By midterm I'm determined to do well in all my classes, to test above remedial tracking and perform better than many of my white counterparts. While in reading, Long, a white no nonsense older teacher, struggles with Beanie. Long can be direct: "You should know these words by now. Can't you get help at home?" It's inconceivable we should know certain words and be further along given what we have not learned from outdated textbooks at segregated schools. Long expects and likes to bring up that point, that scores confirm what we already knew—that we were unprepared.

While Johnny is smart, enthusiastic and a bit temperamental when he studies, he needs discipline to get caught up. Beanie, on

221

the other hand, is passive, lacks confidence and is not interested in studying at all. "I got to pick oranges to help my family out, hustle like Teddy, do something," Beanie says. Both have problems identifying synonyms and word meanings as Ms. Long grows impatient. Both are 15 years of age, the two oldest boys in the class, and their interest wavers with thoughts of quitting. "You can do it. Let me come by and help you all," I always plead. I knock on Johnny's door. "Johnny ain't here. I know he failin, I got a letter from his teacher, he out there somewhere. He keep me worrying, see where his books are?" his Mother pleas. Johnny comes home from school, leaves them on the open porch and hits the streets.

In English, Ms. Kluppleburg is an older demonstrative teacher who is wise and helpful when she sees that you are making an effort. Hardly any young teachers are as patient, considering more than 50,000 Florida teachers threaten mass walkouts and over 31, 424 turn in resignations. Substitutes come and go and then resign because our overcrowded classes, school conditions and racial tensions remain problematic.

Kluppleburg asks Johnny to read. Sadly, he hesitates and momentarily stares blankly at pages and then reads in a soft whisper. Johnny's voice trembles nervously mispronouncing words. I grit my teeth, slide low in my desk, embarrassed for my friend as the teacher stops him in midsentence. The class is silent, even whites are compassionate. Not a giggle can be heard. "I want to continue," Johnny says. "Alright Johnny." He takes a deep breath, pauses, then mispronounces more words. Feeling a sense of obligation, I whisper out corrections and the class follows. "Go ahead, you're doing fine, you're almost done," a white girl whispers encouragement. Everyone claps and cheers. Johnny gets through his exercise and for once smiles with confidence.

Beanie and Johnny live on the periphery of Avenue D. From the front porch of their shotgun homes you can see a juke joint and a number of gambling houses. These businesses are calling to those not strong enough to ignore an itch that calls you to the streets, even when your heart tells you to go to school.

One morning when I'm walking an admirer to class, I notice

several black and white boys laughing while peeping into a classroom. "Look at you now. I told you so!" The white boy points and teases a seated white boy. "You just a dummy, retard that's all!" Another white boy laughs. A brother standing nearby watches. "What's that all about?" I ask, peering inside. "You haven't heard? There are rumors. They gonna move all the dummies to this special class. That white boy got his friend in there crying." I look closer and see more blacks than whites seated in the classroom. I get this heightened suspicion that Beanie and Johnny and others blacks will be shuffled along too—like Ms. Wright said. This is the school's way of getting rid of the so-called troubled and misunderstood black child that insensitive white teachers don't have the time nor patience to teach. While underlying issues of assimilation, the adjustment process and racial tensions create a hostile climate for learning, black and white students are crying out for help and the lily white naïve administration doesn't have a clue how to address it.

In Kluppleburg's class I see that whites also have problems with standard English. Much attention is given to correcting grammar, but the focus some days goes beyond teaching standard English to the use of superlatives and street vernacular or slang. Is there a language barrier when black classmates speak? A need to use *gone* instead of *gon*, and to replace *mo* with *more*? Is it Ebonics (later coined) or a lazy tongue Mama speaks about?[29]

Beanie and Johnny's absenteeism will likely lead to failing English and Reading. Beanie, by way of using colorful slang, blows every opportunity he has to pass. They jive and play in class, causing outbursts of laughter. Long is clueless; she doesn't understand street culture.

---

[29] In the 1990s much attention is given to African-American vernacular or dialect as a language known colloquially as Ebonics, which stirs controversy in public schools. Many linguists expressed frustration over public misconceptions, with anti-Ebonics invariably setting the tone for racist stereotypes. Ebonics is simply the product of tongue laziness, street slang: Is it a dialect or a language? Linguists determine it has its origin in various English and African languages. Should a black vernacular language be acceptable in contrast with Standard English? William Labov, *Language in the Inner City: Studies in the Black English. 1973.*

"What do you think of Beaver (the television series *Leave It to Beaver*)? "Maann he be coolin it all decked out," Johnny answers Kluppleburg. Beanie and Johnny are admonished for their use of slang. It seems they are destined to fail. Carl Sandburg, an American poet, finds his subjects in people and landscapes, and makes a career in ordinary language acknowledging that slang has its place: "Slang is a language that rolls up its sleeves, spits on its hands, and goes to work." The mastery of street slang does have its place, but not in Long's or Kluppleburg's classes.

One day, in a rare moment, Kluppleburg asks Beanie to conjugate a proper verb, necessary to correct a sentence on the chalkboard. In his typical animated and playful self, Beanie uses his hands to articulate a point, reading in a rhythmic cadence. He substitutes certain words in sentences with street slang. The class explodes in laughter. "Stop it!" "Stop it!" "That's not funny!" Kluppleburg snaps. "Why you be so uptight, run it by me again?" Beanie cracks. She refuses to repeat the question, knowing that Beanie's stalling. "Ahhh! Why you blowin me off? You blowin my cool. I was just jivin you!"

Kluppleburg gives Beanie more than enough chances. She is one of the few white teachers with patience who reaches her limit with his flippant outburst. It's embarrassing for me as other black classmates see through his disguise—his way of masking fear and shame. He and Johnny are a disruptive force that lights up the class.

I stop by with books in hand, ready to help with assignments. I make a visit, and no one shows up. "Where's Johnny?" I ask his mother. "I can't find him. Beanie not home either." She tried to stop both. "I'm sorry, Beanie won't listen to me." I wait a few minutes, but the street is in eye shot of Johnny and Beanies' homes and its allure is impossible for them and me to ignore.

I peep into Busy Bee Poolroom and I see them shooting pool. "We ain't gonna study man. Forget it." Johnny insists. "Y'all gonna fail," I plea. "Them white teachers don have time for us. They don care anyway," Beanie reminds me. "Don't make excuses." Ms. Long and Mrs. Kluppleburg try to help y'all." Both are unwilling to be sensible to my pleas. "I got to get a job." "Me too, "Johnny says, always agreeable ever since Beanie saved his life.

I watch their empty desks, hoping before semester ends that they'll change their minds and pay attention to my pleas, but neither does just like Bobby. I stop by Checks 5 & 10 store to buy a notebook. Beanie's father comes out of Dye's Liquor store with a bottle in hand. "How's Beanie? I haven't seen him in a while." "That boy neva home, say he go to school, but I think not. He failin anyway. I saw his report card." His father's drunk and dejected. "Can you talk to him? Help him?" I ask. "What can I do wit ah third grade edgeucashun? My wife too. Da streets got me. I keep tellin um both da streets gonna get um too." He laughs then looks at me in a sad way. "Wan be long that white school gonna do like before—shuffle um both along in same grade, if they eva go back."

Chapter 15

STORIES TO REMEMBER

One hot Saturday in 1967, I sit on my doorstep reading a *Jughead* comic book when a car horn startles me. A new black sleek Jaguar with gangster whitewall tires and a shiny chrome grill with burgundy leather interior rolls up in my front yard. A smiling tall cinnamon complexioned man wearing a black Stetson hat opens the door. He steps out, hunched over negotiating his tall frame. "Hello young man, you must be Kenny. Is Margaret in?" My eyes are locked on his Jaguar. I run my hands across the hood. I have never seen a black man drive such an expensive car. "My sister, young man, is she in?" I see New York tags. "She's cooking." "Uncle Herbert?" "Well, I couldn't have come at a better time. I wanted to tell you, but you're more interested in my car than in me. Don't just stand there rubbing the hood young man."

Uncle Herbert beside one of 3 Jaguars he owned through the years.
(Courtesy of Ronald Jenkins).

I made a detour to feed my pigeons, walking past the kitchen window to eavesdrop on a muted conversation. "Kenny needs his father. He's smart, he's in the South and you gonna have problems." "I already do," Mama whispered solemnly, "I'm worried he's already confronting white teachers and that spells trouble and he's beginning to hang out on the streets." "He needs to assert himself in these times of history," Uncle Herbert replies. "He's angry. Something bothering him, but he won't talk about it," Mama says exasperatedly. I listen closely, gathering my thoughts. It was a conversation I wasn't prepared to hear.

Mama had confronted me days earlier after a family friend reported what she had witnessed. I had gone to a dry cleaner off Orange Avenue to have a stain removed from a pair of pants. The manager standing behind the counter carefully explained the cleaning process, but abruptly abandoned his thoughts and me to wait on a white customer who drove up to the drop off window. "Hey, you were serving me first, what's the problem? My money isn't good as his?" "Sorry, I think he was waiting before you arrived," he said, with a smirk. "You think he was waiting first? You're lying between your teeth!" I snapped, taking a sharpened pencil from my back pocket. (I always carry a pencil and pad to gather my thoughts.) I threw the pencil a foot away and the sharpened lead of the pencil stuck right between his eyes into his forehead. The manager screamed for help. In a state of disbelief at my act and loss of control, it was too late for an apology and I knew that the police (Fort Pierce Police Department headquarters just on the other side of Bamboo Park) would surely be at the scene in a split second. I abruptly dashed off into Bamboo Park towards home.

I was careful and prepared to go along. Uncle Herbert had come to visit his family and now he was taking part in a story telling scheme devised by Mama to probe and pick my brain, possibly to get me out of Fort Pierce and into the Big Apple (New York) for, according to Mama, a more favorable environment.

After dinner my family gathered in the living room for storytelling. I heard many stories about Uncle Herbert, some I vaguely remember. "I have fond childhood memories of this old house," Unk says in a reflective moment. "You were a good child. I can't think of nothin you did bad," Grandma muses. "Herbert's my favorite brother. I'm the youngest and closest," Mama proclaims proudly. Uncle Herbert keeps my sisters and me laughing as he recounts mischievous childhood pranks. He then unexpectedly becomes solemn. "Tell a story Margaret, one you can remember about back then." Mama gets quiet a moment. After Alberta became a nurse and marries Uncle Eddie, Mama went to live with them in New York City. She enrolled in nursing school and worked for white families to support herself. "Once an old white man selects me at an employment agency and touches me on my leg. I get out his car and hide while he stops at a store, leaving without me. Young black girls desperate for work line up and white men come looking for maids and nannies. Most have wives and children and behave decently. Some have other motives and want more than housework. Many black girls take offense to sexual advances, and some are taken advantage of," Mama adds disgustedly.

My mother Margaret on left and friend Faye with Uncle Herbert home from the Navy, circa 1944. (Courtesy of Hurst family archives).

228

Grandma catches hell trying to make ends meet after Granddad dies right before the Great Depression years, Uncle Herbert leaves home, joins President Roosevelt's Civilian Conservation Corps, a program designed to provide work relief for young men. "You have to send 75 percent of what you make sent home to help your family. The work's hard but the racial prejudice you never get over." Segregated, blacks do all manual labor that included cutting down trees and clearing land to construct roads while whites hold technical and mechanic jobs. Anguish in his voice reveals the pain suffered from the depths of yesteryears.

I listen and wonder if I could survive during such a segregated time. Uncle Herbert became a decorated World War II veteran. It is rumored he was honored at the White House, where he stood before President Roosevelt. This is where he met Aunt Norma working as a secretary. "Kenny, I see a rebellious side in your eyes. Of course, in those days a black boy must know how to navigate through the clutches of Jim Crow segregation or face grave consequences."

Uncle Herbert returned home after the war and finished high school. This is exceptional because he graduated in his early twenties. He leave the South for good. "Margaret, tell the story about the chicken." Uncle Herbert laughs. Mama and her childhood friend, Naomi Butler, decided to kill, cook and eat Grandma's pet chicken, Irabella, but can't get it done burning up several pots. Grandma unexpectedly came home, calling out, "I can't find Irabella. Where is she?" "Oh, she ran away." Mama and Naomi repeatedly look guilty at each other. Grandma smelled something burning and went out to their playhouse and found Irabella blackened in her frying pan! "This got them both a good spanking."

Aunt Norma looking elegant at the War Department on 17th and Pennsylvania Avenue, Washington, D.C. Circa 1945. (Courtesy of Ronald Jenkins).

"Boy, where ya headed in this car?" Uncle Herbert employed with U.S. Postal as a tractor trailer operator in motor vehicle service made good wages. "Once I leave Fort Pierce and the South, I know returning can mean my life. I prepare myself for every possibility." Most times driving down south, white cops suspecting one of his expensive cars are stolen routinely stop Uncle Herbert. He always has his license and registration papers for such a stop. During these occasions, Aunt Norma is often humiliated because of her light skin. Cops think she's white and taking up with a colored man. She gets a few flashlights in her face as cops try to discern her identity. She never goes south without identification and a birth certificate. "You would think these incidents are quite a departure now, but I still get stopped in the South. They think a black man driving an expensive car must have stolen it." I sit listening, coming into enlightenment as I realize questions of race are always relevant—just around the corner.

Family members relaxing at home; Top row left, John Hairston, Uncle
Herbert, Norman Hairston, a World War I and II veteran and member
of the historic black infantry regiment, Harlem Hell fighters. Bottom row
left, Edna Hairston, unidentified women with baby and Aunt Norma.
(Courtesy of Ronald Jenkins).

Race can be served up in short order, or perhaps long, even as
an appetizer for white folks have been known to disrupt your life for
no reason—unexpectedly and unlawfully without having probable
cause, at any time.

"What yawl doin with that white baby?" On a visit back home, gets
stopped by a white Fort Pierce officer, not for a traffic violation but for
kidnapping a white baby. Calvin, his young son, is light skinned like his
mother, Aunt Norma. Uncle Herbert tries to explain, although a black
man isn't supposed to initiate conversation, or do much explaining in
the early 1950s. His New York tags make matters worse.[30]

On this occasion, the cop insisted he's a Yankee kidnapper,
rather than accept proof. Uncle Hubert gets interrogated and
harassed at the police station. Even after evidence is produced that
Calvin is his son, he gets accused of car theft, driving an expensive

---

[30] Uncle Herbert met Aunt Norma at the White House honored for his
heroism while she worked as a Secretary at the War Department and attend
night school at Howard University in Washington, D.C.. She eventually
became an educator in New York City public schools for 33 years.

car. This time the cops "play" a game for fun. "I always get angry afterwards, because we're delayed seeing relatives and it is so discouraging traveling by car," Uncle Herbert reflects.

"Kenny, you ready to tell your story?" Mamma looks on. "Not yet." I'm not about to get caught in the trap she has set. Regina shies away from her story, Sheryl's too young, and Gail has nothing of value to share. But then she quickly lights up. "Oh! I have a story to remember! Mr. Webster!" He worked for the city back in 1964, driving tractors to level new soil on dirt roads in all the black neighborhoods full of pot holes following a down pour. A pleasant man, Mr. Webster sometimes stops his tractor in front of our house when Gail and I are reading under the mango tree. We listen to his words of wisdom: "Be kind and generous to others, it comes back to you." Another time, "Dream big, you can be and do anything." "Don't fall victim to this evil system, keep studying and be somebody." "He was always kind," Gail recalled.

One day he digs up $25,000 in a buried rusty safe deposit box. The caption in the newspaper read: "Good Samaritan finds $25,000 turns it in." The money was abandoned for years, no one claims it. Webster gets his name and picture posted on the front page of the *News Tribune*, with honorary mention for loyalty and years of service. But what of the money? Rumors circulate that whites keep it all for themselves. "Silly fool!" "You don't get one red cent!" Black folks' mocking becomes Mr. Webster's poison. He stops passing by for a while. "One day, he stops his tractor in front of our house, looking troubled. "My own people are against me when I do good, and the white man don't care one way or the other," Mr. Webster says sadly.

Sometimes man is beholden to be honest and righteous, just as Mr. Webster was. But to everybody else it is wishful thinking. They believe he should have kept the money. In the end, whispers are too difficult to overcome. Beset with disappointment and grief, old man Webster succumbs to a heart attack and dies. Rumors say that his death came prematurely from a heart broken by unforgiving black folks.

I listen to stories late into the night. Hoping Fort Pierce will change like every small southern town must do in America.

"Scaldee can sit and listen to a good story all night," Grandma says. "Then what's your story Kenny?" Uncle Herbert slyly asks. "I never get to tell one." I reflect. "Be careful Herbert, Scaldee got a third eye just like me. He can see things." Everyone laughs. "Since a little boy he sees clowns, horses, all kinds of folks in his bedroom," Grandma continues. "Mama, you haven't been telling Kenny those ghost stories and talking about spirits you see in this old house!" Herbert interjects. "You been saying you see things since Daddy died." "Nooo, this is different." Grandma responds smiling.

Aware of being set up, I was careful to avoid getting implicated in any story. I feel compelled to speak about spirits lurking in Grandma's old house. Dark shadows duck and dodge some nights when I least expect them, hiding from me behind an old hutch, peeping behind doors. Once I awaken to shuffling and watch the dark figure of a man standing behind my bedroom door, peering in as if hiding from me. I never can make these figures out. Grandma says it's the spirits of my Granddad, Ollie Jay and his first wife Julia. "Don't be scared Scaldee," she tells me. "They good spirits, ya family. They never left this house, though they bodies in that cemetery down the street."

My Granddad dropped dead while spanking his daughter, Aunt Alberta, at the foot of my bed. Some evenings when the sun goes down and sometimes after the rain casts a dreary look inside the old house, the spirits hover. Their presence intensifies sometimes when Grandma lets me sit up with her and watch Boris Karloff's television series, *Thriller*. "It's ya magination cause ya scared child seeing this movie," she says. "What about when I ain't Grandma?" Her face and thoughts drift to a far off place. "Scaldee what ya see in this old house is real. I see them more days than you. I speak but they never answer."

The dark shadows move about peeking at me and Grandma from behind corners. Grandma says we have spirits of ancestors under the house. I crawl underneath the old house on cinder blocks but never can find any spirits. She seemed to know it and laughs. I don't think it's funny at all. She teases me to lighten the mood. Grandma is far from crazy, lives in her spiritual realm of thinking. I come to believe, in some way, because of her persona there's something special in me, as she likes to proclaim.

"Kenny tell your story, you got many!" Gail says. I want to tell what Grandma wanted me to. I dare tell it to my scared sisters. With trepidation, my mind shifts to a moment of anger and revenge towards a white man in Bamboo Park. I dare tell this story with the idea of giving hope and inspiration. A story of Grandma and me, when times seemed timeless and never void of adventure. A simpler time in Grandma's stories when colored folks have skills passed down from generation to generation, out of slavery times and as far back as Africa. The will to overcome enduring struggles and hardships borne out of segregation empowers people with limited resources to rely on the gift of the human spirit. In doing so they find ingenuous ways to create and develop the necessities to survive.

Joy of tender years comes not from the obvious host of playful things, but in remembrance of those things learned and cherished by one's watchful eyes. Anything alluring to the eyes will eventually captivate the heart, imagination and stimulate the mind. I'm Grandma's favorite of my siblings. Born with alert and watchful eyes, third eye Grandma says, and a low maintenance baby seldom cries or wants of anything. It's said that I lay in my bassinette and am fixated on everything that moves. My eyes light up and I smile every time Grandma comes near and speaks to me. It's why I get the Hebrew middle name "Ira," which means the observant and forever watchful one, befitting of my personality. It doesn't take Grandma much to convince my parents I'm special. I should spend time with her.

Colorful commentary, gestures and constant moving about keep me glued to the kitchen chair and my eyes on Grandma's every move. Grandma can flat out cook, bake, make soups and can preservatives, grow vegetables, and as an herbalist, rely on the healing effects in the secret life of plants, concocting portions of wonderment from their medicinal powers.

Quiet and quick-witted, Grandma can get lively on her sewing machine, humming a gospel tune, and then at a moment's notice take a tail spin into weaving out a scary ghost story, a folktale or dig deep into her consciousness about family history. I get caught up in her command of life stories, which are a source of entertainment and knowledge that help me shape my understanding of a hostile world I'd yet to encounter. Stories so mesmerizing about enchanting travels in time into the old world of her ancestral past. I often interrupt her cooking routines, hanging on to every word pleading for more as I fight off growling hunger pains. Always a challenge sitting still, I have trouble staying quiet. Sometimes when I don't interrupt, she rewards me with a delicious slice of hoecake bread from her wood burning stove. The love and reverence for Grandma and her life stories leave mental impressions that I can't forget if I wanted to. Eger to watch her cook as a pretense to listen to another interesting story, I earn the befitting name, "Little Pot-Watcher." I love watching her move about with cooking while telling stories. I become her little sentinel—the watchful one in the kitchen as our special relationship continues throughout her life.

"Scaldee you won't never get to know real hard times like me," she says, peering over wired rimmed glasses as she ties on her apron. "Flour, meal and sugar cost 1-cent. My Mama born in slavery made all her chillin clothes for school out of croaker sacks. Those sacks made you itch when it gets hot, so we didn't like wearin them." "Course back then," she added, poking in her dentures, "you wear the same clothes back to school the next day if they not too dirty."

Grandma walked three miles to school, and three miles back home. "Cause Mama and Poppa had too much work to do. Poppa never was no sharecropper. He own a 152-acre farm." "We walk to school in all kind of weather. White folks take their chillin in wagons to a better school, ours just a stuffy one room shack. Sometimes white chillins pass us on a dirt road in wagons with their mama or pappa teasing, and call us n..gas, and the chillins join in too. If we ain't careful they spit tobacco or splash mud on us and laugh. Course I only went far as third grade, far as they let us get educated, course I learn to read and write. Colored folk got treated awful bad back then, awful bad and couldn't do nothin about it."[31]

---

[31] On a genealogical research trip in 1985 to Waterboro, South Carolina, I discover my relatives retain 152 acres of land, although it is no longer

Viola Clayre Jay, proud soft-spoken bow-legged fresh-water Geechee, devout Christian, more mysteriously spiritual than religious. Born in Walterboro, South Carolina and later became an unassuming community activist. Her Eastern Star Lodge sisters and church elders of the Pallbearers Association, and The Women's Negro Improvement Association hold meetings on our front porch. I sneak and hide behind the living room door, listening to discussions on race relations, fund drives to bury the poor, social and humanitarian issues affecting black folks. I sit and listen to ten or more women on any given night speak so passionately about the struggles of survival, listening with a watchful eye, staying up long after my bedtime.[32]

On weekends, I enjoy walking beside Grandma as she pulls her two-wheel wired cart to the grocery store. When Grandma does business in "white town" (as if it is another city because of Jim Crow segregation. There is a suburban area of Fort Pierce named White City so ironic), she takes time and care explaining to me in detail historical landmarks. This is how our trip starts and ends, as she is a tour guide paying close attention to every detail. She drills and indoctrinates me on the do's and don'ts (black codes) of expected behavior around white folks. "Watch your manners and everything will go fine."

Grandma, left Charleston, South Carolina in 1922 with her son Herbert and her wealthy white socialite employer for their summer vacation home in Fort Pierce, Florida. Upon arrival, her employer had not informed Grandma that there were no separate Maids quarters. Because of Jim Crow laws, the pastor of Mount Olive

---

farming land, it is testimony of my ancestry's will to succeed and retain our family legacy, in spite of racial intolerance.

[32] Gullah people of West African retain much of their culture, and staple diet of rice, okra, pigeon peas were brought to the new world for their specialty for rice planting. This point can't be understated. South Carolinians and Englishmen place value and positive emphasis in selecting Africans from race-growing regions keenly aware of Africans technical knowledge to produce rice. West Africans early as 1500 possessed skills of cultivating rice. *Rice and Slaves, Ethnicity and the Slave Trade in Colonial South Carolina*, P. 99-114 1991. Daniel C. Littlefield gives one of the best scholarly accounts.

Baptist Church directed her to the colored section of town for racially segregated accommodations. There she met a widower, Ollie Jay, who needed help raising two of his younger children. She accepted his offer and eventually they got married.

Grandma and Uncle Herbert, age 5 after arrival to Fort Pierce circa, 1922. (Courtesy of Hurst family archives).

We make trips to Moore's Creek, which meanders like a snake several miles east and west of the city, dividing black and white communities. Grandma lays it down on me: "This is the color line," holding my hand, "it's a symbol of division, separated by colored and white folk. I think whites dug it for that purpose. I don't go over there unless I got business." She points to the south side of the creek where there are white homes with manicured lawns and a panoramic view of the creek, in sharp contrast to those on the other side. The creek for me is a reminder that we can look but we can't cross unless it's absolutely necessary. These kinds of reminders keenly sharpen my consciousness: How obviously disadvantaged and devalued blacks lives are in a system called Jim Crow.

"Listen and listen good, when we walk on the sidewalk and you see white folks you look them in the eyes and if they speak, you speak, and you answer 'yes' or 'no' like I taught you, not know 'no sir' and 'no maim' and you stay close to me and don't wonder off." No different than any other visit downtown. I try hard being a good little grandson, excited if I do good I'll get an apple strudel pastry. But this day in my mind, I have enough of her black code etiquette put to memory.

I listen, but have something distinctively different in mind. I recognize implicit warning signs from approaching eyes and facial expressions. The stares, smiles, frowns—looks of anger, hatred and resentment. Whites address Grandma respectfully as Ms. Jay. She proudly lets me know she earned it. "You know I never like dignifyin white folk with 'yes maim' and 'no maim, ' 'yes sir' and 'no sir.' They love hearin colored folk say it to make a living. Now I don't say it, gives them power and control over you. I didn't say it much workin in hot kitchens takin care of their young'uns either." (My sisters and I address our parents and adults respectfully, with yes or no as we were taught to do.) Grandma believes some no God-fearing uppity colored folk in Fort Pierce are fooled by white folks—give whites respect and reverence, never get any back. "Feel good saying maims and sirs, most whites ain't nothin but devils. Stay close to me and don't wonda off you get your apple strudel," she insists.

In summer of 1962, I take my first leap into reality on a trip to the A&P grocery store. Overcome with thirst, I simply ignore grandma rules sneak over and take a sip from a "whites only" pretty-green water fountain. The rusting silver fountain reserved for "colored only" never have cold water or a strong flow to quench my thirst. I gulp the cold refreshing water before grandma discover me missing. "You better get that boy right now!" Someone yell. I look up into eyes of a white lady snarling at me near the cashier with customers staring as grandma yank me around. I come to my senses understanding why she spend much time rehearsing. Her words reverberate in my ear from too many questions: "Scaldee how many times I need to tell you? Some things colored folk ain't allowed to do."

In my rebellious way, I couldn't resist temptation being told I can't drink water from a fountain when water is free. Reality struck me that moment caught in the clutches of Jim Crow segregation.

The manager come over towards grandma, "Maim, that boy's old enough to know better." "You gonna get a spanking for your disobedience...no apple strudel for you." Grandma says apologies to the manager. Her words, I suppose remove astonishment from the lady and manager faces at boldness of my undertaking. Embarrassed not for myself but having disappointed grandma. All I could do is wipe away my tears.

"All glory be to God," as grandma would say, it takes but a minute to see resentment and anger fade from white customers faces into a look of satisfaction as they commence doing business. The fact that a rusty "colored only" water fountain never worked properly doesn't matter. The need for a child to quench his thirst doesn't either. I violate a state law. A child, grandma warned, a colored child can go to jail.

Grandma promise spanking never materialized. Of course not! She sit me down with words of wisdom, "Child I ain't gonna listen to no demands by those devils spankin you for a drink of God's water for a moment of pleasure...they gotta answer to God."

I grasp wisdom in why Grandma apologized to the manager and his customers meant as words of consolation to appease and ease anxieties a bit because a little colored boy encroach upon their comfort. I got my apple strudel, and a new understanding how black folk use psychology in Jim Crow segregation as means to survival.

Some summer nights, Uncle Herbert likes to stretch a bit. We go outside in the fresh air to kill time, throwing and catching my football. Unk has a peculiar way of sizing me up with questions about things. I know it's part of Mama's scheme so I play along. I'm feeling like one of his four sons. He's a no-nonsense guy who keeps me thinking on my feet: "What if you don't make it in football or basketball?" "Your future?" "College?" "What will you do in life?" I feel overwhelmed by these probing questions that I have no answers to. "Don't waste your life. I see potential in you."

Uncle Herbert isn't lame, but unlike Grandma he doesn't possess something mystic, although I think he is a bit strange. He sits alone and still in an awkward position with his legs folded like an Indian Chief for long periods of time and says nothing. One evening, I walk past his bedroom and I can smell incense, and I can see a makeshift altar with symbols and ornaments and Unk sitting in meditation. Another profound moment I hear him mantra chanting. I'm surprised since I know nothing of his departure from Christianity. The Hindu faith he embraces sets me on my own quest for information about other religions.

One evening before his departure, we sit under our giant Australian pines to catch a slight breeze off the Atlantic Ocean from the humid night. "When I was young living in this old house, we always tell family stories to remember that last a life time," Uncle Herbert recalls. "You're smart, prepare yourself, you you're your father, exposure to new environments other than the South, it will help expand your mind with new ideas and interest." He insists. "Come visit your Aunt Norma and cousins in Long Island anytime. For me, a gracious gesture, he knows it must be difficult for me, and others like me growing up in the South without a father to reel me in if I lose my way. I get numb, turned off, not looking for pity. Rather, I want to sound tough, to throw him off. "No Unk, it don't mean a thing to me." Instead, it comes out differently. "Tell you the truth Unk, I used to feel sad seeing my friends with daddies...I got over I," whispering like it's an embarrassing secret someone I don't want hearing is listening to.

"Don't let it be a hindrance, keep your head up. I try to fashion a life for myself around moral character," he says. "Will help you stay grounded and you can turn back to it if you happen to go astray." For me, it's a great story to remember; a rare moment spending quality time with a black male authority figure.

Uncle Herbert revelations about his growing up are similar to mine. As a young man when Grandma divorced, he never knew his father. He never overcame that empty feeling, the void created by the absence of a father-son relationship. Until now, I had never given any thought about Daddy, other than being angry at him for being angry at me. "You can forget about Charles ever coming back south," I again overhear Uncle Herbert tell Mama. Might be in your best interest through passage of time to divorce." Nothing forceful, just an advisory chat a brother has out of concern and love for his sister. If he only knew, neither Mama nor Daddy wants a divorce. Mama I suppose doesn't for religious reasons. Daddy has been gone so long that I suppose it's about his ego staying in control. Mama's against any man visiting, so too is Grandma. But there are times when a few men come over who know Grandma for the purpose of getting to know Mama. I see a twinkle in their eyes. But me and my sisters make sure the twinkle doesn't stay long.

My sisters and I are overly protective. We sit, watch, frown, make unfriendly faces and do anything to make Mama's guests uncomfortable until she insists we leave the living room. We peep and spy around corners. We make it our business to sabotage any man replacing Daddy. We act indignant, we don't speak, we crumple paper and throw it at any random male guest. "You better treat my Mama nice cause I'm gonna tell my Daddy," Sheryl says innocently.

One night, Mr. Emerson, a handsome and muscular, mocha complexioned man with a perfect set of pearly whites comes over. He smiles a lot like daddy, a very nice man, but I think he has a sneaky side. I'm suspicious. He jokes trying to butter me up and get on my good side. Once, when I come home he's about to leave and stands in the doorway obstructing my path. With an intimidating manner, he whispers, "I know you don't like me. I like your mother, so nothing you can do about it, get used to me coming over." "You don't scare me one bit. If I find some dirt on you, something, anything I don't like I'll tell it. I'm watching you," I warn. "By the way, my Daddy's coming home soon." He gawks, shakes his head in disbelief. Turns out, Mr. Emerson is a nice man, but I don't like his idea coming over, ever. After that confrontation, he never does again. I grapple with the need to protect Mama, for a father I know little about.

Chapter 16

FORBIDDEN FRUIT

Sports do more to bring blacks and whites together than integration itself. Sports are the great equalizer—you must have a competitive edge to win regardless of color. Sports, too, help break down the racial barriers that separate us. My junior high's intramural teams three years earlier allowed me to release anger on the field. Black teammates take it out on white boys. We hit so damn hard to knock them out. Coaches yell, "Great tackle! Way to bust their can!" (Their asses) He doesn't have the slightest idea hitting is good therapy. "I'm busting your ass now cracker. How you like it? Who's superior now?" I say to myself, smiling as they get up grimacing in pain. White boys catch on fast, some change positions, dare play halfback, receiver, and quarterback again; they don't want any part of the football.

I bring spiked cleats and a uniform home to wash. Neighborhood buddies who attend segregated Lincoln Park are in awe; they have no intramural teams. They want to see and touch the cleats and uniform and hear what our games are like. I'm embarrassed to brag, because segregation cheats black schools of opportunities in every way.

Playing team sports with white boys is unlike playing with my neighborhood buddies. I can't get used to uncoordinated white boys who can't play worth a damn, and interrupt a game for trivial rule infractions. Brothers have a fit and don't tolerate it, especially in hard-nosed sandlot games. Some white boys competing against blacks don't like the idea that blacks have dominance. White boys want brothers to know, if they can't beat us playing, they can with cunning, use the rules. It's implicit: "You might have athletic superiority over us, but we control the game with intelligence." "We know the rules." Although I don't like interruptions, I come to admire this shrewd strategy.

We play freestyle team sports in our neighborhoods with basic rules. But Eugene "Jinx" Jenkins, a true lover of popular sports, knows rules, and team and player statistics more than most coaches. Jinx gives me a crash course while watching games at his home. At school I discover in full court basketball games some white boys don't know diddly squat. It's more a superior attitude, the shame of losing to blacks. I join them, arguing over rules just as much as they do. I don't like white boys thinking I'm dumb, so I argue my point. Soon I have them siding with me.

Before gym class, I stop by Coach Valentine's office about something I now can't recall. I overhear his peculiar conversation with Coaches King and Burleson about racial distinctions between black and white athletes. Valentine has the sports section of the newspaper opened on his desk. Coach Haley (black) comes in and discusses standout black athletes. King's the loudest, and he's big and burly, perhaps he played football in his day. The discussion gets intense, often separating black athletes by speed agility and power. Marveling over the speed of past and present Lincoln Park Academy track star speed demons Jack Hemi, Jimmy Fowler and Calvin Henderson; football stars sure-handed receiver, Sammie Sykes, elusive halfback Robert Crutchfield and many others. "That quarterback Marcellus Brown is a smart kid, you don't see that from the Negro at the collegiate level," King muses. "Lincoln Park always has great athletes, if white schools give um a break," Coach Haley adds.

Some days, I stand near the door out of view, listening to debates over black athletes like halfback Iverson Williams and wide receiver Jackie Kelly making their mark, already shattering records at recently integrated John Carroll High School. "What would a Notre Dame be like?" Valentine weighs in. "Or University of Texas," Burleson chimes in with his southern accent, western string tie, cowboy boots and crew-cut. "All out recruiting the Negro? It's not happening yet, maybe in a few more years," King adds. Until then I give little thought to their hypothesis. Black athletes like Joe Louis, Jessie Owens, Jackie Robinson and Jim Brown are all at the top of the white man's game. There's something special about our athletic prowess that forces racism to step aside. The strategy is to integrate all schools if they want to share in the black athletic dominance.

Brothers shooting pool at Nappy Chin's often get into heated debates over past Lincoln Park athletic greats who were overlooked. They resent the missed opportunities, being shut out of big rich white colleges because of segregation and prejudice. The great ones come a dime a dozen at black schools. Coach Valentine, King, Haley and Burleson weren't unrealistic in their debates. Integration slowly makes it possible. These coaches might have attended Lincoln games at Jaycee Fields. Some whites do. You can't miss specks of white in a sea of black folks slipping out minutes before a game's end to avoid being in the mix with black fans.

But for blacks, walking home once the game ends is part of the celebration except that we are accompanied by an unwelcomed police escort. Chief Christianson has his map out and is steering us clear from downtown, away from white businesses, as if we might break in and steal something. Christianson's officers tail beside us in patrol cars. We get loud and boisterous like a pep rally, while walking through white neighborhood as we endure police harassment. While inching along behind us in their cars, the cops yell, "Quiet down and stay the hell on the sidewalks!" Cops are shouting through bullhorns. We dare them to find a reason to arrest someone. "Kiss my ass!" brothers yell back. It's unrealistic for anybody to stay quiet after a football game. The crowd explodes in laughter. Cops speed off realizing that a little football fun is alright.

Our pep songs disturb white folks out of their sleep. Our way of protesting: "Hell, let us walk our own way home, you won't have this mess." White folks come outside, angry at the cops not at us. "Cop is harassing y'all acting like damn fools with bullhorns," a white liberal lady complains. Perception is that blacks can't be trusted walking unsupervised downtown without looting white businesses.

We resent the implication because we have never looted their businesses. We have more than enough suppressed anger, if we'd wanted to destroy properties, if we hadn't been so powerless.

At an early age, I learn that there are no lunch counter sit-ins in Fort Pierce's Woolworths, despite the passage of the Civil Rights Act in 1964 that guaranteed equal access to public accommodations. No protests at the Sunrise Theatre, at hotels, businesses and other segregated public places other than an incident at the Greyhound Station that turn into a riot. Perhaps Chief Christianson is edgy haven't forgotten. Small groups articulate their disapproval, but large-scale organized protests don't exist. There's a kind of passivity to protest that exists among Fort Pierce's black leadership. De facto segregation persists long after the passage of the Civil Rights Act until Dr. King's death. Protests then take a different approach that had unexpected results in major cities.

Cops follow us until we cross over Orange Avenue to Tenth Street and Avenue D. Once reaching the black district, white cops don't give a damn what happens, so they retreat into the white district. We tolerate their after-game control patrolling for a long time. I take note of such things beyond school desegregation. Cops make sure we stay in our place, and we're basically complacent with it. But I witness the anger reflected on silent faces. I know I'm not alone. The hatred for white folks' system of segregation that persists after the introduction of school desegregation, limits, cripples, controls and inconveniences the quality of our lives. This we all find to be unsettling and unacceptable.

Most mornings before class I spend time hooping with Ron and the Alford brothers, Charles and Oscar, and "Ballie Boo" Davis and a host of other schoolmates. Brothers take over all two goals honing our skills. A white boy doesn't stand a chance playing unless he's there early and brings a ball. Some brothers seem to come to school just to play ball. St. Lucie Junior High has ninth grade Gators junior varsity in football, basketball, and track and field. We have four intramural teams: Blue Devils, Cardinals, Golden Bears and Hurricanes in football and basketball and one rinky-dink team for smaller guys in football and basketball. Players line up for speed drills because you're selected by swiftness of feet and how you handle agility drills. Coach Valentine looks at a player's coordination and athleticism in drills—speed, catching, blocking, tackling, shooting, jumping and rebounding. Newly arriving blacks from segregated Lincoln Park Academy aren't used to hearing white coaches give praise. Many get a bighead.

Some pampered stars get lazy academically. All the hoopla about talent and new attention from whites distract them from keeping "eyes on the prize"—to get a quality education. Their focus shifts from the classroom to athletics. Atrophy sets into their brains, convincing themselves that they don't need to study. Some fall victim to the dumb jock syndrome—not because they are, but because they get the bighead; all the attention is intoxicating.

It doesn't take long for signs of jealousy and resentment to seep into black athletes showered with this special attention. I won starting position at split end for the Cardinals. Some white teammates resent speaking to me on the field or in the locker room. It doesn't bother me one bit. It is our turn to spread our wings in the sphere of equal opportunity. Even so, I see the effects from freshly written racial epithets, "dumb n....r jocks" carved into the walls of bathroom stalls.

Coach Valentine calls a meeting to break the mounting tension, but some phantom fool keeps it up. Coach assigns a guy with locker duties to monitor the johns and threatens suspensions. In some way, graffiti awakens a few brothers academically. In class, some refocus their eyes back on the prize. Perhaps the graffiti is a reminder why they're at school in the first place. Others can't handle the aggrandizing sense of importance granted them for their athletic prowess. Pampered and star struck, some experience the beginnings of their academic demise.

White fans flock to our games, watching up-and-coming black star athletes for the first time. And we don't disappoint. Few whites refuse to watch a winning team dominated by black stardom making headlines.

Some white teammates pout on the bench, snubbed by Coach Burleson not letting them play, even if it means disappointing their parents. Coach rarely gives in. Only when a few angry dads criticize his strategy does he give in, allowing their sons playing time, but only if we're winning. Some mothers come down from the bleachers to give Coach Haley an earful. "I got to play my starters, my best play first!" he yells back over the noise. He says we're his stars. I wasn't naïve falling for the hype.

I catch a pass for a touchdown, scampering down the sidelines. All racial attitudes change when I walk past our all-white cheerleading squad. The largely white crowd goes wild and cheerleaders come running over, patting me on the back. For a moment I watch their smiling faces caught up in the excitement. I know under ordinary circumstances I'd be rejected and wouldn't be touched for the color of my skin. I know better. I'm invisible, nothing other than a reflex action that cheerleaders ordinarily do in a moment of celebration.

The Golden Bears intramural squad from 1968 St. Lucie Junior High Gators yearbook. Top left, Coach Burleson, childhood friends 52, Clemmie Hill, 53, Mickie Collins and I, 54. Surprisingly little Mickie shown here grew 6'10" to dominant on the high school and college level.

In St. Lucie Junior High, few white teammates make an effort to introduce themselves, not until my popularity increases on the gridiron or on the basketball court. This is when I sense what is at first implicit before full disclosure. Race and fear is the issue, but sports has the tendency of bringing out people's humanity. Even for the black athlete, I discover, if you're at least halfway smart and play some ball your stock increases in popularity with the girls. With each game come smiles, giggles, wiggles, winks and kisses from the sisters. White girls are no different. What's considered taboo only means keeping a low profile.

This "forbidden fruit" begins to stir up the black athletes' curiosities. Blacks not cutting it academically get caught up chasing a white trophy. All the attention being "the big man on campus" adds another distraction away from hitting the books. The bright lights of the gridiron with cheerleaders and cheering fans calling out your name and number, for a black or white athlete is electric.

Unfamiliar white attention and recognition can, without question, bring a sense of new found importance and acceptance. In the world of sports, one must be careful of the "rose-colored glasses" it promises. But I see greater benefits for studious "black jocks" who acquire greater merit and attract triple the attention when they excel academically and on the field. They are the boys who get the girls.

I appreciate and do better when I receive such remarks as "Good job" and "Well done" on and off the field. I get an appreciable amount of attention from white girls sitting next to me in class. They're friendly and smile and are willing to share notes.

The Freeman brothers, Harrison and Coleman, are attractive and well-dressed. They are from a middle-class family and they can't escape the white girls' interest. Harrison, older is athletic, cool, laid back and quiet, while Coleman is livelier and more outgoing. Harrison has sharpen his football skills and grows into a dynamite halfback at the intramural level. The white girls really dig his clean image. The Freeman's are two of the first blacks to boldly exhibit openly, interracial dating, causing quite a stir as they swing Sandra and Betty on their arms in the school's corridors in full view, like attention-seeking peacocks. The disdain of whites parting the breezeways in shock and awe to the occasional hateful words "N….r Lovers."

Some faculty members don't conceal their building resentment as some black athletes stroll the corridors with white girls. It's like watching a Macy's Thanksgiving Day Parade. The swagger obviously brings prejudiced remarks and nervous whispers. I sometimes tease the brothers. "Maann y'all gonna get lynched!" Coleman is the youngest, playfully animated and takes it in jest. Harrison takes it in more seriously. "Kenny, don't be joking like that. We're just having fun."

Obviously, flaunting their innocence in a racially forbidden manner draws for many whites, a disdainful display of anger. Teasing from the brothers is tolerable, but not the remarks coming from white boys who perceive this racial mixing as encroaching on their territory. White girls are a symbol of white purity and white boys are rattled that blacks are taking their place. To protect this purist image, Sandra and Betty get downgraded to "white trash." These girls are popular with blacks, hardly a day passes without a call to account for their behavior from the administration. "You can't walk around like that, it causes problems." "Like what?" "Well you know, what will your mother and father think?" "It's not your business," they snap back, sashaying away.

White free-spirited hippies are independent thinkers, rebellious, against old southern traditions and they welcome spirited conversations about integration, interracial dating and other racial issues. They sit with blacks at lunch tables, in the library and in breezeways between classes. This is how I meet Amy. We have shared classes together throughout junior high. She is friendly, smart, attractive and curious. Amy always displays a positive demeanor. "You should lighten up. You're too serious, and smile, I like your smile," she tells me. "I have little to smile about," I remind her.

Amy sits directly behind me in eighth grade general science class. We share notes, and chat before class in a superficial kind of way. My big neat Afro—popular in a Jackson Five style, on occasion obstructs her view taking notes from the chalkboard. She asks politely to move my head, but it never helps much. Whenever Amy needs to see the chalkboard, she pulls my hair playfully. One day she whispers in my ear, "Since your hair covers so much space let me put a fence around it, take care of it if you walk me home." This eventually leads to some deep conversations. I find myself walking her to class, but I have my suspicions. Amy's open-mindedness, I suppose, wants to kumbaya me to show that she isn't prejudiced. I get this morbid thought— perhaps she's compensating with a guilty conscious for her ancestors' slave ownership.

The more we talk the more I am convinced that she isn't disguising her racial hang ups. Rather, she wants to discuss them up front. Sometimes on our lunch break we find a secluded spot on a bench not to attract attention. She's very curious and bombards me with questions, especially questions about blacks' anger towards whites. She can't understand the powder keg of anger from years of frustration that has been building and when it is unleashed it targets the color white, regardless of the name of the innocent. "We have no traditions here. Nothing to remind us of our school traditions and culture, we're always taken for granted," I remind her. "You should be happy to integrate," she tells me, something I hear whites say too often. It is clear to us that whites' effort to welcome blacks is—superficial. "I don't think we'll ever become color-blind." She ponders over that quietly. "I still think black is beautiful," she proclaims. I laugh, surprised to hear her admit it.

Amy and I delve into deep discussions on race, sometimes shy away to ask controversial race questions that stir her curiosity. She doesn't understand an incident between two black girls in the locker room that almost turns to fisticuffs. "Why is it dark-skinned blacks are teased about their skin color by lighter ones?" "And why so much anger?" I'm caught off guard, always in the habit of referring to historical information from black history books I read. I put it to her in one word—*self-hate* caused by slavery and racism. I break it down in simple terms, focusing on the former question. Segregation causes misdirected hate, just like during slavery. The lighter skinned black feels closer to his oppressor, and feels superior to darker blacks who often feel inferior about themselves. I touch on slavery as chattel property, who are treated as being less than human. The only things back then relieving our misery are God, prayer, and song.

Amy gets quiet thinking about that. She believes integration is causing whites to reevaluate their own prejudices. "I want to do my part and make a difference," Amy says. I admire her for that. Though she doesn't understand why with greater opportunities for better education some blacks aren't taking it seriously. Carter G. Woodson's *Mis-education of the Negro* and Elijah Muhammad's *Message to The Black Man in America* are books I reference to Amy and among the books I vigorously reread with regularity. She has obviously never heard of them. "You see why we need to include our history in class? We're miseducated and misguided about our glorious past," I explain.

What little of our history appears in textbooks gets rushed and skimmed over. Teachers stay on the topic of slavery too long, only to mention a few well-known black leaders—it is cultural "whitewashing." The history that is taught purposely devalues our contributions after slavery, while smearing their contributions to history in our faces.

One day from the depths of my consciousness, I release what I have no intention of letting slip from my lips. I tell Amy that I hate white people. Her dark eyes watch me, waiting for me to flip the script into a practical joke. But it never happens. So, when she punches me on the shoulder thinking I'll come to my senses, I assure her that I'm not kidding. Amy goes quiet a moment. "Kenneth Ira Hurst, I don't see you that way," saying my full name like I made a solemn oath of dishonesty. "Because you don't know how I live my life." I snapped. She grabs my hand like I need comforting and I snatch it back. I feel terrible, but I can't tell her from where my hatred really originates. How it got started in a city park. There's silence as she looks as confused in her thoughts as I am in mine. I apologize, and I do so quickly to recover my own surprise at how unintended words slip from my subconscious.

One day Amy promises me there won't be problems walking her home. Football practice is cancelled for the day, so I get to leave school early. But I am skittish about walking to her home on Sunrise Blvd, a few blocks from school. I get nervous thinking about what might happen walking with a white girl in broad daylight in a middle-class white neighborhood. Somehow, I get my nerve up for the experience. With every passing car, I psyche myself up— don't let it be the Klan. We get a few stares, and when cars slow down, I tense up, ready to do battle with a redneck, but nothing happens.

Amy introduces me to her mother. I feel nervous, like Sidney Poitier must have felt in *Guess Who's Coming to Dinner.* Her mother smiles and doesn't show any outward appearance of shock or anger. Amy invites me in, but I don't want to step into such a delicate experience that I'm not quite ready to undertake. We continue our friendship on campus. Romantically involved, we keep a tight undercover relationship. I don't allow myself to cross the threshold, taking the forbidden fruit of interracial dating into the open. There's much to discover in my own culture; too much racial hatred to put myself in harm's way; and too many fine sisters to take myself out of circulation.

White girls are undertaking avoidable risks, trapped by their black love interests. They're mostly despised and shunned between two worlds as prejudiced whites hound them with threats and fights while resentful and jealous soul sisters get uptight over pursuing potential boyfriends. Outraged rednecks like the Ag Boys and Swamper varieties scratch racial epithets on freshly painted-over graffiti on bathroom stalls, walls, in schoolbooks, on school desks and anywhere to make their point. Humiliate by placing a name beside phrases: "Cindy is a n....r lover, treat her like a leper."

After school and on weekends, Carol and Diana, two white hippie girls, trek across the tracks venturing into some dangerous hot spots off Avenue D. Older cats cruising, stop to hit on them and they get a lift to who knows where. Both boldly lay themselves on the line, defying all odds for a little while.

These two hippies hang out at house parties with a few black girlfriends in pursuit of the forbidden fruit. Carol can hardly sip an ounce of beer without getting wasted. Diana, tall and husky, keeps it more together. One rainy Saturday afternoon at Jinx's house watching Notre Dame whip up on Michigan, Carol shows up at the door smelling of alcohol, her dress sticking to her body drenched from a heavy down pour. She had been walking and looking for some brother. Someone gave her a ride, a few beers, and came on too strong, so she jumped out at a corner nearby. Jinx gives her a towel to dry off and a glass of water. She sits long enough to stare blankly at the game for a restless moment. "Why you walking the streets looking for some brother?" I ask, genuinely concerned. "I feel safe, lots of blacks know me." "Carol, you don't understand, it can be dangerous with these older cats. Who were you riding with?" "Don't worry me, not your business, you got some weed and beer?" Jinx doesn't do either and I drink occasionally.

The rain lets up to a slight drizzle. Jinx's family doesn't have a phone. We watch her stagger to a phone booth down the street. But before reaching it, she jumps back into the very same car she got out of. The car rolls into the driveway. Two brothers inside with Carol are drinking beer to the O' Jays' "The Backstabbers" blaring from an 8-track cassette player. An argument ensues, and she jumps out once more, stumbling intoxicated towards the house. The brothers back out of the driveway kicking up dust. "White bitch, ya can't ride unless you give it up!"

Carol lives up to the rumors twirling around campus—that she's promiscuous. "Can you stay awhile until you sober up?" I ask. "Nooo leaaave meee the hellll alooone!" She apologizes, "I know you care about what happens to me." Then she leaves anyway.

I'm home a short while afterwards when I hear a voice outside. It's Charlie! Jinx little brother. "You better come quick, that white girl come by again. She gonna get raped!" He pleads with me. I find Carol with two brothers in an abandoned house nearby, with her panties pulled down. I try to intervene. "Leave me alone!" she yells intoxicated. "It ain't your damn business, she likes it this way," one brother says. His gratifying smile widens with each word. I can't believe it. "You heard her brotha, back off, we gonna pull this train," the other chimes in and pulls out a knife. Carol is searching for the forbidden fruit and she finds it in an unlikely place.

It's not uncommon hearing the latest gossip at school that some white girl or black girl gets a train pulled on her during a weekend party. These tragedies or escapades happen, getting high in back bedrooms of house parties. And some aren't naughty school girls.

Just naive and innocent girls caught up trusting young hip hardcore streetwise dropouts whose motives are to turn white or black chicks into ladies of the night. Some, like Carol and Diana, are open to a black experience, whichever way they can find it. And the brothers are more than accommodating to whatever stereotypical appetites white girls may have.

I overhear two brothers rap in a restroom, one bragging to the other how much in love a white girl is with him. She gives him money. Her fascination with his dark skin, the way he moves, his sexual prowess. He speaks as if she's his trophy much as he's her prized possession.

It reminds me of a series of novels I obsess over, somewhat the same situations that two white authors write about. All deal with slavery and plantation life: *Mistress of Falconhurst, Mandingo, Falconhurst Fancy, The Mustee, Flight to Falconhurst, Drum, Master of Falconhurst, and Heir to Falconhurst.* I can't put them down. Slave breeding, brutality, lust, envy. In a story plot the plantation master's wife is jealous of her husband's interest in female slaves and the way the author exploits the wife's insecurities. She lusts over this one black physical specimen—this big buck with sexual prowess—who her husband buys off the auction block. In her private moments, her lust turns to love. And in it, she discovers this oppressed slave is a man, a proud independent thinker with emotion, compassion and aspiration. She falls deeply in love, or is it lust? Unable to let him go, and unable to control her feelings for him, a slave, she jeopardizes her marriage, inheritance, and his life.

These novels put my awareness into action. Between classes, I catch the inviting eyes of white girls looking at me as I walk down the corridors. I smile. If a girl smiles back, doesn't turn away or frown, I know she's open-minded and unlikely to hold prejudiced views. I strike up conversations. Get her name and get to know her. In time I am able to see what her motivations are. I'm excited how readily they're willing to talk openly about almost anything.

After some baiting, I pose a question to see if they're willing to try the "forbidden fruit." Some laugh uncomfortably when agreeing. Others won't for racial reasons, while others dig brothers already, too nervous and cautious to approach. My buddy, Ron and I come a long way from the first days of integration, touching their flat white fannies.

I'm soon obsessing over another series of fictional novels about plantation life: *Child of the Sun, The Black Sun, Golden Stud, The Mahound,* and *The Tattooed Rood.* The authors' audacity makes fictional books come alive. All have similar plotlines—miscegenation, lust, brutality, violence, unspeakable acts of breeding slaves, and the typical fascination with the black man's sexual prowess. The story lines are graphic! Real and identifiable with what happened during slavery in America. I think the authors are pulling skeletons from their own family histories. Each story and character deviate little from the standard plots. Especially in the earlier mentioned *Falconhurst Fancy*, when an overpowering master, and his wife with lustful passions pursue a slave when his fate is doomed. I can't ever imagine encountering, in my young life, such fascinating and emotionally charged story plots that come alive, all in one weekend.

Me, Darnell and Charlie go fishing and crabbing. We take a short cut across U.S. Highway 1 from Avenue E. Passing Trevor, a white man in his early 30s, sitting on his porch drinking a beer. Typical redneck, crew cut, cowboy boots, T-shirt and denim jeans. He's rather friendly, waves to us on our way. We're suspicious at first, until he asks to see what we catch, and then buys a few fish and crabs. Sometimes a few beers get Trevor talking more than we have time to listen. His funny dirty jokes gets Charlie, a jokester himself, excited.

One day, Charlie goes behind a bush about to relieve himself. Trevor says, "Charlie go inside, my wife will show you to the bathroom." My antenna goes up, knowing how protective Jinx is of his little brother. Charlie's fearless with a cutting-edge temper and he's known not to bite his tongue nor back down to older guys. Tenacious, he'll chase you with the knife he carries. "Charlie's ok out here," I say cautiously. But Charlie's not having it. "If Trevor doesn't mind lettin his pretty wife show me to the bathroom, I don't either. What's the hell wrong with you?"[33]

Inside a cracked screen door, a tall, pretty blonde lady stands smiling. She opens the door and motions Charlie inside. Darnell looks nervous and I am shocked. I'm thinking, damn Trevor rather stay put talking to us while this mannish joker goes inside alone with his wife. Within a few minutes, Charlie comes out smiling. Leaving, Charlie says, "Maann, Trevor's wife asked me can she watch." "What you say?" "I told her 'hell yeah come on in." We believe Charlie's lying, because he usually exaggerates to impress.

The next weekend, Trevor stops us and proposes that we come sleep with his wife while he watches. It all seems a joke to Darnell and Charlie. Trevor looks serious and I believe we're walking into a scurrilous game. Y'all pack the real McCoy!" He smiles and offers to pay a studding fee for an exhibition. I restrain, but Charlie's overly excited, eager to take Trevor up on the offer. "Maann you must be crazy thinking we do something like that!" Darnell says. "Sorry, I thought you guys are up to it." Trevor recoils, embarrassed by Darnell's rejection, awkwardly realizing we wasn't as he'd hoped.

I think of the *Falconhurst* novels that white authors write are more a white fantasy borne out of slavery than a fictitious one. It was clear, Trevor breathed life into these stereotypes that persist to the present. Lest we forget innocent black men who are lynched when falsely accused of lusting over and raping white women, more often out of her design. The white man's insecurities about protecting the purity of his woman from miscegenation—a southern cracker's worst nightmare, moves him to resort to violence and murder.

Trevor wants to bring life to his fantasy. I sit on his porch gawking. Wondering how the hell did we get into this. I think of the novels, this fascination with black men's sexual prowess. Trevor really wants to purchase us as studs for hire as he sits, watches, and fulfills his fantasies. Perhaps he'll even ask to bid for the right price, like we're on auction blocks for the sake of livening up his sex game. His wife comes to the door with the audacity to ask, nervously, "Hey guys, can I size you up?" Darnell laughs then looks at me. It's happening

---

[33] Charlie dies young by stabbing with a knife.

too fast. Just what I read comes to life—their fantasy. A slave owner's wife's role in an auction block examination scene is playing out in my reality. Before purchase, the slave owner takes us back to a private spot to fondle for size and studding before sealing the deal.

There I am young, feeling invincible, willing to try almost anything, but not this. While Trevor plays it down laughing, joking with his wife, we watch as she rubs one large breast with her hand. "You guys don't know what you're missing," Trevor says, with an enticing stare at his wife. "That's right," she adds giggling, winking her approval and cracking the screen door for a clearer view of the imprint of her erect nipple in a tight halter top. I see in it hidden dangers, yet I have an awful time convincing Charlie that his willingness to take the plunge is not a good move. I am concerned that he might just go back to test that forbidden fruit.

Chapter 17

SAME OLE CHANGES

Numbness is what I feel toward integration. You can't expect seeing it where you look for it—it's invisible. On campus, it's personal—an individual thing. You make your own interracial experiences wherever you find them. It sure isn't utopia. It's like looking through the illuminating lens of a kaleidoscope expecting to see beautiful images, by comparison, no real social freedoms, justice or equality happens in my neighborhood. I'm not hopeful at all.

There are times I want to pack up and leave Fort Pierce, leave America go to Africa. To leave America is whimsical thinking of frustration my people built much of America—blood soaked and mixed into the soil of this country. I understand integration's purpose, but it doesn't give me joy in the morning waking up for school. I don't feel my spirit shouting "Integration is a good thing!"

My sole purpose is to get a good education. The integration thing will only happen when white people allow themselves to feel it in their hearts and minds. I'm unconvinced that diehard whites will ever change. Rather than giving integration a chance, they pull their children out of public schools and put them into lily-white private schools in other counties. Minds are changing, but some blacks are reluctant to put their children into integrated schools, not to reject integration but to avoid the violence integration brings. Most middle-class black parents don't want the stigma on their child's family name with a criminal record should violence result in arrests. Time will stand still, and Hell will freeze over before integration is a success.

The federal government keeps a close watch on how racial problems are handled at St. Lucie County's public schools. Teachers are under great stress to perform despite overcrowded conditions and racial tensions that integration creates. I witness rigidity in teaching styles and boring lesson plans. A hot topic turns into a debatable racial issue. Students who are eager to discuss relevant topics don't get the chance as cautious white teachers quickly diffuse potentially explosive discussions. I find it, at times, difficult to stay focused, as do most. I have not had one black teacher going into my third year of integration. I miss their creative energy and teaching styles. Boredom in class lures me into the streets. Just enough study time to get by as my B average takes a nosedive.

One day, sitting on a bench outside the Busy Bee, with a book in my hand, waiting for an open pool table, a brother from Detroit watches me. "What's you reading?" *"Black Like Me,"* I say. "I notice you reading in the strangest places. I got something you'll like." He goes to his car and brings me a book. "I like to see brothers filling their heads with knowledge." *Dark Ghetto: Dilemmas of Social Power* by psychologist, educator and social activist Kenneth Clark. Clark delves into issues of abject poverty, lack of hope in the underclass, and the plight of black life on the streets, a subject that interest me. Living near Avenue D, exposed to street life, I like observing common folks, their behaviors and social conditions. The book becomes my bible, exposing hidden truths how black folks struggle to survive.[34]

---

[34] In Brown v. Board of Education, Topeka school desegregation case Dr. Kenneth Clark "Doll Test" (a black and a white doll) was persuasive enough for U.S. Supreme Court to overturn the Separate but Equal Doctrine. Dr. Clark had long before Brown, used his groundbreaking experiment proven the psychological effects segregation has on black children self-esteem and how one feel about his or her race, color and academic achievement. Each time a black child was asked specific questions e.g., the best, the prettiest, the best to play with preference a white doll was disturbingly picked. The Supreme Court held, in essence, the Separated but Equal Doctrine was inherently unequal. To separate African-American child solely because of race, similar age and qualifications creates a badge of inferiority. The doll experiment is still used today reflect a tendency of a

I equate it to life of migrant workers struggling to earn a meager existence; how inequities turn many into wineheads living for the bottle. It makes me wonder why an old lady living near the streets just nods her head when I speak to her, staring blankly at me from her porch each time I pass. Street life can make you suspicious and restless. To the impoverished and their impressionable minds, the street is a powerful trap into what Clark calls "the pathologies of the ghetto."

In early 1968, there is high teacher absenteeism and resignations, others are threatening to strike. Students are absent from school as a result. Many poor parents as domestic workers are unable to afford childcare stay home. As a result, some of my friends' parents lose their jobs. During this crisis, many poor and illiterate are unable to assist their children with homework. In a rare moment, I tag along with Mama on her appointment to volunteer with the Vista program to help poor and uneducated parents learn how to read.[35] As we wait in a small office, a pale lady with a New England accent busy on the phone cut into a city official. "What you're doing is not enough...black families need more housing...that's the biggest problem." (A 70-unit federal housing project is projected by city officials not yet under construction. The housing authority say is a beginning although there are 500 applicants.) Minna Barlow get our attention as she address discrimination practices and disparities between blacks and whites that linger in Fort Pierce.

Mama and I amusedly listen to Barlow debate the official on welfare starvation budgets the poor get from Welfare departments

---

large percentage of blacks to favor light skin and white characteristics. Rather than celebrate or unique characteristics, we may subconsciously justify reasons for style, choice or individual taste to wear blonde hair or blue contacts or other Eurocentric identifiers. Invariably it is much deeper, rather a psychological dilemma that extends far into our enslavement as a people. The paralysis of mental slavery still lingers.

[35] Volunteers in Service to America (Vista) is a national service program founded in 1964 design to fight poverty in low income communities. Vista coordinate volunteers with various organizations to address illiteracy, healthcare concerns, unemployment, deficient economic neighborhood development, and lack of quality housing. Volunteers work directly with the poor to improve their quality of life.

and not just black folks whites too. Barlow explain to the insensitive official, poor women as a result of loss of jobs are without food some forced into prostitution to feed their children has no effect on the listener. Mama whisper, "this is why I worry about your sisters but you mostly…this white male dominated society is uncaring about the poor…will be crueler to you later as a strong, proud smart black male…with an education you will be seen as a threat."

Barlow ask the city official a strikingly honest question, why blacks don't deliver mail in Fort Pierce, work in the post office, as bank tellers, or sales clerks must of cause the city official voice to stuttered with indecision. "I'm waiting for your answer." Bartow repeat. And none came at the end of the call. It was quite obvious selective discrimination. "I talk to these officials enough, she tells mama, and get excuses they must move slow with blacks…you think 100 years since Lincoln's Emancipation Proclamation is long enough."

Barlow is a determined, this white savvy principled women hone her skills dealing with city government big-wigs in impoverish areas of Harlem. She seems the ideal advocate for the poor in the Lincoln Park community to confront good ole boys in city government. I have not met a white person like Barlow speak truth to power about social and economic injustices towards black folk. I suspect she relinquish her racial biases long ago to do this work so genuinely natural and honest in her comments.

Racial injustice, Barlow understand are systemic in white positions of power meant to move slow to suppress black progress. Just as in Brown, the 1954 Supreme Court school desegregation case was a restrictive decision to give leverage to whites in power to "deliberately" move slowly then and embolden city officials now to do just that at all cost. Barlow affirmed what I and Blacks already know. The movers and shakers downtown Fort Pierce don't give a dam—dare come to look at the conditions of my people in our neighborhoods. Politicians down in City Hall, I dare any to set foot, to see, hear, smell, breathe, and feel the depth of poverty in the community inner city, where people in despair are neglected. Unpaved streets with potholes, broken streetlights, no drainage system, mounds of neglected garbage and trash piles from negligent city services, no community libraries, a small outdated community recreation center, no tennis courts, ballparks or swimming pool to cool off. We pay taxes, don't we? Where is the empowerment zone Barlow speaks about should revitalize poor neighborhoods with better housing? Where are the Man Power Programs for job skills and employment opportunities to help eliminate sources of poverty and despair? We can still hope and dream.

As Barlow points out, local government racist attitudes and policies restrict black advancement as it surely does on the federal level. Barlow with her experience is not surprise Fort Piece city officials implement discriminatory practices with well scripted excuses. Her fight for the poor, open my eyes wide with a keener vision of awareness at a critical stage in my youth. I come to believe there are other whites willing to fight with us. I just wasn't sure who they are.

Although Jim Crow is legally abolished, white supremacy surface in attitudes and actions of some white schoolmates and even older teachers bought up in that era. Whites of the Jim Crow era down town have always govern black lives—racist then and racist now. City officials in their lofty positions have attitudes Jim Crow still exist. In their minds remains a necessary evil to try and keep a foot on our necks.

I often sit on a bench at the Busy Bee Poolroom on Avenue D and study the tale-tale signs poverty and despair does to my people deprive of an education miss out on social and economic opportunities. We can never be free until this unjust white power structure is fair and just. We can no longer be naïve in believing our city government will relinquish its vice-grip of unfairness over us any time soon without a fight. Malcolm X brilliantly emphatic in his message say it best, if we are to achieve freedom, justice and equality we will have to take it by any means necessary. This is as much my mantra as it is young brothers and sisters throughout the U.S. frustrated and impatient for change.

I feel the pain of the elderly, and it saddens me not of my condition, I was young determine to get an education and move forward, but I know the squalor and wretched conditions many live in. I see them drift about trying to make ends meet. Even in a time of black consciousness and racial pride, the paralysis of mental slavery in them lingers. I see in their lifeless eyes deprived of even a glimmer of hope because of racial injustice have never known how to hope.

I beg the question to many on the streets: What if you had that same chance afforded to whites? Like Victor, an excellent self taught shade tree mechanic unable to read or write. Jim Crow denied an opportunity to reach his full potential. "I be educated way ahead by now...have my own shop....make ah good livin fa my family...why you ask dis question? No I ain't got no schoolin...I'm ah old man now...that chance long gone." Jim Crow snatched away his humanity, a chance for an education, to be sure, an opportunities to advance the quality of his life. From the inception of America and the framers of the constitution guaranteed human rights and civil liberties to white citizens with exception to black folk.

Mama says I am mature beyond my 14years; she must also understand it is so because I am hardened by the environment I am exposed to. I am critical of America with her racist history. I am not hopeful America will ever be truly fair to her so-called black citizens. Mama will never accept the classification of second class citizenship and let that status control or strip her humanity, nor give her a sense of inferiority. I suppose, I inherit my parents pride, I come to understand pride flow in the blood of my ancestors. I love black people and we can't afford to wait for governmental fairness. I am willing to risk speaking against systems of oppression even in my classrooms.

At a desperate time for social change in America, I remain motivated by voices of protest; I read about Fannie Lou Hammer, Huey Newton, Bobby Seale, Eldridge Cleaver, H. Rap Brown, Angela Davis and many others. Young brothers and sisters are conscious and engage in the struggle for racial equality on campuses of integrated schools, in St. Lucie County and throughout America. The local NAACP and black leadership are organized in our communities. We are destine to vote out racist school board members, city officials, politicians and vote in progressive thinking blacks to address or needs and concerns.

I come to believe integration will never be a cure-all to our problems. Integration is a first step, but won't solve problems on our streets and neighborhoods, until we can get concern city officials and politicians to address real issues of racial inequality. Barlow look squarely into Mama eyes with deep reflection of work she so passionately dedicate her life to in Boston out of retirement to do here in Fort Pierce. "Mrs. Hurst I must tell you and your son listening to my response is what you already know this downtown system of Florida crackers only value blacks as second class citizens."

Mama has never identified with the term second-class citizenship, let control or life our humanity, nor give us a sense of inferiority. Black citizenship in America has always come into question. It is an inherently dangerous and racist term ever since the 1857 Dred Scott Supreme Court decision.[36]

What will it take for America to come to terms with her legacy of slavery she remain indebted to her black citizens. Mama says I am mature beyond my 14 years. She must also understand it is so because I am hardened by the environment I am exposed to. I am not hopeful America will ever be truly fair.

America labels me her citizen, yet she dare treat me equally as her own is hypocritical. I struggle with this belief of true freedom, justice and equality all through my youth. At a time Civil rights activist Stokely Carmichael chairman of the Student Nonviolent Coordinating Committee question democracy as America's great

---

[36] Dred Scott v. Stanford became the first Supreme Court case to bring black citizenship into question. Scott was enslaved in Missouri a slave-holding state sought freedom after his owner took him into free territory of Missouri that was part of the 1820 Missouri Compromise. The Supreme Court ruled blacks have no American citizenship deserving of any rights under the constitution. During slavery blacks are considered chattel, inferior, less than human. After slavery was abolished in 1865 the 13th amendment was instituted into the constitution against involuntary servitude and 14th amendment right of citizenship to include all its citizens. However, Jim Crow segregation a form of servitude or semi-slavery introduced to keep blacks in their place as inferior unworthy of first class citizenship many still have this belief today.

contradiction. What little patriotism I retain if any at all in my innocence years pledging allegiance to our flag, which in no way do I proudly proclaim or compare equally is of a different strand as most whites give devotion to it and America now, are long past lost.

In early January of 1968, Coach Baylock Benjamin and his staff, Coaches Wesley Dixon and Emanuel "Sam" Green take action after the city commissioners fail to fulfill their promises. Tired and weary but determined to make their demands heard: "It's time ya'll spend our tax dollars on *us*! We play on a makeshift field at Lincoln Park Academy without bleachers, lights, concession stands, on a dirt and rocky field our boys get injured sliding stealing base!"[37]

On our way to play games out of town, we often pass a newly built white ballpark on Twenty-Fifth Street and Delaware, ironically sitting behind the school board's administration complex. With games in progress, we make our voices heard from the back of the coach's rickety old truck. "How y'all like playing in a Nice ballpark!" "You got it made in the shade! Bleachers! Grass! Dugouts! Lights!" We'd yell to white players, who stop their play, wave, and smile in approval. "All that and you still can't beat us!" Passing by on several other occasions, we make it our business to yell out. Players pat their butts and shoot birds at us.

Coach must have seen an opportunity. He stopped by to talk with one of their coaches to organize games between teams, but it never happens. A well-funded Babe Ruth League, and our struggling North Side League, Coach Baylock likened the idea to an experiment. The white team backed down, had nothing to prove playing a black team—we have everything to prove.

By February, Jackie Caynon, the lone black city commissioner, keeps the issue on the table, once again presenting a proposal

---

[37] Albert Benjamin envisioned the risk young black boys take playing baseball in the streets of Fort Pierce, but they need to harness their energies constructively. Benjamin and Wesley Dixon organized the first little league baseball association of the Fort Pierce Northside Community, named "The Pony League." Later with other community leaders the two men organized for girls, the Bobby Sock League. For a historical reference, see Annie Kate Jackson, *Treasure Coast Black Heritage: A Pictorial History. (Donning Publishers: Virginia Beach, Virginia* 1996), 72-73.

trying to persuade council members to vote in favor of the construction of a Northside ballpark in Lincoln Park for the black community. Politics turns into a race issue. The white commissioners, after months of construction delays and political wrangling, play hardball refusing to allocate funds to contractors who give excuses "exorbitant estimates." This is not true nor is the allegation that the cost of our ballpark will exceed the city's budget.

"We demand our fair share of funds for this project now!" Black leaders cry foul, considering all the project construction in white communities, especially in light of the ballpark we pass on Twenty-fifth and Delaware. The excuses and penny-pinching get the attention of black businessman Horatio Grisby Sr., who steps up to the plate and delivers. To cut expenses, Grisby donates his land for our ballpark.

Dedicated men like Coaches Albert "Baylock" Benjamin, Wesley Dixon and Sam Greene, joined by other teams organized by coaches Gordon, Cutler and their staff, chip in money and expertise to design and build our ballpark. Coaches and others in the community contribute time, planning, skill in construction design, masonry and painting. My teammates and I help until the final piece of sod is laid. Our ballpark is as good as any.

The Northside ballpark becomes a catalyst for speaking out against community neglect. It motivates additional community activism by black leadership and highlights inadequacies in our community to the "good ole boys" downtown.

We owe a debt of gratitude to Horatio Grisby Sr., Benjamin, Dixon, Green, Gordon, Cutler and their staff. They are dedicated family men who take time out of their busy lives to teach the game of baseball, and to some, including me, without fathers at home, more importantly teach the game of life.

Fort Pierce is a city primarily made up of powerful citrus growers and farmers who influence city government, and who are dependent on transient black laborers. They would rather keep progress at a snail's pace than open the floodgates for social change.

In early March, we have our groundbreaking ceremony, thanks to our community leadership. I don't see one commissioner in attendance. Shame on them! Not having a white commissioner in a photo with our team, coaching staff, and leaders breaking ground is not our embarrassment, it is our victory.

If not for baseball, I might not have had the opportunity at a young age to travel to similar segregated neighboring towns like Okeechobee, Port Salerno, Hope Sound, Indiantown, Pahokee, Stuart, Riviera Beach, Palm Beach and many others, to see and compare how my people live. I find greater appreciation for black folks' ability to survive in the worst conditions. Wearing a Panther uniform, the camaraderie and team spirit are irreplaceable. The aforementioned strong black men help community youth to stay clear of trouble and make success possible. Much is given, much is required.

St. Lucie County school board members remind me of soldiers hunkered down in their bunkers waiting for a bomb to explode. Racial tension is the bomb and every parent's concern about their child's safety needs to hear only favorable news. But the board finds it necessary to play on mainly white parents' emotions and fears, prolonging the "school choice" concept. It seems, as I keep abreast of the news accounts, the idea of whites 'preference for taking their child out of public schools to private ones is a sad commentary, especially for them. Black parents hardly have that luxury, much less consider it. Their only option is to play it safe and keep a child at segregated Lincoln Park Academy or at other segregated schools or counties. Considering, school choices some black parents do decide to send their children to an integrated school.

The dilemma for the school board is how to appease whites who are opposed to sending their children to a black school. Rather than reassuring and calming all parental anxieties, the board defies federal legislation to fully integrate and does nothing while racial tensions persist, hidden behind a smile and a frown.

By the start of my second semester at St. Lucie County Junior High, my education is becoming tenuous and hijacked by the precepts of a racist school board. Rumors resurface that teachers are threatening another strike and getting ready to walkout. Each morning entering class, I suspect I won't have a teacher. A teacher shows up one day and misses the next, and some aren't enthusiastic about being there at all.

One day, when I come to class most of my regular teachers had already turned in resignations. Two hundred frustrated teachers in St. Lucie County public schools are angry over inadequate salaries, insufficient instructional materials, equipment, and outdated textbooks, and school in general. Lingering overcrowded conditions plague our school because of integration. Our teachers join the more than 35,000 resigned Florida educators. The strikes and walkouts paralyze Florida's schools, unprecedented in our history. I sit among noisy classmates eager to go back home.

Jesse Mullins, our fair-minded principal resigns, had given me fair justice on several occasions. I thought I was the only Hurst on campus, that is until a red-headed nuisance, Bruce Hurst, shows up. Teachers and administrators are ready to rid themselves of this problematic student and eagerly accuse me of his wrong doings rather than investigate. "I hadn't pulled any white girls hair nor punched any white boy," I pleaded. "Hold off a minute," Mullins tells assistant principal Billy Ratcliff, "Bruce Hurst is white, Kenneth isn't who we want." Admittedly, I had gotten into a few spats when I detect racial slights, but I had not pulled hair or punched white boys. On this occasion, Mullins apologizes with a smile. I admire him for that. Well respected by the school board for his leadership, his resignation shocks black and white parents alike.

Mullins spent 28 years in the public school system, fifteen as principal. The board desperately wants him back. Scurrying about for a suitable replacement, many overlook capable blacks. As racial tensions mount with only a few black teachers on campus, it is clear that additional black teachers would have a calming effect. Surely there are others who are worthy. Mullins had seen enough of the board's ineptness. "I don't want to return and undermine the integrity of my students. I feel the best way to call these matters to the attention of the public is to resign." Mullins had witnessed in the past ten years that the state of Florida was doing less and less for schools. "More money was appropriated," Mullins says. "Less now to go around because of growth in student enrollment." Even less for black schools, every black parent knows.

Classrooms built to accommodate 20 are overcrowded with 35 or more. We have no gymnasium, and an outdated building for assembly during inclement weather. The Physical Education building, designed for 75 students, defies fire codes cramming in 175 students. Don't ever get ill since there's no clinic for the sick to even lie down. How are we to learn with all these deficiencies and distractions? I anticipate changes, but I'm surprised to get what I had become accustomed to when I was a student at segregated schools. I laugh at white classmates complaining one day about not having their own books. "You get a taste what it's like for blacks at our schools all the time." All hushed up and didn't complain again for the remainder of the year.

How ironic, before integration Florence Robinson used to say we'll have the best supplies and books, but what we have is *déjàvu* all over again, little has changed.

On top of these distractions, the federal government monitors how the school board allocates funds. The board finds itself under greater scrutiny and pressure to replace striking teachers or to meet their demands and the ultimatums of the feds.

How quickly the spider weaves a web and stifles its victim into immobility and a slow death. Seems a particularly appropriate metaphor that comes to mind. I say this because I will never forget all the sacrifices made and hardships endured by black teachers under a segregated school system. The board has an inept proposal to revamp the educational finances in areas of school administration. Money isn't being spent where it needs to be spent— higher salaries for teachers, bus drivers, janitors and lunchroom workers Black schools are suffering long enough, but they are about to suffer even more.

Each day I come home from school there's a dramatic school event on the news. The quality of our education is a question of grave concern. The National Education Association announces that it plans to slap sanctions on Florida's public schools.

Grandma gets weaker and can hardly keep her eyes open, dozing off on the sofa. It has been a while since we sit and discuss anything of interest. So, as she dozes off, I listen as the spokesperson for the National Education Association warns teachers throughout the U.S. not to enter into contracts with Florida County school boards. Rumors swirl that another strike is imminent. The board panics and circles their wagons; to lose federal funding will be catastrophic. According to most estimates, St. Lucie County's educational system is quickly going down the sewer. I sit and watch much of what I can before my sisters bicker over a program and turn the channel. Then I make a mad dash into the streets.

One morning I wait impatiently with classmates to see if our teacher's going to poke her head into the classroom. A voice comes over the PA system, "Your class is cancelled, you're dismissed for today!" There is an uproar of cheers, the news is like waking up and smelling Grandma's hoecake bread! In the first days of the strike, the four teachers left at school to teach hundreds of students resign.

For weeks, teachers and the board remain at an impasse, negotiating new contracts. Letters are mailed out to parents—school remains closed indefinitely. Some resigned white teachers tutor classes at community centers and the Veterans of Foreign Wars Post to a small number of white students. Mama and a friend drive my sisters and me, deciding if we should attend. "I don't think it's a good idea, she tells a friend, teacher walkouts add to the racial tension." It does when a barrage of anonymous callers threaten tutors who are accused of breaking rank. "We just want to help students, I guess some nuts think it compromises the strike," one teacher surmises.

Mama makes daily phone calls to the board, school administration, and teachers, to anyone who will listen to get updates about the strike. She doesn't like having her children out of school. The strike has no effect on my baby sister Sheryl's black elementary school. As she rises for school, we remain in bed. She thinks she's being punished.

Policemen who guard white tutoring locations are ineffective, as a bombardment of bomb threats intimidate weary teachers to rethink and retreat. Sessions are ineffective with the few tutors and students who are left. But for my community no such thing happens until neighbor and retired teacher, Elizabeth Espy, hanging cloths on her line, looks across the fence. "Kenneth, you need to stay busy, tell your mother to call me." My heart drops, thinking of her as my tutor.

My neighbors, Espy, Gustarva Hussain, and other retired black teachers, parents and senior citizens all volunteer to organize private and public tutoring sessions in homes and at Lincoln Park Recreational Center. But in short order, overwhelming demands by students in a quaint outdated center pose familiar safety and fire code hazards. Although tutoring is a success, the potential safety risks cause many to stay at home.[38]

Gustarva Hussain my neighbor and community leader taught for more than 35 years in St. Lucie County public schools.

---

[38] Gustarva Robinson Hussain took care of business and got things done. A trailblazer in her own right was one of the first to be appointed to the Florida Council on Elementary Education. The first women appointed to the Board of Trustees at Mount Olive Missionary Baptist Church where I and my family were members. First black and first Democratic Women from Precinct 4A to run in and win an election. First women to sit on the Democratic Committee in St. Lucie County. First Basileus and organizer of the first Greek Letter Organization, ETA Omega Chapter of Alpha Kappa Alpha Sorority in the Lincoln Park area. First President of Club Utilitas in Fort Pierce and in 1945 in her duties as a teacher at Lincoln Park Academy organized Lincoln Park Marching Band. Annie Kate Jackson, *Treasure Coast Black Heritage: A Pictorial History. (Donning Publishers: Virginia Beach, Virginia 1996), P. 44.*

Disillusioned, I should be back in school rather than listening to Mama's constant nagging about opening a schoolbook. She makes out assignments for essays, reading, and math problems, whatever it takes to keep our minds busy before leaving for work.

Mama comes home early one strike day. I think of a good excuse to get outside, to hang out with the fellas. Before I can slip away, she cramps my style. "Why don't you take advantage of the library on Indian River Drive. Get a library card like your sisters from that downtown library. I see a few black children come and go, it's not for whites only. We must change how we think. "Colored Only" signs have long been removed." Mama's right. Black parents need to purge the stigma of segregation from their psyche by encouraging a child to actively engage in public forums. Our tax dollars are at work to make these forums happen.

There's no library in our community and I haven't given one thought about a library downtown. "Until you do, you want to invalidate yourself as a second-class citizen, Mama says seriously behind a smile, "and that something we never considered ourselves being."

I sit on the sofa, dazed momentarily because I know she's slyly coaxing me into going. I haven't given any thought about a white library across the tracks. There's a book advertised in Jet magazine that I so desperately want, but it's not offered at the school library, which makes it all the more reason to visit the downtown branch. I get Jinx to come along because he has a studious itch about him too. We always exchange comic books. I like reading history and some fiction and he's a science fiction and sports buff. I always remind him that he'll make a great sports announcer since he has a genius mind remembering sports statistics.

The library is crowded with white students, some I recognize working together quietly in groups. A few blacks are in attendance. White students take advantage of the library during the strike. I'm disappointed we don't have such a facility in our community. I feel guilty we don't take advantage of theirs, which is ours too.

A gray-haired librarian wearing bifocals smiles as we approach the counter. "Can I help you boys?" I want her help, although it may be an innocent offer of assistance, I frown at her "you boys" address.

"I like to check out," then I suddenly can't get "spook," the racial epithet out my mouth, and I am too embarrassed to ask for The Spook Who Sat by the Door. I look to Jinx for help, and the librarian looks at me as if I'm stupid as she waits for my reply.

I can't shake off the mental block the word is causing me. Jinx looks puzzled and shakes me. "Kenny give her the name of the book." Luckily, I haven't told him. He might have blurted it out. "You don't know the name? I can help you find it. What's the title? Who's the author? Oh, we have some selected books by Negro authors." She asks these questions in succession, probing. I evasively ask to look at what she has, hoping to throw her off me acting silly. "Any subject interest you? I'm glad to help," she proclaims. "I prefer to see what you have," I say cautiously. I'm hoping I'll finally get rid of her.

She leads me to a card catalog and a shelf with a small selection of books on black subject matter, similar to the school library. Searching, I can't find the book I want. Most I have already read, and others are by white authors. Disappointedly turned off reading books not written by us and for us from our own perspective, not by most white authors with bias.

I prepare to leave, but Jinx reminds me we should get library cards. He checks out a science-fiction novel. I approach the librarian, this time with fire power: "You need more books by black authors." I brace myself in a defensive posture. "Ah, a very good observation young man," she rightfully says. I agree. "Make a list what interest you, and I'll make an order." Her cheerful offer with such candor and a smile releases my tension. "We've never had a Negro, I mean black, nervously correcting herself, come here with that kind of question." I promise to complete a list in a day or two and return, and in a month, an order does arrive with The Spook Who Sat by the Door and various other books by black authors. That book was the lure that got me to return to the library and read the others across the tracks on Indian River Drive.

Mama's right, we as a people put ourselves through the same old changes, must initiate real change. We can't wait and blame anyone but ourselves. We, and I must effect change for my own and others' benefit. I believe we are taking token steps upgrading the black history section. It is a significant bit of progress in the right direction. It will, I hope, increase patronage and readership in black history and bring forth a new birth in racial pride.

I need to catch a hustle to make enough to buy a new style of Levi button up bellbottom jeans at Richard's Department Store. I can't find a decent after school job so I psyche myself up to pick tomatoes I dislike. I resent lining up against a bus being counted and examined like a slave. It is demeaning to see helpless old black men and women examined, being asked if they are capable of picking and lugging tomatoes from a field. That scene gnaws at my consciousness and irritates me. I stay above despair with hope for my newer generation.

The weather forecaster predicts a hot and sunny day to a cold October morning. I talk my way onto this short nappy-bearded gin-drinking contractor's bus. He jives and teases me, thinking at 14, tall and lanky, I can't pick one box and carry the weight of grapefruits in a sack by myself. "You don't even own a fruit sack, how you gonna fill a box?" Shorty asks, laughing. I don't mind teasing since I had only picked a limited amount of oranges briefly with Junior before. Shorty is convinced that going up and down a ladder for eight hours is going to be too much for me while handling heavy grapefruits. Older experienced pickers laugh and make jokes, which livens up everyone's spirits away from the cold morning. I take the brunt of teasing in jest with a smile. I must have impressed Shorty that I'm tough enough and that I can take criticism, since he hires me and lets me borrow his personal sack.

Instead of filling boxes, we have big tubs called bins. We get $10 per bin, which is equivalent to a little over 30 filled sacks. I somehow find myself working in a setting of eight trees alongside a Jamaican brother. In his early 30s, he is tall, lean, and muscular with sooty black skin and pearly white teeth. He has a serious look about him. He throws his ladder and before it snugly lands between two branches, climbs it with the balance of a tightrope walker. His hands pull grapefruits with the efficiency of a boxer hitting a speed bag.

Before noon, he finishes a third bin to my half-filled first. Out of his league, I stay my distance. Just before lunchtime, he catches me admiring his style and comes over to greet me. We sit under a tree eating lunch. Ras Enoch loves cooking as a chef of ital (natural) foods back in Jamaica. I mention my love of pigeon peas and rice, a Bahamian dish Kenny "Pookie" Knowles' grandma makes, the best I ever tasted. The brother is of Rastafarian faith, something I know nothing about growing up around a second generation of Jamaicans assimilated into American culture. "American blacks mon tink I natty hair stand up on I head ir wild and crazy," Ras Enoch says.

Ras Enoch laid it on me about practicing his faith, while we sit under a grapefruit tree hidden from the sweltering sun. I listen to many stories of his life as a Rastafarian in Jamaica. "Yah mon, a mon like Marcus Mosiah Garvey (paraphrasing in the spirit of Garvey's message to rise up you mighty race! We can accomplish what we will!) ah true lion of dir peeple! Ah mon fir all seasons un brotherhood! A mon wit ah vision un love fir Afrika!"

In his thick and rich patois Ras Enoch gives thanks and praise. I listen while emptying my fruit sack, watching him climb his ladder up a tree to its highest peak, picking grapefruits. Descending, emptying his sack, pulling off his woven cap to wipe his brow. His adorned long horned and matted dreadlocks fall shoulder length. (His are unlike the neat, stylish, dreads worn without any historical, spiritual or cultural connection or significance by some blacks today.) His locks epitomize the spirit of a cultural warrior, in the image of a lion's mane. A true Rasta man's dreadlocks look good and in the natural rebellious spirit against oppression wherever it's found, in his native land shunned and despised for his Rastafarian beliefs.

Ras Enoch has been in America for five years. I continue listening to his strong beliefs. "Yah mon Jah Rastafari will bring about justice, ir be ah fire this time tir destroy dir wickedness!" That the bibles speaks about fire destroying earth and everything laid bare. His claim, unlike that of the Black Muslims, encompasses all oppression no matter what color. By his interpretation, I dare dispute what he says. I understand the essence of its meaning. The oppressor causes much suffering in the lives of black folks.

At end of the day, I make believers out of Shorty, the contractor, and the other men too. Filling two bins to Ras Enoch's six, earning $20, not bad for a neophyte.

Perhaps picking beside Ras Enoch I'm inspired and hopeful, determined by his message. On our trip back into the city, I keep thinking of things Ras Enoch says as I watch him doze off two seats ahead. The Rastafarian movement, and Ras Enoch believe that Haile Selassie, Emperor of Ethiopia, is the true King of Kings, Lord of Lords. The enslavement of African people throughout the West Indies, as in the Americas, and throughout the Diaspora, prolong our misery and suffering in a hopeless hell.

Now, springing forth out of our people, a hunger to reconnect to Africa becomes a movement that is taking hold of our consciousness. We have been robbed of our culture and language, and we focus on regaining our equilibrium to sustain us here in the bowels of North America. I envision that it can happen with a sense of purpose, in ways Grandma speaks about ancient Israelites exile from Egypt in search of a promised land—Ethiopia is Rastafarian promise land. And Ras Enoch believes this exodus will occur. When our people repatriate to mother Africa, if not permanently but long enough to gain dual citizenship, we will connect to our original culture and we will be able to nurture our shallow and detached spirits as we strive for peace, justice, and equality with tranquility into the future.

Deeply impressed by Ras Enoch, I am left with an indelible mark on my mind—his African-centered consciousness. I think about what he meant by a "fire coming this time." And I think about the misery in this kind of living. And I think about the misery of our reality. I see it in the faces of worn out, tattered and smelly men and women—my people sitting near me. The sullen gloom and doom in the eyes of my brethren, and Ras Enoch having to leave his island nation and come to this God-forsaken place to sweat and toil in the scorching Florida sun; climbing up and down ladders, picking fruit, dumping sacks and sweating, doing work white people won't do. Black people work too hard for nothing in this unforgiving town. They too as I at school go through the same ole changes— devalued. Our realities are shared: my experience as an invisible black student at school and their daily drudgery as exploited pickers, amount to the same thing—we are devalued.

Chapter 18

A FIRE THIS TIME

On Thursday April 4, 1968, less than a month after Florida's teachers' strike ends, my school days are once again interrupted, this time by Rev. Martin Luther King Jr.'s assassination. Dr. King, like John and Robert Kennedy before, was most black folks salvation. Blacks nationwide hung photographs in their living rooms of Dr. King, a testimony to the reverence they felt for him. Unlike Malcolm, who was maligned and misunderstood and did not get respect from older black folks, Dr. King admired Malcolm as he did Marcus Garvey for speaking the unmitigated truth to power. Now his assassination is bringing blacks together in grief. At his death black youth intensified our studies of Dr. King, Malcolm and Garvey and honor their messages.

Now with the loss of Dr. King, I find myself compelled to do my part honoring him. I'm watching CBS Evening News with Grandma when anchorman Walter Cronkite interrupts his news report. Looking a bit stunned, Cronkite expresses shock and sorrow telling us that Dr. King has been shot and killed. Cronkite doesn't hold back because King is a black man and a man for all people.

Mama repeatedly cries, "Oh my God! No!" Our eyes are glued to every word coming from Cronkite's quivering lips. Many whites are crying too. It occurs to me that like it did when President Kennedy was assassinated (and Robert Kennedy later), shedding tears really isn't about a man's color, but what a man symbolizes. Mama doesn't want to go to work the next morning, but Grandma talks her into it. "You got to pay the bills," she says.

On the way to school, Fort Pierce is quiet as everyone moves in a daze, in slow motion. In all my classes, white teachers are forced to confront the race issue, however uncomfortable they feel. Overly cautious not to interrupt, black classmates who want to vent frustrations, but each time they try the teachers utter generic statements: "He was a great man." "He did great things for this country." They keep the lid on hot button issues to avoid racial conflicts. During Civics class, a black classmate interrupts Ms. Green in the middle of a class assignment, posing a blunt question: "Why are we discussing civics, lets' talk about why you think that white man killed Dr. King." "I can't say why, I guess that's for the police to find out," she says, a bit surprised and firmly evasive. Her eyes give a nervous flicker revealing that she is 'anathema' to lighting a stick of dynamite.

Blacks throughout the day are irritable and pushing for a discussion. There have been several fights when some white boys are accused of saying that they're glad Dr. King is dead. With all the rioting on the news, teachers, faculty and administration are on pins and needles. Before lunch, anyone who wants to go home is given permission to leave early. Most blacks, including myself, and some whites leave early on Friday.

I'm about to enter Richard's Department Store, when I see Sneaky sitting on a bench outside the Busy Bee. He yells for me to come over. "Hey Kenny, there's gonna be a march for Dr. King. If the cops won't let us have one we gonna raise some hell man," he says excitedly. "Who's organizing it and when?" I ask. "I heard some soul brothers at Gibson Poolroom putting it together." "I'm down if it's orderly, for a good cause," I say. Squirrel pops up: "I know Kenny's talkin serious shit." "I just don't want a riot. I like a march for unity," I insist. "Damn right!" We gonna do what's right!" Sneaky agrees. I'm not so sure.

As much as I rap about black unity, Sneaky, more than Squirrel, is interested in hustling, cheating a brother out of his money. "Lets' just go see what it is about," Sneaky says, banging his fist against the bench. The streets are crowding up fast. Music from juke joints vibrating off windows and people riding up and down Avenue D yelling: "We gonna burn this mothaf..ka down!"

It's Saturday evening and I'm feeling excited about marching, but not sure we can pull it off with a rowdy crowd. There are no gatherings at Gibson Poolroom, only a few men shooting pool to our disappointment. We go to Nappy Chin Poolroom down the street, the owner, a tall dark burly man with a long bushy goatee stands outside talking with several men. "Nappy Chin?" "You know about ah meeting tonight?" "A march for Dr. King?" Sneaky asks. Nappy Chin turns and displays his enormous girth which gives the impression he's pregnant. He yells back, "Ain't no meeting in here tonight, it's Sunday night." "Won't be one here if y'all gonna act like n..gas destroying the neighborhood. I'll hang lead in yo asses before I let that happen." Nappy Chin's a leveled-headed brother you don't want to cross unless you're ready to die.

Later in the day, I go to Check's 5 and 10 Department Store to buy some notebook paper. I stop by Gibson Poolroom to check out the scene. The place is crowded now. I stand outside listening to some older cats rapping. "Maann, they better kill James Earl Ray before I do," one older man says. "Yeah brother man, somebody betta do something. It's ah damn shame." Another man, with a pipe stuck in his mouth, laments while playing dominoes. "I know from the beginnin some cracker did it. Just like the FBI killed Malcolm." "Correction, one of his own did it, a paid FBI informant," a man reading the paper says. "But they set it up. Something gonna go down so you jitterbugs betta be ready," an old head listening outside says. He's sitting across from the pipe smoker, and winks at me as he slaps the bones (dominoes) down hard against the table. He pauses to reach behind his chair and picks up a bottle of Thunderbird wine, and takes a long swig licking his lips. "You know how n..gas can get. Got to get that anger out like the Watts riots in California," he says, smiling slyly at me as I smirk, detesting the n-word.

White reporters I never expected to see around here are riding shotgun through the neighborhoods, looking for reactions to King's death. An old winehead known as "The Professor," because he claims to have taught at a black college before ending up on skid row, walks up to a young white reporter. "I'll give you a story young man, but you should ask what's my pleasure." He hustles the reporter, following him around for a bottle. Everyone laughs, "Alright now Professor, don't take him to school!" we all laugh.

The reporter walks towards us. He wants to get our feelings about King's death. "You want a story?" the man reading the paper asks. "I'm damn angry about it!" "We all angry!" "What's the government gonna do about it!" "Will his death be in vain, will black folks get justice?" Another brother chimes in as streetwalkers mill about listening. A young reporter listens intensely then speaks, "Do you think there'll be retaliation?" "By who, us, black folks?" a tall man wearing dark shades asks. "Of course, you know what I mean," the white reporter responds. "It might," the man retorts. "In what way do you mean?" the reporter scribbles fast with pen to pad, a bit uncomfortably as the crowd closes rank breathing down his neck. "By any means necessary," the man says in Malcolm's words.

The reporter thanks him, wasting no time getting into a waiting car. The crowd laughs and jokes, but I'm convinced he'll fill his story with lies. "I betcha Mayor Tucker, or some cracker downtown sent these reporters to get our opinions. White folks feel threatened, gettin nervous and wanna spy on us, know we angry bout Dr. King's assassination." "Ain't gonna be no violence, we gonna march with dignity," The Professor adds, taking a swig off a newly purchased bottle of Irish Rose from pocket change the reporter gave him.

In less than 24 hours after King's death, a wave of destruction paralyzing cities sweeps across America. More than 20 people die in the rioting. Fort Pierce's Mayor Milton Tucker asks for calm with hopes to save Fort Pierce from a similar fate. The mayor hears swirling rumors that rattle whites. They fear black rioters will cross over Moore's Creek, which separates our communities, and burn their nice homes and businesses to the ground. I wasn't so sure what might happen as I listen to angry brothers on the streets.

Grandma's not in a good mood. Her health already declining isn't talking much of late. She spends more time in bed. I often sit beside her and talk, moments before sneaking out into the night. One night Grandma is depressed. She had two huge mason jars mysteriously go missing from her bedroom, one filled mostly with silver dollars and coins, the other with bills—her life's savings. As a common laborer, this was money she toiled for in the tomato fields, the strain of toting baskets ruining her health.

Two carpenters who had remodeled our house over the summer had access to Grandma's bedroom are under suspicion of stealing. When she confronts them they deny it, but never return to work. The head carpenter, Mr. Prince, knows Grandma well and he seems genuinely remorseful about it. "Ms. Jay, I'm sorry, you can press charges. I hired both as reliable carpenters, but they are long gone and that raises my suspicion enough." Grandma believes both stole her money and cops downtown without proof can't find the men and probably hadn't even looked. She thanked Mr. Prince, but it doesn't get her money back.

Mama has known about Grandma's saving for years, insisting she open a bank account. But Grandma doesn't trust banks after the 1929 stock market crash that resulted in the closure of banks during the Great Depression. Many black and white folks lost their life's savings. "God knows those men stole my money," she whispers to me. Her voice is weaker than the day before. "Don't worry over it Grandma. God will punish them for it," I say often, reassuring and calming her.

"Herbert took my gun, didn't he?" "I can't find Ole Bessie," she says getting agitated. "Your gun is missing?" "No Grandma, Uncle Herbert left before the carpenters began remodeling the house last summer." "The carpenters took it too." "Old Bessie" a 22-caliber pistol she carries in her apron for security when a stranger comes along. I find out about it when I was about seven years old. A widow living alone in a wooded isolated neighborhood needs protection.

Drifters occasionally pass on the trail in front of Grandma's house before the city widens Tenth Street. One night, a stranger comes knocking, asking for a glass of water. Ordinarily, Grandma helps strangers, but not at night. "I can't help you! Go away!" But the stranger persists to bang loudly, creating a ruckus. "I just want a glass of water, give me some damn water!" The stranger shakes the doorknob, banging and yelling. It's late, suspicious Grandma thinks he's up to no good. I'm startled, standing near her and the front door when she reaches in her apron and yells, "You betta get off my property fast mista! I'm gonna shoot if you don't!" She pulls the gun from her apron. "You gonna feel the hellfire of Ole Bessie and her seven sisters! Get off my property now!" The noise ceases and I can see out the window the drunken man staggering in haste. "Yes maim, I'm leavin, don't shoot!" He stumbles and falls on the exposed roots of our Australian pines.

One New Year, I get the chance to see her shoot. She holds a firm grip and steady hand around Ole Bessie, firing one of her seven sisters into a pepper tree out back. I wonder what might have happened if she fired Ole Bessie at that straggler. I kiss her cheek as she smiles and dozes off. I tiptoe from her bedroom, anxious to hit the streets. "The devil is walking to and fro, waiting to devour someone," her voice startles me. She only makes statements about the devil when she thinks I'm full of mischief. "Be careful and come home early tonight," she whispers. I crack the door, promising I'll be alright, but she's already fast asleep. I wonder why she speaks of the devil now. Grandma can be quite mysterious and being ill she reads her bible more than ever. Not giving it much thought, I step outside to the Atlantic Ocean's fresh nightly breeze sweeping across my face. My thoughts are focused on the upcoming march.

Most Sunday mornings, I walk with my sisters to Mount Olive Baptist Church. People are piling into every church on the way, I suppose, eager to hear a great sermon honoring Dr. King in the wake of his death. A few well-known wineheads I never thought I'd see dressed sharp as a tack are in their Sunday best. When I come to church, I can sit and listen to our Pastor Reverend R. J. Cliffin all day. He has such command of the bible and have captivating oratory skills. I think most people join our church for that reason. And he gives resounding eye-opening fire and brimstone sermons. His baritone voice echoes throughout the hallowed walls of church. But this Sunday's morning sermon is subdued and premeditated. At the end he asks the community not to overreact with malice and hatred. "Let us remain calm and respectful in the days ahead, not turn our pain into revenge and destruction."

Rev. Cliffin activism, a prolific orator influence my family, neighbors
and teachers Hussain and Robinson and many others. After Rev.
Cliffin delivered my baptism at age 7, I fell ill with the flu and a 103
temp, prayed at my bedside for a quick recovery I value and
appreciate today.

I sit listening tentatively. Rev Cliffin's eyes wander out over the
congregation, and suddenly they seem to stare directly into mine,
as if he is speaking to me and no one else. It was, I suppose, a
warning, like Grandma's warnings. As president of Fort Pierce's
NAACP local branch, Rev Cliffin must know something I don't about
the march in the making.

That evening I'm anxious to leave home, but Mama pays
attention to the news special on Dr. King, and keeps a close watch
on me like white on rice. Riots break out in South Florida and
throughout the nation; cities are on fire. Mama suspects trouble and
doesn't want me out. I, too, am anxious about the planned march.
Scaldee, an idle mind is the devil's workshop. I'm reminded of
Grandma's many sayings. Mama suspects my mischievous side is
about to surface. "Stop pacing around looking out the window. Go
read a book, or go outside, but you better not leave this yard!" she
warns.

"You never around when Mama finishes cooking dinner. We

gonna have chicken tonight," Cowchee (Sheryl) announces, making sure I stick around. Cowchee is an inquisitive and nosey little sister always getting into my business, although I can't complain because she's my gatekeeper most nights when I get home late. Mama doesn't trust me with a key. While my sisters devour their chicken dinner, I step out to feed my pigeons, and give my pet boa constrictor a mouse treat. I try hard to do the right thing, but excitement of a march can't keep me still. I slip away.

A crowd of about 300, mostly teenagers, gather early Sunday evening on Avenue D and Twelfth Street and on Avenue C near Nappy Chin's place. Squirrel Nut, Beanie, Johnny and Sneaky Pea are in the crowd and some others from Twentieth Street I recognize from school are whooping it up. "Keep it quiet! This gonna be a peaceful march respecting Dr. King! No violence!" an older man shouts. Many return the reminder. There are no rank and file community leaders taking part. I'm hyped as is everyone. We walk several blocks east on Avenue D picking up stragglers along the way. There's intermittent chanting: "Justice for Dr. King!" but overall demonstrators are surprisingly solemn and orderly.

The Quarterback Club (monitor police against unreasonable acts of violence) appears in white hats and shirts, with the emblem of a cross, and for safety their carrying flashlights. Some young brothers get riled up. "Look at those Uncle Tom Negroes workin for the white man!" "Yeah look at those stooges!" "You jitterbugs don't know a damn thing. They're here to observe, make sure you don't get your head bashed in by the pigs," an older brother says.[39]

One Quarterback Club member whose fed up with the teasing hecklers shines his flashlight into the crowd and yells back, "If it takes Uncle Toms to stop any violence then we're Uncle Toms. We pray there'll be more Uncle Toms!" Quarterback Club members smile, pleased with his response. "Keep it orderly!" Someone in front snaps, carrying a placard that reads: "March for Peace." The crowd chants "Justice for Dr. King!" It picks up momentum until someone

---

[39] The Quarterback Club advocates boosterism as a social and political organization that gives support to youth programs and a voice for Lincoln Park's black community.

yells, "Hey everybody, the pigs are waiting with billy clubs ahead of us!" "This is a peaceful march, stay cool!" we're reminded once more.

Sneaky comes over with a crocodile smile: "The pigs think we gonna start something." "Don't you do anything stupid!" I warn. Nearing Ninth Street, a large group of cops gathers on Eighth Street in full riot gear, buckling helmets in a show of force anxiously hitting their hands with batons. I sense the cops are edgy, ready to bash some heads. I'm apprehensive, but it's too late to turn back. I keep marching, knowing that it's for a worthy cause. We approach within 100 yards of the cops moving in a slow shuffle towards us. "Stop and disperse! This is an unlawful assembly!" a cop with a bull horn yells. "This is a lawful and peaceful march!"one of the older organizers confidently boasts."You have no city permit, nor did you notify authorities. Disperse now or you will be arrested!" "We have rights!" "We don't need no permit!" "This is a peaceful march!" the men in front respond in a fevered pitch.

Suddenly, cops fire a canister of exploding tear gas. Pandemonium breaks loose as everyone scatters blindly into clouds of smoke, rubbing their eyes and gasping for air. We are sitting ducks blindly running into the arms of cops, kicking and yelling as we're shoved into waiting paddy wagons. "Somebody help me, my eyes burning. I didn't do nothing to deserve this!" a girl yells, rubbing her eyes, blindly bumping her head on a lamppost before ending up in the arms of a cop. I see Sneaky running behind a building where Squirrel, Johnny and Beanie wait. Each pick up many planted bottles filled with gas and paper fuses which they light and throw as firebombs into buildings, which quickly are engulfed in flames. A cluster of boys rain down rocks and bottles on helmeted cops. Several cops fire their guns into the crowd and hit their mark. (Several boys we discover are hit with rubber bullets) One cop shrieks in pain when he gets hit in the back with a massive rock. "Get that bunch on the sidewalk!" I hear an echo from a bullhorn as various businesses' windows shatter.

"Burn baby burn!"a group of boys yells. A short while later, I watch Squirrel get cuffed, jacked up by his pants literally thrown into the patty wagon. I run, duck and dodge about, eyes stinging, coughing, finding cover behind a parked car a safe distance away. "Dap Daddy!" "Hey Jit!" I look around. "You wanna go to jail?" "Get in here!" I hear from a kindly man as a car door opens. Without hesitation, I gladly jump inside to the chagrin of an old man and women. "You runnin round like ah chicken wit his head cut off?" The man said laughing.

"Look at those hoodlums, you part of this?" "No!" His eyes are piercing and voice stern. "The cops started it with teargas," I reply. "Dr. King never wanted violence, never this way." "I'm so mixed up." He continues. I look at him curiously. "It's anger, years of it. Black folks angry at the Mayor and white politicians downtown overlooking us. I'm angry too," he says in a reflective voice. I, too, was feeling angry, but can't acknowledge it as sirens blare from police cruisers and fire trucks dart pass as we watch demonstrators turn riotous three days after King's assassination.

Monday after school, I go survey the damage. There are many boarded-up businesses with broken windows, all on Avenue D between Ninth and Thirteenth Streets and further on Twentieth Street. A local unit of the National Guard stands watch. Law officers from Indian River and Martin Counties are called in to assist Fort Pierce's Sheriff and Police Departments. Check's 5 and 10, Richard's Department Store, Whiddon's Grocery, United Furniture, the Amco Grocery, Western Meat Market, Dixie Dime Store, Clark Furniture, Sammy's Shop and Midway Sundries nearly all white businesses that are charred by Molotov cocktails. Quite a historical departure from the usual indiscriminate destruction, considering no lootings or killings took place. A departure from what happened in other cities, with 24 deaths resulting in the wake of Kings' assassination.

I bump into Jesse, standing on the corner of Ninth Street and Avenue D along with curious everyday street people hustling to survive. "I didn't see you at the march last night," I say. "I was up front man when a cracker cop threw teargas on us." "Did you say anything to anyone about it yet?" "What for? I got a juvenile record. Who gonna believe me?" "I was hoping for a peaceful march. That was what Dr. King was about," I remark. "Maann you crazy, plenty n..gas dead already tryin to have peaceful marches. Crackers in Fort Pierce afraid to let us demonstrate, that's why the cops gassed us. I'll check you later at baseball practice soul brother," he says, giving me some skin and a soul shake. Jesse is a free spirit and a hellava baseball player, he tells it like it is. Even at Dr. King march hecklers turn it into violence.[40]

I spot Moon Glow, a small-time hustler on the corner getting his shoes shined. Never thought I'd see him reading a newspaper. Sweating bullets while jiving with the shoeshine man. Gets his street name from his heavy sweating while gambling, which causes his charcoal black skin to shine under the moonlight. Moon Glow's decked out in purple pants and matching shirt, looking for any reason to get angry. "Brother, you see what I mean, these crackers killed John, Bobby, Malcolm, and now Martin and they aim to kill our black asses too, that's why I carry my roscoe. Ever since two crackers jumped me at the Greyhound Station last week, I'm like them Black Panthers, I'm for real. I'll bust a cap in their asses," he went on.

A white man driving a white "deuce and a quarter" (Buick Electra 225) rolls up to the curb with Tootie a prostitute sitting in the front seat. She gets out, dressed in leopard print tights showing off her curves and watching me give her a disappointing stare. "How you doin pretty boy?" "You old enough yet to be my man?" she says teasingly. "What's that all about?" I ask, nodding towards the white man timidly pulling off. "I know what you thinking honey. I ain't like that! Don't do white men baby. I just get um drunk and take their money." "I bet you do," I say sarcastically.

Later in the afternoon, before curfew closes businesses at 9 pm, I get a date to go to the Lincoln Theatre on Avenue D with Sylvia, a fine red-boned sister who recently moved into the neighborhood.

---

[40] Jesse, smart, a jokester, always smiling, an excellent baseball player fall prey to the streets. After completing 9th grade, Jesse was in and out of reformatory school, spent 5, 10 and 3 years respectively in prison. Jesse was often beaten by prison guards and as a result unleashed his anger onto inmates. Jesse is the brother, my friend and neighbor I speak of in the introductory chapter.

The theater is crowded with teenagers, who need a diversion from the inconveniences curfews cause. Lincoln Theatre's a great place for teenagers to meet and socialize. Even better for smooching during boring movies. We sit down below on the aisle by the wall for our private moments. I pray that my tell-tell sister Regina and her welcoming committee of girlfriends won't show up. I want to make a good impression, but I'm out of luck. Regina and her friends unbeknownst to me Sylvia invites, pops up cramping my style and throwing my romancing plans quickly out the window. It breaks my heart having to watch Doris Day sing in a lame musical comedy instead of having my time with Sylvia. After the movie I see that any possibility of luck with Sylvia has disappeared. It's hopeless. Sylvia's mother rolls up to the curb, loads in the girls, gives me an evil eye, and leaves me standing speechless. Her mother pulls away, smiling at me through her rearview mirror.

I tackled an English assignment, unenthusiastic about finishing and dozing off in bed. Mama gets home early and bangs on my door to wake me up. "Get your lazy butt out of bed!" I roll over groaning. "Get up and come look at this afternoon's headline." "You slipped off!" "Is this where you were last night," she points to a bold caption on the front page of the *News Tribune*: "Firebomb Ignites Negro March." I go into my dance, explaining how the cops sabotaged our peaceful march with teargas. She pauses. "I hear that too from ministers and Sgt. Pat Duval earlier today. "I don't want you rioting. This summer I'm sending you up to your Daddy!" "I've had it with you!" She thrusts her arms in the air and walks away.

Mayor Milton Tucker is in cover-up mode, shifting the blame for the violence. He is covering himself as much as he is covering up for the cops who threw tear gas. Somebody didn't want a peaceful march. The mayor goes so far to call demonstrators "irresponsible unthinking elements" in the Lincoln Park community. The mayor and his cronies spread rumors of "outsiders" from another city leading the march. It's what they do to shift blame. Law enforcement, I'm convinced, sabotaged a peaceful march. I discover while organizing on the lower end of Avenue D, a rowdy bunch of 200 youths on Twentieth Street and upper D earlier in the day throwing a gas bomb that caused heavy fire damage to Bass Groceries. The crowd refused to go home. Sgt. Pat Duval of the Sheriff's Department, well respected in the black community, persuades the youth to stage a peaceful march from Twelfth to Eighth Streets. By the time I join the demonstrators, city, county and local state enforcement agencies were waiting for us on Eighth Street.[41]

Years later, I discover family friend Deputy Sheriff "Pat" Duval keep a watchful eye and report back to Mama my street activities. In 1952 Sheriff J.R. Norvell in photo recognize Duval's intelligence and investigative skills in a Jim Crow era to become the first Deputy black or white is impossible to imagine.

History tells us when powerless people unite and rise up it makes the powerful uncomfortable. Even King was called an outside agitator for his disrupting the peace and tranquility of white business districts. Some black community leaders back up Mayor Tucker's accusations of outside agitators. I suppose it's easy for "the powers

---

[41] Deputy Sheriff Pat Duval became the "first" deputy sheriff of Saint Lucie County Sheriff's Department. Duval climbed the ranks of Lieutenant and Saint Lucie County Sheriff's Department first black detective and headed the department detective bureau. Duval became a legend in his own right for his investigative skills in vice and narcotics.

that be" to cast blame on outsiders, given that Fort Pierce's black community historically had not been violent. This time we had exercised our constitutional right to peaceful assembly. The isolated firebombing on one end of Avenue D by a bunch of hoodlums, I think, disrupted what should have been a peaceful demonstration. With cautious monitoring by law enforcement things became tense and sensitivities became heightened. Panic ensued provoking an overreaction of law enforcement officers who resorted to tear gas, rubber bullets and aggressive physical contact.

Hours before curfew, I stop by Warrick's to get new heels on a pair of shoes. "Young man, that march was planned to get the attention of City Hall about the "have nots" in the Lincoln Park community. Politicians overlook black folks." Mr. Warrick is a community activist who chats with me from behind his shoe buffing machine. I knew nothing of the march's intended purpose. At 15, I just felt compelled to participate in the memory of Dr. King's legacy. "Pray ain't gonna be no more rioting tonight, least gas stations can't sell gas in cans," Mr. Warrick notes. Always upbeat, he shrugs it off, not worrying whether his business will go up in flames.[42]

I spot Beanie and Johnny rolling dice on the side of a juke joint. Beanie is already juiced up arguing with Johnny over the few dollars he lost. Mayor Tucker declares a state of emergency for Fort Pierce. Just an hour before curfew, alcohol sales are prohibited from 6 pm to 7 am. Beanie is irritable. Beanie is a 16-year old dropout, already an alcoholic and asks to borrow $2 to buy another bottle of liquor. After I refuse he curses me out. It isn't the first time and not the last.

During rioting, Sneaky Pea and Squirrel get arrested for disorderly conduct and the destruction of property. Luckily neither get caught with their gas cans. About 50 adults, 15 juveniles and 2

---

[42] My father's friend, R. M. Warrick is a community activist, a member of Prince Hall Masonic Lodge No. 96, and a participant in the City of Fort Pierce Citizens Advisory Committee. His community activism leads to the naming of the first beach for blacks, Frederick Douglass Memorial Park during segregation; and has Warrick Drive named in his honor. Warrick is also a Sunday school superintendent at my church, Mt. Olive Baptist. His wife Agnes Warrick, teacher at Lincoln Park wrote "Dear Lincoln," the school song for historic Lincoln Park Academy.

girls are arrested. I'm pleased when the cops report no lootings or killings.

Some Fort Pierce churches continue to have memorial services for Dr. King. The Governor of Florida Claude Kirk has National Guard reserves on standby for Gainesville and Fort Pierce. Nearby cities, including Gifford, Stuart, Pompano and others are hit with smaller incidents. Police in riot gear are deployed to every busy intersection on Avenue D, on the lookout for suspicious activities. Mayor Tucker imposes a citywide curfew to keep 16-to 21-year-olds off the streets by 7 pm. I come to grips with the mayor's words "irresponsible and unthinking element," hoodlums destroying our community. Not wanting any part of it, I go straight home before curfew.

Standing in my front yard, I spot an unusual number of white people looking lost while riding through the neighborhood in luxury cars. Staring neighbors cause some to get a bit giddy, panic and hit the gas-petal. An elderly white man and woman cruising by in a silver Lincoln Continental smile at me. Four soul brothers approach as the white couple reaches the stop sign at Tenth and Avenue H. The white man suddenly panics, shifts into reverse and floors it. Spinning dirt —his rear end aims at me. I jump back, barely miss getting hit as he slams his brakes. "Maann! You almost hit me!" He rolls down his window. "I'm lost, can you help me?" His face panic-stricken about to croack. "The problem is, I don't know where I am. Sorry, I guess I'm a bit nervous, panicking because of that bunch." He points to the brothers approaching. The brothers pass by talking, unaware of what just happened. I give him directions to Friendship Baptist Church. "Sorry it's this area." "What's wrong with this area?" The white man looks embarrassedly at me, knows I already know the answer. Mumbles some inaudible explanation, thanks me and speeds away to avoid further embarrassment.

How ironic, only King's assassination can bring out a few good white folks. Mama and a few of her friends also go to listen to Reverend Cliffin speak with his usual fervor to a mostly black congregation at Friendship Baptist Church. "Let us not let emotion and lack of thought confuse our goals," he says, appealing to rioters to stop the burning of businesses. "Your weaknesses are our (America's) losses and your strength is America's greatness," Rev. Martin Devereaux of St. Anastasia Catholic Church tells the audience. A local rabbi reads from Dr. King's famous 1963 March on Washington speech. Black and white ministers speak, one after the other.

Days earlier Mayor Tucker expressed his regret at having failed to appear at a tribute to Dr. King. Jackie Caynon, the only black commissioner who is believed to be the mayor's stooge, apologizes for Mayor Tucker's emergency absence. A number of black youths grumble and are agitated in response to the announcement that he won't be appearing. We believe that there is nothing of greater importance than paying tribute to our fallen leader. "Please have a tough mind and a tender heart," Rev. Russell Palmer of First Christian Church addresses the angry youth in attendance.

Before the night ends, weeping sirens fill the air. Somebody out there didn't hear a word the ministers were saying. Smoke seeps through my bedroom window. I look out into darkness and a short distance away the smoke billows upwards into the moonlight. Avenue D is on fire. Thinking of Ras Enoch's prophecy—"a fire this time" seems appropriate. This fire, however, is misguided and is destroying white businesses in black neighborhoods. It seems symbolic to me. It is making some evil whites very uncomfortable—will they ever listen?

My sister, Gail, startles me as I pull a mango off the tree. Her school's principal, like most others in the area, gives students asking to leave early permission if they want to watch King's funeral on television. "I didn't think he'd say 'No.' since he's nervous already because someone set fire to a classroom," Gail says.

Mama takes the day off, although she can't afford to. Regina and Sheryl eventually come home early too. We all huddle in the living room, fixated on the tube. We watch Martin Luther King' Jr.'s simple wooden coffin being pulled by two mules as it slowly proceeds down the streets of Atlanta. "A lunatic killed Kennedy and strikes again. Dr. King was a man of peace not hate," Mama says sadly. "Good always prevails over evil, James Earl Ray will meet God's not man's justice," Grandma adds. I have stirring doubts about justice.

My mind drifts from sadness to hating white people for all their evil and destruction, although it is not part of my upbringing, it is my experience. Hate festers inside me. I go read to help take the edge off. I'm in a new realm of enlightenment. Receiving new and clearer revelations about periods in black history I knew little or nothing about. I discover one day at school that our library has no resources available from which to order black history books. I'm suspicious of anything white folk say when it comes to advancing the black cause. We get integration, but we don't have updated black materials, which librarians claim are relatively new to publishers in the South.

I discover it is school committees that select text books and library books from publishers. It appears little effort is given to black authors, as if black folks haven't done anything great. The few pages on slavery in our history books, or the watered-down versions of Frederick Douglass's and Nat Turner's contributions make me even angrier.

These accounts are so biased that they do nothing to foster racial pride. All this material does is lift the guilt whites "might" feel and increase the anger blacks feel. I believe that we should never insist on learning to accept insults when our history is compromised. Dr. Carter G. Woodson proclaims, "To mislead your fellow man. . . is to lose your soul." The hidden ugly truths and mistruths about Lincoln, Jefferson, Columbus and others are the myths whites dare to print in textbooks. I supplement my readings to stay ahead of my teachers, especially in black history. Authors like Lerone Bennett's *Before the Mayflower: A History of Black America, 1619–1962*, teach me that what is kept in the dark shall eventually come into the light—the ugly side of American history intentionally and surreptitiously hidden. Yet watching Ms. King and her children in mourning, it appears she will never hate the man who killed her husband, the father of her children. For me it was much more difficult to reconcile.

"Are you satisfied now, Mr. Big man!" "Are you?!" "Is this what you want!" Little Johnny from Cocoa Beach, one of several so-called outside instigators, yelled at Sgt. Pat Duval. Judge Roger slaps Little

Johnny with a sixth-month sentence for unlawful assembly and resisting arrest. He yells repeatedly, kicking and screaming as the deputies drag him away. I arrive just in time to witness his act of defiance during the hearings at the St. Lucie County Courthouse.

Popular black disc jockey and manager Jimmy Barr of WOVV FM radio station, who's signature intro keeps the groove: "Be he round . . . be he square, we go sounds to rock a bear!" Barr was saying all along on air that 75percent of the rioters are out-of-towners. I don't know if that is true. Beanie, Johnny and I keep our fingers crossed during sentencing. Sneaky Pea and Squirrel Nut are out of jail on bond, and when they go before Judge Rogers, he goes off on a tangent. "I won't hesitate giving time to anyone participating in setting fires, breaking the seven-day curfew as well," he says firmly, looking down from his bench. Thirty-three fires are set during three days of rioting. Sneaky and Squirrel are about to pay. Judge Rogers has a change of heart as he considers the age of juveniles without prior serious arrests. Sneaky and Squirrel think luck's keeping them out of jail, so they yell out: "All right!" Slapping skin, hugging, smiling over at us in jubilation. "Silence in my court young men. I'm not finished with you yet!" Judge Rogers orders. Their smiles fade when they're hit with a two-year sentence at Okeechobee Boys Reformatory School. Sneaky and Squirrel slump low in their seats, shaking their heads in disbelief.

I stop by Richards's Department Store to buy a blue velour shirt. Richard isn't in a good mood. The walls in front of his store are charred from firebombs and several broken windows are boarded up. I ask why he's closing early. "Ain't no money being made, my merchandise is smoke damaged. Why they take anger out on me?" "I'm Jewish!" "I didn't kill Dr. King," he reasons. "People been holding anger a long time. Dr. King's death made it all come out," I say. "I understand that!" "I'm just disappointed, doing business in a Negro area for years, I thought blacks respected me, that they won't damage my store," he says dejectedly. "All the credit I give your people," he adds sadly.

Richards doesn't get it. Rioters didn't do it against him personally. He represents the white system, a system run by white men who keep black folks at a disadvantage. Years of promises, years of scheming uncaringly creates a powder keg of explosive anger, set off by cops throwing teargas canisters. Richards has a fearful, less optimistic look about his future. A look I have never seen in a white man. All these years around black folks, thinking he figured us out. The belief that loyal customers would gladly overlook firebombing his business. I never go back to get that velour shirt. Within a month, he closes business for good, following the closure of other remaining white businesses up and down Avenue D.

Chapter 19

MULE TRAIN

In the summer of 1968, I meet Charles "Mushmouth" Patterson in a tomato field. Hyperactive, funny and animated, he's always bouncing about in motion, the brother's never serious. His wide motor mouth never misses an opportunity to crack a joke for a laugh. Mushmouth's silly, but I'm intense—the serious type. I initially underestimate the brother's abilities and talent, the next Flip Wilson or maybe Richard Pryor. Mushmouth's smart, likes books, a big dreamer like me, he's hoping someday to get admitted into aviation school and join the Air Force as a pilot. Although he's always in survival mode, I find him easily distracted living among distractors in an area on Ninth Street called "The Bottom." Not because of black folks, but where it is near the border line of white town. Although I think the name invariably stigmatize its inhabitants. It is a notoriously dangerous and poverty-stricken area whose residents are mostly migrant workers.

Moore's Creek, meanders through the Bottom. The migrant workers who live here are mostly first- and second-generation unskilled common laborers from the Caribbean, who came looking for a better life during the 1940's at the start of World War II. They work in the fruit groves, and in the flower and vegetable fields. The Bottom has its share of dingy shotgun houses, shacks, rooming houses, storefronts, poolrooms, and juke joints where crowds gather after a hard day's work to drink and dance to blues, reggae, soca and calypso tunes on a jukebox blaring from open doorways.

Mushmouth's hip and streetwise by age 14. He already smokes, drinks and gambles. He knows the pimps, prostitutes and hustlers who hang out in the area. Mushmouth likes to impress me by hustling someone to buy him drinks from the Blue Front Lounge on the corner of Avenue D and Ninth, a block from his home. He gets a thrill showing me how easy it is sneaking inside a bar. Blue Front has a notorious reputation, and most weekends someone is being carried out on a stretcher shot or cut up.

In elementary school hustling shoe shines, I once inquisitively ventured into this depressed but vibrant area where people struggle to survive. I was ignorant of the complexities of their lifestyles, and found my curiosity taking me to see what it was like. White reporters get a kick with their front-page cover stories of Negroes killing Negroes: "Negro Dead. Argument Turns to Deadly Gunfire." Senseless killings, like a man over a piece of pork chop, and another over a few pennies. I get angry at negative news commentaries, and put unrealistic pressure on myself to correct these wrongs. I prepare and arm myself with knowledge about social and economic injustices to come to those that can't come to their own defense.

I hear subtle racism in writers' commentaries. I get angry at their high-falutin sarcasm poking fun at the disadvantaged. When I meet Mushmouth after venturing into the area, I come to understand the anguish of these invisible and powerless islanders who are afraid to confront Mr. Charlie at work. It is safer for them to take their frustrations out on their own. It's like that— people in the Bottom living on the edge of one extreme to another day after day. Get drunk to release mask anger, fear and pain directed at Mr. Charlie— the white man they blame who keeps his foot on their necks to keep them powerless. They resort to gambling, drinking and dancing and to distract them from a meager hopeless existence.

One Saturday morning in the spring of 1968, I get a job picking staked tomatoes—a process whereby tomatoes are suspended above ground by vines that grow about three feet tall, staked with sticks in rows two feet apart. I expect to pick cucumbers that day, but Mushmouth persuades me onto a neighbor's bus. The Melton's, Henry, Sr., a contractor and his wife Ms. Odessa Melton, are neighbors. I put Mushmouth on notice about Odessa's manner as a no-nonsense straw boss. I hate picking tomatoes, especially with the Melton's slaving us in the hot sun. Odessa rides me: "Kenny you can pick better. Stop foolin round or I'm gonna send you to the bus." She doesn't cut any slack. Mr. Henry Melton is reserved, personable, unlike Odessa, who behaves like an overseer and doesn't take to slackers.

My day starts out good, but by lunchtime I have problems keeping up. Odessa warns that she might not allow me to come back. I bite my lip, suck it up, knowing she'll probably tell Mama if I get sassy. But the white man doesn't take kindly to me hanging back talking to Mushmouth and some other teenagers. Odessa separates us, but when she does she creates problems. Mushmouth disapproves and protests playfully, throwing tomatoes at me.

One good thing about picking tomatoes aside from getting paid, is that it motivates me to get out of bed in the morning to meet girls. I met Jennifer, a slender but fine girl with a gorgeous smile, on a contractor's bus a month earlier. We can't keep our eyes off each other. Her parents are separated. Her mother works the graveyard shift on school nights. Jennifer rotates between her mother's home on Twenty-third Street, and her father's small second floor apartment on a creepy side street off Douglas Court and Avenue D.

Jennifer's living room window gives a clear view of noisy streetwalkers and the house is in earshot of music blaring from nearby juke joints. She doesn't like the area, and only goes out to a store on the first floor. Her father strictly enforces his rules, forbidding her from standing on street corners. Her curfew is 9 pm, she must complete her homework every night and she is not allowed to invite boys over. After weeks of talking on the phone and dates at the Lincoln Theatre, she invites me over one evening. Jennifer warns of her father's mean streak against dating and cautions that he might threaten me with violence. I can't stay long and must leave before he comes home, but she never knows when. Typically, he goes fishing with buddies after work, however he once popped up unexpectedly to my disappointment.

We're watching television one afternoon when a mean-looking, stocky- built, dark-complexioned man nicknamed Frog with bug eyes steps inside. "Boy what da hell you doin here with my daughter?" He gives me the 411 about raising a decent and educated daughter who won't be walking around with a comb stuck in her hair and pregnant with a baby on her hip and another on the way. "I want her to stay away from street hoodlums like you!" he snaps. I listen, waiting for a chance to explain. Hoping, at some point, I can make a good impression out of a bad one.

I listen hoping to convince him I'm not what he thinks he sees, but before I can cut in, he asks me politely to leave. "The next time I catch you over here I'll put some lead in your ass. You understand me?" He says it smoothly with conviction in his eyes. A rumor circulates on the streets that Frog killed a man while serving a stint in prison. I nod my head in agreement, hoping he doesn't change his mind, get a gun, take aim and shoot at that very moment.

I invite Jennifer out to lunch at The Step Up, a restaurant on Avenue D—a popular spot with an outdoor patio and jukebox where teens meet, eat and socialize. Jennifer's afraid someone might tell her father. I have this crazy notion that he'll come around to like me, but Jennifer isn't convinced. With my persistence winning through— she invites me over again, though I can only stay a short while. Jennifer's father unbeknownst to us snoops around hoping to catch me there. I leave just in the nick of time. But Jennifer worries he's on to me and will carry out his threat. If he catches and hems me in with only one way out, I'll be forced to jump from the second floor living room window.

A store clerk downstairs warns me that a man keeps asking if he ever sees a tall bushy headed boy with his daughter. "His daughter comes in here often, I told him, but I neva see you wit her," the man says. "Of course, I lied. I saw ya'll the other day. Her daddy will mess you up if I tell," he warns laughing. I thank him kindly. But it's not funny thinking of my brain splattered on their living room floor. Each time I visit, I open the living room window for safe measure. It will be a miraculously great Houdini escape, jumping from the second floor—quite painful too. I'll probably get shot in the back or break my legs on the sidewalk below.

Blind love and stubbornness is a dangerous mix. One night,

caught up in a moment, we lose track of time stretching a minute into two, five, ten. Jennifer keep nudging me to the door. Before I can get there, it opens. Our eyes meet, startling each other. He comes charging at me like a wild boar. "What the hell!" Let me get my shotgun!" Sidestepping away, I leap over a sofa and make my move for the window. But somehow he already has his shotgun. As he loads and cocks, I have just enough time to bolt for the door. I run down the stairway a short distance away. I just know in a matter of seconds I'm dead, or he'll light my ass on fire. I leap over the balcony wall onto the ground below. I hear Jennifer scream: "Please daddy don't, he's nice. I love him!" She laughs about it later. It might turn out like I imagined had she not held him long enough for me to escape.

Here we are, Jennifer and I together finishing up a vast field of tomatoes. Odessa threatens to separate us for talking more than working. We move to another area right after lunch to pick cucumbers. I'm warned to avoid cucumbers because it's boring work. Odessa separates the girls from the boys since we teens are talking more than we're working. The white man comes cruising by on a dusty trail in his silver Ford pickup truck with a huge antenna swinging on top. He motions to Henry, sitting in the middle of a mule train, to get to moving this humongous mechanized contraption of steel and tubing stretching outwards like wings on a plane.

An old man shakes his head, not wanting to leave the bus after lunch. "Workin hind that mule train, neva stop is slave drivin work." When we're put in position behind the mule train, the old man says to me, "you wan never forgit how this jackass kicks yo ass by days end." I say rather confidently, "Well, it moves too slowly to tire me out." "That's da point," he says, with cunning laughter, "It neva stop, da white man neva wan it to." Curious that this is an ominous warning, I ask him to explain, but before he can Odessa shifts him to another row.

I prefer not to have fun poked at me around girls, so I grab my basket, bend over and start picking. It dawns on me this mule train has its own mind, moves at a snail's pace, takes no breaks, waits on no one, no time to rest, stretch or get a drink of water. It keeps going, as I catch up after Odessa stops me for not "pickin um close."

Preoccupied with Jennifer, I don't notice the white man parked and watching until a static voice comes over his CB radio. "You betta keep up, stop talkin, the white man's watchin." Jennifer warns. Jarvis is too busy rappin to a pretty girl wearing a muti-colored scarf and bangle earrings to notice my warnings. The white man exits his truck. "We gonna finish this here field today!" he yells, somewhat worriedly. He announces a storm in the forecast, which is a sign of relief and rest for all. But he, the white man is worried about profits. "Get that mule train ah runnin fasta!" he says in a Florida cracker drawl.

We come to a massive unfinished field worked by another crew the day before. A light drizzle and wind starts, a downpour will destroy and rot much of crop, yielding a smaller harvest. Ms. Odessa's talk about a storm gets everyone's attention. The planter watches a short distance away and loathes the fun and laughter we have killing time just to get through a possible stormy day. Every minute or so I catch him yards ahead staring behind dark shades in deep thought. A big man, over 200 pounds, short in stature, built like a Pillsbury dough boy, all day reluctant to come into the fields. Never raises his voice above a whisper, which I suppose is why he waves Henry over to the edge of the field. Unlike most planters, he lets his straw bosses control workers rather than getting directly involved himself. But, planters pay our salaries and he has had enough of our shenanigans.

The planter springs towards Henry, and I imagine him saying, "How dare you n..gas drag about half pickin my maytas." It's obvious to all, although we're yards behind the slowly creeping mule train.

"Maann, I think this is the end of the road for us, we gonna get fired," Mushmouth says with a look of disgust. "I don't see any point pushin myself to exhaustion either behind a heap of slow-movin steel." I added. The white man whistles to Henry to stop the noisy engine of the mule train. "I want um to keep up, if they can't, put um on the bus!" Odessa gives me a stern eye. She and Henry are firm but fair, giving young people a chance to earn a wage, but they do have a reputation to uphold. Before the day's done, Odessa points me to the bus. I decide before lunchtime that it will be my final day behind a mule train, even my last time for sure picking tomatoes.

I get on the bus angry at myself, expecting a pay cut although I am relieved from facing further humiliation. Two middle-aged men already voluntarily conceded to what I'm thinking. One smiling man says, "Hey brotha, don git down on yo self you won't be tha last." He passes a bottle of gin to the other. The other takes a swig, smacks his lips, reacts to a lethal dose hitting his gut. "That white man can get away with this shit...ain't no labor laws out here," he says, showing a bad case of decaying front teeth.

We sit listening and believing him. That mechanized contraption is a backbreaker, no time to stretch without getting left behind. Most workers are old, powerless and silent. Some moan and groan, some bend down crawling on their knees picking, complaining to themselves, yet somehow tiredly getting tomatoes onto the conveyor belt.

Odessa orders Mushmouth and several younger brothers to leave the field for the bus, but they refuse. "Push um, push um. Make it go faster!" the white man yells at Henry Melton, who revs up the engine, but the mule train by design isn't built for speed, just efficiency. Henry knows that, but anger snatches away the white man's reasoning. What everyone knows is that rushing workers risk bruising or overlooking tomatoes dangling underneath vine beds.

Mushmouth, in an act of defiance, plays a game throwing tomatoes like baseballs onto the conveyor belt. Each time he strikes he lets out a cheer like he's winning the grand prize at a World's Fair. The white man's enraged. From the bus, I take notes, scribbling on a piece of paper. Such an act of defiance inevitably elicits the planter's reaction. "Hey, ova thir stop throwin an bruisin my maytas!" "Yah wanna git paid but yah ain't workin!" "I don need yo damn tomatoes... you gonna pay me alright for what I done, and you ain't gonna keep rushin me behind that damn machine. I ain't yo slave." The petrified white man's eyes widen, looking at Henry to bail him out. But Henry's smart, he knows that the ultimate power rests with the white man. He's not going to clean it up for him. Workers stop picking, stunned by the action of a young cocky brother like Mushmouth, and the planter's inability to challenge him.

Everyone waits for Mr. Charlie to make his move. "Get on the bus!" he finally orders. "I move when I decide, not when you tell me," Mushmouth rebuffs, all the while gaining confidence from his entourage of accomplices with repeated outcries of "Yeah! He goes, we go!" The younger brother yell in unison.

From my window, the white man's neck shrinks as his ruddy skin goes pale, clearly embarrassed. I imagine he has never encountered from a younger generation such defiance when ordering workers back to work. He gets back in his truck and heads off to survey workers in another field. Watching Mushmouth impresses me more than when he acts the silly jokester. It's the first time I see him approach a situation, especially this one, seriously. Within an hour, the bus gets a few more protestors, including Jennifer and some of her girlfriends who, too, have had enough of the mule train.

On the bus, we keep it lively considering where we are. Tune in to a transistor radio, dance to soul music in the aisles, play bid-whist crackin up at Mushmouth's jokes. We had two hours of fun that Henry and Odessa would rather have prevented, but it goes on uninterrupted.

After harvesting a section, the planter comes over to Henry, smiles and extends his hand. This time it appears, happy youngsters don't influence older workers to join and sabotage a decent yield of tomatoes behind his mule train. Migrant labor is a harsh, dispensable and marginalized life. You move about the season like pawns regardless the condition, you have little say in the matter.

The planter is relieved. Henry Melton, Sr., an efficient contractor has workers on the mule train grading and packaging tomatoes in boxes on a conveyor belt while a majority of the workers finish picking. The field is completed just before the impending storm.

Before day's end, a crop duster overhead dives low, spreading a foul mist of pesticide over workers. Workers complain among themselves, coughing and gasping for air, and pulling what clothing they can manage over their face and skin and get back to picking. The planter who is shielded from toxic chemicals sits coolly watching from his air-conditioned truck. I count the number of times the crop dusters haphazardly spill their poison on me over the years. One of Mushmouth's buddies on the bus says, "We gonna be $2 short of making 8." I don't care about pay. I feel helpless, angrier about the abuse than about the docked pay.

Later in the evening, I watch the television with Grandma. Chet Huntley and David Brinkley on NBC Nightly News and Walter Cronkite of CBS News televise Dr. King promoting a Poor People's Campaign. Dr. King envisions a mule train dramatizing the desperate plight of farm workers and the unemployed before his assassination: To take a mule train of poor people to camp out on the steps of the nation's capital, Washington DC.

After King's death, Rev. Hosea Williams fulfills Dr. King's dream. I watch believing that Fort Pierce desperately needs an ironclad law to protect farm workers from the inhumane conditions. With conviction I tell Grandma that it's the last time I'll set foot in a tomato field.

Mushmouth becomes for me an open window of opportunity to venture into the Bottom. I love the pulse and liveliness of its migrant people and return home writing late into morning about its characters. Black folks in the Bottom are poor but hopeful, not always edgy, rejoicing happily in drink and song after a hard day's work.

I see cultural distinction between American blacks and our brothers and sisters of Caribbean descent. While we're both discriminated against, islanders are far more likely because of their distinctive social and cultural barriers, to experience intensified disrespect and rejection. In the Bottom, I notice self-hating American-born blacks unwelcoming, resentful and prejudiced against Caribbean blacks. While American-born blacks are far more likely to navigate through a discriminatory system, many migrant islanders are not aware of what it takes to do so. The sing song cadence of their Patois pronounced Patwah (the Creole language of West African influences) somehow brings them closer to the African consciousness than the American blacks who have more or less assimilated to Eurocentric culture. My neighbors, the Knowles family and their island friends, retain much of their cultural traditions through their patois, their unique cuisine and distinctive art, clearly with an African influence that romanticizes Africa. I become fascinated with their music, particularly the drum and become aware that the traditional struggles of black folks throughout the diaspora are shared.[43]

Many islanders have proudly retained a closeness to Mother Africa long before the late 60s, when American blacks are awakened to their connection to the African continent. I notice many older Jamaicans, Barbadians and other islanders who are yet to totally assimilate into white culture are far removed from British colonial rule. They made the break when their own countries won their independence. Although many have fond memories of their homeland's traditions, I notice that others choose to assimilate into Western culture and have little or no interest in their island identity.

I hear over the news someone gets shot and killed on Ninth Street the night before, near Mushmouth's home. I investigate and find blood splattered on a walkway with fingerprints smeared against one wall of a dingy rooming house. My knocks on Mushmouth's door go unanswered. Mushmouth is a guarded brother who says little of his parents who appear to be Bahamian. I suppose he is ashamed to invite me over to a partially furnished living room with mattresses

---

[43] Florida in early 1900s had the highest concentration of black immigrants dating back to the colonial period with enslaved Africans from British North American Caribbean colonies. The United States entered World War II in 1941, and found itself with a shortage of citrus workers while agricultural production increased disproportionately. The need for a larger labor pool prompted an editorial outcry: "Black men are in the armed forces instead of the fields where they belong." The agricultural labor shortage, primarily in Belle Glade's sugar plantations, prompted a "New Deal." The US government waived immigration restrictions for guest worker schemes meant to improve conditions, salaries, and accommodate Bahamians, Jamaicans and Barbadians, and other island workers. By the war's end, conditions had become intolerable, leading to strikes and worker resistance. See a scholarly account of this in Nathan Daniel Beau Connolly's *By Eminent Domain: Race and Capitol in the Building of an America South Florida,* UMI Press, 2011. For a comprehensive account of economic hardships endured by islanders and forced slavery by the U.S. government, see Cindy Hahamovitch's *No Man's Land, Princeton University Press, 2011.*

on the bedroom floors that smell of sweat and fertilizer, the same smells you get from fruit trees after a hard day's work. I'm 16, Mush 14, a proud brother. "I wanna fly. I wanna make my parents proud," he tells me with a wide-mouthed smile. "You can do it," I say to him.

I hear drumbeats nearby. I hear a brother chanting, but can't make out what's being said. The drumbeat leads me to two houses down from Mushmouth's, behind a long wooden shotgun house with a spacious backyard. A brother with his back to me is playing a drum. I speak and he answers, "Irie mon." I don't recognize Zachariah with his matted dreadlocks (unlike the trendy well-groomed styles of today) until he speaks of my family, having not seen him in some years. Years ago, he would come along to visit his father's old friend and my neighbor, Mr. Strawberry Knowles, to talk about the good old days in the Bahamas. I'd listen inquisitively rather than go play outside with his grandsons, who had arrived on planes to America as guest workers.

I watch fascinated how Zachariah plays his long drum, called akete in the rhythms of Nyabinghi drumming with African origins. I don't know of any hand drummers in Fort Pierce, so it's refreshing seeing a brother in his mid-20s acknowledging his African roots. "I'm Rasta now. Jah Rastafari in the bowels of Babylon here in America." I smile, reminded of similar sayings by Ras Enoch in the orange grove.

Zachariah lives in a communal setting among several other families. Women nurture their babies, cook and prepare raw vegetables, known as itals (natural unsalted) as the Wailers pluck reggae guitar chords from a phonograph inside. Outside a liberation flag hangs from a stick with a conquering lion symbolizing Haile Selassie I, Emperor of Ethiopia—their Lion of Judah. Rastafarians study Selassie's teachings and worship him as the second coming of Christ. I sit quietly as Zachariah speaks of the akete, one of three sacred drums. Ras Owen, an older brother visiting from Jamaica with hair traditionally locked thick, long and wooly like a lion's mane, speaks with wisdom. I smell ganja (used only in rituals), and listen as Ras Owen shares his knowledge of the Rastafarian lifestyle. "Yah com mon fir the almighty blessings of baby tonight un feast yir welcome. We black mon of Africa chant rid our minds of Babylon, no tribulations. Peace and love fir all mon kind blok ur white. We chant fir life praise thee almighty Jah Rastafari."

I return late after a "kumina" a word in the Ashanti tongue—Twi is a ritual service ceremony for the rights of passage, including illness, birth, and death. Baby-naming ceremony for Ezekiel, who was brought into this cruel world days earlier by an elderly Jamaican midwife. I watch a young brother my age with tiny dreads just starting to sprout and matt, play a long bass drum is the heartbeat or holds the timing too Nyabinghi drumming. Zachariah holds down the middle-pitched drum called a funde, while Ras Owen plays the lead drum polyrhythmically while chanting:[44]

"Go down no mo Babylon
Go down no mo taste dir fire
Of ah evil...no taste no mo in
dis life fir ever...oh Babylon
Go down all yir evil...go
Down...lift mir people up Jah
Rastafari ir rise up...no mo
Babylon no mo..."

The rhythm pulsates and the dancers twist and twirl trance-like into a frenzy of spasmodic movements. Stomachs contort and hips shiver in perfect timing with the approval of Mother Africa in their

---

[44] "The Rastafarian cult is a messianic movement unique to Jamaica. Its members believe that Haile Selassie, Emperor of Ethiopia, is the Black Messiah who appeared in the flesh for the redemption of all Blacks exiled in the world of White oppressors, the movement views Ethiopia as the promised land, the place where Black people will be repatriated through a wholesale exodus from all Western countries where they have been in exile (slavery)." Leonard Barrett, *The Rastafarians,* Beacon Press, P. 1, 1977. The name Nyabinghi derives from a fearsome African warrior Queen Nyabinghi, victorious against European colonial powers. She was known for playing a drum of mystical trance-like powers. Nyabinghi refers to ritual gatherings or drum use at gatherings. See a scholarly account by, Ras Steven Amirault, *Rastafarian Mysticism: An introduction to the Mysteries of Nyabinghi*, Infinity Publishing, P. 45-64, 2013.

genes. Their possessed spirit is set free by the hypnotic healing power of the thumping bass and the syncopation of sacred healing drums. A small crowd gathers around a pile of burning wood, as sparks flicker descending high into the night's pitch-black darkness. All sit inhaling ceremonial ganja as smoke fills the air up towards the stars.

I'm absorbing every bit of this strange and new ceremony, and loving every bit of it. Adult souls dance as small children mimic their parents. I wonder if this Rastafarian movement will take root and sprout outwards into the city. How will it be accepted? It doesn't matter. The belief is real as I listen to chants for Ethiopia and Marcus Garvey. I know that this African-centered way of life that Rastas recapture is truly theirs and ours.

After we eat fresh itals—vegetables, rice and curry goat, spicy beef patties and a mango salad I sit next to Ras Owen and Zachariah for a follow-up. It's late, a brother gives me a piece of paper, so I cram as much information in short order. I try to keep an open mind, although the ceremony is strange and cult-like just as Garvey's message was considered when he was misunderstood and denigrated.

We rap far into the night as reggae music fills the air. I sit in the presence of natty dreadlocks, a symbol of defiance, like warrior tribes in Ethiopia referenced in the Bible. "Read yir Bible," Zachariah, the new convert says. "I wear my hair now this way because scriptures say mon shall not cut his head or facial hair." "Rastas flush out shame ir people in Jamaica tink fine straight hair of dir slave masters tis best than wooly," Ras Owen interjects. All add truth to hair problems blacks face, perhaps everywhere steeped in self-hate. I find Rastas' hair has great symbolism. To many it is offensive, but Rastas wear dreads for others to confront their own shame and self-hatred. I sit and learn a good lesson: an African-centered lifestyle will, perhaps, awaken others who will learn to embrace it.

I leave early morning and Mushmouth still isn't home. The streets are alive with gunfire. Perhaps another senseless life is taken again. Perhaps these Rasta brothers will bring change and togetherness into the Bottom. I walk clearing my head, thinking about what Ras Owen schooled me. What the Rastafarians have in their possession is the history of a drum—the heartbeat of African people brought by the transatlantic slave trade throughout the diaspora (scattering out) onto every continent. I learn drumming has healing powers, and can communicate and deliver messages across great distances. The complexity of a polyrhythmic structure was played back and forth by slaves, transmitting information through resonation of tone and pitch. Our ancestors spoke to each other rhythmically through a drum, which was thought strange and primitive to slave-owners who soon realized that it was a source for potential slave revolt. When this happened, slave-owners barred by law the playing of drums in America.

I visit Zachariah, often to escape, infatuated by stories of the drum so essential in every aspect of life to keep Africans globally balanced and in harmony—the heartbeat of our people.

Listening to Ras Owen, I learn that the drum is what has brought us together, the first instrument to do this work. Ras Owen says that the African drumbeat is the pulse, our equilibrium and protection in the bowels of North America.

It was the lure of Mushmouth that brought me to the Bottom. I am moving further into my personal awakening. I discover an unlikely communal group of African-centered Rastafarians in Fort Pierce who are juxtaposed with blacks, integration and social progress. By the mid-and late-60s, a revival of interest and pride in African drums emerges in our music from a long history of Eurocentric acculturation. I want more than ever to play my drum. Maybe I, too, can make a difference.

Chapter 20

MAGNIFICENT MOMENTS

"Life is like riding a bicycle. To keep your balance,
you must keep moving."
Albert Einstein

My embattled thoughts are defiant after Dr. King's assassination. I'm unhinged, restless, bored, and I know why. I read and the more I read, the more I come to believe something's wrong with this segregated town I live in. At the height of the Civil Rights Movement, I am preoccupied by the indifference in all I see. I can't help but think about the inequities of the poor and disenfranchised in the backdrop of white advancement in wealth because of America's exploitative history of people of color. I can't sit still—I got to keep moving.

My thoughts race through my brain and I move swiftly out into the darkness where black folks are as restless as I am, in survival mode, aimlessly wandering the streets. I was unaware of a planned summer to Cleveland, Ohio. It's Mama's hope of saving me from myself, in what she calls a "need for a behavioral change." It's Uncle Herbert's idea of exposing me to something different from the segregated South. With Aunt Ruth's fondness for me and Uncle Jesse's hen-pecked frame of mind—anything she says about a trip up north Unk is convinced for me it will be enterprising. I'm convinced both are part of Mama scheme to get me out of Fort Pierce quickly as possible. With my restlessness, and Mama's worried about me hanging out on street corners, I suppose she think trouble is lurking just around the corner.

Late in the summer of 1968, I arrive at an integrated middle-class neighborhood with manicured lawns and flowered-filled yards. A lovely home with plastic-covered protected sofas, Aunt Ruth and Uncle Jesse are in a cheerful frame of mind. After lunch, I go for a walk to check out a much too quiet and clean neighborhood. I spot a group of white boys getting ready to play softball in a park. "Hey, you over there! You want to play!" I ignore a chubby sandy-haired boy who won't let up. "Come play with us!" He comes over and greets me with a conventional handshake. I discover Lars is not your average white boy. "You live around here?" "Just visiting," I reply to Joey, a blonde-haired boy. Zach and Douglass, two black boys introduce themselves. "Where are you from?" Lars asks. "Florida, Fort Pierce."Lars got his first orientation in the South visiting cousins the previous summer. "They really talk country in Mobile, Alabama, but not so much in Cocoa Beach, Florida. You don't." I awkwardly wait, expecting some old country bumpkin joke, but things get back to normal.

For me everything has racial implications. With every disputed foul ball or base hit, I expect racial slurs, but none come. Not even n....r between Zach, Douglass and the other black boys. We agree to meet and play each Saturday. "You should come over sometime." Lars wastes no time giving me his phone number and directions to his home for lunch. My guard is up, but I nod in agreement. "Noon time tomorrow, not a minute after," Lars says with a smile.

A lunch of crusty veal with garlic potatoes and spinach is beyond my expectations. I proceed cautiously. "Me, Zach and Douglas are best of friends," Lars says, in the company of his buddies, waiting for my reaction. I give none outwardly, but inside my mind races with calculated speed. My suspicion is that Lars wants to impress me with his color-blind attitude because of my southern experiences where racial problems are pervasive. His mother and father are ordinarily friendly. His younger brother and sister innocently smile, and to my surprise she gives me a big hug and a kiss on the cheek. My visits to Joey's home is much the same, and Zach and Douglas in the company of Lars and Joey are so natural. I sit in awe, wondering if there are any problems between the blacks and whites in the Midwest.

Uncle Jesse, an electrician, long retired from his career as a Navy man like Uncle Herbert and Uncle Eddie, considers himself an inventor. He gets up early, tinkers in the garage on a security system he expects someday to patent. He shakes me out of a peaceful sleep. He and Aunt Ruth plan a surprise trip to Niagara Falls. Over breakfast, Unk gives me a geography and history lesson about Niagara Falls. We pack bologna and cheese sandwiches and sodas in a cooler. "Hurry up Ruth, don't forget the address book!" "It's 326 Clarissa Street, I know it by heart!" she replies. As we climb into his 1967 Chevrolet Impala I quickly realize it's Daddy's address. A sudden feeling of excitement and anger comes over me.

I sit quietly reading highway signs flashing past my window as we head towards upstate New York. "You excited about seeing your father Ken?" "It's another surprise," Auntie says. I nod with a superficial smile as my stomach churns. In some ways I suppose, I was hoping, higher than ever to see Daddy after all. Niagara Falls, a three-hour drive from Rochester, my thoughts run wild as mile signs get closer to Rochester.

Unprepared to see Daddy, having suppressed my feelings for so long, I realize an eerie feeling than ever before. I want to get to know Daddy. How will I react? What will I say? "Does he know I'm coming?" I say finally breaking silence. "Of course!" both reply emphatically. Both realize I'm struggling emotionally. It has been nine years since I last saw him. I don't know whether to be angry or happy. Traveling on the New York State Thruway there's complete silence for a while, except for the wind blowing through the windows whispering in my ear that everything will be alright.

Lightning from a thunderstorm distracts my deep thinking. Rochester's heavy rain gives the city a stale smell. Uncle Jesse rolls into the driveway of a big white house. A man of average height wearing an opaque raincoat comes out in the light drizzle to greet us. I recognize Daddy by his thick mustache and the cigar tucked into the corner of his mouth. Dapper as ever in a brown Fedora

313

gangster style hat, beige long-sleeved dress shirt, brown slacks, suspenders and brown Stacy Adams. I have inherited a strong resemblance alright. We greet, and he smiles clumsily, attempting a hug. I reluctantly return a cold limp-like hug to his peculiar stare.

Daddy lives in a second-floor apartment of a rather spacious old two story Victorian wooden house. It reminds me of one of those grand houses from the antebellum South. Daddy serves up fried chicken dinners, but Uncle Jesse is craving beer. Aunt Ruth restricts him from drinking because he's the driver, and Daddy rarely, if ever, drinks.

After Aunt Ruth turns in for the night, Daddy takes Unk to a bar across the street. Daddy lives in the inner city, and his house borders the street life. I'm just where I like to be, in the middle of screaming sirens, blowing horns, neon lights and loud streetwalkers. By midnight, loud drunken patrons, music and neon lights from a club across the street with flashing billboards come inside my room and keep me awake. Restless, I get dressed and tip toe out the front door to get a firsthand view of Rochester.

It's 2 am and I am sitting on the front stoop with the morning dew in the air. People are still moving about from a night of partying at a local bar down the street. An elderly white couple sitting on their porch, waves and smiles. I can't believe how comfortable they appear in an integrated neighborhood. The elderly man gets his wife's attention and points at someone coming up the street. A black man wearing high-water elephant leg bellbottom jeans up past his ankles, loud red socks with white tennis shoes and a green pullover shirt, totally absent of any color coordination, staggers towards me on the sidewalk. He tries to shake off his blues from last night's partying, talking to himself and tripping over his feet. A black sedan rolls up beside him. "Hey Bama! You look like a walking Christmas tree lit up! Take your country ass home!" I laugh a little as he walks past, not even noticing anything around him, arguing with someone in his head.

Before we head back to Cleveland late the next day, Uncle Jesse takes Aunt Ruth out for breakfast to give me some time alone. My visit with Daddy is filled with awkward moments of superficialities.

One moment he hands me a *Dashiki* he purchased to lighten the mood. "Your mother said you like African prints." I conceal any sign of my surprise. I say thank you and nothing more. Daddy doesn't know what to say further and how to say it. I wait for him to say something, and realize I should be saying something too. Another moment he finds me browsing through his book collection and sees an opening. "Here, this book is a good read." He hands me *Richard Wright's, "Native Son"* he purchased. "I thought you'd like this subject matter...saw you browsing through my book shelves...I had it when you were young." He muses. Then finally, later on he shift into silence, to a reflective and troubled expression. "There are things I regret and will do anything to change, if you give me a chance to explain." "You don't have to, Mama already have explained your excuses." I interrupt. "Son, you have a right to be angry. I see it in your eyes." "It's too late for excuses, you left, and Mama catching hell, forget money you send." He sits attentively as I pace the floor nervously, not angry but numb by this solemn ordeal. His nine-year absence from my life must have played over in his head many times. We both struggle, trying to find the right words to say.

It takes a moment to grasp the vastness of Niagara Falls, bordering between Upstate New York and Ontario, Canada, flowing from Lake Erie into Lake Ontario. It's a magnificent moment to hear the sound and force of water gushing over the edge of enormous cliffs. It's so powerful that Horseshoe Falls blows fine mist into the air, forming large rainbows overhead. Hearing its roar from one cliff in Thunder Alley traveling over vast areas excites everyone while soaking them.

Niagara come from Native American words Onguiaahra or Ongiara spoken in an Iroquoian language is said to mean *strait* or *neck*, similarly translated to *thunder of waters*. Standing there, I am amazed how lucky I am for such an experience, able to leave the US and cross the border into Ontario, Canada. It might not have happened if Mama had not given Auntie my birth certificate for identification.

Canada is a beautiful country and has an abundance of wildlife, birds and plant life. "You don't seem excited Ken," Auntie says. "Oh,

I am!" "You can come with us on a boat ride with other tourists in raincoats to the edge of the waterfall," Uncle Jesse insists, pointing below. As much as I would have liked to, I decide to check out the views from a cliff. Walking alongside other tourists, I discover I'm the only black around. No white person is watching, no one seems to care I'm black.

I venture into a novelty shop to look around. There are postcards, tourist books of Ontario, T-shirts, coffee mugs and porcelain figurines— a tourist trap that is selling everything with Niagara Falls imprinted on every single object. Oddly, in the midst of the porcelain figurines, a wooden African statuette catches my attention. As I get close, a white man sweeps it up, smirks at beating me to it. The carving captures my attention. I am spellbound—I must have it. "How much? The tag's missing. It's an astonishing piece, a bit amateurish but good quality," the man says to the clerk. "$15!" "Surprisingly, it's the conversation piece of today!" the clerk adds. "I'm a collector. Not bad, Nigerian, perhaps Yoruba, Ibo fertility piece." I'm in waiting, like a vulture honed in on a meal below, as the collector puts it back and leaves.

I examine the intricate details. I am captivated by the craftsmanship of an elongated women standing erect, expressionless but proud with a basket on her head. "How much is it?" I ask, even though I know already. "$15!" the clerk blurts over the noisy customers, paying me little attention, preferring to attend to impatient tourist with items ready to purchase. Fifteen dollars with tax equals two days slaving in the fields. I am a few bucks short. On impulse, I tuck it underneath my shirt and walk out with her. Just turning 15, far away from home, I take a risk on a foolish impulse, in a foreign country.

Shock comes over me as the clerk's facial expression changes while watching me leave. I keep walking, scared, knowing I'm doomed. I try to quickly blend into the crowd. I find a secluded bench behind a bush, sit and watch the door. Any minute the clerk will come out with Canadian police in tow. "I caught this Negro stealing!" My heart pounds, I'm terrified at the thought of seeing Aunt Ruth crying. Uncle Jesse is disappointed as he sees me carried off in handcuffs. But moments later, no one appears.

I can't explain what comes over me, acting in such a cavalier way for a carving I had to have. I suppose I was driven by having the opportunity to finally possess something of African origin and feminine beauty. I detect her subtle facial expression of ethnic pride. I suppose she casts a spell on me to take her home, where she can be admired without interruption.

"Where did you go?" Aunt Ruth asks. "We were worried, the clerk said you left 20 minutes ago in a hurry." I breathe a sigh of relief. Not until entering the Niagara Falls Museum on the Canadian side do I stop looking over my shoulder and feel safe. "It's Jesse's idea," Auntie says. Exposure to something distinctively historical, catchy, and thought provoking. Unk gathered from Mama my obsession with Mother Africa. The museum appears in a state of disarray, unimpressive at first until I see stuffed freaks of nature—a 5-legged pig and 3-headed calf, Egyptian antiquities and artifacts of daring stuntmen who survived going over the Niagara Falls in a barrel.

A moment to reflect young, black, free of the segregated South with Uncle Jesse and Aunt Ruth in Toronto, Canada. (Courtesy of the author).

To witness a collection of mummies thousands of years old in decorative coffins is a magnificent moment. "Even when you die, white folks find away to get to you and make a buck," Unk says. It makes sense in the movie, *The Mummy*, when Boris Karloff puts a curse on Europeans excavating royal Egyptian burial grounds. "You're a history buff like me. I couldn't pass up this opportunity." We stand there with a few whites nearby discussing Elizabeth Taylor's portrayal of Cleopatra, with dark makeup on her lily-white skin. There's a controversy over whether "is Cleopatra black or white." Hollywood rather stretch and distort the controversy than give balance or any semblance of history. There are whites think Hollywood was ignoring the controversy and just making Taylor look brown. Others believe she was a top paid actress and stunning so perhaps it didn't occur to them to dare use a black actress, I wonder. When whites can tell their own story, we must be vigilant in telling ours. "Look at the facial features of these mummies, they aren't white, they're black if you ask me." Uncle Jesse impresses me with his thinking. Amazingly while in the Navy in the Pacific in 1943, when the white man would not accept a black man in a position of authority, Unk became enlightened by some white men's willingness to tell unbiased accounts that included blacks in world history.[45]

"Reel him in, you got it!" Unk says, watching me struggle with a feisty rainbow trout on my rod. Yet another magnificent moment on Lake Erie. Fishing is boring, and I only come along to bond and listen to whatever Unk wants to chat about. With only three days remaining in Cleveland, I want to make the best of it. Aunt Ruth packs a hearty picnic basket of fried chicken and lemonade and beer for Unk, to keep us away so she can watch her soap operas. Cleveland is located in the Great Lakes region, and is great for anglers with miles of shoreline. Most people can practically cast a reel from their front doors.

---

[45] I gazed upon an unknown mummy. Ramses lay in state out of his tomb away from Egypt 140 years much at the Niagara Museum of Canada. A collection of mummies was sold in 1999 to the Michael C. Carlos Museum at Emory University in Atlanta, Georgia, where I later visited. After medical research discovered that the mummy was Pharaoh Ramses I, it was returned to Egypt in 2003 as a gift of good will.

Uncle Jesse home from the Navy with Aunt Ruth circa, 1939.
(Courtesy of Hurst family Archives).

Out on Lake Erie in Uncle Jesse's twin-engine boat, I discover there is an "emerald necklace" of parks encircling Cleveland. "I notice you're quiet. You don't have to be so serious." Unk reminds me, pulling in my fish with his net. "I was just like you. With the absence of opportunities, I joined the Navy after school. Now Ruth and I have a good life." Uncle Jesse met Aunt Ruth as Aunt Alberta met Uncle Edgar while living in New York. I sit on the bow of the boat listening, thinking. My mind is adrift, shifting to something Lars said. After a softball game, Zach, Joey, Douglas, Lars and I are hanging out. We stop by a local store and Lars purchases a newspaper for his father. On the front page is an article on Carl Stokes, Cleveland's first black mayor, on the job less than five months. "Hey Zach, now that we have a Negro mayor, you think he'll look out for every Negro?" Lars asks with sarcasm. "Yeah man, I hope so. I need some money. After school jobs will help," Zach replies seriously. "Give all the Negroes money, we're the ones suffering the most," Douglas chimes in. Lars and Joey react unfavorably, "Not for whites?" I sense racial tension, the first time in their squeaky-clean interracial relationship. Zach and Douglas don't catch Lars' reason for asking. I sense Lars' question is a bit sinister with racial implications. I want to respond, but at the same time I'm reluctant to overreact. If Zach and Douglas can't figure it out, so be it. Being from the South, I'm too critical and have a heightened sensitive antenna for racial subtleties. Unlike them, I'm in the trenches of racial tensions and violence where whites and blacks aren't so comfortable hanging out together.[46]

Before realizing it, words get ahead of my thoughts. "So, Lars, what you're saying is Mayor Stokes is prejudiced if he looks out for all Negroes, he'll forget about all whites?" I fasten on every word with proper grammar, knowing southerners are the brunt of their jokes. Joey stops in his tracks, giving me an angry stare. Lars is caught off guard by my question and freezes up in silence, struggling to respond. I suppose not expecting such a provocative and divisive question from me, he befriended to say such a thing. Douglass comes quick to his defense. "Maann, you're crazy, Lars doesn't mean that!" I'm stuck with an awkward feeling of anger.

In the final days I stop hanging out at the park and spend more time with Unk. "I got one!" I snap out of a daydream as Unk pulls in a perch. "Unk, do Negroes have racial problems here?" Race becomes the centerpiece of my preoccupation and much of our discussion. I read about the 1966 race riots where major companies moved out of Cleveland while Negroes' demands for better housing and jobs go ignored. I see the patterns in every city—blacks are firmly entrenched at the bottom of the totem pole.

There's psychological alienation among Cleveland's inner city blacks, a reality shared by all blacks living in cities. As Kenneth Clark points out in *Dark Ghetto*, "the privilege white community is at great

---

[46] Carl Stokes is the first black mayor of a major American city with a predominately white population, He catches hell putting an end to job and housing discrimination. Some blacks who feared change are against him, while others unite and join unions, strike, and protest for change. Uncle Jesse, who became an electrician and then a supervisor is grateful to Mayor Stokes. Stokes seized power, building black and white coalitions aiding the poor. At this time, no other black man in America has control of city government and its policies.

pains to blind itself to conditions of the ghetto, but residents of the ghetto are not themselves blind to life as it is outside of the ghetto." I noticed in Cleveland the lack of opportunities and inequities in housing and jobs because of discrimination. As Clark establish, "They observe that others enjoy a better life, and this knowledge bring a conglomerate of hostility, despair, and hope." There is this ugly reality among blacks in most major cities like Cleveland and small ones too were set on fire.[47]

"Of course, Unk says, as I am deep into my thoughts on Clark, my central theme, whites in Cleveland don't show or express racial indifference as much as southerners." I sit listening as a fish nibbles on my bait. "Whites won't tell you outright what they're thinking, long as you don't talk about race," he adds. Unk's intelligent, a damn good electrician, middle class, could have easily grown content or complacent about the plight of majority of poor forgotten blacks. With beer flowing, Unk gets more open and candid. "I keep them thinking on my job. My boss is white and he's no electrician. He can tell me what to do alright but not a damn thing about how to do it. Imagine that!"

Unk's company would rather pay him as much or more than the most senior union electrician rather than have him in charge of less competent white electricians, just to avoid racial tension. "My boss hates getting stuck with electrical problems others can't solve, so they all must come to me. He can't do a damn thing about it."

In the final days before my departure from Cleveland, I stay away from the ball park. Aunt Ruth can see I'm anxious to get out and do something. What I envy most during my stay up north is the interracial relationship between Zach, Douglas and their white friends. Considering racial problems do exist in a city like Cleveland, my life experiences from the institution of segregation makes it difficult for me to reconcile that their relationship has redeeming qualities. How can whites and blacks get along without racial friction seeping in from the past? Although segregation laws are abolished, I still live in defacto segregation; the constant reminder that little if

---

[47] *Dark Ghetto: Dilemmas of Social Power.* Kenneth Clark. (Harper & Row: New York, 1965), 12

anything really has changed. The ugly words of diehards remind us of the deeply entrenched southern racism—the "South shall rise again."

I'm reminded of this diehard belief sitting on the back of Coach Baylock's truck on our way to a weekend game in Okeechobee, I look out on a cow pastor at an old rickety and dingy outhouse with a sign that reads: "For Coloreds Only." Someone plants an outhouse in defiance of the abolished segregation laws for all the world to see. Surely it is there to instigate a reaction. Most of my teammates hardly notice it or fail to capture its symbolic significance. But for me and a few others who are more in tune with Dr. King's resounding message: We shall overcome, that "For Coloreds Only" sign, in a metaphoric sense, calls out for black folks to overcome complacency in integration. We could very well again have to use that outhouse after being blindly lured to sleep in the new era of integration with its superficial conveniences.

In another instance of a huge porcelain caricature of a dark black man with thick red lips smiling while eating a watermelon. I stumble upon it in a backyard. Such lawn jockeys holding lamps in front yards are prevalent and cause me to pause just a moment as I cut through white folks' yards on my way to football practice. They represent the diehards who are longing for the Ole South, defiant as ever.

Mama says her sister Ruth is so stingy that she'll keep a penny until it rusts. Growing up poor, she meets Uncle Jesse in New York City, gets married and never looks back. Aunt Ruth insists on taking me to, of all places, an Eagle Army-Navy discount store for school clothes. Still penny-pinching, I'm afraid to embarrass her, I don't wear redneck and hillbilly fashions. Uncle Jesse reads my facial expressions and comes to my rescue. "Ruth, Ken's a jitterbug, he doesn't wear that. Take him to a store he likes." Despite Unk's fussing, she doesn't heed his advice. She purchases several pairs of white boy-style khakis, plaid pullover shirts, and underwear. Auntie gets her way. Unk, being a hen-pecked man, rebounds in a manly fashion and slips a $50 bill into my shirt pocket.

Back home life has new meaning. I'm grateful to Uncle Herbert for planting the seed a young man needs to spread his wings and encounter new experiences. Getting to know Daddy gives me that. I was thankful to Mama for a needed escape. I was especially happy for the opportunity when many boys I know had never left Fort Pierce nor could afford to. I could now see in myself what Mama and I could see in other black boys on the brink of losing hope. I am grateful to Aunt Ruth and Uncle Jesse for their patience and for giving me some magnificent moments.

Chapter 21

BUS STOP MOMENTS

When I return from New York, Ms. Naomi Bryant and her son Alex from Apopka, Florida had already moved into the neighborhood. Naomi's a tall husky pigeon-toed professional gambler with a big down-home smile. She has two gold front teeth, diamond rings on both hands and long fingernails. Alex at 15, who is crafty and slick, has learned some of her gambling skills. A chip off the old block in resemblance—gold tooth, long fingernails and pigeon toes with the same love of hip fashions as I have. We hit it off immediately. We're both tall with similar features, many claim we can pass for brothers.

Living close to the main drags—Avenue D and Thirteenth Street two of the business hubs of the black community, Alex has his card tricks and loaded dice down pat. He thinks his tricks are foolproof. It is like playing a game of Russian roulette, a dead give-a-way to a quick death. His gambling reputation takes top priority before school starts each morning.

Our bus stop sits at Avenue I and Thirteenth Street, at a cross section of thriving black businesses and a migrant loading zone. I watch worn out common laborers prepare for the drudgery of a long hot grind in the fruit groves. It is also where wannabe pimps, small-time hustlers and gamblers gather. I wait at the bus stop, taking note of the ugliness of street life—the smell of stale beer and urine, trash- littered sidewalks which are bloodstained from last night's cuttings or shootings. Our hangout, Barnes

Poolroom which sits at the crossroads, can turn from good times to a crime scene with the drop of a hat.

At the bus stop, the tired and lost are always passing by. One morning this fine young hooker passes after a night of tricking, and forces a tired smile. She stops to pull off worn out high-heeled shoes to stretch her tired feet. She is walking barefoot as her cheap wannabe pimp staggers behind. It's already hot by 7 am and he's not wearing a shirt. Although she's walking right in front of him, he hollers, "Bitch ya betta keep up with me!" The sister shows signs of wear and tear by the brother beating her down with his abuse. I get deep in my thoughts at these scenes of wasted lives. The couple disappears, like vampires before sunrise into a back-alley rooming house.

Most mornings at the bus stop, Alex and I stop by Barnes Poolroom if gamblers are still at it from an all-night blitz of cards. We play pinball until our bus arrives with classmates on the lookout for the bus arrival. Jack, a moody and decrepit houseman, (manager) drags behind him a bum leg from an old bullet wound. Everything Jack does is in slow motion like a sloth even talking—slow and short on words, he can be one ornery joker if you test his patience. He reminds me of Daddy, a slick dresser, always with a huge cigar poked between his teeth. His Fedora hats, suits, shirts, suspenders and wing tips make him look like an old gangster.

Most mornings, he's not in a good mood, coming off a night of drinking and gambling. Often, our noise gets to his nerves. "Leave!" We leave without question. One morning while we're playing pinball, Jack catches a man cheating in their card game. He asks the man to leave, but he refuses. Jack pulls a long barreled 45 that he keeps snug in his pants' waistline and pistol whips the man bloody in slow motion as he staggers out onto the street.

A now boarded up poolroom and barbershop next door (also on front and back cover) on 13th Street. Where I hone my skills watching pool sharks and sometimes dodge gunfire from a crocked gamblers' card game. (Courtesy of Jamie Ortiz)

I'm fascinated with the underdog—the downtrodden, and those even down lower, who will come to their aid. How and will he or she rise up like a phoenix from the ashes and find their way—undaunted, will they emerge once again out of the environments from where they come.

Brothers and sisters at the bus stop are hyped over last night's crimes in their midst at the notorious Silver Slipper Juke Joint just down the street. "Let's rap about street life," I say, about familiar surroundings to lighten my schoolmates' fears and anxieties. I discuss street scenes of people's stations in life.

I observe men I know standing in front of Baker's Flamingo Bar and Grill Night Club and Hotel. A joint once made popular to the likes of Sam Cook, James Brown and others. Still hyped, rapping loudly over last night's disagreements over women, liquor and money. I engage schoolmates in my thoughts on other characters I know or who I have observed on the streets at the bus stop. People getting by using their strengths and weaknesses. I label street characters as big fish and little fish. The big fish who are upwardly mobile have cultured mannerisms and stable lifestyles, well as an overall good reputation on the streets and in the community. Little fish, in contrast, are unrefined, incorrigible and involved in deviant acts. Will a little fish be devoured by a big fish, and if so, how? And if not, how will a little fish's life play out? How will the little fish overcome the deficient hand life has dealt him? We get into heated debates. Which big fish will show his humanity to his down-trodden brethren? Will he take advantage of and victimize the little fish? Which little fish will rise up and overcome life's insurmountable odds? Who will be rehabilitated from their inevitable doom? Will it be the big fish's greed to take advantage of the little fish weaknesses? Will the big fish succumb to haughtiness and dislike for the wayward? Will he/she show no compassion for a lost soul— the little fish? Will a certain little fish continue downward spiraling into a tragic life of physical abuse, addiction, prostitution and the like? Who will overcome and rise up from insurmountable odds? We all agreed life on ghetto streets is a self-absorbing game of manipulations and conflict—the strong and clever prey on the weak and vulnerable. We all agree there's poverty and despair all around us. It is how you maneuver through it. Like a game of chess—a continuous game of clever moves.

Poolroom and barber shop sit next door to a night club. Artist like James Brown, Sam Cook, Betty Wright entertain at the Flamingo Club on 13th Street which include a lounge, restaurant and hotel in the rear. Big name entertainment and a vibrant night life as school integration provide a pathway for the drug trade into the black community. The club no longer serve its intented purpose ironically renamed The Love Center for drug addiction. (Courtesy of Jamie Ortiz)

"Kenny, man you got some imagination," Howard Hall muses. "Yeah man, he hangs on the street too much," Marvin Johnson chimes in. "Kenny, you know I live right around the corner… and you live on the corner. I stay away from the corner I live by…the streets in your blood not mine." Marvin adds, breaking the intensity of the matter.

It's about the underdogs on the street, unexpectedly overcoming odds of some life's misfortune. They wipe themselves off and clean themselves up and start afresh, which absolutely amazes me the few times it happens.

I'm at the bus stop when Bobby Williams comes out of Bob Casey's Grocery Store. Bobby is looking older than 16, and takes a swig from a bottle of wine. "How you been doing?" I'm serious. "You and your stupid questions, you really want to know?" Bobby's indignant. His clothes are dingy, tattered, smelling of yesterday's sweat. He takes another long swig and wipes his lips. His industrious spirit, mechanical wit and love for learning is long gone. A blank stare of nothingness darkens his deep-set sad eyes. Bobby, my childhood friend, is deep in despair have lost his way.[48]

"I ain't doin well Kenny, can't you see?" His rotting teeth and wine consumption create a noxious mixture of a foul odor. The benevolent side of me comes seeping through to help. Bobby's numb, guarded, untrusting from a hard life on the streets, and he's deteriorating fast.

I'm no big fish, yet I try lifting his spirits about old times, which are only a blur in his mind. He doesn't care to look back on old memories nor does he remember earlier good times. I listen, wondering if what's said about huffing glue and gas is true—they killed his brain cells and now he's resorted to wine. "That stuff's killing you man, give it up." "It ain't easy Kenny, granny's dead. You got your family, I got nobody." Bobby's voice is somber. "Hang in there, Bobby, we go way back man." He smiles sadly. We slap hands into a soul shake. "And don't start with me about damn school, okay!" Before I can sneak in a few more encouraging words, he slips away. Just another unsuccessful attempt at Bobby, I refuse giving up.

---

[48] Bobby Williams died young from health complications.

Like Bobby, it's like that at the bus stop with childhood friends, many aren't doing well after Congress abolishes segregation. Segregation and inequities remain and continue to create life's challenges. The absence of opportunities in jobs, insufficient earning power, the breakdown in family values can contribute to the loss of hope and focus. One can easily get distracted and slip through the cracks, reinforcing hopelessness and any sense of direction.

One morning at the bus stop I watch Sneaky Pea coming out of Bob Casey's Grocery. "Kenny, don't start with me!" His signature smile recedes into a detached look of suspicion. Two weeks free after a 2-year's stint in Okeechobee Reformatory School for Boys. A small-time hustler, Sneaky's biceps and chest bulge from pumping iron. I persist, asking about Squirrel Nut and school. "Squirrel is out too. Kenny, you just don't quit about school, I give you that. You always care, brother. I ain't goin back! I was workin on my G.E.D. in the pen. I ain't got time now, gotta hustle, make some bread." Sneaky Pea literally runs away to keep me off the subject. When we meet at the bus stop, it is the only chance I get to try and turn a buddy around.

Chapter 22

SAY IT LOUD

There're times in life you feel invincible. You believe something out there is calling you to do something. The civil rights movement has put blacks on center stage. I say to mama, "thank God you bought me into this world at the right time blacks are getting themselves together making changes."

Still anger is never far away. With so many racial distractions, I don't invest enough time to finish homework. Injustices feed my anger and glaring at me from the tube—news scenes of police brutality. Cops unleash Billy Clubs, tear gas and dose fire hoses on protesters. All for a simple demand for dignity and treated as human beings.

There are whites resist to their graves than let blacks enjoy same privileges, and defy the 1964 Civil Rights Act. It's inordinately frustrating watching blacks tirelessly march demand to sit at the same table, attend same school, same private clubs anywhere white people are protesters picket for weeks in front of businesses with same ole outcome; a white business leader negotiate and reach a settlement to a token negro thrust in a position with little or no meaningful power.

I watch our leadership, Roy Wilkins Director of the NAACP shake hands skinning and grinning fronting, faking a Cheshire cat smile before the cameras. Saying to all parties involved: "We've reached an agreement." Who those crackers think they're fooling!

Embedded in the white negotiators eyes and facial expressions say to all: "We still don't give a damn about you Negroes or your civil rights." "We will never have your interest at heart." I recognize what else we can do to bring attention and pass laws. I admire our national leadership equally and shamefully frustrated by behind door deals to be on par, it seems, just to sit with and eat crumbs at Massa table.

Yet, we must compromise what is ethical for sake of business integrity. Knowing it can spell financial disaster for whites not doing business with blacks. Just give them a little bone to bite on will please them for a little while. White businessmen eyes seem to be saying. Grandma knows we have power in our dollars. I learn very young, often enough with grandma generation shopping at downtown businesses—white folk may hate you, but in the end, accept your money with respect regardless, although you may or might not get your way through the front door.

Watching news is a keepsake between grandma throughout my childhood is our together time, she won't let me avoid. She enjoy these moments as I try not getting upset at images of protest. "Scaldee change happenin fa us colored folks all ova America...we finally waken and standin up too." Grandma says through loosen dentures.

In her twilight years, it's her way of rejoicing in hope. Her last hurrah from all the torment and suffering endured during her life time. We sit, watch and feel good inside. I alienate from family discussions in social and political dimensions is a no-no, and cause of concern, as I move further exploring the streets. Lately when grandma ask for me before my sisters can turn and look, I'm out the door.

The U.S. Dept. of Health, Education and Welfare (HEW) stepped up its enforcement of desegregation plan under the 1964 Civil Rights Act prohibiting federal aid to school districts still practicing discrimination. When I start integration, federal government latest statistics suggested only 5 out of 67 school districts in Florida accept federal school standards. Only 16 districts are under a desegregation plan by court order. While 46 other districts are under an acceptable "voluntary freedom of choice" plan good until 1970 school year. Of 46 acceptable districts, 24 are under review for compliance, since "school choice" barely change racial balance. Finally, 3 of the 24 school districts are found in non-compliance lose federal educational aid. For 1969 school year only 18% of blacks in Florida attend desegregated schools. Only Texas 26.1%, Virginia 20.4% and Tennessee with 18.4% surpass Florida.[49]

After considerable numbers of blacks bravely break the color barrier, numbers soon decline in St. Lucie County. Primarily reports of racially charge incidents between black and white students increase. Black parents believe their child circumstances are of unequal treatment. Withdraw and enroll their child in another county with no or few racial incidents. Many parents bring attention blacks receive harsher punishment to their similarly situated white counterparts.

The veracity of black parents clams in many of my experiences bare out in preceding chapters. Such stories are reported repeatedly to principals, teachers and even news reporters. It's plausible these stories spread to other black families with alarming reluctance to integrate.

I listen angrily at a diehard white parent on local news adamantly justify her reason not sending her child to all-black Lincoln Park community schools. "I wouldn't dare send my child to those inferior schools." She dare recognize academic excellence, spite of inequities at black schools. There's an undercurrent of ignorance and driving force of fear behind her and others 'outbursts. More reasons black parents lack confidence, and assurance crossing the threshold to integrate. At least one of my white teachers from the beginning, Nancy Colcord and a few others, I can attest, have black students interest at heart.

Attitudinal change is why the federal government stepped up its plan because of grave disparities in desegregation statistical numbers; and not just in the south, throughout the United States. Since the 1954 Brown decision, and subsequent 1964 Civil Rights Act, few if any whites register their child at all-black schools in St. Lucie County.

A cry of discrimination because of conduct is not uncommon, to a greater degree believable in a racial climate.

---

[49] Based on 1969 Department of Health Education and Welfare statistics.

Beanie drink liquor heavily now and smoke pot. Johnny more agreeable to return to school get a letter he'll continue taking remedial classes doesn't mind that, as much but don't like the idea of special education. "I ain't dumb...they discriminate you know it Kenny...them white teachers just makes me angry ignoring us!" Both at 16, retained twice before, perhaps socially promoted because of age, Johnny doesn't have confidence without Beanie. When Beanie quit, so does Johnny before first day of school begin. Like Bobby, I hound both to get back in school.

One day getting off the school bus on 13th Street, I notice Beanie and a group of boys sitting on bicycles in front of Braynan Restaurant. A tall Baldheaded rail thin no-nonsense Bahamian businessman has a calm temperament dealing with customers. I notice Beanie and his boys loudly disturbing customers entering. "Boys please don't block dir entry way...my customers con't get by." Braynan speaks politely. "Go to hell n...ga!" Beanie snap sit on his bike to roaring laughter. "Young mon did yir parents not teach yir manners?" "I ain't got no parents!"Which is a lie? "What cha gonna do about it?" Beanie says his buddies egging him on. "If yir don't move, ah call..." "Call the damn Police!" Beanie interrupts. His redden eyes widens into a glaring stare. Braynan look at him a moment shakes his head disgustedly walks back inside.

Beanie keep a hand stuck in his back pocket. "What's going on man?" I arrive interrupt his thinking. Beanie look up at me frown, snatched a pint of gin from a buddy's hand and take a swig: "None of your damn business!" "What the hell you want!" He stares at the restaurant door. "I aught ta kill that n...ga!" He says. "Beanie listen please...don't do nothing foolish...he asks you nicely to move." Beanie look at me with eyes rolling back intoxicated. "You see Kenny, I can't go back to school...I'm angry what them crackers did to me...I might kill a cracker!" "Don't tell me nothin else bout school!" He rides off angrily yell back throwing the gin bottle barely missing my head with his buddies in hot pursuit. I see the handle of a 22-caliber pistol hanging out his back pocket. Booze sneaks up on Beanie turn him into a monster. It frightens me seeing him like that even after he apologizes soberly days later. I just can't give up on neighborhood buddies.

Mama still tries to clamp down on my staying out late with less than desirable grades not turning in homework assignments. Days into first semester, I fail to heed Ms. Green, my Civics teacher warnings: "If you're not prepared, I'll fail you without question." The first semester she gives me a C and I barely pass my other courses with C's and an A in Physical Ed an easy course. You got C's and an F in Science…what's wrong it's unlike you." Mamma says. I'm unfocused pull between two worlds—the streets and indifference in school. I needed to make a quick decision. I love school, but teachers, students, everyone looks disinterested, unmotivated. I catch myself daydreaming in class, like early years. Realize I need a change of scene. I start hanging with Ronnie Briggs—not a studious brother, but smart well-grounded with a since of direction.

Ron and I started experimenting with our names in eighth grade. I shortened his from Ronnie to Ron; he shortened mine from Kenny to Ken although I tell him someday I'll change it all together. Ron laughed for suggesting it. "What your parents gonna think?" He'd joked. "You crazy man…you read too much!" Ron knew I was always into some deep reading of Pan Africanist movements of Delaney, Garvey, Du bois and Malcolm. Ron had no social status or peer pressure doesn't drink nor smoke, and not a lame brother matter of fact. He's hyped with a glib for jokes we become tight buddies he unknowingly keeps me for a while away from street distractions.

Most mornings, Ron and I catch a ride to the Annex with older brother Bill, a junior at Dan McCarty High School. I arrive at Ron's home hearing him sing a new hit: "Say It Loud! First time I hear Soul Brother #1 James Brown's anthem of black pride. We're surprised such a politically black conscious song's playing on WIRA, a popular white radio station. "Watch out!" "The white man tellin us somethin!" Bill proclaims. "Yeah! Black people gettin themselves together!" Ron chimes in.

When our community radio station WOVV isn't playing our favorite tunes, Bill switch to WIRA for an occasional popular black song. For some peculiar reason "Say It Loud!" blast through the speakers most mornings on our way to school bring a breath of fresh air gets me, everyone refocused. I'm feeling it preoccupied with a deep indispensable sense of racial pride for my African ancestry and blackness. With Brother James chanting: "Say it loud!" To our refrain: "I'm Black and I'm Proud!"

I know I can never get rid, nor do I ever intend to, my since of blackness at a moment in time, in history, it surges and crest for all to witness and experience. "Say it loud!" Ignites brothers and sisters, still confuse, in denial of who they are—to believe from depths of their souls. "Say it loud!" I'm Black and I'm Proud!" Let those never again be ashamed! "Say It loud for weeks stay number one on R&B charts. Pump our fist "Say It Loud!" Lift voices; elevate spirits to face another day of integration. Say it loud! Is our anthem—our wakeup call—our rallying cry. Push a movement for equality, our call for "black consciousness." Moving and grooving to Brother James plea telling it like it is:

"We're people; we're just like the birds and the bees
We'd rather die on our feet, than be living' on our knees
Say it loud! I'm black and I'm Proud!"

We raise extended arms and clenched fist out Bills' car window. "I'm black and I'm proud!" Causes white students to stop in their tracks and stare, surprisingly others cheer.

Second semester report cards come out, I pull my grades up to a B average in Ms. Green class. One day after class, she stops me. "Kenneth I'm not surprise you removed that F you got last semester." I thank her for the compliment, although it doesn't motivate me to change my ways. I still come to her class tired from hanging out late. Not showing enthusiasm an initiative, just enough to get by.

I'm restless. Searching for something to get excite and motivated about. Then it happens in Greene Civics class. There isn't much discussion on black issues. And when we get to a chapter on "Slavery in America," she quickly skims through pages touching on a few minor linear notes: "Producing tons of cotton made plantation owners wealthy…slaves as chattel cost owners lots of money…more land had to be cleared because textile companies put more demands on producing more cotton…cotton is king…plantation owners need more slaves to pick cotton."

I sit angrily lowering my gaze while some black classmates bury heads into their books ashamed. I have an arsenal of responses. Like you skip over black people treated like animals; white people believe slavery as a necessary evil not willing to repent and end it. Lest discuss these points. I feel compelled to put shame where it belongs. But I say nothing without the courage, missing an opportunity.

I sit watching somber white faces looking straight ahead avoid eye contact with blacks; I suppose any misinterpret expression might trigger black classmates negative responses. Ms. Green meticulously cautious rather than openly discuss, like previous chapters avoids the real evils of slavery. We go through the Negro history chapter so quickly make my head spin would serve class best reading it at our leisure.

Ms. Hill's my Science teacher like most whites stuck on saying Negro. Until one day, speaking, I raised my hand. "We're black." I say candidly. "It's just a matter of preference." She replies nervously. "Well your preference has played out…we define ourselves as black now." She yields, and I suppose, dignify my response with a Cheshire cat smile slumping into her seat, taken aback a moment with an ok.

Even some black teachers I encounter struggle with the new term Black. Once overhear several discuss on hallways. "I'm not black, I'm Negro and proud of it." "I'll never call myself black." I suppose, that moment, I think of Godfather of Soul, Anthem "Say it loud!" I'm black feeling proud about it. I hear my calling; I'm conscious and race in America matters.

Some of my friends aren't as fortunate abiding by the old negative saying: "If you white, you're right, brown stick around, black get back." This inferior message we give validity impose on ourselves, still pervasive in our communities, institutions, inflicts greater harm on family values.

As mentioned in an earlier chapter, my sisters and I are taught against using the "N" word. And the word "Black" in a negative manner. We're taught to turn "Black" as a pejorative into positive meanings: "black cat" crosses your path means good luck; "black sheep" of the family means you are the nicest child are some of many examples. I once let street environment creep into our home. Get angry with my middle sister Regina darkest in our family: "With your black self!" (As Sheryl did earlier) I yell angrily slipping it out. Mama goes into rage immediately pick up a shoe throw it catching me upside my head. No explanation needed. I knew better.

Some of my friends aren't as fortunate. Being call black and "Tar Baby" is a pariah too many like Larry a neighbor can get mean and volatile. I'm always vocal to my hood buddies to lay of the negative racial terms.

But there are others with disconnect for black pride have low-self-esteem and self-hatred. The pathology of slavery and its effects past through generations cripples. We must not be critical but reach out and uplift by education of our glorious past before and beyond slavery.

Too often playing sandlot football, an argument ensues into a fight; in this instance, one calls the other big lips and nappy-head. Self-hatred creeps into our daily lives and experiences for far too often. If we only believe our physical prototype is God given attributes of the African genetic-type uniquely ours!

We must embrace and celebrated our beauty. God's in control and what is well known in the tropics of Africa, melanated skin and its variety of shades shield and protects against ultraviolet rays; our unique body types, full lips aid in retaining moisture; cooling off (circulatory) the body; our broad nose increases oxygen intake in Africa's humidity; our kinky or wooly hair types insulates and protects our scalp; our round buttocks and natural muscularity for endurance, and I suppose against the dangers in the African bush— uniquely ours unlike any other race!

Perhaps Madame C. Walker may not have anticipated the negative and inferior implications when inventing the straightening comb to de-kink our hair let lose a trendy trend for the ages. Even today, "straight hair is good hair." Mama wouldn't dare allow my sisters to entertain such ignorance. She says: "Straighten or curly hair isn't good hair. You can't eat it—place greater value on one type over the other." So how is it good? There's no such thing—just grades from kinky, coarse to straight, none better than the other our people must appreciate without distinctions."

I was coming into ages reading black literature slavery and the white man's blood in us has warped many minds into believing any characteristics we possess—the straighter or curlier our hair is good—better; lighter our skin is good—better; keener our noise and thinner our lips is good—better; bring us closer to being white.

Equally, in the same realm black men in the early 60's straightened their hair into wavy Conk styles widely popular with black entertainers. When "Say It Loud!" hit the airways James went natural to an Afro feeling black and proud as ever.

After sitting in class listening to a poorly delivered rendition of black history I realize my calling. Learn more black history than I already know, and beyond that bit of history meticulously selected in school textbooks, it seems the intent is not to offend whites but embarrass blacks.

There aren't any black bookstores in Fort Pierce. Not one, I suppose will consciously evolved, and perhaps be advanced, like Minister Leonard X, in the interest of the so-called Negro dare open such a needed book store.

What hold us back ourselves? There're many in our community more than financially capable. I grapple with that question many times at Warrick shoe shop. "Son there're many who are capable, few serve their community and many who serve only themselves."

We can only look not too long ago at our accomplishments before integration. I haven't even thought to investigate the school library. So, I go during my lunch break ask a librarian to assist me. "We have a section, but it's limited." She says pointing to a shelf of books in a corner. The section on the shelf has less than 20 old and outdated books. Most are previously stamped "Property of Lincoln Park Academy" stamped over with Dan McCarty High. I realize we will continue being marginalize if we don't look out for our best interest and bring attention to things need changing.

I check out two books, "Great Negroes Past and Present," on

historical contributions. Martin Delaney, abolitionist, physician, explorer and scientist leading the first party of freed slaves back to Africa; noted for saying: "I thank God for making me not only a man but a black man;" Daniel Williams performing the first successful heart surgery; Charles Drew revolutionary ways of preserving blood plasma; Toussaint L'Ouverture Haitian General defeating France General Napoleon Bonaparte's army; Haiti first black nation in western hemisphere. Black like Me", a white man darkening his skin traveling through America experiencing how it feels to be black—as if he truly knows. Before end of first semester, I read all black history books on library shelf. I found my niche reading black history kept me focused improved my grades and last three semesters got straight A's in Ms. Hill Science class.

One Saturday, a neighbor drops me off at Doctor Benton's office to get a cast on my left leg examine. I break it somersaulting over citrus crates a few weekends earlier after returning from Cleveland, Ohio. I sit waiting patiently listening to several Black men way into their golden years critiquing the young generation insistence being identified as black. A short man with salt and pepper hair and wire-rim glasses can't agree on anything. "That's the problem with colored folk, always wanna change who we are…we colored always will be." "You think I wanna be called black?" Jawing on an on until a middle-age woman interrupt. "Excuse me sir but we're trying to get away from thinking like that." "Most folk don't use negro anymore anyway." "Calling yourself colored is far outdated too." Her voice seems to whistle speaking. "Amen!" A balding muck black elderly man says.

The muck black man looks up from a magazine. "I know I'm black…everybody else call me black all my life…I can't call myself nothing else." His remark brings forth laughter. "Now take this young man right here, he continue nodding at me. "He's at the front end of integration." "He ain't takin no crape we old coots took pickin cotton." That's right, a chubby man interrupt. "Gettin served in da back door…being disrespected an all." "You right." "Young people nowadays ain't going to take no mess now." The slender women add. "They're at the front door kickin it in to get what they want."

Y'all see what's happenin at them white schools…they make white teachers call them black!" The slender women continue. The muck black man chimes in. "Is that right young man?" "What you like being call?" I look up at him with a wire hanger stuck in my cast scratching my itching leg. "I prefer being called Black." "You see what I tell ya!" He ain't like most ya'll scared Negroes don't wanna be called black!" "This boy is livin for today not yesterday!" Mucky black reminds all.

I sit listening feeling good from the attention. "Well I don' care what y'all say." "I'm ah colored man." "Been one all my life." "Be one till I die." "Ain't gonna change now cause it's fashionable." The short stubborn elderly man insists.

Dr. Benton sticks his silver head of wavy hair out the door into the waiting area on a hot topic and smiles interrupts their discussion as he always does when it gets hot and deep. Dr. Benton's a witty man, known to tell funny jokes when you're in pain on the examining table. Which put me at ease and distract from discomfort, never mine his patient's debating in the waiting area? Long as discussion respectfully keep in order.

"Do you gentlemen care to hear my opinion?" Dr. Benton customary says with an intro into a discussion. "Go right ahead Doc!" Everyone say in unison. "Change can be good…you older men seem to have forgotten, not long ago, and even now, a man my age with all my education and social status…there are whites think I'm still a boy, not yet a man…put that in your pipe and smoke it." He laughs pokes his head back in the doorway as Nurse Helen calls back the next patient.

Chapter 23

RACE MATTERS

Ron and I try out for the Junior Varsity football squad, not freshman squad at the Annex, but at Dan McCarty High Junior Varsity for tenth and eleventh graders before school starts. Most days we walk through white neighborhoods two miles twice a day for two daily spring football practices in the scorching Florida sun. Some days we are entertained by white boys waving rebel flags and shooting birds. We reply in our normal fashion—"Yo mama!" None of them ever dares to stop us. I suppose wearing football gear deters them from tangling with us.

More than 200 boys show up to make the Junior Varsity squad. There are dozens of ninth graders from the all-black football powerhouse Lincoln Park Academy. Most are polished in football agility and skills. Some who are not athletically inclined try out because brothers they're tight with ask them too. White players I'm familiar with since junior high are good to average. Some stand out with solid athletic skills. Even white bookworm types with no athletic ability try out. They make coach laugh at their poor performance since they can hardly do a push up or throw a football. Nerds show up only because their daddies encourage it. Why not?

Head coach James Blalock whips players into shape for stamina and endurance, running laps, sprinting, exercising and doing repetitive reflex drills. Rumors swirl since integration that white coaches have the inside scoop on persuading black players and their parents away from powerhouse Lincoln Park. Promises of a safe environment and better learning resources, even stipends, are on offer just for the sake of future college pursuits, notoriety and fame. This new wave of black athletes immediately becomes Coach Blalock's favorite. Their athletic talent is used as the standard coaches use to determine who has it and who doesn't.

I quickly notice black and white teammates who have already integrated receive less notice. Coach Blalock salivates over what he can do with the speed and agility of Lincoln Park's athletes. After a week of getting in shape, we face agility drills, catching, hitting and tackling. Coach James Tuttle warns, "I'm gonna make this an everyday hell for you! My goal is to separate wanabees from the serious."

The sun is at its highest peak. I see heat waves in the distance while we run ten laps around the track. In a week, white boys who were doing it for daddy quit, brothers out to impress buddies quit, bookworms and nerds too. The locker room becomes less crowded.

Two practices daily in the South Florida sun can make you cry. The sun dances a mirage until green grass moves like the Atlantic Ocean. The scorching heat reaches 100 degrees by noontime. Players load up on water awaiting their term to be a dummy in a tackling drill. A white boy behind me makes muffled sounds like he's crying. His eyes are red and he's shaking like a leaf. I ask if he's alright because it's very hot. "I'm ok. I'm just afraid to get hit." I chuckle, a bit out of surprise. It's his first time trying out. "You better get familiar with this drill. You need to get hit to know what it feels like." Hiding under his helmet, tears trickle steadily down his cheeks. "I don't like football. I'm only here because of my dad," he says, as if hoping I have an answer he likes. "Maann, if your heart ain't in it you gonna get hurt. Just quit." "You don't understand," he says whimpering. "I don't want to let my dad down." "Well, you got to make a decision, stand up to him. He's gonna be disappointed anyway."

I get tackled, which makes this scared white boy jump, wincing as if he got hit. His turn comes, he's about to get tackled, falls back anticipating the blow, to avoid full impact. His wide eyes are stricken with fear like a deer frozen in headlights. "Son! What you call that? The Flop! Do it again and don't move!" Coach Blalock yells. The boy stands visibly shaking and scared. As a tackler plows him into the ground, he screams like a girl panicking from the sight of a spider. No one laughs as they're too exhausted. Shaking and scared, he does it three times more before Coach Blalock is satisfied. As he slowly gets off the ground, I'm convinced he'll quit. But he keeps coming back each day for more punishment. To my surprise he makes the team.

On weekends, if I don't catch a hustle in the groves, I hook up with Jinx and especially with Calvin, an easy-going brother. Calvin lives two blocks away on Avenue F. We're always on the hunt for a decent job. First we try businesses in the Lincoln Park community, but older blacks hold jobs for life it seems with little or no turnover. A decent job in Fort Pierce is always hard to find for a brother, even harder for black youth.

Integration should give blacks equal access, but most white business owners aren't of that mindset. For a young brother, it's discouraging. I jump through too many hoops, not just filling out applications, but having to provide a photo ID, and damn near every family member's name, number and address. And if that isn't enough, they ask suspicious questions. Why do you want to work here? Can you be trusted? Will you abide by company policy and rules? Are you honest? It was like interrogating a criminal who'd wipe him out of his inventory.

We know how to hustle, selling most anything. Jinx and Calvin can't stand the heat, picking fruit and vegetables in the Florida sun. When I swing by some mornings, the jokers refuse to get out of bed. One Saturday morning, Calvin and I get an interview for the same position at Sambo's Restaurant. Our local NAACP threatens a discrimination lawsuit against its name, which they feel is egregious and offensive to blacks. A national boycott is in place to force the restaurant chain to change its name. Black patrons complain about being ignored and receiving bad service. Because of the suit, I have reservations about an interview. To work for a company that doesn't respect blacks, I don't want to come across as a pacifist blocking the way of protesters seeking justice.

Calvin's interview is 30 minutes ahead of mine. This is his first ever interview and he isn't ready. So, I think it's best we practice one Friday after school to familiarize him with the typical questions asked. I also want to help Calvin with Standard English. Calvin has a tendency of using git for get, naw for no, and yeah for yes. "Maann that's lame. I can't change my accent talkin white." "You're not, we just don't want to sound what they expect—dumb. We need all the help we can get." Calvin thinks I'm implying that he is dumb, but I'm more concerned about him attending an integrated school the next year. Like Beanie and Johnnie, the sly jokes, giggles and teasing he's sure to get from whites is going to unsettle him. He'll have an awful time expressing himself. Daddy reminds me, "Slang has its place on the streets. Leave it there." He believes that Standard English whether among whites or your own make a good impression to advance your chances.

We live in a white man's world and we're forced to communicate in King's English to get a foot in the door. "It's a stereotype. White men already against us will feel less threatened," I say. I just hope proper grammar gets the white man's attention and us both a job.

The summer of 1968, Donald Spence, a hip and smart brother from Milwaukee, Wisconsin, moves into the neighborhood to live with his uncle, Parnell Adams, a World War II veteran. Donald comes south because his parents believe it will keep him away from big city lures that rob and poison hopes and aspirations. Donald approaches us in Calvin's front yard debating the issue of proper English. Donald gets teased often about "talkin white" with his midwestern accent. Brothers even think each time I return from New York, I change my accent talkin white. Up north, southerners, especially those from Georgia, Mississippi and Alabama, get teased for their deep southern twang. In my circle of northern friends, a typical southerner is considered dumb. I never want that attention and certainly not the "country" label many transient brothers up from down south get.

I work on what Mama calls "lazy tongue syndrome." Stop dragging words, saying "as" instead of "ask." "Rememba" instead, accentuate the "ber" in remember. Donald's vocabulary is well-polished as he enunciates every syllable.

Sisters in the neighborhood are attracted to Donald's midwestern accent. Donald tries convincing Calvin to work at pronouncing difficult words, but he won't budge. "Maann, I don't care what y'all sayin, y'all talkin white, and I'm talkin black." "Brother please!" Donald replies. "Look soul man, if that's the case whites to speak bad English. You think they're talking black because of using bad English is a good thing?" Donald adds, "Because of my Midwestern accent, jealous dudes think I'm taking their chicks. They tell me I 'ain't nuten.' How can they keep a chick when they're mispronouncing the word 'nothing.' I'm just too smooth, suave and debonair for those jokers." Donald laughs.

Calvin needs a job just as bad as I do, and he keeps a sense of humor about it, overly confident and braggadocious with anything he does. "Soul man, I can't wait to get that job. I'm perfect for it, bet I get it before you, bet my last dollar on it. Wait and see," Calvin says.

That Saturday I come by early to make sure Calvin's up and ready to go. He comes to the door. "Sorry Kenny, maann I ain't goin." "Why? Brother maann, you can't back out now." I'm puzzled. Calvin gives a lame excuse being sick. I probe. "You're lyin, that can't be the reason." "Naw maann I'm not." "Come on, it's your job to have if you want it. It's meant for you." "No, it ain't." "What you mean?" "I can't work there. Maybe I'll be teased, you know, by the protesters, that name Sambo." It dawns on me. Calvin's dark complexion. Afraid he'll get the job, and then protesters and anyone else who sees him will call him Uncle Tom, or worse "Sambo" and laugh.

Since early childhood, teasing from the story *Little Black Sambo* creeps back into his consciousness. "Come on brother, every human comes from the blackest of black, be proud of ya blackness. The blacker the berry the sweeter the juice, black is beautiful, it always has been. . . some of us don't know it yet. Be black and proud," I plead, continuing with clichéd phrases, with the hope of convincing him to get over it. His emotional scars are deeply embedded. "Naw, you go ahead. I'm too black, you're not." Dejected, he closes the door in my face as I stand silently, feeling sorry for my friend.

The dishwasher-busboy position doesn't appeal to me anymore. I want to back out just for Calvin's sake, but I can't. I need a job. Whenever I don't like a job or my chances are poor and my enthusiasm diminishes, I don't get it. I wear a dashiki instead of slacks, white shirt and tie. Do my own protest. I'm sure to get a white manager's attention and reaction in my interview.

I step into a smoke-filled heated debate going on in my living room. Mama has some colorful characters over. Through the years, her attendance in social organizations slows so she can care for Grandma, and has established good relationships with all types of people. She remains benevolent in her duties, finds time to give hot meals, write or read letters, give away old clothes, fill out job applications, tax forms, anything to help a soul in need. It's not uncommon having po-folks over challenging professionals who happen by. The professionals are outnumbered and hemmed in while the indigent are in attack mode.

I walk in, speaking politely and rush to get ready for my job interview. Mama's refereeing as Cousin Cleveland and Mr. Joe have Attorney Bill Benton bobbing like a prizefighter against the ropes. "Look, I don't let nothing worry me. I can't change!" Cousin Cleveland says. I rarely see him when he isn't drunk; his speech slurring as usual, but always clear-headed, cool as a cucumber, and on point. I smile to myself, thinking how rational his argument would be to this day. Many years fighting the bottle, he ultimately quit drinking. I learn a lot about life watching and listening to such lively debates.

"Your battles you're fighting are different! I'm fighting a long-standing legal system. It's almost impenetrable, routinely discriminates, and makes doing business under the law impossible!" Attorney Bill Benton says passionately, pointing at Cousin Cleveland before he flips another swig of whisky from his flask. He looks to be a beaten and sleepless man with bags under his eyes. A longstanding racist judicial system in Fort Pierce and its judges render inequitable decisions against blacks. It appears the system has beaten him down deep into the bottle. But he's sharp and witty, a fighter not a quitter. Like his father, Dr. Clem C. Benton, he comes from a successful and proud family helping the poor.

"Yeah mon, but my point tis yah con't chonge it within, yah must chonge it without!" Mr. Joe Smith says in his distinguished highland thick Jamaica accent. "Mon like Garvey say we must do fir self, con't chonge dir seeystem. Build first from within ir selves mon, get knowledge who we aur tir stay out dir seeystem. Thir no justice in it mon, unteel it reespeect us as ah peeple un we see reeaal chonge, un chonge wit dir times!" Mr. Joe gets my attention as usual. He comes around from time to time and brings Mama delicious hot, crusty breaded and spicy Jamaican beef patties. Mr. Joe's a 33rd degree member of the Prince Hall Freemasonry Imperial Counsel. He appreciates young people learning our rich history and culture. He always indulges me to rap about it. He tells me, "Mon feed dir history tir um, if they no wan tir hir it mon, no stop, ur peeple need medicin to heeaal."

Listening, I'm not sure what point's being discussed. But it got my attention as Cousin Cleveland looks up. "Hey Kenny! What's your opinion? You young people wanna change the world!" he echoes. "I think you all make good points. I don't have time; I got a job interview." Mama catches a glimpse of me. "Oh no! please! Don't wear that dashiki! You should have cut your hair!" "I'm just busting suds. I want to see how this white man reacts. He'll hire me if he really wants to," I say smiling confidently.

I catch a glimpse of the news days before. Sambo's Restaurant is feeling the heat from picketers. I want to make a statement in some small way. "Why ruin your chance, you want the job, don't you?" Mama asks, puzzled. "He's alright Margaret. You know these jitterbugs nowadays, they're doing their own thing," Cousin Cleveland boasts smiling. "No, he isn't. I'm teaching this dap-daddy to dress and look the part, play the role until he gets the job!" Mama retorts. "Let him learn for himself, Margaret. He's in an experimental phase," Attorney Benton smiles. "The white man needs to see young blacks evolving; we old heads should be out of our stagnant state into our own culture. It's a new generation." "Yah Margaret, let um be umself, stir up dir restaurant tir chonge ah Sambo name, heel learn from it," Mr. Joe interjects. I dash out smiling, happy and confident all concede to my position, except Mama.

I arrive early at Sambo's on U.S. #1 in a moment of brisk picketing. A few brothers and sisters out front pace with raised picket signs that read: "The name Sambo is racist." "Change the name." A picketer observes me entering, "Join us brother, not them!"

A short white burly early 30ish manager introduces himself in the lobby. "Nice dashiki." He smiles, extends a hand, and leads the way to his office. A few black waitresses smile as I walk by. Roger closes the door to his office. His smile quickly vanishes into sinister looking eyes—a new character appears—a new role to play.

I sit watching him look over my application, questions turn to usual discouragement. "Can I trust you?" and "Are you serious about working here?" and "How do you get along with others?" "Yes, of course. I certainly do," I say with enthusiasm. I want to ask sarcastically, "How the hell you get along with others as picketers pace outside your damn window!"

I pay attention to my speech, making sure I pronounce and round off every syllable in every word. "I make friends easily with any race, if that's what you mean." I've done enough interviews that I'm familiar with not so subtle race questions. I watch him sizing me up and down, looking for anything to hang a weak excuse on to keep from hiring me. I'm thinking maybe I shouldn't have worn my dashiki. But it's too late.

I'm accustomed to interviews being just a formality with white managers. A few questions to a quick ending, out the door and the phone never rings. This interview is no different—within minutes he's done. Unexpectedly, he leans back in his recliner into comedy hour. "The Cowboys this weekend can't beat a rinky-dink team if I play quarterback, all 250 pounds of me." I sit there watching him, annoyed by his rather stale comedy act. I experience it too often and prepare myself for the unlikely, but this is too much.

Roger goes further, into jiving like he's down with the brothers. "You like the Bengals?" I nod. "What the hell John Stoffa thinks he's doing running around like Houdini, he can't hit an elephant ass with a pass, can't carry my jock strap, ain't that right dude?" He perks up into a silly grin. "Excuse me, I want to finish up. Are you interested in hiring me or not?" I say bluntly. Surprised, he quickly gathers himself with that grin vanishing into a look of disdain. I want him to understand this black guy can think, speak and should be taken seriously. And I'm hip to his game. I'm not going to be the stereotypical n....r he has in mind.

At school with its racial climate, I have enough experience to sense when something isn't right. I sense in Roger's eyes that he doesn't want to deal with a race conscious brother. As I speak about shift availabilities, his eyes study me carefully. Perhaps I'm overreacting, I tell myself. Maybe he's just unprepared for this brother. But I feel resentment and tension in the room. A lack of interest, my dashiki, maybe my big bush Afro or my wild boar's teeth necklace turns him off. But that was my intended purpose, wasn't it? My style was an implicit protest of Sambo's, to get a reaction.

Roger decides to let it all hang out renouncing me. "Who do you think you are coming in here with that get up on? You might be a good worker," he says intensely, but calmly. "I just can't trust your type." "What's my type?" "Ah you know, the black militant, ah the radical type causing trouble." "You mean the way I'm dressed?" "You're wrong. I'm just into my culture. Makes you uncomfortable?" I say with intensity and a restrained smile. "What kind of trouble?" I keep probing, watching his eyes evade mine. "I don't know. Just don't want to hire no agitators around here. We got the NAACP on our backs for a boycott. Your type talking this black power lingo," he says, forcing air from his lungs like he can't hold it back any longer. "I don't want any trouble out from my 'negro' employees," he added. Few blacks I observe, far from it, look happily content.

"Do you have an open mind at all?" Roger looks at me curiously and puzzled, not knowing how to answer the question. I suppose encountering someone quite young, black and astute to his game makes him nervous. "I don't know what you mean by that." So, I answer for him. "Fear is your problem. You should learn to know and appreciate people as you find them." I leave his office abruptly, with the sound of his voice calling out, "Wait a minute! I didn't mean it like that! You're right! I'm interested in you anyway!" I want to turn around and go back, but then I think of Calvin, foolishly too proud for my own good. I keep stepping.

After my interview, still without a job, I think of Calvin and this episode for a long time. It reminds me how much race matters. How we as a people can't and shouldn't escape being black. We can't afford to. No matter that whites and even those of our own race prefer, we must embrace our identity. I'm not discouraged by the white manager's revelations. He's no different than some brothers I know who are stagnated by the fear of the unknown. It's as Carver G. Woodson emphasized, "How can you get where you're going until you know where you've been."

The white manager doesn't care about how the name Sambo offends blacks because it perpetuates negative stereotypes. The psychological effects of slavery and Jim Crow segregation attribute to a black inferiority complex as we come of age into black consciousness. I choose proudly to express and celebrate rather than suppress and dismiss my cultural heritage. It's not a play thing—a fade in vogue today, replace by another fade in some cultural thing, tomorrow. I wear and choose my cultural expressions for life. `

Race matters. When we were children, Mama read to my sisters and me folklore stories of "Little Black Sambo" and "Tar Baby." Never once did she express black as distinctively inferior. Nor does she proscribe to it as others come of age in black consciousness and view those stories as offensive and racist. We're shielded from notions of black as an inferior color in every way possible.

My parents never stifled their children by low self-esteem issues about one's shade of color. Although by grade school, black jokes and stereotypes from the outside and from school inevitably creep into our home. Yet, I was already awakened to understand what W.E.B. DuBois so poignantly put: "The problem of the twentieth century is the problem of the color-line." People of color have been exploited and marginalized and bear the psychological scars attributed to the color-line, and we inflict hatred unto ourselves. Look in any standard dictionary for a definition of black (revised for today's politically correctness doesn't change one's misguided perception) and its synonyms. They are negative, bad and sinister, while white is defined as pure and good. Just think of a little white lie, meaning nothing serious, and black market referring to something illegal. The imagery is deeply engrained in our psyche.[50]

My middle sister Regina is dark in a family of multiplicity of colors. Regina and my youngest sister Sheryl who is of a lighter hue get into a skin color argument. "With your black self!" Sheryl says, ending her argument. Mama goes into a rage, throwing a shoe that barely misses Bee Wee (another of Sheryl's nicknames) and frightens her. "Don't ever let me hear you say that in my house! The color of your skin is no better than your sister's! Don't you ever forget it!"

A family friend, Annabelle, comes by to visit. Mama hasn't seen her in weeks. She's known for her occasional negative black antics and slinging around the n....r word. My 8-year old niece, Natrice, comes into the living room. "Hello smoky with yo black self!" Mama pushes her out the front door. "And don't you ever come back inflicting self-hate in my granddaughter's mind!" Annabelle apologizes, pleas she never meant anything by it. "Friend or no friend, I won't let you put poison into her mind." Mama's passionate in these types of things, things rooted in self-hatred since slavery. She slams the door on Ms. Annabelle.

Race certainly matters. As a child, Grandma witnessed some disrespectful blacks acting a fool. She says, "The white man molded us with self-hatred and broke the mold." As I mature in understanding, I realize she meant those of us beyond reproach. When help is offered, there are those who prefer to wallow in degradation. She witnesses this type of behavior in her social organizations. In one such organization, the Negro Women Pallbearers Association, they raise funds to help bury the indigent. "That n..ga don't deserve a red cent," an inconsiderate member speaks out. That member is quickly admonished by Grandma, of course. Grandma comes to terms with this kind of talk, but she does not accept it. She says, "You can't change behavior of a person until they are willing to change, even ones you think should have polished

---

[50] More current dictionaries have changed with the times when defining black. They have adopted a more positive race conscious definition.

behavior you got to straighten um out now and then."

Race must matter. We need to change our attitudes teasing the darkest brothers you hang out with and who take the blunt end of negative black jokes: You black mothaf...a this...you black son-of-a-b...h that. We allow others to sling n....r at our friends, not come to their aid. Many of our people with low self-esteem dignify the word. No respect for themselves and others. Just as the oppressor plans and fashions it to be done in slavery, many of us have adopted those ways. There are those who say, "a n..ga ain't shit...a n..ga ain't this...a n..ga ain't that..." Referring to all blacks, and many believe it, are full of it, don't, won't, love, desire, or identify with anything black.

Many are culturally malnourished with low self-images. They don't realize they harbor self-hatred. It's a disease and it spreads and it's contagious. It's why my parents prevent my sisters and me from catching the inferiority complex self-hating disease. When we use n....r and other negative stereotypes against ourselves, we can't cry foul when other races use it against us. It's like the old axiom Grandma often says, "The pot calling the kettle black." There is no reason anyone can justify the use of the word given the harm that has been done with its impact on our community. It is not an affectionate term nor a term of endearment. In my opinion, blacks who use it are ignorant, unaware, and don't know their history.

Race will always matter in my quest for understanding how enduring segregation continues to create systemic social conditions of crime, joblessness, hopelessness and despair. How its lingering effect passes from one generation to the next; the inferior thinking of oneself, whereby people despise their color and are ashamed of their culture.

I discover my interest in Peaches fully blossoms into one I try to keep platonic in our rendezvous, fending off her solicitous pimp-game moves. Peaches believes wearing blonde wigs makes her look and feel elegant—among other things, beautiful, graceful, dignified—refined. "But what of the Afro wig?" Peaches sits on the edge of her bed, pulls the blond wig off her head and stares at it. For the first time, I see a lush thick healthy head of neatly braided hair can be her own Afro. She caresses and strokes that blonde wig, searching deep into the recesses of her mind for something, anything.

Hollow silence amplifies street noise below. An expression of doubt and vulnerability plasters Peaches' face. I can't get her to extrapolate her thoughts into words. Not until a knock interrupts her already subdued quietness does she become animated. "Oh hi Joy!" A lascivious charcoal black Amazon lady of ill repute enters. By now the moment is lost, but the effect my question has on her remained. Peaches forces a smile, turns her attention to Joy, who is about to sit next to me. Every bit of her 200 pounds shakes and compresses an already badly-worn velvet sofa. Peaches says, "Joy? Girl please explain to Foxy Black here, why we wear this here wig." Joy rolls her eyes, and her frown turns into a stare of consternation and exhaustion from turning tricks on a hot summer night. Sweat beads up after trickling down from beneath her shabby platinum wig, meandering into crevasses on her shiny black forehead. Joy, ten years Peaches senior, is a dark chocolatey hue revealing remnants of beauty her profession has sapped away.[51]

Joy twice shunned my interview advances about her life—shut them out. All I can get is a traumatic childhood of humiliation and pain in Mississippi, the land of cotton where she picked lots of it. "I got called "Tar-Baby" and was teased by my mama and daddy, sisters and brothers, day and night and at school. I quit school and ran away from home." I watch and wait, thinking Joy might have been a beautiful "Tar-Baby" to some foolish lucky man. The sweat enhances her black skin into a silky radiant glow of beauty, but that platinum blonde wig looks ridiculously pitiful against her dark skin. It reminds me of a dab of chocolate floating in cream—not a good contrast.

"Go ahead Joy, tell Fast Black why we wear blonde wigs," Peaches insists. "What the hell for?" "N..ga please!" This wig attracts

---

[51] Street name Peaches coined for my hip style of dress and rap, she boast someday I'll become her pimp. She uses "Foxy" and "Fast Black" interchangeably. Peaches is impressed by my ability to get her to open up for my vignettes—a description of her life.

all the suckers. Besides, you need to stand out and look good, that's what this wig do honey." "But why not wear an Afro?" I ask. "Lyin there trickin them fruit pickin n..gas? Don't wanna rub up against no nappy Afro, like they hand through this white thang and fantasize, you know? Wearin it I'm closest they get to a white bitch." Joy's words stir up deep thoughts of anguish. Her smiles fade into a shade of gloom. "Besides, brothas so damn mix up in the head for this horse hair shit!" She rubs her fingers through it, caressing stroking copying Peaches. "But hell, you can sho as hell make mo money with it than without it," Joy muses. "Black men sho messed up in the head."

I think how beautiful Joy would look naturally. How ridiculously pitiful that blonde wig looks against Peaches' café au lait honey-toned skin.

Peaches gets up, neatly places the blonde wig on top of her dresser. She opens a drawer carefully and pulls out, to my surprise, a black Afro wig. She stares into a mirror while placing it snuggly on her head. "You see Fast Black. I can wear it now that I ain't workin. I'm wearin it just for you daddy." She smiles teasingly. "You look like my sun goddess," I reply jokingly as she smiles. "You always say the sweetest things to me. That's why I'll turn a trick for you anytime, whenever you ready daddy." She and Joy burst into laughter. It's sad commentary, but real. The depths of self-hatred saturate the oldest profession and play out a harmful role.

Self-hatred starts first with the black man's psyche. Many negative self-images turn inward and play outward onto the black woman's psyche. It is this poor self-image and rejection of cultural identity that explain why whiteness signifies a superior standard of beauty. The blonde wig and it's "lengthy hair" highlights what white beauty is. The black man's cultural hatred and disillusions with black woman and black standards of beauty have been internalized. Depravity of positive self-images are overshadowed by historical dehumanization inflicted on our women from the times of slavery. Now is the time to lift our women up!

I can't get over waiting for Peaches' answer, as I watch her grasp and massage the blonde wig's stringy silky softness. Years of segregation and cultural depravity, paraphrasing Dr. King, distort the soul, damage the personality, and give the segregated a false sense of inferiority.

Race matters when negative jokes made about blackness of skin can have a crippling paralyzing effect on one's psyche for a lifetime. This pathology of self-hatred is passed down from generation to generation. Calvin internalizes teasing with emotional passivity, in a nonaggressive way with subtle signs of humiliation absent of anger. While another neighbor, Larry, has heightened sensitivity about his dark skin, and teasing unleashes an explosive temper and rage. He, in contrast to Calvin, acts out his aggression with violent acts.

Some weekends, Lon Knowles, Eugene "Jinx" Jenkins, Ray Isaac, the Richardson brothers, Harvey, Levi, Adrian, and their cousins Aaron and Larry Richardson and I have some serious basketball games of "21." Whenever Larry gets ahead in points he has a tendency to talk trash, dishing it out but unable to take it. Levi is tired of his jawing and yells out, "Shut up Blackie!" While Larry's back is turned, Blackie gets Larry rattled and conjures up emotions of embarrassment and shame. "Who said that? Tell me!" He gets teary-eyed as paranoia sets in. His eyes search for a culprit.

Larry hears snickers and whispers, but can't identify the offender. "Tar Baby!" Levi sneaks it in again. "Who call me that!" Larry screams. No one answers. I shoot free throws, smiling because I move ahead of Larry in points. Noticing my smile, he thinks I'm the guilty culprit. "Kenny! You call me that?" He picks up a 2x4 and approaches me in attack mode with uncontrollable rage. "No man, you know me. I don't jive like that. It's Levi!" "No! It's you!" Larry's convinced. "I'll kill you!" He charges, swinging the board. Once before I had dodged his knife attack, this is not the first fight we have.

All the Richardsons know their cousin's dark skin is his weakness. They take pleasure making him angry for their advantage. I manage to outmaneuver and take him down into submission. Once Larry gets up, he's even more dangerous. "I'm gonna kill you. . . wait and see!" He runs home crying. "You know Larry, you better leave Kenny. He just might do it," Harvey warns. "I got your back Kenny. Go home and stay until he cools off," Ray adds. Ray is always neutral. We're Pisces, born on the same month and day. Considering Larry's' reputation, I take Ray's advice without question.[52]

Race should matter until time immemorial as black people reject the idea that the color black is inferior. Mama says, "In this house we turn black away from negative into positive." She takes this from Grandma, who religiously says that a black cat crossing your path is good luck; that the black sheep of the family is a good child. She turns any with negative connotations of black into good.

Getting off the school bus one day, I spot Squirrel Nut and Sneaky Pea standing on the corner of Thirteenth Street, both were kicked out of school for fighting before entering ninth grade. It's been a year since I last saw them, both in and out of jail on petty crimes since reform school. Squirrel has aged, now with cold eyes and a mature mustache. Sneaky is hardened by more years of jail time and his signature glowing smile a mere glimmer of itself. "What's happenin school boy, give me some skin!" Squirrel says. Our hands slap, very pronounced this time into a soul handshake. "You still into that school thang dude? What good is it?" he continues. "Don't jive man," Sneaky Pea interjects, "you know Kenny's a serious brother about school." We rap for a while. Every few minutes a car rolls up to the curb. Sneaky runs up to it poking his head inside and returns stuffing bills into his pocket. Sneaky's influence has Squirrel hopeless. "You dudes ought to get back in school." "Why should we when the bread's good," Sneaky says, laughing as he pulls out a wad of large bills. "We can make this sellin weed," he brags. "Cool it man. Don't blow our cover," Squirrel snaps. "Kenny's alright, he just ain't down like this." "I'm hip. We doin our own thing now brother maann," Sneaky adds, running over to another car rolling up for a sell.

---

[52] A few years later at Busy Bee Poolroom, a misunderstanding and argument develop between three of my playmates, Larry Richardson and Jeff and Raymond James lead to a shootout. Jeff was killed. Uncontrolled anger was the contributing factor. Another friend with untapped potential dies young.

"Kenny, what's it like now at that white school?" Squirrel whispers, out of Sneaky's range. Squirrel likes school, but Sneaky's influence is too deep. Squirrel has low self-esteem and gets teased about how his mouth hangs open with protruding lips, a habit he worked hard to break, but he can't. And Squirrel is ashamed of his short kinky hair that curls into bee-bee shots (tight curls) when he sweats, concealing it under a hat. Unlike a neighborhood friend, Clayton, "Peas" Jordon, nickname appropriately given to his tightly curled hair smile answering to his nickname. Peas, mom, Naomi Jordan, Mama's childhood friend is educated, culturally conscious raise her children similarly with culture pride without the stigma best hair types.

On one occasion, Squirrel and I rap in my front yard when Mr. Preston, an elderly dapper neighbor, happens by. Preston hips me on the latest fashions and gives me color coordinating tips in clothing. He notices sweat beads up and rolls down Squirrel Nut's face. "Young man, take that hot hat off your head and let it breathe." Squirrel Nut doesn't respond—doesn't dare show off his nappy hair. "What's your problem brother?" Preston frowns. Squirrel reluctantly takes off his hat as sweat runs down his face. "Son, you need a brush!"

Preston recommends a brittle brush hair tamer to relax his hair naturally, so his head can breathe without sweating. Squirrel Nut gets enraged, thinking he's the brunt of teasing. "Old man, I'll f..k you up!" Preston jumps back startled. "What's wrong with your friend?" Preston quips. "I'm not teasing. Frequent brushing tames the tight kinky hair, guaranteed that it'll loosen up naps and make it manageable." Squirrel Nut isn't convinced nor impressed in the least. He thinks nothing will relax his hair. "It won't happen, no way! I rather have good hair like white people got," he says angrily.

"Wait a minute! There's no such thing as good hair, it's just different textures, either straight, curly or coarse, which we call nappy. None is better than the other," I interject. Squirrel Nut doesn't believe me either. "I don't care what y'all say, I hate naps." Years of teasing give him a poor self-image. "Sorry old man." Squirrel goes somber. "I get so angry. I don't know why, like I'm gonna explode."

"I get angry about things too brother," I remind him. "We gonna work it out."

Race does matter a lot. I try to reach out and help brothers like Larry, Squirrel Nut and others. Free their minds and get them to read about our history and take pride in it. I want to prove to all that our history opens doors to new worlds that whites have kept hidden from us at school. It will help instill confidence and racial pride. I can't get through to Squirrel Nut, not just yet. The brother rejects reading anything black. "What good is that black sh..? I ain't black, I'm Afro-American!" he snaps. "That's cool," I say, willing to compromise to get him reading. At least he comes to know the term Negro is outdated.

We have come so far that no longer should we allow our oppressor to define us. I think I make some progress. "Brother, we're living in better times to be black and proud." "Black is beautiful, get connected." We debate until I get a headache. "To hell with James Brown's 'Say it loud!' I rather be a Negro before I say I'm black and proud." Even in an era of awakening, there're still lost souls. I don't give up on Squirrel Nut's deep self-hatred. Never do I give up to reach understanding.

Race matters. In an era of integration with school nearing, news networks spew propaganda that makes parents cautious over the race issue. "Will racial problems be at new Dan McCarty Annex?" I keep an open mind, hoping to stay out of trouble. There will be unfinished business as usual, that I know. Many whites feel entitled, not willing to budge, rather keep things lily white, while blacks find ways to fit into the deeply entrenched white system. Gail's heading into her junior year, Regina, now in the seventh grade, and Cheryl is at an integrated elementary school having behavioral problems. Cowchee can't handle being teased and called skinny.[53]

After basketball practice, I hang out with Jesse, Beanie and Johnny shooting pool at Busy Bee. Jesse quit ninth grade and

---

[53] Sheryl, my youngest sister, has several nicknames; Cherry, Bee-wee, Fresh, and Chowchee pronounced CowChee given by my Grandma from her Cherokee ancestry. Our family affectionately uses these nicknames interchangeably, depending on the mood of the moment.

served time in jail. Beanie and Johnny smoke and drink and are lightweight hustlers. Johnny, the oldest at 17, served a month in the county jail for stealing. Beanie somehow has a white connection selling weed with no time for anyone but weed and money. I want to check Beanie out and get into his head. Like Jesse, Beanie's smart, has more interest in school than Johnny, his partner. I probe Beanie about his plans to get back in school. Shooting pool, I strike but he's hip to my game. "Maann I ain't got time for yo shit! Don't com ova hear preachin bout school. I ain't interested!" he rebuffs.

I reach out to brothers on the brink of heading into the pen. Many brothers in the neighborhood quit school early. I feel their frustrations and anger, the pull and vices of the streets all around the neighborhood, the absence of guidance and no sense of purpose are commonalities shared by many underprivileged youth. I'm just lucky still holding on.

Cautious when I'm out on the streets, I stay clear of weed although I occasionally hit a cigarette. More of an "in thing," sneaking a beer or taking a swig of Mogan David wine from the fridge, where Mama keeps it for guests. I amass a large collection of black history books on a variety of subjects. My reading keeps me grounded, although I am still disillusioned by inequalities in my community. The changes and struggles I witness my people go through every day are troubling. Especially disheartening are those on the streets with the advent of drugs two years earlier now permeating the minds of those who were already hopeless. So many distractions coming at me in such a short time.

Ron and I stop by the gym to check a list of names for final Dan McCarty High Junior Varsity cut. Certain of making the team, we want to see if any capable brothers get cut for a mediocre white boy, for the sake of having an integrated team. We notice two white boys fuming over the list. The taller one we believe utters "n.....s." We restrain our anger to probe. "Y'all make the team?" No response. Both whisper and ignore us. "Don't see your names?" No reply, as both finger up and down the list. "I guess y'all don't make it." "No, we don't make it! the taller one reacts. "It's unfair," the shorter one adds. "Why?" we ask. "Most you guys make up the team. We're going to talk to Coach Blalock about it." Both walk away.

The two are wrong. Blacks, too, get cut, and some quit. Our Junior Varsity squad is mostly white after the cuts and the quits. I say to Ron, "They're blaming brothers, looking for some racial excuse for not being good enough."

It becomes news at practice. Coach Blalock received flak from some black players, but mostly from whites who are unhappy being cut. "I'm fair," Coach Blalock says. "What we have here are proven guys black and white who work hard and make the cut." Some white players aren't convinced.

Race matters in athletics. No one expects to win with mediocrity. To win you must put your best talent forward. Unlike one's mental acuity, with physical abilities you can't overlook, disguise or conceal them. Racist theorist and historians claim blacks are mentally inferior to whites. Borne out through some acknowledged standardized test at the start of integration. It ultimately is proven to have a cultural bias, especially in the vocabulary portions that are suited to white social orientation. You can't measure and quantify an entire race's mental acuity by testing. But they do it so they can say we are mentally inferior, less civilized, underdeveloped mentally when compared to other racial groups, without first understanding our social orientation.

There are black students, I'm certain, and white students too, like myself who scored low and are placed in remedial classes. But scientific data fails to delve into the root causes for blacks scoring poorly and the complexities attributed to enduring years of Jim Crow segregation. Many racist historians, for too long, perpetuate the falsehoods that black Africans have no ancient relics nor have invented anything of value, and have concluded that we are a backward, primitive, and uncivilized people. This fallacy is a racist construct used to conquer and divide civilizations. And it has been used handily here in the United States to keep people of color down.

What integration does for a segment of culturally and socially disadvantaged blacks languishing in mediocrity at so-called inferior black schools is put a spotlight on academic and behavioral problems. This comes at a time when notable white theorists are unwilling to acknowledge the accomplishments of blacks who have succeed in spite of the unfavorable conditions they are relegated to.

At the inception of integration, I dread standardized testing with the suspicion that my score will be scrutinized differently than that of my white counterparts. What will the scores prove and what will the professionals conclude? That blacks truly are inferior to whites? That blacks are ignorant? That blacks are uncivilized and underdeveloped mentally? That black culture and social orientation is beyond reproach?

Ever since junior high, Coaches King, Valentine and Burleson have debated black athletic physical prowess. Who's the best athlete? Black athletes undoubtedly change the rules of major sports. Our domination stirs controversy, causing the media, and some whites to play the race card: "Does race matter in high profile sports?" In 1963, Iverson Williams and Jackie Kelly, both academically sound, break color barriers at Fort Pierce's Catholic school, John Carroll High, with few wins before Williams and Kelly's arrival as eighth and ninth graders. Williams breaks school records, winning every award possible, as does 6' 5" Kelly, pass-catching honors and his contribution as a placekicker. John Carroll posted an over-all 26-2-2 record, winning two league championships and a title during Kelly enrollment.

Williams and Kelly lead the way for other greats like Jackie Robinson of Dan McCarty High. A big and fast power runner, so good that he is allowed to wear the unthinkable white shoes. Robinson breaks numerous rushing records and is responsible for bringing out huge integrated crowds to Jaycee Field Stadium. Kenny Durham, a 6'6" defensive lineman, who the *News Tribune* (a white newspaper) crowns player of the year; and Henry "Joe" White, who averages 35 points per game shatters every possible basketball school record. Many others follow, making their mark at predominately white schools; many are 2-, 3- and 4-sport athletes who excel academically. And what of the possibilities missed by all-black Lincoln Park Academy's great athletes? Jim Crow segregation cheated us. One can only imagine what such accomplishments we might have achieved with equal opportunities.

White coaches can't possibly win without black athletes. This reality leads the way to recruiting black athletes from powerhouse Lincoln Park Academy. The revenue black athletes bring into white schools is enormous—white coaches can no longer turn a blind nor prejudiced eye.

In 1967, for the first time in John Carroll's Rams' history, a few black star athletes play basketball and football games against Lincoln Park Academy's Greyhounds. I'm lucky to get tickets to the sold-out gymnasium and to Jaycee Field. The news media's stigmatization of the Lincoln Park community as "crime-ridden" play the race card frightens away many whites. Yet, clusters of loyal whites who are undeterred by the media hype gather, with not one criminal incident reported by the media. The games are so important that people stand outside awaiting the outcome. With a Basketball game played on the segregated side of the tracks there is much news propaganda about if John Carroll High beat a predominately black supposedly superior segregated school will go down in annals of basketball history.

Race always matters whenever a white or black in sports plays against each other. The marginalized have little to cheer about in a segregated world. We know, as do whites, the superior natural ability of the black athlete. Sports, music, entertainment is said to be our exclusive domain because of less discrimination in these areas.

When Muhammad Ali (then Cassius Clay) defeated the next "great white hope" we cheered; in 1966, when the all-black little known Texas Western basketball team defeated legendary Adolph Rupp's all-white Kentucky team, cheers reach a high pitch in my living room and in the houses of our neighbors. Similarly, in earlier years, we cheered when Jackie Robinson breaks the color barrier and hits a home run; when Joe Louis defeats Germany's native son Max Schmeling in a title fight, we cheer; when Jesse Owens at the 1936 Olympics wins four gold medals to defeat Hitler's belief that an Aryan-race with blue eyes and blonde hair is superior, blacks cheer louder.

For the marginalized and disenfranchised in America, it has always been this way—race matters. We are prone to fantasize such momentous accomplishments as our own personal victory—a black defeating a white opponent. We pray, and we play and fight twice as hard for a victory.

The oppressed take their repressed anger and frustrations and unleash it on "Mr. Charlie." We can yell and shout, exhilarated every time points are scored, a metal is won, a knockout is delivered—it's a victory for the black race! Every time "Mr. Charlie" cheats us out of pay, charges too much, refuses to hire us, fires us, denies us housing, rejects our application for a loan, whatever the situation— we hang on the aforementioned victories as our own for all times!

The black community is pressuring the Greyhounds to win with its reputation of having superior athletes. News media overreact on issues of race *"when race matters."* Lincoln alumni reacts: "We can't let a white school come into our house, even with a few black players, and beat us." Lincoln Park routs John Carroll both in basketball and football. "The game of the ages" leads to stories in local newspapers—*when race matters*:

Negroes Dominate High School Basketball and Football. . . as they are dominating college and professional levels. A white writer in the Fort Pierce *News Tribune* goes on to theorize reasons for black dominance in national sports:

> The Negro is hungrier than the white athlete. . . better desire to excel because it is the only avenue out to advance his socio/economic status. . . the Negro often feels that his physical talent is the only thing he can count on for the future. . . while white athletes are not so strongly motivated.

> Another theory writers harp on with an implicit air of racism: The average Negro youth can't afford to do much else than play sports like basketball. . . you don't need to purchase much equipment. . . with movies to see, books to read cars to drive white youngsters may not be inclined to compete in sports at all.

The latter opinion illustrates what sports writers find as the most acceptable racist concession for black athletic dominance. A stereotypical characterization that impoverished black athletes thrive with their singular preoccupation with sports, absent of any cerebral focus to get ahead academically in an unequal society. This belief the black athlete was gradually putting to rest at integrated schools.

Many of my teammates are studious, go to movies and drive their own cars. Writers whimsically believe when black athletes, especially blacks in American society, are accepted and their socio-economic status improves, their dominance in sports will recede. What white coaches realize is integration brings about parity. A lily-white team can no longer compete nor win without inclusiveness nor say it is or was the best ever without competing against an integrated team that is an equal opportunist—open to all ethnicities. How can any ethnic group measure greatness without openness to all ethnic groups?

Rumors swirl even more around campus that white coaches prefer black players. Rumors of disgruntled white parents whose sons lose starting positions to blacks. Fathers accustomed to seeing their sons in key roles and positions, especially as quarterbacks, are angry because they want their sons to star and succeed so the dads can relive their own glory days. The coaching staff finds itself on the defensive. Angry parents, on occasion, show up after practice to question their son's playing time. "It's unfair my son isn't playing. . . all starters are black," I once overhear a parent say in the bleachers. But it isn't unfair! The best happens to be all black.

When taking the field against mostly white schools, I see a prevailing trend from integration—teams slow integrating, we destroy. And those schools that are fully integrated are stiffer competition. A black starting quarterback on a predominately white team is scrutinized unfairly by white fans and the media alike as not smart enough. In some instances, they make these claims having never witnessed him play.

Some of Lincoln Park Academy's old all-black high school nemeses close. Gifford High in the city of Gifford, Woodrow Wilson

High in Stuart and others are forced to close their doors because of integration. There again, the school board closes black schools and keep white schools open under the guise forcing whites to integrate black schools across the tracks. Justify closing black schools under badges and instances of black schools and its students there as being inferior is how it's done. Black leadership understands this old school board ploy, but not without a fight. Black citizens file law suits that delay that process as sports at the height of integration becomes a unifier of the races.

Standing at the bus stop after school one day, I overhear two white teachers whispering: "A victory isn't a victory if a white player isn't contributing," one teacher says. "Come on, you don't believe that. It's about all have an equal chance. . .and the competitive edge is black for a change," he laughs. The other concedes. "I guess you're right, times are changing." The best really matters.

Chapter 24

LONESOME DOVE

I get a summer job in June 1969, working at Dan McCarty High School's in a Neighborhood Youth Corps program. The federal government legislates a grant for unemployed and disadvantaged youth—a decent hourly wage when compared to field work pay. My goal, as usual, is to make enough money to buy my own school clothes and supplies. Whatever's left I save. Mama never asks for a dime. She believes that what you earn is yours to do with as you please, smartly of course, encouraging us to save just as much. For black boys, finding a job staying out of trouble is hard enough. Black businesses usually reserve jobs for adults with mouths to feed. A brother must "keep moving," step out of his element, up his game, and get lucky across the tracks finding work with white businesses.

I step into an office where a white man is sitting behind his desk. He immediately asks, "Will you do what I ask? Will you listen? Be on time? Not cause problems?" He's cautious and picky. "You don't have to worry, I come here to work," I assure him. The News Tribune advertises school janitorial jobs, moving and hauling furniture out of classrooms, office clerical, and inside jobs at select schools throughout St. Lucie County. I want to get out of the sun for a change, and move into an air conditioned office. The bulletin board has nothing of interest, nothing other than outdoor jobs. I know a few brothers get hired, but better jobs go to whites, and then to blacks from prominent families with money and connections, while the poor and disconnected get the leftovers.

"I'd like a clerical job, that's what I applied for," I say with assurance. "Sorry, all those are taken, except one," Jerry says, pointing to a hoe and a rake propped up against the wall. All enthusiasm and interest I come in with disappears, and he realizes it. "You did say you come to work, didn't you?" I hear sarcasm in his voice.

I set out trimming hedges, hoeing, and raking weeds out of the flowerbeds. Within minutes of getting started, Jerry comes and stands nearby, checking my work. "Go back, you're not getting out all the weeds." I go back and jump on it. Jerry returns minutes later. "I need you to stop that and do this." I go jump on that. After a while, I catch him peeping from behind the trees and corners.

One hot day his shadow startles me. I turn and there he is, a few feet away leaning against a wall watching. Old time migrant workers say that having a Negro straw boss is bad enough, but having a white man standing over you while you work is double humiliation, and is equal to calling you a dumb n....r. Your work in the hot sun is productive enough without question. I suppose he thinks I'm too dumb to do the same simple task right, unless he watches.

I understand this mentality. In the white man's eyes we're not thinkers, we're mindless. It reminds me of Eldridge Cleaver's brilliant narrative in *Soul on Ice*. "The white man turned himself into the Omnipotent Administrator and established himself in the Front Office. And he turned the black man into a Supermasculine Menial and kicked him out into the fields. The white man wants to be the *brain* and he wants us to be the muscle, the *body*."[54]

This kind of humiliating technique, it appears, is used today by design, just as potent as it was for the overseer during slavery. The psychology of it is keeping the slave in a constant state of flux and fear—questioning his own worth. The slave was dependent on the overseer standing over him to check, question, and punish at his discretion a slave's productivity.

A slave devalued and helpless has no choices. But I do, so I ask, "Is there a problem?" "Oh no!" he says. "Then why are you watching?"

---

[54] Eldridge Cleaver, *Soul on Ice*, Dell Publishing, New York, New York, P.162. 1968

"Just checking." "For what?" He leaves without comment, but continues his clandestine spying at a distance.

That white man tries, as Cleaver points out, to get into my head, where he thinks I'm weak and unnerved. After work, I go to his office, ready to quit, and give him a piece of my mind. Later I decide to opt out of my mindless emotional overreaction to his cerebral challenge. "Look, I do my work, you don't have to check up on me. I'd appreciate it if you didn't." I say this politely but seriously. Jerry gets up from behind his desk and looks out a window, thinking how to respond. "I've had a number of Negro boys working, and all quit on me for no reason, so I thought you would too." "What happened?" "They do good work but did a lot of talking, singing, laughing. I don't understand that."

There's a saying I learned from my father that has been proven in our history: Never let Mr. Charlie catch you on the job laughing among yourselves. It's Mr. Charlie's perception that you're hardly working, or not working hard enough to earn your pay. When it's time for a raise, Mr. Charlie disagrees because your behavior sends a misleading message—Negroes are content with the little work they are perceived to be doing and satisfied with the little pay they get. I believe there's truth that whites see us this way. It's a biased perception: We are happy in the "big house." We harbor that plantation mentality—happy Negroes at work, content with low wages. I learn early on never to congregate gossiping with boisterous laughter.

Laughter's a smoking gun on the job. Jerry doesn't get it. Working outside for blacks, talking, joking and laughing, singing, and toiling in the heat gets you through the day has historical roots. African people, wherever they may be, have always used song and dance to cope, to keep their sanity through difficult times. We are a rhythmic people. Everything we do: work, sing, dance, art, music, walk, run, talk, dress, sports, making love is rhythmic. By constantly checking up on brothers, and then further separating them by giving them different tasks, broke their spirit. I suppose this is why they quit.

Sometimes blind insensitivity can make you overlook the reasonable side of an issue. Sensing I might be on the verge of quitting, he shifts his mindset. "You're a good worker. I hope you stay on." I get an upsurge of satisfaction knowing Jerry's encounter with black boys prove futilely flawed—I suspect he expect I will quit too. I leave with a tingling sensation. I win a small victory in perception and Jerry, after all, won't be checking my work.

Before the end of June, Daddy calls and invites Gail and me to come visit him for the rest of the summer in Rochester, New York. After receiving our Greyhound tickets, we can't get much sleep. Besides a brief moment previously with daddy, has been nine years of any quality time together. I give Jerry two-weeks' notice before my last check.

Grandma gets weaker each day, spending more time in bed. She never complains, doesn't speak much but reads her bible. My sisters and I spend moments with her at her bedside. I kiss her cheek, hold her hand, and talk to her. She listens, smiles, but says little. Her mind slips into a child-like state. Mama has a difficult decision to make. Should she admit her into the once white, now supposedly integrated, Easter Manor Nursing Home, a week before our departure? "She'll die Mama, white people won't care for her like their own," I plead unconvincingly. Mama says her mind and body are tired. I don't want to know what that means.

Gail's independence and confidence might challenge Daddy's authority. Mama's concerned because Daddy's explosive temper can spell trouble. Nothing indicates a hint of this during my brief visit with Aunt Ruth and Uncle Jesse last summer. I promise to keep an open eye.

When we arrive at the Greyhound station in Rochester on July 12, 1969, Daddy smiles ear-to-ear. We embrace and get a bite to eat at a fast food joint. Just as we get inside, put our luggage down, his phone rings. Daddy answers and his smile quickly fades. Grandma has passed away. It's an awful time. Gail and I want to return home immediately. Obviously we don't want to miss her funeral. But Daddy can't make up his mind, so Mama decides. Returning to Rochester after her funeral is too costly, and it will ruin our visit. Staying is ideal for Gail, since graduating in June she has plans to get a job in Rochester and save money before starting college in September. This sets me off emotionally. I have saved enough money to buy a fare back, so I grab my footlocker, and decide I'll get to the station someway. Daddy talks me out of it.

"Kenny is in the kitchen." These are the last words Grandma uttered before passing, according to Mama. She was feeling better thinking of me. I lapse into crying, thinking of those fond times and stories in my childhood spent in the kitchen with Grandma—her little "pot watcher."

Many species of birds—especially blue jays, mocking birds, black birds, seagulls, cardinals, woodpeckers, sparrows, robins and mourning doves flock in our yard feasting on grass seeds, fallen fruit and their seeds. Grandma's superstitious about birds that come and sit on our window sill. She believes if it pays attention to you, it comes to deliver a message—sometimes not always a pleasant one.

Once I catch an owl and keep it in a cage in a tree above my pigeon coop. The spooky hooting not only causes my pigeons to stir noisily, but also disturbs neighbors going to sleep. Grandma believes owls aren't meant for capture. They symbolize wisdom and embody a spirit to forecast future events by way of their hooting. She insists I release it back into the wild where it belongs. I rightfully do.

One morning, a few days before departing for New York, I am awoken from an eerie dream by the sound of mourning doves outside my window. One lonesome dove breaks away from the flock and flies up into my window sill. I clap and knock against the window, startling it. But the dove flies just below my window, make mourning sounds. It seems to stare at me. Each time I tap my window pane, it flies away briefly and then returns to the same spot, again mourning. That night I have a weird and abstract dream about someone dying. It doesn't make sense and I think nothing of it. I sit on Daddy's front stoop thinking of that dream and the lonesome dove mourning at my window. Grandma's superstition comes true. That dove comes to deliver me a message that Grandma was dying.

The neighborhood bustles with city life. People are sitting on stoops, entering and leaving storefronts, going to the cleaners, liquor stores and bars. It has a reasonable mix of black and white residents. Daddy drives cabs and doesn't get home until midnight. Gail and I have time on our hands. We go walking uptown site seeing and window shopping for hours. We visit the Travetts, cousins we've never met. Some days, I walk or catch a transit bus to lower East or West Main Street. I find some hip clothing stores run by Jews who're willing to bargain with me so I can get a lower price. Daddy often stops to check on us. If a problem arises and we can't get him right away, Lindsey Jacobs, an elderly man who lives right across the street, will help. Lindsey's like a sentinel, sitting on his rocking chair on his porch and watching everything move all day long.

Daddy makes good money and stashes the bills in a Tampa Nugget cigar box, with a silver metal coin-holder, that he sometimes carries on his waist. He makes it a habit of counting his earnings at the dinner table. He gives us $10 or $20 apiece every day—good allowance back then. We find where he keeps his stash, easy to do since he never actually hides it. It sits exposed on the floor of his closet. Each day, we each take $20 or $40 to add to our daily allowances for shopping. Although Gail is conservative, I buy the latest hip fashions no one will have back home. Daddy soon catches on to out lavish spending. "By the way, the money you been taking from me is for your school clothes, thought you'd like to know," he says jokingly. We sigh with relief, dreading a show of anger Mama warns us about.

One afternoon, I come home and Gail's sitting on the front stoop talking with this brother. Right in the presence of Lindsey Jacobs, who is bound to squeal to Daddy like it's a cover story in a gossip magazine. Reggie's introduction comes with a soul-shake and a cruise. We all cruise through the city as he points out some hip spots where teenagers hang out. We play a few games of basketball at the local YMCA. He takes me at my request to Alkebulan (Africa's original name) one of the book stores Daddy shops, a black cultural haven near downtown where I purchase *The Autobiography of Malcolm X*. It's common sense brothers are naturally protective of their sisters. Every chance I get, although Reggie comes across nicely, I want to know what his game is—I want to get into his head. I ask questions to find out if he's worthy to take Gail out on a date. The brother wears glasses, comes across intelligent, is enrolled as a freshman at the University of Rochester. I notice the school insignia on his bumper and biology textbooks on the seat. I suppose he's smart enough to figure me out and fake a good impression, but I believe him.

Lindsey breaks the news to Daddy that it isn't ladylike for Gail to invite strangers over to sit outside. Though Gail doesn't dare to invite Reggie inside, she doesn't think it's disrespectful sitting outside on a stoop. Rightly so, he knows Gail's an attractive girl who will catch the eyes of a stranger who'll certainly stop to chat.

Gail has a date with Reggie to a movie, but Daddy decides he doesn't know a thing about him. I find Reggie a respectable brother. Daddy wants to meet Reggie first, but never takes the time to do so. Daddy comes home from work one evening and finds that Gail decided to go anyway. For the first time, I see the side Mama warns about. Daddy goes livid, pacing like a caged animal. "Dammit! I told her to stay home! Where did she go with that Reggie guy?" I conceal the tension I'm feeling, "She's at the movies with Reggie. Don't worry, Gail can take care of herself." "How the hell you know?" he cut in. "You don't know anything about this city!" "I know my sister and she's respectable." Daddy stands over me in a threatening manner as I sit on the couch. His eyes are fuming red and I know his temper is flaring up.

Everyone in Rochester isn't bad. I think he's overreacting. I understand being a bit overzealous to protect is a fatherly reaction. But we need space to get out and explore on our own, even if it means encountering what he considers "bad elements" of the city. We try to make good choices so as not to let him down.

Like one afternoon in late August, trade winds are whipping up a cold breeze from Canada. I run into Willie C. Whitehead, a slick, hip brother from Fort Pierce, standing with this brother at a convenience store trying to keep warm. The brother isn't having much luck selling off a gold watch to a customer leaving the store. Willie C. spots me a short distance away, walking with my back to the wind. Dressed real fly (street term for hip) in leather pants, white ruffled Tom Jones shirt, leather blazer and black boots sporting a bad bush Afro. Still looking strong and together talking a good street game.

Not that he knows me personally. When I mention that I am from the "Fort— Fierce Pierce— the City with no pity" (street name given to the city of Fort Pierce because of its mean inter-city streets if you are tuff to survive there, you can be successful anywhere.) and that I attended school with one of his younger brothers, Willie's eyes light up. Willie C. was a savvy hustling pool shark, slick dresser with a smooth and suave game and reputation rapping to street ladies. I admire his taste in rags—dressed in the finest expensive clothes and shoes. "What's happinin brother? Dig it maann, my partner needs to get a fix. Help him out." I own a watch and I'm not interested. Here he is, over 1,000 miles from home, and hanging out with a junkie hooked on heroin. I wonder about him. His friend looks desperate and he comes over hustling me for an expensive watch, or the sheepskin black leather jacket right off his back for 50-bills, far below its value. Quite tempting, but risky getting my money snatched or robbed. The brother is jonesing—shaking, feeling miserable. Both strut away. Willie C. swings his arms in the wind, the last I see of him.

When Gail doesn't return by 9 pm, Daddy gets worried, and leaves infuriated. I awaken the next morning to an ensuing argument. He pulls his belt off and strikes Gail with the leather then its buckle. At first, she's surprised and holds her arms out to block the lashes to her legs. He makes adjustments and she hollers and cries: "Daddy, please stop, you're hitting me with the belt buckle!" What occurs at that moment is precisely what Mama had warned us about. "Stop hitting her with the buckle!" I yell, with serious authority in my voice. Quickly adjusting the belt, he commences to inflict more lashes. Daddy's out of control. I'm afraid for Gail. I grab him by the arms from behind as we tussle and fight. I tackle him to the floor, somehow landing on top. He doesn't use much force resisting. I pin his arms to the floor. Our eyes lock, and in mine he sees rage, and I see the rage in his turn to shame and guilt. "Get off me." His voice is monotone and unusually faint. I come to my senses, hurt and frightened by who I become—a reflection of Daddy filled with rage. He grabs his hat, jacket and cigar and leaves without saying a word.

Gail and I are eating breakfast the next morning, when Daddy comes home unapologetic about losing control. Considering that Gail did leave against his permission, he had reason to be angry. But he should have listened, and given Gail a chance to explain. She deserves a chance to explain how she carries herself in a respectable manner. Daddy spends a lot of time playing catch up in our lives, stuck in our early childhood years and now overcompensating. As teenagers, we don't need to be told how to bathe, brush our teeth, put on deodorant, make our beds, or comb our hair. Regrettably, he missed valuable time in our lives that he can't recover, change or undo. A setback when we had just become comfortable.

Daddy still wants to play catchup. He wants to expose us to his taste for the performing arts. Never will I likely get a chance to see black artists, like the critically acclaimed Garth Fagin's "Bottom of the Bucket BUT Dance Troupe" or the plays at the Xerox Performing Arts Theatre, in a now de facto segregated Fort Pierce. Gail feels hurt and shamed and wants to leave. I can take the bitter with the sweet. I prefer to stay.

One evening Daddy, still unapologetic, takes Gail out to get a bite to eat. I stay sitting on the stoop, watching crowds and cars pass by. I go across the street to chat with old man Lindsey Jacobs in his rocking chair. He tells me Daddy often talks to him about good and bad times down south, his family, but mostly about me. He worries about me growing up down south. He hopes that I finish school and get the hell out, that I go off to college and do something with my life. "The best decision I ever made leaving the South, crackers down there ain't never gonna change, not in my lifetime," Lindsey says.

Lindsey likes telling stories like Grandma did, and he has more to tell and I like how he tells them. The old fella can weave and spin a story like Grandma did, deep into family history. Lindsey's father caught hell sharecropping tobacco. Lindsey doesn't want to replicate his father's life and leaves Durham, North Carolina for

Rochester in the early 1930s and moves in with a cousin. He gets a factory job, saves his money, marries, buys a home on Clarissa Street and raises four children after his wife passes away. Lindsey listens to news of rioting and protesting down south, and it reminds him of a troubled childhood in the Deep South, which makes him angry. "It's racial up north too, but more to do with jobs and economics. We ain't protesting where we want to go to school, eat, sleep and be entertained . . . that's white madness down south."

I notice a white couple has lived above Daddy for years, and they get along well. I also notice an elderly Jewish man, Ezra Weissenberg, who lives next door, stops to chat with Daddy some mornings. When Daddy tells him I enjoy reading, he invites me over to see his book collection. I get uncomfortable because of his broad knowledge of book topics and their authors. I'm surprised to see in his book collection several black authors. He says: "I can read anything that is thought provoking, black, white or written by Hitler himself. It makes no difference," he says, "Long as it stimulates and feeds my intellect." Ezra has an open mind and I never once get a hint of a racist attitude in the least.

I live by Ezra's message today. One must read and understand the mind of one's enemy to advance a just cause and avoid repeating a wicked past. Daddy must have urged him to invite me over. Daddy, like Mama, is a voracious reader.

One afternoon, Lindsey calls me over. Listening to one of his stories causes me to think about Grandma's hard life in Jim Crow times. Grandma worked as a maid cleaning white folk homes, and a common laborer picking tomatoes. They both took a toll on her health. Overcome with sadness, my heart opens and tears build up in my eyes. I abruptly get up and leave. I haven't grieved since her passing, and as I go walking the floodgates finally open and I feel relieved.

In the days before our departure, I want to know what Lindsey thinks about Daddy. My objective to asking probing questions is to get bits and pieces of information about his life in Rochester. I know he's productive and think he has a girlfriend in Baltimore. But Lindsey's a wise man, catches on to me quickly, and doesn't disclose much. However, he praises Daddy as a hard worker and a proud and honest man. I keep at it until he stops me. "Son, if something's nagging you, best you ask Charles yourself. He's your father. That's the best advice I or anyone else can give you." He's right. Deep down I know at some point I must have a father-son chat before leaving. I want to know Daddy better, but I still hold a grudge. I'm still angry for what he did to Gail. I have avoided him since our fight, not yet comfortable to approach him.

Daddy's always on the go and the clock is ticking. Then it happens. He takes Gail and me to finish our shopping. Sitting on a bench in a mall, he understands where my anger comes from. He notices it right away, from the time of my arrival. My reservation towards him is evident. I ask if he kicked me when I was a child. He doesn't remember or doesn't want to. "Do you think Mama lied about something like that?" His eyes turn away from me onto the floor in deep thought. He then looks up at me and says, "I might have. Yes. I did. You were maybe 5-years old and put my cigar in your mouth. I'm sorry. I was going through some changes," he says in a whisper. "I have no shame about you leaving Daddy. I admire you standing up for justice." But it's his unavoidable absence in my childhood that is eating at my conscience. It is unforgiving and I can't overcome it.

Daddy's defiant outspokenness in Jim Crow segregation towards indifferent whites takes a toll on our family. We talk about his past life, his pride, his chronic job losses that drive him into a deep depression. "Son, that was the time I kicked you. Please forgive me, it's inexcusable." His frustrations were rooted in his military experience overseas in France, where he experienced freedom and equality. Once he returned to the United States, he realized that racial equality for blacks was a dream deferred. I forgive him for that past, but I find it awkward how to say it for our fight.

I understand what Lindsey Jacobs means when he says that Daddy's a proud man. Not the type to bow down and bootlick to white folks. And I understand the pressures he must have been under as a black man in the South. He kicked a white man during Jim Crow era and risked going to jail and dying, jeopardizing his family's welfare. "Bringing blood out that white man…I'd do it again rather than be disrespected as a man." "Dangerous thinking, that night waiting, I was ready to die. Margaret asked me to leave for you all sake." Daddy's guilt caused hardships, abandoning Mama and our family. Mama never wanted to move to Baltimore nor Rochester where he settled, leaving Grandma alone with no one to care for her. I take the bitter with the sweet. Daddy never misses his obligation sending money via Western Union—he's always there for us in that sense. I see a lot of myself in Daddy—some I admire. But the other side, his intensity frightens me because that part already exists in me.

When Gail and I embrace Daddy before getting on the Greyhound bus, I notice his eyes water up and he exhales a sigh of relief. Like a heavy load removed from his conscience. And for me, our talk brings relief to questions only a father can answer for a troubled son—a starting point to a new beginning.

A pretty and fine sister with long legs comes and sits next to me. We talk about our vacations, share laughs and phone numbers. Before the bus rolls into Harrisburg, Pennsylvania, she gives me several big juicy kisses putting the icing on the cake of my almost two-day journey back down south.

When I arrive home, I walk up Thirteenth Street and Orange Avenue to Easter Manor Nursing Home, with vengeance on my hateful mind: "White people killed my Grandma!" I cried out. She was well when I saw her last. I pace outside with indecision, in front of a glass door as white nurses and a few black orderlies move about inside watching. An old black janitor emptying garbage approaches. "Sonny you alright?" "No!" "Those crackers in there killed my Grandma!" "Wait a minute now," he says, alarmed. I explain, and the old man listens with compassion and regret. "Just terrible. Terrible. It's gonna be hard to prove, we die in these places. Maybe you got a point, but whites die too." The old man doesn't dispute factual injustices done to our people every day. Yet he doesn't go far enough for my satisfaction. "I just ah janitor don't pay me no mine, but I see um smiling, actin properly towards us different in this home than when we out in public." Somebody's responsible I tell him, convinced of it. "Sonny, if ya go in there threatnin they gonna arrest ya, a black boy won't stand a chance, ain't gonna see no justice. Go home now. You hear? God ah handle it." His voice and words calm my thoughts a little, like Grandma's soothing tone does when I am troubled. I leave still troubled, still vengeful towards white folk.

I have an awful time sleeping. The house is quiet—in mourning. The house Grandma lived in for much of her adult life. I look at her bed made up neatly. It strikes me she's gone for good. I think of her in a state of rest, sleeping in another time and place. When I awaken, I look out my bedroom window and see a flock of Black birds pecking out a meal in the grass. Suddenly they fly away. There is no sign of a lonesome dove. I think of Grandma again and realize I love and miss her, and she loves me and that's all that matters.

Many birds like these Seagulls take flight after feasting on fallen fruit from nearby orange trees in my yard. (© Courtesy of the author).

I was feeling empowered with an African-centeredness, knowing Grandma's in heaven smiling down on me with pride for my activist spirit and racial pride, to be able to stand up to the truth. I was studying sometimes into the wee hours, reading about revolutionary civil rights and pan Africanist heavyweights and others such as

Douglass, Malcolm, King, Muhammad, Du Bois, Vesey, Kenyatta, Nkrumah, Guevara, Marx, Louverture and Gandhi—the agitators in their own way. I plan to carry their voices over into the new school year.

Brothers on the street corners are embroiled rapping about change in this corrupt system of American government. Black voices at a new school will once again be heard in the hallowed halls of learning and in the classrooms of white academia gaining momentum after two years of integration—we won't be silenced.

I feel my mind being cultivated, soaring in strong convictions I read about. I can't stop even if I wanted to. I am empowered by my personal experiences, and recognize that these are human rights not just civil rights. My ancestors were forced into chattel slavery by the sins of this nation, and were robbed of name, cultural identity and dignity. They suffered and died horrible deaths from the first time they set foot on shore in 1619, more than 400 years ago. Years forward, we still have emotional and psychological wounds that are passed down generation to generation. I have come to realize from school segregation, desegregation to integration in my young life that little has changed. In 1969, we are as dehumanized, devalued and discriminated against as we always have been. Civil rights legislation hasn't change the oppressor's heart a damn bit, even to this day. Yet I have gain a glimmer of hope. In time it will come. But, I grow impatient and can't wait much longer.

I make a deposit at a Sun Bank downtown on Second Street when this white man, a customer, was staring at me as he approach the teller. He whisper and the teller glance up at me. I'm always conscious of my surroundings—it's my nature. I was born observant and watchful and middle named Ira, accordingly. I'm up on this customer by his actions, thinking that something is about to happen. I spend a lot of time on the streets cautiously watching my back for the next outbreak of violence—so I suspect something isn't right. The teller leave her post and go into an adjacent office, as I stand in line waiting. The white customer frantically pass by staring at me, not once lowering his gaze as he briskly heads for the door. A plain-clothed man appear from the office where the teller entered and stood watch a short distance away and give me an intimidating stare. I let a few customers get ahead of me (which seem to annoy and make the man on watch a bit nervous) until the teller return from the office to her post. "Excuse me, I say to this young shy teller, I'm not here to cause problems, but I couldn't help but notice the last customer you served staring at me. What did he say to you? Was it about me? I have a savings account with this bank." "Oh, you do?" She sigh, giving a look of relief and exhaling nervously. "He thought you look suspicious." "How so?" I guess how you're dressed, the black militant type." "Taking pride in wearing something of your culture isn't a militant expression at all," I explain. "I don't think so now that you explain it, but I did the way he reacted to you. We're trained to be cautious you know, sorry." She blushed.

My first purchased dashiki from New York get this reaction. Wearing something of my culture, will undoubtedly lead to some false reactions from whites in the South and at school. My color and freedom to move around and to express myself should not create a sense of heighten suspicion, nor an incident in a bank. I should have freedom to go to any public place without restraint or someone threatening me without probable cause. I doubt that man know anything of substance about my culture at all. I expect the same when school starts. My fight for freedom, justice, and equality will be challenged and will never go away.

You can't legislate to abolish racism through civil rights laws and expect change in white folks' hearts. It won't happen overnight. It will take time far beyond my lifetime, I am sure. The hate and guilt of their fathers sins through slavery is passed down. Also passed down are the social and economic benefits gained from slavery granted to whites from one generation to the next. Whether whites acknowledge this privilege or not it is their reality. The flip side of this privileged reality is difficulty blacks have shaking off self-hate and an inferiority complex. Rather than embrace black pride after more than 300 years of slavery, self-hate is still pervasive—it's in our blood and psyche and it persists as mental slavery. It is why Amy was so baffled about shades of skin color that cause a lighter-skinned black girl to feel superior to a darker-skinned girl.

Ron comes by days before school and ask, "brother man, you think whitey is ready for the brothers and sisters next year?" We laughed and thought not. "We gonna change some things with resistance and more resistance," I chimed in. Ron and I have grown enough peach fuzz for a mustache and on our chin, a sign of maturity entering ninth grade at Dan McCarty Annex. We are as radical and militant as ever, culturally conscious and ready for revolutionary social change. "Look out whitey! Watch us now! The flood gates are openin up with new guinea pigs! They comin! We comin! It's happenin! You gonna be dealin with a lot mo soul brothers and sisters next year just wait and see!" Ron laughed.

Acknowledgements

For the better part of this project, I was intrigue by many family stories my mother, Margaret Hurst, shared with me. I graciously thank her posthumously. As a pack rat, a hoarder of documents, her stories helped to refresh my memory. She amazingly preserve many of my youthful thoughts scribbled on pads and pieces of papers stashed away in my bedroom many years ago. This proved to be a valuable resource that added texture to this project. I also owe a special thanks to Donnie Allen posthumously for her historical knowledge and for entrusting me with some of her most valuable documents being a good friend of my grandmother Viola Jay, knowing her reputation for trustworthiness, I can do no wrong. I thank Sam Carter posthumously, teacher, businessman, and historian sat me down under a shade tree in his backyard to help align my thoughts about how to approach this book. I owe a debt of gratitude to librarians, Hajara Mohiuddeen for her resourcefulness and willingness to do the leg work necessary to locate an article or book from some rarely used file cabinet or shelf and to Barbara Pastman for her guidance and patience navigating microfilm. I owe deep appreciation to Nan Lasher Ball posthumously of Best Photo Restoration and Jovey Hayes of Phojoe Restoration Studios, for their amazing skills bringing back to life badly faded and damaged photos. I am most grateful to my editor, Lynne Feldman, whose gentle encouragement gave me the confidence to move forward. I would not have gotten this far without her prodding questions and suggestions, which helped to shape and reshape my thoughts down the final stretch. I wish to thank Bouchra, my lovely wife, for her unwavering patience and support on this long and humbling journey.

Made in the USA
Columbia, SC
18 August 2021